The Masses and Motets
of William Byrd

Volume I
The Masses and Motets of William Byrd
JOSEPH KERMAN

Volume II (in preparation)
The Songs, Services and Anthems of William Byrd
PHILIP BRETT

Volume III
The Consort and Keyboard Music of William Byrd
OLIVER NEIGHBOUR

The Masses and Motets
of William Byrd

JOSEPH KERMAN

UNIVERSITY OF CALIFORNIA PRESS

Berkeley and Los Angeles

University of California Press
Berkeley and Los Angeles
Printed in Great Britain by
Western Printing Services Ltd

Library of Congress Cataloging in Publication Data

Kerman, Joseph, 1924–
The Masses and motets of William Byrd.

(The Music of William Byrd; v. 1)
Includes indexes.
1. Byrd, William, 1542 or 3–1623. Masses.
2. Byrd, William, 1542 or 3–1623. Motets. I. Title.
II. Series.
ML410.B996M9 1978 vol. 1 780'.92'4s [783.2'1'0924]
ISBN 0-520-04033-3 80-14497

music

Contents

Foreword

The present volume is one of three covering all the music of William Byrd. This comprehensive study originated in an unusual way. It was not the outcome of a grand project conceived in advance by a single scholar or editor who then recruited the present authors. Nor would it be true to describe it as the fortuitous convergence of three entirely independent projects. The authors have long been friends. Over the years they have been engaged with Byrd's music at various levels of intensity, sometimes alone and at other times in conjunction or in correspondence with one or both of the others. There came a time when each began to see that his sense of commitment might lead to an individual monograph, and the larger design then took shape quite naturally. The initial plan to produce one composite volume was emended a little later to encompass three smaller, associated ones.

What it has entailed, then, is not so much a formal collaboration as mutual encouragement, consultation and criticism—for the authors a uniquely valuable and sustaining experience. Whatever the differences between their interests, casts of mind or modes of expression, they share certain assumptions, and these are worth outlining here since they are not spelled out in the books themselves. Most important, we all believe strongly that great music of the relatively distant past deserves the same degree of critical attention regularly accorded to that of the recent past or present. That Dufay, Josquin, Byrd and Monteverdi are on a plane with the greatest masters of later years is a commonplace of the history books, but one that can have little meaning unless the music is more widely heard and understood. The performance of Byrd's music has taken great steps forward in the post-war period. But the growth in popularity of early music that has benefited Byrd has tended to promote general enthusiasm rather than more searching appraisal.

Of course special difficulties arise when one attempts to reach a reasoned critical account of early music, as they do in trying to perform it convincingly. The further back one goes in history, the greater the leap of historical imagination required; and one of the tasks of musicology—perhaps the main task—is to prepare the way for this enterprise. These studies contain much discussion of sources, chronology, authenticity, influences, modal theory and so on. Without such a basis the contemporary sensibility can go very wrong in respect to the past. But without a vital link forward to the present, musicology risks losing touch with the essential nature of the art which is the object of its study. We address the music as music, mediating as best we can between historical vision on the one hand and contemporary aesthetic expectations and attitudes on the other. There is today and has been for many years much generous if somewhat unfocussed admiration for Byrd's genius. We have tried to lay the foundation for its fuller understanding and appreciation.

Philip Brett
Joseph Kerman
Oliver Neighbour

Acknowledgements

This book has been a long time in the making and many persons and agencies have had a hand in it. To thank them for their help is both a pleasure and an occasion for some nostalgia.

I shall not forget the kindness with which several established scholars received me in 1960, when I first returned to England to work on Byrd's Latin sacred music. At Iffley H. K. Andrews brought out his big Byrd note-books and conducted me through them, and at Oxford Frank Harrison allowed himself to be used as a sympathetic sounding board for incipient ideas. Later he presented me with a (the?) carbon copy of his chapter for the *New Oxford History of Music*, Volume IV—which it would have been years, otherwise, before I could have seen. Scholars of a younger generation, most particularly Jeremy Noble and Thurston Dart, were just as friendly and forthcoming. Noble put his invaluable notes on English manuscript sources at my disposal and both men freely shared their stimulating—sometimes positively heady—ideas about Elizabethan music and music history.

With the idea (if memory serves) of winding up this research project before moving on to others, I wrote a number of articles on different aspects of Byrd's work over the next several years. Some of this material has been revised here (though I have, however, changed some of my conclusions): 'Byrd's Motets: Chronology and Canon', *Journal of the American Musicological Society*, xiv (1961), 'The Elizabethan Motet: A Study of Texts for Music', *Studies in the Renaissance*, ix (1962), 'On William Byrd's *Emendemus in melius*', *The Musical Quarterly*, xlix (1963), and 'Byrd, Tallis, and the Art of Imitation', *Aspects of Medieval and Renaissance Music*, ed. Jan LaRue (the *Festschrift* for the late Gustave Reese). My then colleague Professor Edward E. Lowinsky read a draft of the second of these articles, which owes a good deal to his own work, with the greatest of care and perspicacity, and he, too, very generously put personal materials at my disposal—in this case, unique materials concerning the mid-century continental motet repertory.

I did move on to other projects. But renewed acquaintance with Philip Brett and his work, after he returned to Berkeley in 1966, and then a little later with Oliver Neighbour and his, persuaded me—us—that a more com-prehensive study of Byrd's work should be undertaken. As has already been said in the Foreword, our mutual debt is a specially intimate one. I have profited particularly from being able to read Oliver Neighbour's study of Byrd's instrumental music, and discuss it with him, during the preparation of my own book. While certainly it was no part of the original plan that Volume I should lag behind Volume III, this has had an enormously beneficial effect on the laggard.

In its earliest stage this work was supported by a fellowship from the John Simon Guggenheim Memorial Foundation, and in later stages by fellowships from the Society for the Humanities at Cornell University and Clare Hall, Cambridge. A version of chapter 4, on Byrd's Masses, appeared in *JAMS*, xxxii (1979). I am very grateful to Thomas A. Barnes, John Bossy, Robert Ford, Peter Le Huray and Craig Monson for assistance and advice of various kinds, and especially to Vivian Kerman for her invaluable criticism of the near-final typescript.

I should also like to record my appreciation to the choral conductors with whom I have been associated over the years, whose performances have taught me so much about Byrd's music, and who have sometimes allowed me to propose particular Byrd pieces for their repertories. They include Elizabeth Davidson, the late Iva Dee Hiatt, Lawrence Moe, Jeremy Noble (once again), Simon Preston and David Wulstan. I should add George Lynn from my student days and Edward B. Lawton. Performances by Philip Brett, especially, have seemed to me again and again to animate or illustrate Hooker's wonderful words about music, which I first came across in Harrison's carbon: 'a thing which delighteth all ages and beseemeth all states; a thing as seasonable in grief as in joy; . . . The reason hereof is an admirable facility which music hath to express and represent to the mind, more inwardly than any other sensible mean, the very standing, rising, and falling, the very steps and inflections every way, the turns and varieties of all passions whereunto the mind is subject; . . . There is [one kind] that draweth to a marvellous grave and sober mediocrity; there is also that carrieth as it were into ecstasies, filling the mind with an heavenly joy, and for the time in a manner severing it from the body.'

Finally, thanks to the many librarians whose courtesy and willing assistance has in my experience never lapsed: at Duke Humphrey, Christ Church, the Pendlebury Library at Cambridge, the Rowe Library at King's, St. Michael's, Tenbury, Westminster Abbey, Lincoln and Worcester Cathedrals, Sion College, the Pierpont Morgan Library, the Manuscript Department and Music Room of the British Museum (as it then was), and especially at the Music Library of the University of California at Berkeley: which since its translation to Morrison Hall in 1958 Professor Vincent Duckles has made into a rare joy for the research scholar, no less than for the student and the general reader. I am beholden to Frances Yerkes and Larry Archbold for assistance in preparing the typescript and music examples, and to David Kalins for making the indices.

J. K.
Berkeley
3 April 1978

Key to Abbreviated Bibliographical References

The editions, books and articles referred to in this volume are treated in two ways. A certain number are quoted in abbreviated forms, the key to which is given below. Particulars of the remainder are given at the appropriate points, with index references under the names of composers, editors and authors.

BE   *The Byrd Edition*
      1. Cantiones sacrae (1575), ed. C. Monson (London, 1977).

BK   *William Byrd: Keyboard Music*
      ed. A. Brown, 2 vols. (London, 1969–71, 2/1976). (=MB 27, 28).

BW   *The Collected Works of William Byrd*
      ed. E. H. Fellowes.
      1. Masses, Cantiones sacrae (1575) (London, 1937).
      2. Cantiones sacrae (1589), rev. T. Dart (London, 1966).
      3. Cantiones sacrae (1591), rev. T. Dart (London, 1966).
      4. *Gradualia*, book 1 (1605), part 1 (London, 1938).
      5. *Gradualia*, book 1 (1605), parts 2 and 3 (London, 1938).
      6. *Gradualia*, book 2 (1607), part 1 (London, 1938).
      7. *Gradualia*, book 2 (1607), part 2 (London, 1938).
      8. Motets for three, four and five voices (recovered from manuscript) (London, 1939).
      9. Motets for six, eight and nine voices (recovered from manuscript) (London, 1939).
      16. Additional madrigals, canons and rounds (London, 1948).

Andrews, *Byrd's Polyphony*
      H. K. Andrews, *The Technique of Byrd's Vocal Polyphony* (London, 1966).

Benham, *Latin Music*
      H. Benham, *Latin Church Music in England, c. 1460–1575* (London, 1977).

Doe, *Tallis*
      P. Doe, *Tallis* (London, 1966, 2/1976).

EECM   *Early English Church Music*
        general editor, F. Ll. Harrison
        2. *William Mundy: Latin Antiphons and Psalms*, ed. F. Ll. Harrison
        (London, 1962).

Fellowes, *W. Byrd*
        E. H. Fellowes, *William Byrd* (London, 1936, 2/1948).

Harrison, *Medieval Britain*
        F. Ll. Harrison, *Music in Medieval Britain* (London, 1958, 2/1963).

Jackman, *Gradualia*
        J. L. Jackman, 'Liturgical Aspects of Byrd's *Gradualia*', *Musical Quarterly*,
        xlix (1963), 17ff.

Kerman, *Chronology and Canon*
        J. Kerman, 'Byrd's Motets: Chronology and Canon', *Journal of the American Musicological Society*, xiv (1961), 359ff.

Kerman, *Elizabethan Motet*
        J. Kerman, 'The Elizabethan Motet: A Study of Texts for Music', *Studies in the Renaissance*, ix (1962), 273ff.

MB   *Musica Britannica*
        15. *Music of Scotland, 1500–1700*, ed. K. Elliott (London, 1957, 2/1964).
        See also BK, above.

Morley, *Introduction*
        Thomas Morley, *A Plain and Easy Introduction to Practical Music*, ed.
        R. A. Harman (London, 1952).

NOHM   *The New Oxford History of Music*
        4. *The Age of Humanism, 1540–1630*, ed. G. Abraham (London, 1968).

TCM   *Tudor Church Music*
        6. *Thomas Tallis, c. 1505–1585* (London, 1928).
        7. *William Byrd, 1543–1623 : Gradualia, books 1 and 2* (London, 1927).
        9. *William Byrd, 1543–1623 : Masses, Cantiones* [1575], *and Motets* [recovered from manuscript], (London, 1928).

Volumes of *The Byrd Edition* in course of preparation will include the *Cantiones sacrae* of 1589 and 1591 (A. Brown), the *Gradualia* (P. Brett and D. Moroney), the manuscript motets (W. A. Edwards) and the *Masses* (Brett).

A stroke and a number following the symbol for a particular volume indicate a numbered piece within it, e.g., EECM 6/34, MB 19/129a, 1589/22–3. The dates 1575, 1589, 1591 and 1607 used in this way refer to Byrd's motet publications; with book 1 of the *Gradualia* of 1605, where Byrd employed a separate numeration for the 5–, 4– and 3–part fascicles, the abbreviations 1605 *a 5*/22, 1605 *a 4*/5, etc., are used. Wherever possible, references to Byrd motets are given in these general forms in order that readers may apply them to whatever modern editions—TCM, BW or BE—they have available. This has not been possible for the motets recovered from manuscript, which are identified by their BW numbers.

A date with a superscript number (e.g. 1553[9]) denotes a printed anthology listed in RISM (*Répertoire International des Sources Musicales*) BI.

The class-marks Add. (Additional), Egerton and R.M. (Royal Music) followed by numbers refer to manuscripts in the Reference Division of the British Library (BL), the class-marks Mus. (Music) and Mus.Sch. (Music School) to Bodleian Manuscripts. The numeration of psalms follows the Vulgate.

Pitches are indicated as follows: D′, E′, F′ and G′ for the lowest bass range, A–G for the next octave, a–g for the next (including middle c) and a′–g′ for the soprano range. Pitch without reference to the specific octave ('pitch-class') is indicated by capitals: A–G.

References are always to *original* pitches and to *original* note values, even when an edition cited presents the music in transposition, or with note values halved.

List of Tables

I

Motet Texts and Motet Function

Plainchant, the earliest music of the Christian Church, was a functional, rather than a merely decorative, element in the Christian ritual. Hence its great importance for as long as the ritual, or at least the Latin ritual, survived. Plainchant was the way of presenting certain categories of liturgical texts—scriptural readings, prayers, commentaries of various kinds—which were specified in precise detail for the many different daily services. When in later ages certain of the same texts were reset to music in a contemporary polyphonic style, the result was the establishment of new liturgical repertories. The new settings were designed to be incorporated into the services, replacing sections of the Mass or the Office that had traditionally been sung in plainchant. What we call the Latin motet—William Byrd always used the term 'sacred song'—covers all of the smaller items of liturgical composition: hymns, responds, antiphons, offertories and the like, excepting only larger liturgical items such as the Ordinary of the Mass and the *Magnificat*.

From the earliest times, we also hear of non-liturgical categories of Latin sacred music, such as the hymns of St. Ambrose, categories which were sometimes finally accepted into the official liturgy. By the mid-sixteenth century, the situation had grown to be thoroughly tangled: especially on the Continent, but also in Britain, even though here the tradition of liturgical composition had persisted with particular strength throughout the Middle Ages. In addition to liturgical motets, composers also wrote other Latin motets on much the same footing, destined to be performed in other contexts. Not to speak of the small, special category of the secular motet—the humanistic ode, the fragment from Virgil, the encomium to a prince—there is a rather large grey area of music set to sacred texts that do not correspond with any official liturgical items. The words are selected directly from the Bible, or freely composed, or patched together from one passage or another in the service books. But in any case there is no place specified for them in the actual services.

The destination of these non-liturgical motets is often difficult to know. They may have been intended as informal (and strictly speaking, incorrect) additions to the services, if not as loose substitutions for liturgical items. They may have accompanied private devotions, or served as a sort of pious chamber music—or perhaps we have to look farther afield to discover their actual function. Difficult as it is to know, it is also important, for if we hope to understand the Latin motet we should know how the composer conceived of the genre and where and why he meant the pieces to be sung.

The problem is complicated by two major currents that affected composers of the sixteenth century profoundly. One was the steady pressure to bring words, meanings and music into a perfect union: pressure which took many forms and evolved continuously throughout the Renaissance. It became harder and harder to treat a liturgical text simply as a hieratic unit when its intrinsic meaning kept impinging on the heightened imagination of the age of humanism. The other current was of course religious upheaval. Liturgies were reconsidered, reformed, overthrown. Even in a strictly Roman Catholic ambience, a composer such as Vincenzo Ruffo could turn his ideas of Mass composition upside down, as Lewis Lockwood has shown.* In Reformation countries the situation was (to put it mildly) more extreme. In England the first paradox that has to be confronted is the continuing composition of Latin sacred music at the time of the Anglican, vernacular rite. Why did William Byrd write Masses and motets at all?

The paradox turns out to be a many-sided one. Byrd's attitude towards the Latin motet changed several times during his career, and the nature of the music he produced changed accordingly. Before coming to the music we should consider the paradox with some care and try to understand his evolving concept of the motet in terms of text and function. This is material for an introductory chapter, in preparation for the critical analysis which is central to this book.

Not surprisingly, there is also a change in the historiographic problem as attention turns to the different periods of Byrd's activity. In attempting to follow the composer's changing viewpoint, we find ourselves dealing with evidence of different kinds. For the latest phase, the two volumes of *Gradualia* published in 1605 and 1607 provide not only music, and much music, but also documentary evidence of a sort: for the complex selection process that went into this great compendium, and its resulting organization, reveal a good deal about Byrd's position at that time. In what may be called the middle phase we also have a considerable amount of music, including mainly motets published by Byrd in the *Cantiones sacrae* of 1589 and 1591. With this repertory, the special nature of the verbal texts allows the drawing of some suggestive inferences. Much less primary material is available, of course, for a study of the early phases. Less music was written, less survives, and what does survive is always problematic as to date and sometimes

---

*L. Lockwood, *The Counter-Reformation and the Masses of Vincenzo Ruffo* (Studi di Musica Veneta, ii, Venice, 1970).

problematic as to attribution. Here it is necessary to turn to secondary evidence derived from a study of young Byrd's milieu, his likely influences, and the practices and attitudes of his older contemporaries.

Information about the state of English music in the mid-sixteenth-century is not easy to come by, as is well known. Records of various kinds are thin and there is a dearth of musical sources, quantities of which were destroyed as papist books. But recently a number of musicologists have addressed themselves to this problem and a plausible picture of musical life in those obscure, difficult years is gradually being pieced together. Drawing on this secondary evidence, and adding to it some conclusions drawn from the primary evidence, such as it is, we can also form a plausible picture of William Byrd's first phase as a composer of Latin music.

[2]

Little is known about Byrd's early life before he turns up at nineteen or twenty as the newly appointed organist of Lincoln Cathedral.* We know that he was born in 1543 or late 1542 only because of a reference to 'the 80th yeare of myne age' in his will of November 1622. In a prefatory poem to the Tallis-Byrd *Cantiones* of 1575, it is said twice that he was a student of Thomas Tallis: 'Et Birdus tantum natus decorare magistrum . . . (And Byrd, born to honour so great a master . . .), Communemque mihi tecum sic orno magistrum . . . (And thus with a poem I honour with you our common master . . .)'. This was written by another Tallis pupil, the young courtier and amateur composer Sir Ferdinando Heybourne *alias* Richardson. And if Byrd was 'bred up under Tallis', as Anthony à Wood puts it, he must have spent his early years in London, presumably as a choirboy in the Chapel Royal. (This cannot be verified because of lacunae in the Chapel rosters.) He may have been a Londoner born—the son, it has been suggested, of Thomas Byrd, an obscure colleague of Tallis at the Chapel in the 1540s and 50s. Or he may have been a Lincolnshire boy—recruited for the Chapel, perhaps, on account of an exceptional voice; there is a record of such recruitment (impressment would be a better term) by the choirmaster of Magdalen College in those days, the composer John Sheppard. We are probably not wrong, in any case, to locate Byrd in the 1550s in or at the very least close to the Chapel Royal which served under Queen Mary. During her reign from 1553 to 1558 he passed through his early teens from ten to fifteen,

*Biographical information is from Fellowes, *W. Byrd* and *Grove*. With a somewhat different emphasis, the discussion on the following pages follows Kerman, *Elizabethan Motet*.

prime singing years for a choirboy and impressionable years for any boy.

Mary's vigorous restoration of Roman Catholicism entailed a new emphasis on all the arts of the Latin liturgy. The Sarum rite was restored, the rite of Salisbury which had prevailed over most of England and which was one of the most finely articulated of all local variants of Catholic ritual. This meant a rejection of the constrained style of English service music developed for the Prayer Books of Edward VI under the influence of Cranmer, and a reinstitution of the tradition of ornate polyphony that distinguished English church music in late medieval times. But more was involved than a simple return to music as it had been under Henry VIII. It seems clear that deliberate action was taken to establish a new repertory in what passed for the most brilliant style of the time.

This can be inferred from the surviving music, even though the extant sources are few and require careful interpretation.* No more than a single church-music source actually written during Queen Mary's reign has survived, the so-called Gyffard Partbooks (Add. 17802–5), and this is limited to 3- and 4-part music for men's voices. Analysis of this somewhat special repertory and of the composers represented suggests that the manuscript stems from one of the larger London churches, which would presumably reflect Chapel Royal trends at second hand, though with no great time lag. It is thought that the Chapel repertory itself has been preserved in only one source, a large retrospective collection made about forty years later by John Baldwin, the singing-man and scribe of St. George's, Windsor (Christ Church 979–83). There is much else in this collection—including a comprehensive anthology of Byrd's most famous motets, written in the period around 1580. The question is which and how much of Baldwin's repertory dates from the time of Queen Mary.

With the music by composers such as William Mundy, Robert Parsons and Robert White, all of it that is strictly Catholic must have been written under Mary because they were born too late to have written it under Henry VIII. This includes such large-scale compositions as the *Magnificats* of White and Parsons and the impressive Marian votive antiphons of Mundy, the latest known examples of this venerable musical genre. Certain older composers, too, worked hard during Mary's reign. The largest body of Latin liturgical music copied by Baldwin consists of music for the Office, written for five, six or even more voices on the Sarum plainchant as a steady-moving

*See R. Bray, 'British Museum Add. MSS 17802–5 (The Gyffard Partbooks): An Index and Commentary', *R.M.A. Research Chronicle*, vii (1969), 31ff, and 'The Part-Books Oxford, Christ Church, MSS 979–983: An Index and Commentary', *Musica Disciplina*, xxv (1971), 179ff.

cantus firmus. The texts in question are mainly Vesper hymns and responds, which might in some cases also serve for processions. The most prolific composer of this music, Sheppard, produced such pieces for the major feasts of the Church year: Christmas, Epiphany, Easter, Ascension, Whitsun, Trinity, Corpus Christi, All Saints, the Purification and the Annunciation. The next most prolific composer was Tallis. He duplicated a few of the texts set by Sheppard, but on the whole can be seen to have filled in the scheme with some extra pieces in exactly the same categories.

Tallis joined the Chapel Royal in Henry VIII's time and lived on to serve Queen Elizabeth. But Sheppard is not heard of in London before 1552 and disappears from view entirely after 1557. None of this Office music is transmitted in Henrician manuscripts (to be sure, few of them survive to tell this or any other tale) and very little cantus firmus work of the same kind is known by earlier English composers. Taverner's settings of the favourite Easter respond *Dum transisset sabbatum* and John Redford's *Sint lumbi vestri praecincti* are rare exceptions. A great yearly cycle of Office music for five and six parts in cantus firmus style would appear to be the main musical legacy of Queen Mary's Chapel Royal.*

In addition, an appreciable number of occasional motets and Masses survive which were apparently composed during her reign. The text of Tallis's great 6-part votive antiphon *Gaude gloriosa Dei mater* seems to refer to Mary the Queen as well as Mary the Blessed Virgin. Sheppard may have produced his setting of Psalm 127, *Beati omnes*, which figures in the Nuptial Mass in Sarum rite, for the royal wedding at Winchester in 1554. 'All the priestes and singinge men all in riche copes began to singe a psalme used in marriages', wrote the chronicler Henry Wriothesley. Even more probably, Tallis wrote his grandiose 7-part Mass on the cantus firmus *Puer natus est nobis* in connection with Mary's well-publicized false pregnancy towards Christmas of 1554. Several non-liturgical motets with texts extolling the Catholic faith, and sometimes attacking schism, were conceivably written under Henry VIII but more likely under Mary: *Exurge Christe* by William Mundy, *De lamentatione* attributed to John Mundy (but more probably by

*Tallis and Sheppard's 'joint output of both hymns and responds suggests that they had in mind some sort of annual cycle of office polyphony, which must surely have been for Mary Tudor's chapel' (Doe, *Tallis*, 34). Doe has, however, subsequently argued that this music was more probably written earlier ('Latin Polyphony under Henry VIII', *Proceedings of the Royal Musical Association*, xcv (1968–9), 92f). The question should probably be left open. Benham, although he jibs at assigning so much music to so short a period as Mary's reign, still wonders whether certain associated hymn and respond settings by Sheppard may be 'isolated survivors from some yearly cycle of hymn-respond pairs for Vespers at Magdalen College *or the Chapel Royal*' (*Latin Music*, 163, 201; emphasis added).

William, once again), and a curious paraphrase of the Canticle of Isaiah (*Confitebo tibi Domine*) set by Sheppard.*

Exurge Christe appears in the Gyffard Partbooks, but otherwise this source transmits a strictly liturgical repertory, and one that is considerably more various than that preserved by Baldwin. There are Mass ordinaries and even a Mass proper, alleluias, *Asperges*, processional pieces, a *Te Deum* and much else. The Easter season is provided with the most music, by a wide margin. Again cantus firmus setting is the preferred style, and again Sheppard is the main composer; with twenty compositions, he has twice as many as Taverner, who is then followed by Mundy, Tye and Tallis. And the Gyffard Partbooks have a special interest for us because they are the first to include the name of Byrd. This appears in a sufficiently remarkable context. Among the Easter music is a 4-part setting of a psalm with antiphon prescribed for the procession to the font at Vespers, *In exitu Israel*. In accordance with liturgical practice, only the even verses (fourteen of them) are set in polyphony, leaving the others to be chanted—in faburden, as it appears: for the polyphony is built over the faburden of the psalm tone and the antiphon as a cantus firmus. The first half of the piece, verses 2–14, is ascribed to Sheppard, verses 22–8 to Mundy, and verses 16 (*Similes illis fiant*), 18 and 20 to 'Birde'. Verse 18 includes a canon between the two upper voices.

That the Byrd in hand is William was taken as a matter of course by the editors of *Tudor Church Music* and the Byrd *Works*. More recently, however, Thomas Byrd has been put forward as the author by several scholars, including the present writer. The problem is that the piece was patently designed for the Sarum liturgy and this went out of use in 1558 when William was only fifteen. Therefore it seemed more reasonable to see it as the work of a musician of an earlier generation—even though there is no other evidence that Thomas Byrd was ever active as a composer.

However, the existence of some other music of about the same period which is attributed in later manuscripts to 'Mr William Byrd', or to 'Mr Byrd' obviously meaning William, complicates the problem. Among them are some 2-part organ settings in the manner of Redford (see Vol. III, ch. 6)—settings of the *Miserere*, *Gloria tibi Trinitas*, and *Salvator mundi*—and a small (but for the present purpose, important) vocal composition, *Alleluia. Confitemini Domino*. The organ music is primitive in its own way, but the

---

*On the Tallis compositions, see P. Doe, 'Tallis's "Spem in Alium" and the Elizabethan Respond Motet', *Music & Letters*, li (1970), 1ff. The Sheppard and 'John' Mundy pieces appear in Baldwin's Partbooks; for the text of the Mundy, see Kerman, *Elizabethan Motet*, 297. For Wriothesley, see *A Chronicle of England during the Reign of the Tudors by Charles Wriothesley*, ed. W. D. Hamilton (London, 1877, Camden Society, ser. II, No. 20) ii, 121.

Alleluia, although for three voices only and lacking a cantus firmus, is primitive in much the same way as *Similes illis fiant*. The piece circulated fairly widely, occurring in three sources from around 1580 to 1620.*

With the organ compositions, one cannot make the argument that their liturgical cantus firmi imply composition in Catholic times, for it is well known that writing of this kind continued into Queen Elizabeth's reign. The brilliant *Felix namque* settings by Tallis are dated 1562 and 1564 in the Fitzwilliam Virginal Book. But with the *Alleluia* such an argument can and must be made. On examination the piece proves to be a conflation of two separate Easter items. The first is the regular alleluia with verse for Mass at the Easter Vigil on Holy Saturday (a text also set by Sheppard, in the Gyffard Partbooks):

Alleluia. Confitemini Domino quoniam bonus, quoniam in saeculum misericordia eius.

The second item in this composite piece is probably the special alleluia with verse from the procession to the font at Vespers, once again:

Alleluia. Laudate, pueri, Dominum: laudate nomen Domini. Alleluia.

Perhaps the number of voices reflects the rubric in the Sarum Processional directing that the text be sung by three boys: 'Deinde tres pueri in ipsa statione ante fontes conversi ad altare in superpellices simul cantent *alleluia*. Versus. *Laudate pueri Dominum . . .* ' In the service this all takes place directly after a singing of the whole psalm *Laudate pueri Dominum* (another piece set by the inexhaustible Sheppard, in Gyffard) and shortly before the psalm *In exitu Israel*, the one divided up among Sheppard, Byrd and Mundy.

So it becomes necessary to believe not only that the 'Birde' who collaborated with Sheppard and Mundy was the obscure Thomas, but also that the 'William Byrd' who wrote these other early pieces was Thomas too, confused in later years with his more famous son or namesake. It is easier to believe that like most great composers William Byrd simply began composing early. His pupil Morley was writing music at age nineteen, Gibbons at sixteen. At fifteen Monteverdi was already publishing. We should be ready to concede a similar precocity to Byrd, even though we may still have trouble picturing collaboration on an equal basis between a fourteen- or fifteen-year-old chorister and established figures like Sheppard and Mundy. Byrd,

*Christ Church 45, Baldwin's so-called 'Commonplace Book', R.M.24.d.2, and Add. 18936-9 (without text). The text in TCM 9 and BW 8 is in error.

who in later life was obviously a personality to reckon with, may also have been a very persuasive, as well as a very talented, boy.

Byrd's two short alleluias both include canons, like *Similes illis fiant*. At some later time he himself might have brought them together, as a means of preserving examples of student prowess after the liturgical circumstances for them had lapsed. In their original state they confirm the equivocal evidence of the Gyffard Partbooks to the effect that Byrd's first steps as a composer were taken in the absolutely traditional way, within the confines of the Catholic liturgy. We can imagine, perhaps, the great care and fervour with which every element of the Sarum rite was restored in Queen Mary's Chapel Royal. It must have been an exciting time for a choirboy. But more than this, young Byrd seems to have been drawn into a sort of crash programme among the composers of the Chapel to produce new music, most of it liturgical music in cantus firmus style. It is in the light of this early experience that we must understand Byrd's affection for cantus firmus writing in later years, his understanding of and sympathy for liturgical composition, and perhaps also his lifelong devotion to the Catholic cause itself.

Another source of musical excitement in those years should be mentioned, the presence of the Spanish Chapel of Philip II. When this impressive organization followed the King to England in 1554–5, it included 21 singers and 15 'menestrilles', of whom the most illustrious were Antonio de Cabezón and Philippe de Monte.* Many of them were veterans of the so-called *capilla flamenca* of Charles V, whose most famous choirmaster had been Gombert and whose repertory was as much Franco–Flemish as Spanish: that is to say, as much international as local or provincial. No love was lost between the English and the Spaniards, of course; Wriothesley and the other chroniclers are full of tales of intranational muggings and murders. But one could not shut one's ears when Mass was celebrated by both Chapels together. Some of these sounds must have stayed in Byrd's ear; at a later period, in any case, he showed a very lively interest in musical ideas from the Continent. And it has been suggested that as early as 1555 he may have come to know de Monte, who engaged in an unusual musical correspondence with Byrd many years later.

[3]

The death of Queen Mary meant the end of the Sarum rite, but it did not mean the end of the Latin motet in England or even the end of Latin services. Queen Elizabeth, who is known to have retained a liking for the old rituals,

*See J. M. Ward, 'Spanish Musicians in Sixteenth-Century England', in *Essays in honour of Dragan Plamenac*, ed. G. Reese and R. Snow (Pittsburg, 1969), 353ff.

in 1560 authorized a Latin version of the Book of Common Prayer by Walter Haddon for the use of the universities and public schools. This book met with resistance, but the number of reprints into the seventeenth century shows that it was used at least sporadically, at least in certain institutions. Tallis must have written his linked settings of the *Magnificat* and *Nunc Dimittis* in Latin for an Anglican Evensong service in that language; and the institution in question was surely the Chapel Royal. A Latin version of the *Te Deum* ('We knowledge Thee') from Byrd's Great Service survives in the Caroline sets of partbooks at Peterhouse. On a humbler level, two Latin works by Tallis are found in one of the very few Elizabethan partbooks surviving from a parish church, St. Laurence, at Ludlow. There were also Latin Anglican primers, the *Orarium* of 1560 and the *Preces Privatae* of 1564. One of the few Sarum hymns carried over into the latter book, *Christe qui lux es et dies* (*Precamur sancte Domine*), was set to music by Robert White (several times) and also by Byrd.*

However, the greater proportion of Latin music that seems to have been composed in early Elizabethan times cannot be construed into the official Anglican liturgy. It belongs to a special category of non-liturgical motet which had apparently been gaining ground since the end of Henry VIII's reign. This is the psalm-motet—a term that is best restricted to large-scale settings of a complete or nearly complete psalm (or one of the sections of the lengthy Psalm 118, *Beati immaculati*). This definition excludes shorter settings of one or two verses, perhaps taken from the middle of a psalm or from several different ones. Apart from the matter of scale, there is an element of personal choice about motets with texts of the latter type which sets them apart from psalm-motets proper.

Nearly fifty English and Scottish psalm-motets have survived, dating from approximately 1540 to 1580, with an apparent preponderance in the 1560s. Mundy and White are the chief composers. The early impetus for their composition can be traced to Scotland, or more precisely, to the Continent via Scotland, where musical contacts with France had been close since the beginning of the century. From Scotland, too, we get a hint as to the function of at least some of these pieces, thanks to the garrulous scribe of Thomas Wode's Psalter (Edinburgh University Library La.III.483 and Add.33933). This manuscript contains a setting by David Peebles of Psalm 3

*On the Ludlow MSS (SRO 356, Mus. MS 2, '*c.*1570–*c.*1610'), see A. Smith, 'Elizabethan Church Music at Ludlow', *Music & Letters*, xlix (1968), 108ff. On the Latin prayer book and primers, see two publications for the Parker Society by W. K. Clay, *Liturgical Services in the Reign of Queen Elizabeth* (Cambridge, 1847) and *Private Prayer during* ... (Cambridge, 1851). For a recent survey of Latin music in England at this period, see Benham, *Latin Music*, ch. 10.

in a non-Vulgate translation, *Quam multi Domine*, dated 1576 in another hand. The scribe says it was written 'at the command of ane venerable Father in god . . . the letter of this songe was gevin by my Lord of Marche to David Pables'. The Earl of March, Bishop of Caithness, was Peebles's prior at St. Andrews. Presumably he had the composer set his own Latin version of the psalm as a literary or musico-literary experiment, or conceivably as a mild form of Protestant apologetics. This would also be the explanation for Mundy's setting of Psalm 50, *Miserere mei Deus*, in the translation by the humanist François Vatable first published in 1556, and for Byrd's setting of Psalm 150 anonymously paraphrased in elegiacs, *Laudibus in sanctis*, published in the *Cantiones sacrae* of 1591.*

But in more general terms, the function fulfilled by psalm-motets was probably estimated correctly by Harrison, who proposed that shortly before the Reformation they began to take over what he called the 'paraliturgical' role of the old votive antiphon.† Votive antiphons dedicated principally to the Virgin Mary, but also to Jesus, the Saints, the Holy Trinity, and so on, were not specified in the regular service books but had been regularly appended to the liturgy, even being specified in some foundation statutes. The close similarity in style between the older psalm-motets and the later votive antiphons—this can be seen most readily in Mundy's work— lends support to Harrison's view. There is the same basic division into two large movements in *tempus perfectum* and *imperfectum*, the same loosely organized alternation of semichoir and 'full' sections. Then in the later sixteenth century psalm-motets could still have served a similar 'paraliturgical' function in Anglican services. According to the Queen's Injunctions of 1559, '49. . . . for the comforting of such that delight in Musick, it may be permitted, that in the beginning, or at the end of Common-prayers, either at Morning or Evening, there may be sung an Hymn, or such like song to the praise of almightie God in the best sort of melody and musick that may be conveniently devised . . .' Psalms were very popular in the sixteenth century, among Puritans, Catholics and moderates alike. In the company of non-controversial texts, the psalm-motet allowed English composers to pursue a traditional musical technique and a traditional ideal of large-scale, dignified composition.

*On the French–Scottish connection, see NOHM 3, 337ff, and MB 15, xvi. For the Peebles psalm, see A. Hughes-Hughes, *Catalogue of Manuscript Music in the British Museum* (London, 1906–9), ii, 263 and MB 15, 9 and 25. Peebles also set some vernacular psalm translations handed to him by March—just as Tallis and Thomas Whythorne did for Archbishop Parker (see *The Autobiography of Thomas Whythorne*, ed. J. M. Osborne (London, 1962), 208). The Vatable translation was identified by Harrison in EECM 2, ix.

†See Harrison, *Medieval Britain*, 345.

It is less easy to fall back on the Queen's Injunctions to 'explain' some other Latin motets of the early Elizabethan period. Robert Parsons, for example, composed a group of three responds from the Office of the Dead which must be placed in this period despite their apparent Catholic allegiance. Two of them, *Libera me Domine de morte aeterna* and *Peccantem me quotidie*, even incorporate the Sarum plainchant as a cantus firmus—but treated in a slightly new way. In the responds of the Marian Office cycle, Tallis and Sheppard conceived of their task as providing substitutes for the choral sections of the chant in actual services; therefore they omitted from their settings the first few notes of the chant, which were sung by the choir leader as an intonation, and generally introduced the remainder of the chant at the very start of the polyphony. Parsons used the entire chant, including the intonation, delaying the cantus-firmus entry till the last and anticipating it by systematic imitations in the other voices. In short, he made his cantus firmus motets start like homogeneous imitative pieces. This was a small but clear step away from a liturgical orientation towards a technical one.

Evidently Parsons got the idea of setting Requiem responds from Alfonso Ferrabosco, the young Italian musician and adventurer who first appears at Queen Elizabeth's court in 1562. He made a great impression; his madrigals were still being printed in London at the end of the century, and his motets were diligently copied. 'Master Alfonso', too, composed three Requiem responds, and the distinctive opening of his *Credo quod Redemptor meus vivit* served Parsons as a model.* Parsons's *Credo quod Redemptor*, one of his most widely circulated compositions, takes another significant step away from the liturgy. Like its model and like the standard continental respond-motet of this time, it dispenses with the plainchant cantus firmus altogether.

*The two *incipits* are given in Benham, *Latin Music*, 220. On Ferrabosco and his madrigals, see J. Kerman, *The Elizabethan Madrigal* (American Musicological Society Studies and Documents, iv, Philadelphia, 1962), ch. 3. On his motets, see NOHM 4, 489ff. Almost all the MSS which transmit Byrd motets include at least a few by Alfonso, and the following, mostly of a somewhat later period, preserve substantial repertories: Add. 31417, Mus.Sch. c. 45–50, Christ Church 78–82 and 463–7, Tenbury 341–4, 389-James and 1018, the Filmer Partbooks (Yale) and Tregian's Anthology, comprising Egerton 3665 and the Sambrooke MS (New York Public Library Drexel 4302). *Credo quod Redemptor* appears in seven MSS: Add. 31417, Mus.f.1–6, Tenbury 389-James, and the following Paston MSS: Add. 29388–92, RCM 2041, Tenbury 340 and 478–84. Parsons's motet appears in Add. 32377 and 30361–6, Drexel 4180–5, RCM 2041, Tenbury 389-James and Baldwin's Partbooks.

Hereafter references for sources of Ferrabosco motets will generally be given only to Tregian's Anthology, the largest and (because in score) the most convenient source.

[4]

Byrd composed several psalm-motets, in a number of different styles and at different stages of his career. On internal evidence, the two most monumental that have survived were written in the 1560s: *Ad Dominum cum tribularer* for eight voices and *Domine quis habitabit* for nine. Lengthy psalm-motets in Latin must have been sung at some institutions in the 1560s; it would appear that Lincoln Cathedral was among them. Like the more advanced of Mundy's psalm-motets, Byrd's no longer adhere to the Tudor votive antiphon form but rather to a new ideal, that of a continuously imitative structure. His *Domine quis habitabit* seems to invite comparison with several other versions of this favourite psalm, which was also set by Tallis, White, Mundy and Parsons. Byrd's setting is by far the most ambitious.

Byrd also composed cantus-firmus hymns, responds and antiphons. Two of these he published in 1575, one in 1589, two more in 1591 and yet another in 1605, but here too everything points to an earlier date of composition: the nature of the harmony and counterpoint, as well as the employment of a form and technique popular during his boyhood. More precisely, the responds employ the modified cantus firmus form adopted by Parsons, with the plainsong intonation incorporated into the polyphony. In fact Byrd's setting of the Requiem respond *Libera me Domine de morte aeterna* was modelled on Parson's setting of this text. With both composers we have the same paradoxical situation in which a liturgical text (a respond) is set using a quasi-liturgical technique (cantus firmus) for purposes that were evidently non-liturgical.

With Byrd, this non-liturgical orientation is even clearer than with Parsons because of his particular choice of responds and because of certain further details in his treatment of the actual chants. Most of the texts belong to occasions such as Lent (*Afflicti pro peccatis nostris* and *Ne perdas cum impiis*) and midsummer Sundays (*Aspice Domine de sede sancta tua* and *Omni tempore benedic Deum*); this is not the sort of thing that a liturgically-minded composer spends his time with, as appears from the output of Sheppard and Tallis. It must be concluded that Byrd was writing cantus firmus pieces as the outcome of a technical impetus, in order to perfect himself in the traditional arts of musical composition. He may have chosen his particular responds on the basis of the content of their texts, which is sometimes highly coloured (as in the famous Christmas respond *Descendit de coelis*) or didactic (*Ne perdas* and *Omni tempore*) or pathetic (*Libera me Domine*, *Aspice Domine* and *Afflicti*). For the integrity of the liturgical

plainsongs he had little feeling. Many of them are transcribed with errors.*
In *Omni tempore* the long, repetitive chant is subjected to systematic cuts; in
Aspice Domine the mutilations are more complicated and curious. Byrd
starts with the chant transposed up a fifth, but at the words 'inclina, Deus
meus, aurem tuam' quaintly brings it down to its normal position. What is
more, at the very beginning of the chant he changes the characteristic
melodic figure DCFGA to something that will provide him with a more
effective motive for imitation, DFGA. Byrd was certainly moving much
further than Parsons away from a liturgical conception of the respond-motet
and towards a purely technical one.

The most obscure of Byrd's early texts is not a respond but a Vesper
hymn, *Petrus beatus*, which occurs only in York Use for the feast of St.
Peter's Chains (St. Peter ad Vincula). This hymn had never been sung at
London or Lincoln, where Sarum Use prevailed. With the Mass for Sts.
Peter and Paul published in the second book of the *Gradualia* (1607),
dedicated to Lord Petre of Writtle, a connection can safely be inferred with
the Catholic family that is known to have patronized Byrd from the 1580s on.
Conceivably he was already writing for the Petres in the early 1570s, which
is the most likely date for *Petrus beatus*. (This seems to be the only hymn for
the Saint which actually stresses the name 'Petrus'.) In any case, with
Petrus beatus Byrd worked his way through all the stanzas, rather than
setting just the even ones, as a composer of the liturgical era would have done.
White, for example, in his well-known chordal setting of the 7-stanza hymn
Christe qui lux es set only stanzas 2 ('Precamur sancte Domine'), 4 and 6,
leaving stanzas 1, 3, 5 and 7 to be chanted. But when Byrd came to imitate
this very composition, his impetus was purely technical. He determined to
move the cantus firmus up successively through the five voices of the choir,
a stanza at a time; thus he set stanzas 2–6, omitting (symmetrically) stanzas 1
and 7; yet he also set the concluding Amen—reluctant, as it would seem, to
end the total composition with unadorned chanting. This whole scheme is
worse than non-liturgical, it is positively anti-liturgical.†

In 1575 Tallis and Byrd published their famous *Cantiones quae ab argumento sacrae vocantur*, the first publication that either of them had issued,
and their first venture under the music-printing monopoly just granted to
them by Queen Elizabeth. The seventeen musical numbers by each composer are bolstered by a profusion of written matter: a grandiloquent
dedication to the Queen in Latin prose, two prefaces in elegiacs by important
persons praising the composers as paragons of British music, and short

*See p. 62n.
†The hymns discussed in this paragraph appear in TCM 5, 168f and BW 8/9 and 16.

verses entitled *Autores cantionum ad lectorem* and *De anglorum musica*. A tabulation of the texts set by the two composers indicates the transitional state of the English motet in the 1570s (see table 1).

TABLE 1: Summary Contents of the Tallis-Byrd *Cantiones*, 1575

	TALLIS		BYRD	
Responds, *with cantus firmus* 3 ⎫			1 ⎫	
without cantus firmus 3 ⎭ 6			4 ⎭ 5	
Hymns, *with cantus firmus* 2 ⎫			—	
without cantus firmus 1 ⎭ 3			2	(one partly canonic)
Antiphons	4	(two canonic)	1	(canon with cantus firmus)
Introit	1		—	
Prayers (extra-liturgical)	2	(printed as three numbers)	1	(printed as three numbers)
Other texts	—		6	(one canonic)

Tallis, of course, had a larger stock of music available, and a glance at his *Cantiones* motets shows that he dipped into it liberally. Most of his contributions are set to liturgical texts, among them five cantus firmus hymns and responds from the Marian Office cycle composed twenty years earlier in conjunction with Sheppard: *Te lucis ante terminum* (*Procul recedant somnia*) for Advent, *Honor virtus et potestas* for Trinity Sunday, *Sermone blando* (*Illae dum pergunt*), *Dum transisset sabbatum* and *Candidi facti sunt* for the Easter season. But Tallis bypassed other such pieces in favour of four ostensibly later hymns and responds set freely, without any reference to the plainchant, like *Credo quod Redemptor* by Parsons.

This is also the case with all but one of the hymns and responds included by Byrd—though once again, the composer must have had some other pieces available in cantus firmus style. It seems that this style was beginning to be regarded as old-fashioned in English musical circles, at long last. Byrd's one exception, the cantus-firmus Requiem respond *Libera me Domine*, we have mentioned before. He might have included it for a variety of reasons: as a tribute or memorial to Parsons, or to complete a group of three Requiem responds such as Parsons and Ferrabosco had written, or for the sake of its specially high musical quality.

Many of Byrd's motets in the *Cantiones* are similar in type to those of his master Tallis. The two composers must have written some of their pieces in conjunction or at least with reference to each other's work—as seems clear enough with the special (and specially indexed) canons *Miserere nostri Domine* by Tallis and *Miserere mihi Domine* and *Diliges Dominum* by Byrd. Each composer provided as his major effort a long sectional prayer: the penitential collect *Suscipe quaeso Domine* (2ª pars: *Si enim iniquitates*) by Tallis, and Byrd's *Tribue Domine* (2ª pars: *Te deprecor*, 3ª pars: *Gloria Patri*), a collect to the Holy Trinity including an appeal for the augmentation of faith, hope and charity. The latter composition, one of Byrd's most old-fashioned, actually adopts the form of the Tudor votive antiphon. But three of the most modern pieces would also appear to have been composed in conjunction: Tallis's *In ieiunio* and *Derelinquat impius*, and Byrd's *Emendemus in melius*, three unusually expressive free settings of responds for the same Sunday, the First Sunday in Lent, in the Roman rite.* Tallis's cantus firmus responds employ texts and chants from the Sarum rite, of course, and Byrd followed him in this. In England, the choice of Roman, non-Sarum texts for motets is another sign of an essential break with tradition.

That the *Cantiones* was dedicated to Queen Elizabeth, and that she accepted the dedication, may be taken as a hint that the motets were sung at her Chapel Royal. But only as a rather faint hint; perhaps because it would have been tactless to proclaim that the Chapel still echoed to the sounds of Latin, nothing is said about this in the composers' dedication or in the poetic prefaces. And even if some of the motets may have been sung in Elizabeth's Chapel, few if any of them were specifically written for it. Tallis's liturgical items certainly were not—they were older—nor were the special canons. What the two prefaces do say is that the publication was designed to spread the fame of English music on the mainland of Europe. One hesitates to suggest that Byrd composed four of his pieces according to Continental models in order to make his music a success abroad, but whatever his purpose that is what he did and that is what the prefaces claim. In any case, these four motets betray a technical impulse of a particular sort, as does also the cantus firmus respond modelled on Parsons. The hymns *Siderum rector* and *O lux beata Trinitas* adopt basic ideas from a pair of hymns by Alfonso Ferrabosco, *Ecce iam noctis* and *Aurora lucis nuntiat*; Byrd's Requiem respond *Domine secundum actum meum* copies (and improves) the entire opening section of Alfonso's *Domine non secundum peccatis nostris*; and

*Byrd sets *Emendemus in melius* with the verse that goes with it in Roman Use, 'Adiuva nos'; the respond itself also figures in Sarum Use, but with a different verse. With the addition of a second verse, 'Gloria Patri', the respond is also sung just before the imposition of the ashes on the previous Wednesday.

another respond, *Emendemus in melius*, takes over the distinctive texture and the ground-plan of *Qui fundasti terram*, an interior section from the largest of Alfonso's psalm-motets.

It is worth noting that when Byrd set out to imitate *Qui fundasti terram*, a neutral, descriptive text from Psalm 103, he chose a despairing Lenten respond that speaks of sin, death and penitence and appeals to God's Grace for liberation. He set four other equally dejected texts in the *Cantiones*, and was to incline more and more towards material of this sort in his next phase as a motet composer. He was already well on his way to achieving a musical style appropriate to such material, his own powerful individual synthesis of the Continental expressive style—a style almost unknown or at least untried in England. From the textual point of view, however, the clearest indication of Byrd's changing stance in respect to the Latin motet is the appearance of six motets with non-liturgical texts.

Two of them, both in the dejected category, are of special interest. *Libera me Domine et pone me iuxta te* brings together two separate biblical sections:

Libera me, Domine, et pone me iuxta te, et cuiusvis manus pugnet contra me [Job 17:3]. *2ª pars* Dies mei transierunt, cogitationes meae dissipatae sunt torquentes cor meum. Noctem verterunt in diem, et rursum post tenebras spero lucem [Job 17:11–12].

These verses are not so very far separate, to be sure, and a liturgical precedent does exist for their conjunction. Job 17:1–3 and 11–15 make up a Matins lesson from the Office of the Dead, Lesson No. 7, which is followed in the service by the respond *Peccantem me quotidie*. It can hardly be accidental that *Libera me Domine* is followed in the *Cantiones* by Byrd's setting of this very respond. However, Matins lessons had never been set to music in England (except for the special lessons of Holy Week drawn from the Lamentations of Jeremiah) and if they had been, they would have been set intact, not as here in an excerpted form. In selecting the text of *Libera me Domine*, Byrd or whoever did the selecting for him looked at the service books, but looked in a critical spirit and made decisions about them on his own. Another motet, *Da mihi auxilium*, opens with a slightly varied version of an isolated psalm verse (Psalm 107:13, 'Da *nobis* auxilium . . .') and continues with free material, material that is not to be found in the Bible or in the service books:

Da mihi auxilium de tribulatione, quia vana salus hominis [cf. Ps. 107:13], aut aliquid saltem respirandi tempus ut plangam iuventutem meam.

The element of personal literary composition here is obvious. Even the slight variant of the psalm verse, strikingly enough, makes the text more personal.

Free choice of this kind is something new in the history of Latin sacred music in Britain. It represents a change from a medieval attitude to one that is basically modern. To make a personal choice of a motet text implies an interest in and respect for the actual quality of the text in itself, an attitude which sooner or later is bound to affect the musical setting. Things had been different when Byrd's career started, during the last days of the Sarum rite. Motet texts were not chosen at all, in the same sense. One simply set what was provided by one's Dean, what was required to fit the liturgy.

If in a later period liturgical texts continued to be used for motets, that was presumably because it was the way things had always been, and because it did not occur to composers at once to use anything else—though there was no liturgy for the motets to fit and even if there had been, careful examination shows that they were not quite suitable for the liturgy anyhow. An abstract, technical spirit appears most clearly in Byrd's motets involving cantus firmus work and also those involving canons. There are many of these in the early period: besides the ones already mentioned—*Similes illis fiant*, the *Alleluias*, *Miserere mihi Domine* and *Diliges Dominum*—canons occur in the early hymns *Petrus beatus*, *O salutaris hostia* and *O lux beata Trinitas*. In other motets Byrd set himself the technical task of developing his style in certain directions laid down by other composers, as we have seen. The texts of these pieces were a secondary consideration—as was also true in the curious case of the 'motet' *Laudate pueri Dominum*. Originally a fantasia for strings (Fantasia 6/F, BE 17/11), this music was pressed into service for the *Cantiones* by the simple expedient of adapting some miscellaneous psalm verses to its various constituent phrases.

None of these conditions held for *Libera me Domine* and *Da mihi auxilium*. Here the primary element was the text, selected with some originality and independence. There was no pre-existing instrumental piece and no technical project which can be formulated in general terms. The free choice that Byrd exercised (or reflected) for the texts of these two pieces was to manifest itself in a much more striking way during his next phase as a motet composer. It is clear, in fact, that there would have been no new phase without this new freedom.

[5]

The decade and a half following the appearance of the Tallis-Byrd *Cantiones* was the most active period of Byrd's career. Around 1587, as Fellowes observed, he appears to have formed the plan to collect, order and publish his accumulated backlog of material in various musical genres. This project resulted in two books of music to English words, the *Psalmes, sonets, & songs of sadnes and pietie* (1588) and *Songs of sundrie natures* (1589), the famous manuscript book of virginal music for Lady Nevell, dated 1591, and two more publications of motets: the *Liber primus sacrarum cantionum quinque vocum* (1589) and *Liber secundus sacrarum cantionum, quarum aliae ad quinque, aliae vero ad sex voces aeditae sunt* (1591).

In the introduction to the 1589 motet book, Byrd says he has decided on publication because the music has been circulating widely in a confused jumble and in an incorrect state. Earlier manuscript copies are indeed extant for many of the new motets, something that cannot be said for a single one of the pieces published in 1575: manuscript sources of motet repertories from around 1560 to 1575 (three such sources have survived) transmit only one Byrd motet, the early canonic hymn *O salutaris hostia*, together with four of Byrd's In Nomines.* It is understandable that while Byrd was still a young composer centred at Lincoln, not much of his work would enter the main stream of English music, and understandable, too, that more instrumental music would circulate than motets. Things changed after he moved to London in 1572 and after he started publishing music with Tallis in 1575. In sources of the 1580s Byrd rapidly assumed a larger and larger role, to the point where four exhaustive anthologies were prepared assembling up to as many as thirty-six of his motets. While a few numbers of the *Cantiones sacrae* appear to have been composed specially for publication in 1589 or 1591, others figure in manuscripts dated 1581 and 1584. Manuscripts also preserve nearly a dozen motets of this period which for one reason or another never found their way into print.

Taken all together, then, about forty-five motets are known from what we may call the middle period of Byrd's career, from 1575 to 1591. These motets are very different from the earlier *Cantiones*, in musical style as much as in text repertory. Very few have been shown to rely on earlier models in the way that several do in 1575. No arbitrary texts are adjusted to pre-existing instrumental compositions, as in *Laudate pueri Dominum*. The one canon that occurs—in the one piece composed in a 'friendly æmulation' of another composer, Philippe de Monte—does so in a very special context, as we shall see in a moment. Three archaic cantus firmus responds are still printed in the two volumes of *Cantiones sacrae*, and one of the oldest items in these books is another respond, freely composed. But otherwise liturgical texts scarcely

---

*These sources are Rowe MS 316 (King's College), Tenbury 1474 and Add. 31390 (copied later, but evidently devoted to an older repertory).

appear. Byrd has now assumed a fully personal stand in reference to the Latin motet, a stand he had only hinted at in 1575. He is no longer bound by liturgical or technical considerations. He takes texts as he wants them.

Most of the texts he wants speak of depression or distress. Only two or three decidedly cheerful numbers appear in each volume of *Cantiones sacrae*, and they tend to be placed almost self-consciously at the beginnings and ends of the books. Byrd's reputation for unusual gravity stems from this period of his lifetime, the period of the *Cantiones sacrae* and the English songbooks with their 'songs of sadnes & pietie' and their 'seaven Psalmes', the Seven Penitential Psalms. It is not a reputation he could have acquired from the 1575 *Cantiones*, where texts of this complexion account for only about fifty percent of the contents, or from the *Gradualia*, where the proportion is closer to five percent.

Gloomy text material was popular among Continental composers of the sixteenth century, partly because laments, self-reproaches and the like allow for highly affective musical settings. Ferrabosco is typical in this regard, and there is already unmistakable evidence in the 1575 *Cantiones* of Byrd's interest both in Ferrabosco and in developing his own musical rhetoric in the direction of more and more powerful expressivity. However, something other than technical compositional considerations must have influenced Byrd's repertory of texts during this period. For while at first glance the material may strike us as repetitive and conventional, this impression does not hold up under closer examination.

In fact the texts fall into two groups which should be distinguished. The first group, of which we have already seen examples in the 1575 *Cantiones*, is the more homogeneous and the more conventional. It comprises expressions of personal penitence, faith and supplication. With varying shades and degrees of emphasis, texts of this group balance professions of the guilt and distress of the speaker, acknowledgements of the consolations to be derived from God's Grace, and direct appeals to the same. In form they range from the simple statement of *Domine secundum multitudinem dolorum meorum* to the subtle harangue of *Infelix ego*, in mood from the muted confidence of *Levemus corda nostra* to the considerable anguish of *Tristitia et anxietas*. Many of them sound as though they are to be spoken at the point of death; *Infelix ego* comes from the famous exposition or contemplation on Psalm 50 by Savonarola, written shortly before his execution. As to their sources, these texts are thoroughly diverse, some liturgical or biblical, some not. Several of the most complex items—those that required some real literary composition over and above the canny selection of a few scriptural verses—were taken from Flemish anthologies published during Byrd's boyhood:

O Domine adiuva me	1553[9]	1556[9]	set by Petit Jan de Latere
Tristitia et anxietas	1553[8]	1556[9]	set by Clemens
Infelix ego		1556[9]	set by Willaert; also set by Lassus, 1566, and others

They may have furnished some of Byrd's simpler texts, too, though such texts are not specific enough to allow any confident tracing of derivations.

Whatever their sources, the motets of the first group all employ general texts, in the sense that every word of them can be put into the mouth of any Christian sinner. This is not exactly true of the motets of the second group. Containing about as many motets as the other, this group is less conventional in sentiment and also less homogeneous. It includes first of all some motets of penitent supplication that differ in significant small ways from those in the other group. Mercy is now asked for 'us' rather than for 'me', and in a context that seems specified (however obscurely) by references to the plight of 'the City', Jerusalem:

Ne irascaris, Domine, satis et ne ultra memineris iniquitatis nostrae, ecce, respice, populus tuus omnes nos. *2ᵃ pars* Civitas sancti tui facta est deserta, Sion deserta facta est, Hierusalem desolata est [Isa. 64:9–10].

Vide, Domine, afflictionem nostram et in tempore maligno ne derelinquas nos. Plusquam Hierusalem facta est desolata, civitas electa, gaudium cordis nostri conversum est in luctum et iucunditas nostra in amaritudinem conversa est.

2ᵃ pars Sed veni, Domine, et noli tardare, et revoca dispersos in civitatem tuam [cf. Respond 7, 3rd Sunday in Advent]. Da nobis, Domine, pacem tuam diu desideratam, pax sanctissima, et miserere populi tui gementis et flentis, Domine Deus noster.*

Tribulationes civitatum audivimus quas passae sunt et defecimus; Domine, ad te sunt oculi nostri, ne pereamus. *2ᵃ pars* Timor et hebetudo mentis cecidit super nos, et super liberos nostros: ipsi montes nolunt recipere fugam nostram: Domine, miserere. *3ᵃ pars* Nos enim pro peccatis nostris haec patimur; aperi oculos tuos, Domine, et vide afflictionem nostram [pastiche of several responds for Sundays in September and October].

*Only the text fragment 'Sed veni . . . civitatem tuam' was taken (not quite exactly) from the Advent respond; the source of the text for the paragraph beginning 'Vide, Domine' is not known. The system used in this book for identifying literary or liturgical sources is as follows: references, placed in brackets, apply to the portion of the text *extending back to the last new paragraph*, or back to another reference. The 'cf.' in the reference indicates that the text is taken not quite exactly.

Next to imagery suggesting the Babylonian captivity—the plea on behalf of 'the dispersed' is striking—imagery from the Egyptian captivity comes up in a set of three motets which centre on requests not for mercy but for liberty. Once again what is involved is a group or a 'congregation', rather than an individual:

Domine, tu iurasti patribus nostris daturum te semini eorum terram fluentem lacte et melle. Nunc, Domine, memor esto testamenti quod posuisti patribus nostris, et erue nos de manu Pharaonis regis Aegipti et ex servitute Aegiptorum.

Memento, Domine, congregationis tuae quam possedisti ab initio. Libera eos ex omnibus tribulationibus et mitte eis auxilium.

Domine, praestolamur adventum tuum ut cito venias et dissolvas iugum captivitatis nostrae.
2ᵃ pars Veni, Domine, noli tardare, relaxa facinora plebis tuae. Et libera populum tuum [Respond 2, 2nd Sunday in Advent].

The latter text and also *Vide Domine* refer to the coming of God, an idea that Byrd returned to as a central theme in many other motets, in many different moods:

Laetentur coeli, et exultet terra, iubilate montes laudem: quia Dominus noster veniet, et pauperum suorum miserebitur. 2ᵃ pars Orietur in diebus tuis iustitia, et abundantia pacis. Et pauperum suorum miserebitur [Sarum processional respond for Advent].

Vigilate, nescitis enim quando Dominus veniat, sero, an media nocte, an galli cantu, an mane; vigilate ergo, ne, cum venerit repente, inveniat vos dormientes. Quod autem dico vobis, omnibus dico: Vigilate [cf. Mark 13:35-7].

Apparebit in finem et non mentietur; si moram fecerit, exspecta illum, quia veniens veniet et non tardabit [Hab. 2:3].

Exsurge, quare obdormis, Domine? exsurge et ne repellas me in finem. Quare faciem tuam avertis, oblivisceris inopiae nostrae et tribulationis nostrae? [cf. Ps. 43:23-4]. Exsurge, Domine.

Four other texts, united only in their common resumption of references to the Babylonian captivity or some other great communal affliction, are Byrd's most startlingly individual. Two of them were published in the *Cantiones sacrae* of 1589 and 1591:

Deus, venerunt gentes in hereditatem tuam, polluerunt templum sanctum tuum, posuerunt Hierusalem in pomorum custodiam. *2ª pars* Posuerunt morticinia servorum tuorum escas volatilibus coeli, carnes sanctorum tuorum bestiis terrae. *3ª pars* Effuderunt sanguinem ipsorum tanquam aquam in circuitu Hierusalem, et non erat qui sepeliret. *4ª pars* Facti sumus opprobrium vicinis nostris, subsannatio et illusio his qui in circuitu nostro sunt [Ps. 78:1–4].

Haec dicit Dominus: Vox in excelsis audita est lamentationis, luctus et fletus Rachel plorantis filios suos et nolentis consolari super eos, quia non sunt. *2ª pars* Haec dicit Dominus: Quiescat vox tua a ploratu, et oculi tui a lacrimis, quia es merces operi tuo, ait Dominus, et spes in novissimis tuis, et revertentur filii ad terminos suos [Jer. 31:15–17].

One is preserved (incompletely) in manuscript:

Circumspice, Hierusalem, ad orientem et vide iucunditatem a Deo tibi venientem. *2ª pars* Ecce enim veniunt filii tui, quos dimisisti dispersos, veniunt collecti ab oriente usque ad occidentem et verbo sancti gaudentes in honorem Dei [Baruch 4:36–7].

and one was published later in the *Gradualia*, 1605, where it is among the few that stand outside the rigid liturgical scheme:

Plorans plorabit et deducet oculus meus lacrimas, quia captus est grex Domini. Dic regi et dominatrici: Humiliamini, sedete, quoniam descendit de capite vestro corona gloriae vestrae [Jer. 13:17–18].

Reading all these texts as a group, one can hardly escape the conclusion that they refer obliquely to the condition of the English Roman Catholic community during these years. The Latin motet, a prime ornament of Catholicism in its time of ascendency, was now being used to voice prayers, exhortations and protests on behalf of Catholics in time of need. The notion may have been Byrd's, or, if it stemmed from one or more of his patrons, Byrd was the ideal person to put it into operation. The first indication of his well-known Catholic solidarity dates from 1577, when his wife Juliana was cited for recusancy. Thereafter the indications multiply rapidly. From 1580 on, his house figured in lists of suspected recusant gathering-places, in 1581 he exercised himself on behalf of a beleaguered Catholic family, in 1585 and 1586 his house was searched and in 1587 he was bound to answer for recusancy in recognizance of £200. He is several times noted in association with Jesuit missionary priests. In 1581, presumably, he made his consort song setting of *Why do I use my paper ink and pen*, a well-known poem on the martyrdom of Father Edmund Campion and his companions in December of that year. This event shook all England, not only the Catholic community; it may be that for Byrd as for many other English Catholics, 1581 became a year of decision and renewed commitment. But, as we know from some dated manuscripts, by this time the highly expressive 'Jerusalem' motets *Ne irascaris* and *Tribulationes civitatum* and a number of other new works were already in circulation.

In isolation, of course, a text such as *Ne irascaris* would be no sure indication of a strictly Catholic reference, accustomed as the Catholics may have been to hearing their plight likened to that of the captive children of Israel, and their country to ravaged Jerusalem.* Still less could such a motet in isolation be taken as evidence of the quasi-political function that has been suggested above. Jerusalem was a fertile metaphor which the sixteenth century was used to interpreting in a variety of different ways, and there are motets with similar texts composed by unexceptionably Anglican composers of the next generation. But Byrd was not an Anglican and his 'Jerusalem' motets do not exist in isolation. A plea for group liberation such as forms the substance of another three motets, next to them, issues only from a group that considers itself unfree, and the coming of God, treated in five motets, is a theme that one does not expect to see harped on except under oppression. More is at stake than Advent music, surely. The four special texts cited above, on page 42, can be construed in more specific terms. *Haec dicit Dominus* promises the heirs of lamenting Rachel their true patrimony and *Plorans plorabit* foretells the fall of the King and Queen who (in 1605) hold the Lord's flock captive. *Circumspice Hierusalem* celebrates the dispersed children of Jerusalem who return from the East to the West praising God; one thinks of the sons of Catholic families who were sent abroad to Catholic colleges and returned as priests and missionaries. Byrd's own son Thomas

---

*According to the pursuivant who captured Campion on July 16, 1581, Campion had just been preaching 'very nigh an hour long' on the gospel of the day, Luke 19:41–6, which refers to the sorry state of Jerusalem, and he 'applied the same to this our country of England for that the Pope his authority and doctrine did not so flourish here as the same Campion desired' (cited in E. Waugh, *Edmund Campion* (Boston, 1946), 171).

was to spend some time at the college of Valladolid. Most striking of all is *Deus venerunt gentes*, the beginning of a psalm that is rarely found set to music: a cry of horror and shame in response to martyrs' bodies thrown to the beasts of the field and the birds of the air. The quartered bodies of Campion and his companions were nailed to a gate on Tyburn Hill, from which members were stolen by the faithful to be preserved as holy relics.*

In 1582 the publication of the poem *Why do I use my paper ink and pen* cost the publisher Vallenger his ears, and in 1594 one of Sir John Petre's servants came under suspicion simply for copying it. Byrd's setting could not and did not go unnoticed.† But significantly, he felt able to print a few innocuous stanzas when he published the song in the 1588 *Psalmes, sonets, & songs*, even though the poem was notorious and the presence of stanza 1 was certainly a plain enough invitation to sing the others. Evidently it was precaution enough, for someone with Byrd's powerful friends and patrons, to omit the stanzas that were actually seditious. Similarly with Byrd's more extreme 'political' motets, the texts prove to be blameless biblical excerpts. What Byrd and those he was writing for were up to must have been an open secret among English musicians and musical amateurs; but as it happens, the one contemporary allusion to the matter that has come down to us comes not from England but from abroad. Of course, it is an oblique allusion. In 1583 Philippe de Monte sent Byrd an 8-part motet set to a blameless biblical excerpt, once again, but with the verses pointedly rearranged:

Super flumina Babylonis illic sedimus et flevimus dum recordaremur tui Sion. Illic interrogaverunt nos, qui captivos abduxerunt nos, verba cantio- num. Quomodo cantabimus canticum Domini in terra aliena? In salicibus in medio eius suspendimus organa nostra [cf. Ps. 136:1, 3, 4 and 2].

This comes from *By the waters of Babylon*, most famous of all the psalms of captivity. A year later Byrd sent back an answer as though to a challenge:

Quomodo cantabimus canticum Domini in terra aliena? Si oblitus fuero tui, Hierusalem, oblivioni detur dextra mea; adhaeret lingua mea faucibus meis, si non meminero tui. *2ª pars* Si non proposuero Hierusalem in principio laetitiae meae. Memor esto, Domine, filiorum Edom in die Hierusalem [Ps. 136:4–7].

*R. Simpson, *Edmund Campion, a Biography* (1866, 2/1896), 466.

†See BW 12 (2/1963), xxxviii and Thomas Fitzherbert, *Recollections of Fr. Campion*: 'And one of the sonnets [composed on the death of Campion] was presently set forth in music by the best musician in England, which I have often seen and heard' (cited in P. Caraman, *The Other Face: Catholic Life under Elizabeth I* (London, 1960), 282).

Like the psalmist, Byrd found his way to sing the Lord's song. His motet includes a three-part canon by inversion among the eight voices: as though to assure the rest of Catholic Christendom that his hand had lost none of its cunning and that his faith was firm.*

This highly personal use of the Latin motet would not have seemed untoward to Monte. On the Continent there was a tradition for this sort of thing going back to Dufay's famous *Ave Regina coelorum*, in which the standard liturgical text was expanded to include a quiet little prayer to the Virgin for 'your servant Guillaume Dufay'. Josquin Desprez set a humanistic poem to the Virgin containing an acrostic on his own name and also set the psalm *Memor esto verbi tui servo tuo* as a reminder to his employer that his salary was due. In a series of studies Edward E. Lowinsky has amassed evidence for the use of motet texts as political and doctrinal documents in sixteenth-century Italy, Germany and the Netherlands. There is also record of a mid-century French composer who wrote a motet on a suggestive sequence of psalm verses and was hanged as a heretic for his pains.†

In England, however, the motet as a vehicle for personal or political ideas was a new concept, and a far cry from the liturgical genre practised under Henry VIII and Queen Mary. The position in England is dogged by revealing ironies. Only when the motet lost its liturgical bearings did it adopt the Renaissance attitude towards the text established by composers like Josquin at the late *quattrocento* Italian courts. Only when the Catholicism of the motet was called in question did it assert that Catholicism in a newly militant, newly personal, half-surreptitious fashion. The thinking of Byrd's Jesuit friends comes into play strongly here, and it is doubtful that Byrd would have devoted such effort to the motet, and developed it so far, had it not been engaged, broadly speaking, in Catholic propaganda. But one could not express religious or political views in motets without conceiving that

---

*The authority for this exchange of motets is the eighteenth-century antiquarian John Alcock, who scored the pieces with others by Byrd in Add. 23624. Evidently he worked from a set of partbooks from which only the discantus and superius now survive, Tenbury 389 and the James Partbook which has recently come to light. On his copy of *Super flumina* Alcock wrote '. . . sent by him, to Mr Byrd—1583', on *Quomodo cantabimus* '. . . made by Mr Wm Byrd, to send unto Mr Philip de Monte, 1584' (and on Byrd's *Domine tu iurasti* 'This Peice [*sic*] in the Opinion of Mr Bird himself, is the best he ever Compos'd'[!]. Alcock seems to have derived this information from glosses on the lost partbooks; there is no hint of any of it in the two surviving ones. The two 8-part pieces are copied next to one another in Baldwin's 'Commonplace Book' as well as in Tenbury 389-James, and these British sources are the only ones known for the Monte composition. The Byrd appears alone (and anonymously) in Madrigal Society MS G.9-15 (Music Room, British Library) and the associated partbook Add. 34000.

†JAMS, xv (1954), 165, n. 14.

motets could, in fact, reflect personal choice—something that had simply not occurred to Sheppard or even to White and Parsons. Logically enough, when an essentially Catholic artform was threatened by the Reformation, it moved in a direction pointed by the Counter-Reformation. There was no other move to make. And to state a final irony: it was by this move that Tudor church music progressed to its great artistic climax in the later Latin sacred music of Byrd.

[6]

We have yet to address the question of the actual destination for these motets of Byrd's middle years. Where and by whom were they sung? Not in church by Anglican choirs: certainly not the 'political' motets—despite the well-known success of *Ne irascaris* in a vernacular anthem version—and not the long series of highly personal penitential motets, either. The two types of motet appear to have circulated together, without distinction, and evidence for their social context has to be drawn from an examination of the manuscript sources in which that circulation took place.

Some important manuscripts are hardly revealing in this regard. For example, Baldwin's Partbooks were the work of a professional church musician and copyist who seems to have set out to accumulate and preserve the most distinguished music of the last few generations. But other sources suggest a different impetus and a different context. The motet collections Tenbury 341-4 and 369-73 were copied for Edward Paston, whose relations with Byrd will be traced in detail in Volume II: Norfolk squire, amateur poet and compulsive amateur musician, he had dozens of manuscripts copied, in parts and in lute tablature for singing and playing. Another famous manuscript of motets, songs and instrumental music, Christ Church 984-8, has '1581 . . . Sum Roberti Dowi' written on the first page, together with a learned poem by 'Gualterus Haddonus'—the same Haddon of the Latin prayer book. Dow was a Fellow of All Souls who sprinkled his very beautiful and careful collection with classical quotations and *sententiae* of his own praising music (and wine), complimenting individual composers, and defending English music against foreign competition. One thinks of the preliminary material in the Tallis–Byrd *Cantiones*, and indeed Dow quotes from that source.

Manuscripts such as these suggest that Byrd's motets circulated with much other music among groups of sophisticated amateurs of music and letters. They presumably sang and played what they copied, for instruction and recreation, and in the 1580s Byrd was their favourite composer. Possibly the two dedicatees of the *Cantiones sacrae* of 1589 and 1591, whose musical propensities Byrd praises in the customary lavish terms, also engaged in this kind of activity. We do not know; but the Earl of Worcester remained one of Byrd's most faithful patrons, putting a room in his house in London at the aging composer's disposal. As for Lord Lumley, he was the heir of the Earl of Arundel, who had maintained an astonishingly rich musical establishment at Nonesuch, outside London, including an impressive musical library. Lumley still had over thirty music books or sets of parts, and had added some new ones, when this library was catalogued in 1609.*

Walter Woodfill has cautioned us not to overestimate the number of Elizabethan lords, ladies, gentlemen and burghers who actually took part in the singing of complicated music.† However, as he concedes, from the 1590s on there were enough of them to support a modest music-printing trade: a few dozen sets of partbooks, mostly of madrigals, were issued in editions of a few hundred copies. The one clear report that we have of amateur singing on a sophisticated level concerns madrigals, Nicholas Yonge's dedicatory letter in *Musica Transalpina*, 1588:

> Right honourable, since I first began to keepe house in this Citie, it hath been no small comfort unto mee, that a great number of Gentlemen and Merchants of good accompt (as well of this realme as of forreine nations) have taken in good part such entertainment of pleasure, as my poore abilitie was able to affoord them, both by the exercise of Musicke daily used [!] in my house, and by furnishing them with Bookes of that kinde yeerely sent me out of Italy and other places, which beeing for the most part Italian songs, are for sweetnes of Aire, verie well liked of all, but most in account with them that understand that language. As for the rest, they doe either not sing them at all, or at the least with litle delight. . . . I had the hap to find in the hands of some of my good friends, certaine Italian Madrigales translated most of them five yeeres agoe by a Gentleman for his private delight, (as not long before certaine Napolitans had been englished by a verie honourable personage, and now a Councellour of estate . . .)‡

Probably Yonge's singing group was unusual in its transalpine orientation; but probably similar, less cosmopolitan groups had grown up in the 1570s

*See C. W. Warren, 'Music at Nonesuch', *Musical Quarterly*, liv (1968), 47ff and *The Lumley Library: The Catalogue of 1609*, ed. S. Jayne and F. R. Johnson (London, 1956), 284ff.

†W. Woodfill, *Musicians in English Society from Elizabeth to Charles I* (Princeton, 1953), esp. ch. 9.

‡A. Obertello, *Madrigali italiani in Inghilterra* (Milan, 1949), 209.

and provided Byrd's motets with their first hearings. Musical amateurs, such as Dow and Yonge's Gentleman, tend to develop interests that are more literary than those of professionals. Byrd was already investigating music 'framed to the life of the words' in his Latin motets of the 1570s and 80s, just as the madrigalists were to do with English lyrics in the 90s.

It may be, indeed, that Byrd's equivocal attitude towards the madrigal (this too will be discussed in Volume II) arose in part when he saw the amateur circles which cultivated his songs and motets begin to turn away towards new-fangled Italian and Italianate music. In any case, in this social milieu it would have been natural for Byrd to receive motet texts from individual patrons, just as at a later period he is known to have received English song texts from Edward Paston. The texts of the 'political' motets are obvious candidates, as has already been suggested. Worcester, Lumley, Petre and Paston were all Catholics; evidence of Catholic patronage comes up again and again in the study of late sixteenth-century English music. Certain other texts have a personal quality suggestive of a commission or an occasion: for example, *Da mihi auxilium* (cited on p. 36) with its lament for lost youth, and this item from the 1591 *Cantiones sacrae*:

Domine, non sum dignus ut intres sub tectum meum: sed tantum dic verbum et sanabitur puer meus [*Magnificat* antiphon, 1st Thursday in Lent].

Although these words from St. Matthew (8:8) find a place in the liturgy, it is a very obscure one, and they were presumably chosen not on liturgical grounds but in response to some particular domestic crisis. The last of Sir John and Lady Mary Petre's children, Robert, died in infancy on 20 December 1590, at a time when Byrd is known to have been actively in touch with the family.* The date fits well with the modern style of the motet, which unlike most of the others in the collection has not been found in any earlier manuscript sources.

It is sometimes said that Byrd's *Cantiones sacrae* and other motets of the 1580s were written for English Catholic services, in Britain or abroad. The fact that so few of the texts are liturgical speaks strongly against this. What separated Catholicism from the Church of England was not so much fundamental doctrine as the great issue of supremacy on the one hand, and

---

*On the Petre child, see *Genealogical Collections Illustrating the History of Roman Catholic Families of England*, ed. J. J. Howard and H. Farnham Burke (London, 1887), i, 39. Along with such notables as the Earl of Worcester (another of his patrons) and Sir Nicholas and Dorothy Wadham, Byrd attended a two-week Christmas house-party at the Petres' Ingatestone Hall in 1589–90, and two further visits to the Petre manors are recorded in 1590 (A. C. Edwards, *John Petre* (London, 1975), pp. 72f).

multiple questions of liturgy on the other; laxity in liturgy is the last quality to be envisaged in English Catholic services at that time. By the same token, when Byrd in his next phase as a composer of Latin sacred music selects texts which *are* predominantly liturgical, that is a strong argument that the Catholic Church *was* the destination for this new music. In the 1590s Byrd published his three famous settings of the Ordinary of the Mass, and in the *Gradualia* of 1605 and 1607 he provided settings of the Proper of the Mass for the main feasts of the Church year—introits, graduals, tracts, alleluias, offertories and communions. Indeed, the full extent and elegance of the liturgical organization of the *Gradualia*, which was not appreciated until fairly recently,* can be understood only in the context of actual services.

It is known that Mass was celebrated surreptitiously again and again in Elizabethan England, sometimes with considerable pomp. The saintly Lady Montague, whose prodigies of piety seem to have overwhelmed even the authorities, to say nothing of her fellow Catholics, built a chapel at Battle:

> and there placed a very fair altar of stone, whereto she made an ascent with steps and enclosed it with rails, and, to have everything conformable, she built a choir for singers and set up a pulpit for the priests . . . Here almost every week was a sermon made, and on solemn feasts the sacrifice of the mass was celebrated with singing and musical instruments, and sometimes also with deacon and subdeacon. And such was the concourse and resort of Catholics, that sometimes there were 120 together, and 60 communicants at a time had the benefit of the Blessed Sacrament.

This was exceptional—perhaps 'not to be seen in all England besides', as her confessor and biographer puts it—and though Byrd wrote an elegy for Lady Montague when she died in 1608 he was never a member of her circle. But remarkably enough we have record of a clandestine service with music at which Byrd was present. The Jesuit Father William Weston tells of his mission in a Berkshire country house in 1586:

> . . . the place was most suited to our work and ministrations, not merely for the reason that it was remote and had a congenial household and company, but also because it possessed a chapel, set aside for the celebration of the Church's offices. The gentleman [this was a Richard Bold] was also a skilled musician, and had an organ and other musical instruments and choristers, male and female, members of his household. During these days it was just as if we were celebrating an uninterrupted

*See Jackman, *Gradualia*.

Octave of some great feast. Mr. Byrd, the very famous English musician and organist, was among the company . . .

Byrd must have enjoyed high standing in the Catholic community to have been invited on this occasion, for it marked the debut of two recent arrivals from Rome, the most important since Campion's time. They were Fathers Robert Southwell, the poet, and Henry Garnet, superior of the English province from the time of Weston's arrest—only a few days later—until his execution in the aftermath of the Gunpowder Plot. Southwell writes that he was hoping 'we should have sung Mass with all solemnity, accompanied by choice instrumental and vocal music, on the feast of St. Mary Magdalen. This however was put off until the next day.'

Twenty years later Garnet describes another celebration: 'Besides the general affliction [of the persecutions], we find ourselves now betrayed in both our places of abode and are forced to wander up and down, until we get a fit place . . . We kept Corpus Christi Day with great solemnity and music, and the day of the Octave made a solemn procession about a great garden, the house being watched, which we knew not until the next day . . .'. This was in 1605, the date of the *Gradualia*, which includes a Mass Proper and even a processional hymn for Corpus Christi. In this fateful year Byrd is again mentioned in association with Garnet, who is said to have been a keen musician, with a fine singing voice. Of Byrd's immediate patrons, Paston is known to have kept a 'Mass centre' in the woods outside his country house at Appleton, Norfolk, and Petre, a man of infinite caution in such matters, was caught out at least once by an informer who told of a priest fetched from London to say Mass at his Essex manor, Ingatestone Hall, near Chelmsford. When, in dedicating the second book of the *Gradualia* to Petre, Byrd says that its contents 'have mostly proceded from your house (truly most friendly to me and mine)' and when he refers to them as 'these little flowers, plucked as it were from your gardens and most rightfully due to you as tithes', he makes it clear that the liturgical motets of the *Gradualia* had been written for the undercover services run by the Petres at Ingatestone and nearby Thorndon.*

*On Lady Montague, see A. C. Southern, *An Elizabethan Recusant House* (London, 1954), 43. Quotations from the Jesuits from P. Caraman, *William Weston: An Autobiography from the Jesuit Underground* (New York, 1955), 71 and 77, n. 10 and J. Morris, *Two Missionaries under Elizabeth* (London, 1891), 43 (after Jackman); see also Fellowes, *W. Byrd*, 43. On the Corpus Christi procession: in Sarum rite Corpus Christi and Ascension were the two days on which the procession went outside the church; see *Sarum processional*, xiii. On Garnet, see P. Caraman, *Henry Garnet, 1555–1606, and the Gunpowder Plot* (London, 1964), 6, 33. On the Appleton Mass centre, see P. Brett, 'Edward Paston (1550–1630): A Norfolk Gentlemen and his Musical Collection', *Transactions of*

John Bossy has given us a remarkably full picture of Catholic life in England at this period.* It was organized in small patriarchal units centered at great houses in the country (generally further out in the country than the Petre estates). Each unit began with the squire and the resident members of his family. Often, it seems, the wives were the stiffest papists. It also included the squire's servants, or at any rate the main servants, some of his tenants, and other members of his entourage; and it was a common charge that servants and tenants were urged or even forced to become Catholics. The family might have their own resident priest, though this arrangement was more usual in later years. At the Petres' there would have been a community of several dozen persons, who heard Mass together and led a carefully ordered communal life accommodated to the elaborate calendar of Catholic observance in those times. Presumably Byrd joined this community in 1593 when he moved to Stondon Massey, a few miles distant from Ingatestone. Some years later he and his wife were themselves accused of 'seducing' servants and neighbours at Kelvedon away from the Church of England.†

We can only speculate as to the use of Byrd's liturgical music in Catholic services outside of the Petre circle. The fact of publication suggests that it was not intended to be limited to that circle, and the interest and support of the clergy can be assumed at every stage of a project such as the *Gradualia*, from its inception to its circulation. One would not wish to say that Byrd could not have conceived of the idea on his own; still, an undertaking of this magnitude more likely owes its instigation to a higher authority, and the Society of Jesus, with which the composer is known to have been in contact, is a likely candidate. There is a fascinating report of a Jesuit arrested in 1605 with copies of the *Gradualia* in his possession.‡ He may have been a luckless music lover, or he may have been engaged in circulating the books as a matter of Provincial policy. For as a means of ornamenting the service, part-music was both traditional and impressive and also conveniently evanescent, slim octavo partbooks being easier to hide from search parties and easier to transport to attics and Mass centres in barns than vestments, liturgical tomes, or church furniture. Catholic communities would have

the *Cambridge Bibliographic Society*, iv (1964), 53. On Petre, see A. C. Edwards, *John Petre* (London, 1975) and H. Foley, *Records of the English Province of the Society of Jesus* (London, 1875–82), i, 382 and ii, 587ff. Edwards rather surprisingly describes Petre as a 'barely-conforming Anglican', but adds at once that 'his wife, children, and many of his friends and household were firm Papists' (pp. 9–10) and does not doubt that Mass was celebrated at Ingatestone Hall (pp. 74f). For the prefatory matter to books 1 and 2 of the *Gradualia*, see O. Strunk, *Source Readings in Music History* (New York, 1950), 327ff.
  The English Catholic Community, 1570–1850 (London, 1975), esp. ch. 6.
  †Fellowes, *W. Byrd*, 44f.   ‡Fellowes, *W. Byrd*, 43.

needed skilled singers to perform the *Gradualia*, certainly. But Richard Bold
in 1586 had trained some 'members of his household', both male and female,
to serve as choristers; by taking a little trouble—and in such matters the
Catholics were prepared to take a good deal of trouble—other heads of
households could have followed suit.

To be sure, the model for such *Gradualia* choirs would not have been the
traditional cathedral choirs, with their platoons of lay clerks and choirboys,
but rather the informal madrigal groups of the 1580s and 90s. These groups
were already singing Byrd's motets of the middle period. The effect of this
medium on the music itself becomes clearer with the *Gradualia*, principally
in a certain rhythmic agility which in many pieces approximates the metrical
flexibility attained by the Italian madrigalists through the use of the *alla
breve* time signature. This allowed for a subtle flux of metre between the
basic minim and crotchet pulse; it is an essentially chamber-music effect.
Furthermore, in the Masses and the *Gradualia* Byrd for the first time
published Latin sacred music for three voices, suitable for more modest
musical establishments—suitable, indeed, for a trio of solo singers. With its
division into three fascicles containing music for three, four and five parts,
book I of the *Gradualia* follows a model drawn from the madrigal publications, a model set by Byrd himself in the *Songs of sundrie natures* of 1589.

[7]

For the first twenty years or so of Elizabeth's reign, Bossy has observed,
almost all Catholics felt that a Catholic life was 'compatible with some
degree of church attendance; for another sixty this feeling persisted, though
in steady decline.'* The breaking-point for Byrd may have come around
1590. He had already been cited for recusancy, though not before 1586, and
as a prominent member of the Chapel Royal can hardly have absented himself totally from its services. After 1590, though he kept his position, there is
no evidence that he was actually in residence and some that he was not, in
that he now seldom signed the round-robin petitions and memorials recorded
in the Chapel Cheque Book. Withdrawing more and more from the artistic
life of London in which he had participated so effectively in the 1570s and
80s, he moved to Stondon where he perhaps joined a stable Catholic community for the first time in his life. He was nearly fifty. His first wife had
recently died. By assembling and publishing much of his earlier music in
the years 1588–91 Byrd wrote *finis* to a stage of his artistic career, and the
tenor of his sacred music now changes markedly.

*The English Catholic Community, 121.

It is a change, as we have seen, from non-liturgical motets of protest and penitence to music designed specifically to ornament the ritual, functional music to accompany the Mass. At a time when Catholics tended to view the eclipse of their faith as a temporary aberration, Byrd set 'political' texts looking forward to the coming of God, announcing that the children of God would return from the East and that their patrimony would be restored, and lamenting the plight of the City. Repeatedly, too, he dwelled on the theme of sin and repentance as though searching in the individual soul for the sources of the affliction visited by God upon his congregation. In Byrd's turn from motets of anger and anguish to motets and Mass sections celebrating the liturgy in perpetuity, we may perhaps see reflected a new acceptance of the inevitable on the part of his essential public, his patrons among the Catholic gentry. It would be pleasant to see reflected in it also a new spiritual resolution attained by the composer in his late years, the years of his growing affluence at Stondon.

Byrd's liturgical music of the late period represents a new synthesis, of course, distinct from that of the composers of Queen Mary's Chapel Royal: just as late Elizabethan Catholicism was a new thing and not a real continuation of the medieval English Church, despite the nostalgic wish of many of its communicants. The fact that Byrd now sets texts from the Roman, not from the old Sarum Use seems to symbolize a deeper change. Once again, as in his first years as a composer of sacred music, these are fixed texts over which Byrd exercised no choice. But a composer who had developed the expressive language of the middle-period motets and then lived through the madrigal rage could no longer approach every text as an abstract hieratic unit. The force of this remark is perfectly evident from any number of passages in the late sacred music: in the Agnus Dei movements of the Four- and Five-part Masses, in *Iustorum animae, Ave verum corpus, O magnum misterium* and *Tu es Petrus*, to cite only some of the most familiar examples.

Where the words allow, Byrd sheds a wonderful, quiet illumination upon them (and sometimes, as in the case of *Tu es Petrus*, not so quiet). What is also wonderful is the extent of the inspiration he found in these liturgical texts, not only in varied Proper items of the *Gradualia*, but also in the words of the Ordinary, which served Catholic composers on the continent as the commonest of clay for the building of one purely musical structure after another. Byrd was a Catholic composer who could not and did not take the Mass for granted. Still, given the range of liturgical texts, from the most poetic and inspirational in character to the most routine, it is easy to understand that some of them patently failed to strike an individual response from the composer. In his famous programmatic statement in the dedication to the *Gradualia*, book 1, Byrd says that sacred words have 'such a profound and hidden power . . . that to one thinking upon things divine and diligently and earnestly pondering them, the most suitable of all musical measures occur (I know not how) as of themselves and suggest themselves spontaneously to the mind that is not indolent and inert'—but he does not exactly say that this happens with *all* sacred words. Sometimes he composes correctly, beautifully and even imaginatively, but in such a way as to clothe the liturgical text in music which does not differ much from that applied to other texts. This should be no cause for surprise or regret. To a composer working according to the liturgy, the function performed by a certain set of words in the service ultimately assumes more importance than their individual meaning.

The alleluias of the *Gradualia* and Byrd's treatment of them—there are nearly eighty examples—can perhaps be taken as emblematic of his whole endeavour in the late sacred music. He could no longer set this word in the expanding, rhapsodic, ornate fashion of the old Tudor composers. He had neither the time—he was serving lay congregations assembled under somewhat tense conditions, not the leisurely monastic or clerical communities of earlier days—nor the inclination, having himself presided over the dissolution of the old melismatic style into the taut Renaissance idiom of imitative polyphony. Byrd now moulded the alleluias into dense, sharply motivic sections, and these gave him an important new kind of building block with which to construct his concise total forms. He never wrote a *da capo* indication for one of these alleluias, though in many cases the liturgical rubrics would have made this perfectly appropriate; he must have been fascinated by the problem of setting the same word in dozens of different ways, absorbed in the mystery of the inexhaustible renewal of praise. There is a sense of play that is a little abstract as well as exuberant about his manifold solutions. The personal language of the Penitential Psalms echoes characteristically through the texts of Byrd's earlier motets. What stays in the mind from the *Gradualia* is the endlessly repeated, endlessly varied exclamation 'alleluia' and the act of ritual celebration which it embodies.

2

The Early Period

Byrd's Latin sacred music of the early period consists of some thirty motets. Fifteen of them, presented as seventeen numbers, appeared in the *Cantiones quae ab argumento sacrae vocantur*, published jointly by Tallis and Byrd in 1575, when Byrd was thirty-two. The remaining pieces are found in various other sources, some printed, some manuscript. At first glance this may seem like a slow start for a composer for whom the motet was ultimately to become the major genre, like the cantata for Bach and the symphony for Haydn. But it is important to bear in mind the liturgical situation and the dearth of likely opportunities for the performance of Latin motets. On reflection, it is perhaps not surprising that Byrd produced so few motets in his early years, it is surprising that he produced as many as he did. In view of the extensive anthologizing of his music that took place in the 1580s and 90s, it is not likely that many early motets existed which are now completely lost.

Many of the fifteen *Cantiones* items had probably been written just recently and in a considerable hurry, expressly for the publication. None of these motets exists in a manuscript copy antedating 1575—though in noting this, we should also note that very few manuscripts have come down to us at all from the period 1560 to 1580. For example, although the greater part of Byrd's Anglican Church music appears to have been composed at Lincoln between 1562 and 1572, not a single contemporary copy of this repertory survives. Some of the In Nomines for string consort do survive in rather early copies; but few motets. Generally speaking, then, the motets apart from the *Cantiones* assigned to this period have to be placed there for stylistic reasons, since the sources for them are almost all later.

The one exception, the Gyffard Partbooks dating from Queen Mary's reign, has already been discussed (p. 24f). These books contain *Similes illis fiant*, one of two not dissimilar liturgical settings attributed to the very young composer—for if *Similes illis fiant* and *Alleluia. Confitemini Domino* can indeed be considered authentic, they must have been written as early as in the 1550s, when he was still a choirboy. Manuscripts of a later period, Add. 32377 (dated 1584) and Add. 31390 (1578), are the sources of two motets of the early or middle 1560s, to judge from their style, *De lamentatione Hieremiae prophetae* and *O salutaris hostia*. Both of these works show textual affinities with famous works by Byrd's master: with the Tallis Lamentations (though as we shall see, in their text Byrd's Lamentations differ significantly from Tallis's) and with the most widely circulated of the older composer's motets, *O salutaris hostia*. Byrd set this as an unusual 3-part canon accompanied by three other voices.

Still later sources preserve a number of motets based on a long-note cantus firmus. These too date from the early period of Byrd's career, like the cantus firmus motets *Libera me Domine de morte aeterna* and *Miserere mihi Domine*, published in 1575 in the *Cantiones*. At least, almost all of them do; with Byrd one must always be careful to distinguish between the archaic and the archaizing. Obviously he retained a fondness for music in this style, for he published samples of it in all his later motet collections. *Aspice Domine de sede sancta tua*, *Descendit de coelis* and *Afflicti pro peccatis nostris* were printed in the *Cantiones sacrae* of 1589 and 1591 and *Christus resurgens* comes as late as 1605, in the *Gradualia*. The cantus firmus responds *Ne perdas cum impiis* and *Omni tempore benedic Deum* and the cantus firmus hymns *Christe qui lux es* (*Precamur Sancte Domine*) and *Petrus beatus* are known only from manuscripts.

Laetentur coeli, a non-cantus firmus respond printed in the *Cantiones sacrae* of 1589, appears on stylistic grounds to belong with the earlier corpus. And the same is true of the great psalm-motets *Ad Dominum cum tribularer*, entered in a late hand in Add. 31390, and *Domine quis habitabit*, preserved as a unicum in Baldwin's so-called 'Commonplace Book', R.M.24.d.2.

The first section of this chapter will be devoted essentially to the cantus firmus compositions, which constitute a special category and pose certain problems of their own. They will be discussed chronologically or in some other order that promises to provide the most illuminating juxtapositions, and not, of course, in their order of publication or preservation. We shall then proceed to the remaining motets of the 1575 *Cantiones*, and one or two others.

2a

Cantus Firmus and Canon

Similes illis fiant *a 4*	BW 8/6	Omni tempore benedic	
Alleluia. Confitemini		Deum *a 5*	BW 8/14
Domino *a 3*	BW 8/2	Afflicti pro peccatis	
		nostris *a 6*	1591/27–8
Christus resurgens *a 4*	1605 *a 4*/10	Descendit de coelis *a 6*	1591/21–2
Libera me Domine de			
morte aeterna *a 5*	1575/17	Petrus beatus *a 5*	BW 8/16
		Miserere mihi Domine	
Aspice Domine de sede		*a 6*	1575/13
sancta tua *a 5*	1589/18–19	Christe qui lux es *a 5*	BW 8/9
Ne perdas cum impiis *a 5*	BW 8/12		

Several highly unlikely cantus firmus motets are found under Byrd's name in contemporary manuscripts. *Sponsus amat sponsam* (BW 16, pp. 128–9) appears in three sources, and within Byrd groups in two of them, but there was much uncertainty as to its authorship. It is ascribed to Byrd by a peripheral hand in Add.32377; it is ascribed only in the index of Tenbury 389, while in the associated James Partbook the ascription seems to have been later and the 'Byrd' in the index has been substituted for 'Alfons[o].' The music survives only to the extent of an isorhythmic tenor, read in two different time signatures, and an equally improbable upper voice to go with it. Byrd was no antiquarian; his archaizing activities cannot be shown to have reached back any further than the styles practised by his oldest contemporaries. The Bodleian partbook Mus.Sch.e.423, a reliable source, transmits *Sponsus amat sponsam* in decent anonymity.

The large partbook collection of John Baldwin, Christ Church 979–83, which is missing the tenor, supplied TCM and the BW with two questionable Byrd *unica*. That both pieces are set in the liturgical manner—the respond *Reges Tharsis* with the intonation excluded from the polyphony, the hymn *Sacris solemniis* (*Noctis recolitur*) with stanzas 1, 3, 5 and 7 left to be chanted—is an argument against Byrd's authorship, though not a decisive one. It is the extraordinarily crude part-writing of *Reges Tharsis* (BW 8/17) that shocks, and that sent Fellowes into an unaccustomed flurry of emendation. Perhaps we might glumly accept its ceaseless dissonances, parallels and gaping textures as a result of the young composer's first brush with 5-part polyphonic writing. But while the homophonic exclamations 'munera offerent' in *Reges Tharsis* recall 'ex mortuis' in the very early motet *Christus resurgens* (see p. 64), the contrapuntal style recalls an even earlier era. The motives for 'Reges Tharsis' and 'munera offerent' prefigure 'reges Arabum et Saba' and 'dona Domino Deo', and the latter point develops into a sort of imprecise rumination, with the first 'dona Domino Deo' motive followed by a derived motive for the same words, then by yet another, then by the original one running into a new figure for the concluding word 'adducent'. Also uncharacteristic is the repeated-crotchet declamation for 'Domino Deo' and the soprano's dancing sequence on this motive—and the really merciless dissonances throughout. *Sacris solemniis* (*Noctis recolitur*) (BW 8/13) presents exactly the opposite picture. Retiring in harmony, characterless in melody, and far from crude in part-writing—as smooth as soil, in fact, and just about as lively—this style can scarcely be associated with the composer of a hymn setting such as *Petrus beatus* (see p. 77f).

For a more detailed discussion of *Reges Tharsis* and *Sacris solemniis*, see Kerman, *Chronology and Canon*, 378f. Baldwin made numerous other mistakes in attribution. He gave Sebastian Holland's *Dum transisset sabbatum* to Lassus and Lassus's *Ubi est Abel* to Patrick Douglas; the *De lamentatione* and *Aedes nostra* he assigned to John Mundy are more likely by his father William; Baldwin admits uncertainty about *Credo quod Redemptor* ('mr Parsons as some doe say'), hedges on *O splendor gloriae* (naming both Taverner and Tye) and himself changed the attribution of another *Dum transisset sabbatum* from Byrd to John Strabridge. In his 'Commonplace Book', R.M.24.d.2, he misattributed Verdelot's *Ultimi miei sospiri* to Ferrabosco, Peter Philips's *Gaude Maria Virgo* to Morley (though here he was perhaps deliberately misled), Taverner's *Et cum pro nobis* to Tye, and Aston's *Tu ad liberandum* and *Tu angelorum Domina* and Fayrfax's *Rex amabilis* to Taverner. One might argue that in the matter of Byrd attributions, at least, Baldwin ought to count as a first-rate authority, for he copied My Lady Nevell's Book in 1591, he was a member of the Chapel Royal after 1594—when Byrd was perhaps not often in attendance—and he wrote a naive panegyric poem about Byrd in his 'Commonplace Book'. But he also was capable of doing very careless or stupid things, such as scoring Byrd's canonic motet *Quomodo cantabimus* in this manuscript with the canon three semibreves out at the beginning. Baldwin *was* an antiquarian, and it may very well be that he cared less about niceties of attribution than about amassing as many compositions by his celebrated colleague as possible.

Unquestionably authentic is the 4-part *Christe qui lux es* (*Precamur sancte Domine*) given in BW 8/5—authentic as far as the notes are concerned; the words were added by Fellowes to pieces that are textless in the manuscript sources, and so on the face of it intended for instruments, not voices. Byrd's 4-part consort hymns are discussed in chapter 3 of Volume III. Of *Christe qui lux es* there are two sets of verses containing three numbers each, BE 17/24 and 25, and for the 'motet' in BW 8 Fellowes chose and texted set II number 1, II/3, II/2 and I/1.

Both of these consort sets by Byrd are derived from vocal and instrumental settings of the same hymn by Robert White, and Neighbour notes that in set II Byrd takes over the rhythms devised by White to fit the stanzas 'Precamur sancte Domine', 'Oculi somnum capiant' and 'Memento nostri Domine', which are the alternate stanzas 2, 4 and 6 of this 7-stanza hymn. He proposes tentatively that for set II 'Byrd had vocal performance in mind at least as an alternative . . .. A difference in medium between *Christe qui lux es* I and II would explain the existence of two such closely related sets apparently written at much the same time—perhaps even concurrently' (see Vol. III, pp. 53–6). The style of set II is still very different from that of Byrd's other Latin sacred music.

Two very early motets attributed to Byrd are liturgical settings for Easter services in the Sarum rite (see p. 26ff). The 4-part *Similes illis fiant* forms the middle portion of an unusual composite psalm setting written in conjunction with the older Chapel Royal composers John Sheppard and William Mundy. This psalm was destined for the procession to the font on Easter Sunday and during Easter week. The small 3-part *Alleluia. Confitemini Domino* is actually a conflation of two even smaller Easter items, settings of the alleluia at Mass on Holy Saturday and of the special alleluia with verse sung at the same procession to the font.

Both (or all three) pieces include sections in canon and *Similes illis fiant* is built on a cantus firmus. Byrd's earliest motets thus introduce us at once to two characteristic technical concerns of his early composing career. Besides the examples to be discussed in this chapter and later in the present volume, in Volume III Byrd's pursuit of these same techniques is traced through the instrumental In Nomines and hymn settings, and through such splendid *tours de force* as the canonic Pavan G6 from My Lady Nevell's Book and the canonic Fantasia 5/C for strings.

Similes illis fiant and *Alleluia. Confitemini Domino* are compositions with no real scope; they each comprise four distinct sections from 8 to 18 breves in length, interspersed in some cases by plainsong, as directed in the liturgy. In style they differ so far from the music that Byrd wrote later—even slightly later—that it seems hard at first to rationalize them into the composer's musical development. One's first reaction is to be taken aback by the wooden, characterless imitative motives and the pokey rhythms, by the casual treatment of dissonance and the archaic configuration of the all-too-numerous cadences. Yet enough small touches of ingenuity and artistry appear in this music to lend credence to the ascription. Wooden motives, in any case, were absolutely standard in English musical circles at a time when the technique of continuous imitation had not yet been properly assimilated. Byrd still sometimes falls back on them in the *Gradualia*; but one measure of his progress in the writing of cantus firmus motets is the way the motives are gradually made more individual and expressive. And the essential problem of cantus firmus setting, the problem of large-scale organization, is already broached, just barely, in **Similes illis fiant** (BW 8/6).

The cantus firmus of this piece is the faburden of the festal psalm tone prescribed for Psalm 113, *In exitu Israel*, during the procession, plus the miniature antiphon *Alleluia* sung after each verse. Faburden was the ancient English practice of singing chants in three-part harmony, with the chant in the treble and the lowest voice singing mainly in sixths and octaves below it, according to simple improvisation rules. Harrison first observed that a number of late medieval compositions are based on this low faburden voice as the cantus firmus, rather than on the chant proper.*

The cantus firmus follows the same course in each of the fourteen *alternatim* psalm verses set by the three composers. Since it moves mainly in breves and its declamation is almost entirely syllabic, it leaves no time for any real contrapuntal development above it; and since it is placed in the bass, harmonies are rigidly determined. So few satisfactions can be imagined in writing such a piece that we can easily understand Sheppard and Mundy dividing up the task between them. (Did they agree to do seven verses each, and did Mundy then parcel out three to young Byrd?) Sheppard took further short-cuts, repeating music for several of his verses.

In a work of this description we can fairly expect to find our very young composer adopting his older contemporaries' style and turning it to his own ends. As in the later In Nomines, we can watch Byrd closely as he works from a model. The archaic cadences, to begin with, can all be matched in the other men's work: Sheppard liked to move his top voice down from 6 to 5 over the final bass note, and Mundy liked to approach the final *tierce de Picardie* by way of scale patterns outlining a tritone. Byrd followed them, and acquired a taste for eccentric cadences which remained with him for quite a time. On the whole he paid less attention to Sheppard, who seldom employed imitation or elided interior cadence points and never repeated text fragments, than to Mundy, who consistently wrote short-breathed stretto imitations among the three upper voices.

Mundy's last verse, the *Gloria Patri*, seems to have provided Byrd with some specific ideas. He contrived a slightly denser stretto on Mundy's 'Gloria Patri' motive (FFac, etc.) for his own 'Similes illis fiant' phrase; he also took over Mundy's alleluia motive, complete with its unusual touch of E minor harmony, for his own third and last alleluia. A comparison of these two little alleluias can provide a first glimpse of the composer to come (Ex. 1).

Whereas Mundy achieves a sober ostinato effect by starting his stretto entries from E, e, e, b, a, e and C, Byrd starts his from e, c+a in thirds, f+a in sixths, f, and F: a lucid sequence in thirds yielding both an ostinato (f, f, F) and also a relatively intense melodic climax (e . . . f, f). And this climax carries through from the very beginning of verse 3. The opening motive 'Dominus memor fuit nostri' (which, by the way, resembles the actual chant) peaks at b♭ and c in the tenor and at f and g in the two altos; the note g continues to sound during the next point 'et benedixit nobis' and

*F. Ll. Harrison, 'Faburden in Practice', *Musica Disciplina*, xvi (1962), 11ff and *Medieval Britain*, 356f et passim.

Ex. 1

finally moves up to a′ at the crux of the triadic alleluia motive fga′d. Indeed, these are the only high a″'s in Byrd's entire piece.

Byrd's interest in intricacies of contrapuntal technique is manifested most clearly, of course, by his middle verse with its unison canon between the two upper voices. There is no precedent for this in the portions of the psalm composed by Sheppard or Mundy, though elsewhere Mundy wrote some modest canons of a similar sort, involving two voices at the octave over a freely-imitating bass. Byrd must have picked up his liking for canon from his master Tallis.* In *Similes illis fiant*, the way he manages also to fit in the third voice as a free canon earns him more credit, perhaps, than the alto canon itself, which 'breaks' for one note and necessitates two minor modifications in the cantus firmus. It also causes rough dissonances at the alleluia, as the result of a downward-scale motive in syncopated rhythm. But since very similar sounds emerge from a similar motive in the previous alleluia which is *not* canonic, the roughness seems to have been intentional. Was Byrd deliberately rejecting the bland, almost entirely consonant style that he encountered in the work of Mundy?

In any case, motives of this form, which were obviously designed to

---

*Mundy breaks briefly into canon in the course of the long motets *Maria Virgo sanctissima*, *Vox Patris coelestis* and *Eructavit cor meum* (EECM 2, 3, 36, 135); Hugh Benham, who points this out in *Latin Music*, 210, also notes a similar canon in Tye's *Domine Deus coelestis* (*Latin Church Music*, ed. J. Sattersfield, ii (Madison, 1972), 17f). Tallis, in addition to the special prize canon *Miserere nostri Domine* in the 1575 *Cantiones*, wrote canons in the motets *Salvator Mundi* II and *Iam Christus astra ascenderat* (*Solemnis urgebat dies*), in the final Agnus Dei of the *Missa Puer natus est nobis*, in the keyboard Lesson mistakenly assigned to Bull in MB 14/51 (see Vol. III, p. 231n), and in the well-known hymn *Glory to Thee my God this Night*.

produce dissonances, whether rough or smooth, cannot be matched in the verses by the older composers, but are characteristic of Byrd's early work. They turn up again in other cantus firmus pieces: in *Christus resurgens* (see Ex. 2), *Libera me Domine de morte aeterna*, *Aspice Domine de sancta sede tua* and *Petrus beatus*. Two such motives—again for the word 'alleluia' and also in canon—figure in **Alleluia. Confitemini Domino** (BW 8/2). This piece recalls *Similes illis fiant* only too clearly, furthermore, in its cadences. It includes three little canons, all more complicated than the usual type, as exemplified by *Similes illis fiant* and the Mundy trios. The first is between soprano and bass at the octave, the second between alto and soprano at the upper fourth (and at a new time interval), and the third a 3-part canon at the lower octave and fourth.

[2]

Byrd's one other cantus firmus motet for four voices, **Christus resurgens** (1605 *a* 4/10), raises a number of musicological questions of great interest. For one connoisseur, H. B. Collins, it was also one of Byrd's great master-pieces, 'a wonderful meditation on the Plainchant, like nothing so much as some of Bach's Choral Preludes, or the slow movements of his violin sonatas.'* The motet is obviously very early, and the first interesting thing is that years later, in the *Gradualia*, Byrd actually printed it. It stands out as the oldest piece in the collection by far—the oldest and crudest piece, in fact, ever published or anthologized by the composer. The crudity did not bother him, that is clear enough. A setting of the famous Easter processional antiphon was certainly appropriate enough to the general scheme of the *Gradualia*; and we can assume that *Christus resurgens* had its Elizabethan, as well as its Victorian, admirers.

Old: but how old? At first glance the piece seems to fit right in with Byrd's other liturgical Easter music of the mid-1550s. It employs the Sarum chant as a cantus firmus in the antiphon proper (though not in the verse *Dicant nunc Iudaei*) and omits the intonation from the counterpoint, as directed in the liturgy. Other 4-part settings of the same chant, by John Redford and the Salisbury composer Thomas Knyght, appear in the Gyffard Partbooks close by to *Similes illis fiant*. Yet two considerations militate against so early a date. One is the manifest advance in style over *Similes illis fiant* and the other is the presence of two errors in the cantus firmus.† Such errors (as distinct

---

*H. B. Collins, 'Byrd's Latin Church Music for Practical Use in the Roman Liturgy' *Music & Letters*, iv (1923), 257.

†On the words 'vivit Deo' (BW 5, 68, bars 2–6) Byrd has CDECE EDD instead of CDEDF EDD, and on the last 'alleluia' (69, bars 5–10: repeated on 75) CDEFED

from ornaments; they can easily be distinguished) never occur in genuine liturgical items. They do occur, however, in several of Byrd's cantus firmus compositions of a later period, when he was writing this quasi-liturgical music in a technical spirit, after the liturgical conditions for it had lapsed. *Christus resurgens* seems to be the earliest of these compositions. Significantly, the text was one of the most popular for cantus firmus as well as free settings. Contemporary 5-part versions by Christopher Tye, William Parsons of Wells and John (?) Tailer are known, as well as the 4-part settings in Gyffard.*

In the cantus firmus sections of *Christus resurgens* the dissonance treatment is still crude, and one boisterous cadence erupts to conclude the alleluia (this cadence also returns to conclude the whole motet—with the insertion of an extra semibreve!). One particular dissonant configuration, which may be called a 'consonant seventh' or 'consonant second' by analogy with the 'consonant fourth' described by Jeppesen and others,† is shown in Ex. 2 as produced by the descending syncopated motive which we have already encountered in Byrd's earliest alleluias. For better or worse, this now becomes a standard means of making cadences in Byrd's cantus firmus writing. The motives in *Christus resurgens* are still mostly colourless, with the exception, perhaps, of 'Quod enim vivit', and in addition Byrd gets into unaccountable trouble with voice spacing. At half a dozen places gaps of more than an octave appear between upper voices.

Ex. 2

But the piece marches, vigorously even if sometimes a little clumsily. The cadences are solid and the harmonic plan serviceable. Treating a melismatic cantus firmus, rather than a syllabic one as in *Similes illis fiant*, Byrd has much more space for contrapuntal development; and the most novel feature

instead of CDEDFED. Other such errors occur in *Libera me Domine de morte aeterna* on the words 'movendi' (BE 1, 219, bars 40–4), FGAB♭G etc. instead of EGAB♭G, and 'terra' (bars 46–7), EFDC instead of EFED, and in *Omni tempore benedic Deum* (BW 8, 129), where the first note of the verse is A instead of G. Cf. *Sarum antiphonal*, pp. 241, 583, 317.

*The three 5-part pieces appear in Mus. Sch.e.423, Tenbury 807–11 and Christ Church 984–8 (also Huntington Library H.691) respectively. No Christian name is given for 'Mr. Tayler' or 'Tailer', but a John Taylor was master of the children at Westminster School in the 1560s. He has been cautiously identified with the 'Mastyre Taylere' of the Dublin Virginal Book. Redford's composition is printed in C. F. Pfatteicher, *John Redford* (Cassel, 1934) and the beginning of Knyght's in NOHM 3, 344f.

†Andrews, *Byrd's Polyphony*, 121 (Ex. 205d) and 200 (Ex. 403[a]).

of the motet is the way he takes advantage of this resource. Prior to the alleluia, the cantus firmus falls naturally into six phrases to accommodate imitative motives, phrases lasting 11, 23, 11, 15, 19 and 8 semibreves. But Byrd unlike other composers does not accept this implied sectionalization; he subdivides the antiphon into three longer, double sections of 34, 26, and 27 semibreves, and carries two sharply defined imitative motives along simultaneously in each long section. This is a primitive form of double imitation, something that is very seldom found in earlier English music, and never systematically as here. There will be a good deal to say later about Byrd's refinement of this technique, which is one of the most important of his innovations in the 1575 *Cantiones*. And things are already handled well in the last double point of *Christus resurgens*. After the motives 'Quod enim vivit' and 'vivit Deus' have worked together several times, each returns in stretto and then 'vivit Deus' acquires a lively melisma (and an inversion) for the cadence.

If this cadence sounds decidedly curt, that is in character with the rest of the music. The peremptory tone struck by the homophonic exclamations 'Ex mortuis' in *Stimmtausch* at the very start of the counterpoint—exclamations which seem to be echoed by the first few alleluias—is kept up by the almost entirely syllabic declamation of the voices other than the cantus firmus. This all sounds very different from the typical leisurely, melismatic cantus firmus motets of Byrd's older contemporaries.

The alleluia is undoubtedly the clumsiest section of *Christus resurgens*. The verse 'Dicant nunc Iudaei' is undoubtedly the smoothest: so much so, indeed as to raise the interesting possibility that it was added later, as an afterthought or a substitution for an original cantus firmus section. The ranges of the voices are smaller and no untoward gaps develop between them. The dissonance treatment, though still sometimes irregular, is more sophisticated. Some quite mature touches can be observed: the half-canonic, half-homophonic phrase 'nobiscum dicentes', the quiet but expressive progress of the point 'quomodo milites', and the way G minor harmony is introduced, maintained and quitted towards the end. The sequential motive 'Quare non servabant', and the combination of this motive with 'petram iustitiae', recall the style of the *Gradualia*; the sporadic plainsong paraphrase in the tenor (at 'Dicant nunc Iudaei' and 'ad lapidis positionem') can also be matched in the *Gradualia* hymn *Pange lingua gloriosi* (*Nobis datus nobis natus*) (1605 a 4/8). There are admittedly some problems in upholding this interpretation, for as an example of the 'verse' style of the *Gradualia*, 'Dicant nunc Iudaei' is unusually quiet, in fact unusually dull. But there are greater problems in trying to accept this music as written by Byrd around 1560.

Byrd would doubtless have known the earlier, Gyffard settings of *Christus resurgens*. But he did not learn anything important from them, not even from the impressive Redford piece, though this composer certainly influenced his organ compositions of the same period (see Vol. III, ch. 6).* The case is different with the 5-part **Libera me Domine de morte aeterna**, the one full-scale cantus firmus piece included by Byrd in the *Cantiones* of 1575 (No. 17), when one suspects he had already kept it by him for some time. It is a remarkable composition, both in its own terms and also in terms of the progress made since his earliest music.

Presumably this is the work that established the pattern for Byrd's other responds, for that pattern is borrowed here from the 5-part setting of *Libera me Domine* by Robert Parsons, the man whose place Byrd filled in the Chapel Royal in 1570. An interesting minor composer with a decidedly original turn of mind, well calculated to appeal to Byrd, Parsons had joined the Chapel in 1563. Not much else is known about his career, but the employment of words from the First Prayer Book of Edward VI in his First Service shows that he was already composing in the early 1550s. And for what it is worth, some geographical affinities can be traced between the two composers. Stainton, Lincolnshire, where Parsons was granted a Crown lease on a rectory in 1567,† is four miles from Hainton, whose lease Byrd had obtained in 1563, and Newark-on-Trent, where Parsons drowned in 1570, is the next large town to Lincoln. The influence of the older man on the younger can be traced in instrumental music as well as in motets (see Vol. III, pp. 46ff, 74f, 116).

Parsons was the first English musician to compose a group of responds from the Office of the Dead, in which choice of material he was followed by Byrd, and was himself probably following Alfonso Ferrabosco. His responds mark an advance over the traditional model established in the Marian Office cycle by Sheppard and Tallis. In *Credo quod Redemptor meus vivit* he even abandons the cantus firmus entirely, and concentrates on 'affective' setting;

*At most Byrd may have picked up his motive for 'vivit Deus' from Redford, and perhaps also the idea of concluding his motet not with the second alleluia of the chant but with a da capo of the first one. This non-liturgical plan must have been widely sanctioned, for Tye adopts it as well as Redford and Byrd. (Only one part of Tye's piece has survived, the countertenor (Mus. Sch.e.423), but it is undoubtedly a cantus firmus setting, for the part fits with the plainsong. And since the setting stops after the verse, with the words 'Aut resurgentem adorent nobis dicentes', the first alleluia is evidently to be sung da capo.)

†*Calendar of the Patent Rolls. Elizabeth I*, iv, 1566-9 (London, 1964), 142; information kindly supplied by Mr. David M. Baker. Byrd is cited as an authority on Parsons in the Chirk Anthem MS; after copying Parsons's *Deliver me from mine enemies* and ascribing it to Strogers, the scribe adds: 'Some say mʳ parsons: mʳ Byrde affirmes it to be truth' (Richard Macnutt, Music Catalogue No. 101, p. 36).

so does Byrd in many later responds, of course, including *his* Requiem responds *Peccantem me quotidie* and *Domine secundum actum meum*, printed in 1575. In *Libera me Domine* and *Peccantem me quotidie* Parsons keeps the cantus firmus but treats it in a slightly new way which is distinctive enough to make Byrd's dependence clear. Since in the 1560s respond motets were no longer designed for the liturgy, there was no longer any call for the first notes of the chant to be delivered as an intonation. Parsons could incorporate them into the polyphony along with the rest, and smooth over or disguise the entrance of the cantus firmus. In this he was adopting a venerable Continental practice, as exemplified *inter alia* by the one cantus firmus motet by Ferrabosco, his 5-part setting of *Da pacem Domine*.* Instead of starting with the long-note cantus, Parsons leads off with the other four voices; they present a solemn point of imitation— 21 semibreves long in one case, 18 in the other— using a motive with the same melody and same even rhythm as that of the cantus *incipit*. So when the cantus firmus turns up last in order, it sounds like an innocent final imitative entry. And just when the listener is beginning to suspect that this entry may not be what it seems, one extra entry in the bass confuses the issue ingeniously.

All this is followed by Byrd (with improvements: the motive 'de morte aeterna' is introduced earlier, and the extra bass entry comes on a fresh scale degree, the subdominant). Both composers use relatively neutral-sounding imitative motives, but a comparison can sharpen our appreciation of the quietly expressive quality of Byrd's 'quando coeli movendi sunt', 'dum veneris iudicare' and 'de morte aeterna', even though the latter conforms to the melodic stereotype illustrated in Ex. 2. Byrd parts company from Parsons by placing the cantus firmus in the soprano rather than the tenor, by omitting the verse 'Dies illa',† and by harmonizing the Dorian chant melody much more richly. He takes full advantage of the resources of the Dorian mode, using the flat and sharp forms of the sixth degree in a ratio of about 5:3. (The chant as transposed to G includes only one E♭ and only two E♮s, one note apart; Parsons's other voices tend to stick to E♭ except in the immediate area of those E♮s). Indeed it is the harmonic treatment, and especially harmonic treatment on the large scale, that stands out as the most remarkable feature of Byrd's motet.

Listening to the long opening section, we are struck at once by the

---

*Egerton 3665 (Tregian) No. 16. Alfonso's 6-part setting of the same text (Sambrooke MS, No. 4) lacks a cantus firmus.

†Both composers omit the two other verses, 'Quid ergo miserimus' and 'Nunc Christe te petimus'. White in his 4-part setting includes 'Dies illa' and 'Quid ergo miserimus' (TCM 5, 131ff).

extreme vagueness of the harmony. We expect this quality, perhaps, during the slow opening imitation with its modal-sounding *incipit* GFG. But it persists as successive points consistently avoid forming cadence patterns and instead contrive to undercut the local tonic; in the phrase 'de morte aeterna', for example, the tonic G tends to be underpinned by subdominant chords, while dominant chords are repeatedly turned minor. The bass seldom moves by fifths. Likewise the phrase 'in die illa tremenda' coalesces around F, but Byrd manages this without the usual cement of syncope cadences, with a resulting effect that is curiously unassertive. Only at 'Quando coeli movendi sunt et terra' does the music move decisively to B♭ in order to support a preliminary climax in the chant on the notes d'e♭'. 'Dum veneris iudicare' begins as though to acquire even clearer definition, with delicate cadences after 3 and 6 breves and even the suggestion of a repeated period after 7. But Byrd carefully draws back, and after launching the phrase safely lets it float where the chant melody takes it; the true soprano climax on the characteristic Dorian semitone f'e♮' is echoed poignantly by the 'dum veneris' motive in the other voices at the top of their ranges. Again, the passage is almost entirely consonant, without syncope dissonances.

These are reintroduced beautifully at the first entry of the final subject. Yet with this same stroke Byrd blends together two long points without any clear point of articulation. (Parsons does something similar here.) This final motive, 'saeculum per ignem', recalls the earlier motive 'de morte aeterna', and the harmony, too, which was already clouding over at the 'iudicare' climax, falls back to the soft, unarticulated flow of the beginning. The ultimate plagal cadence has no trace of any preliminary dominant. The 'saeculum per ignem' motive converges into a brooding ostinato on the notes GF, the same notes which seemed to generate this vague harmonic style in the first place.

The harmonic style of *Libera me Domine* is certainly far from primitive, though it is very unusual for Byrd and may make us think vaguely of earlier generations. There is nothing like it in *Christus resurgens*, nor incidentally in Parsons's *Libera me Domine*, a portion of which can be seen in *Tudor Church Music*.* From the respond melody Byrd derived his basic scheme; the harmony bears out the melodic implications of the chant, with its 'modal' beginning, its cadence on the lower seventh degree at 'in die illa tremenda', its climaxes on the upper sixth and seventh degrees, and its modal conclusion. But the crystal-clear structure is clouded by surface detail. What is most elegant is the way the structure is *selectively* clouded, the way the

*TCM 9, 303f, misattributed to Byrd.

harmony seems about to take root in the climactic central sections of the motet, only to return to the prevailing obscure idiom at the conclusion.

[3]

Libera me Domine is one of four Byrd motets in the 1575 *Cantiones* provided with aberrant key signatures. There are eight more by Tallis. Either the signatures are inconsistent among the various voice parts of a piece ('partial signatures') or they actually change during the course of the individual parts, or both. In *Libera me* all the voices have two flats in the signature except the soprano bearing the Dorian cantus firmus transposed to G, which has only one. It is astonishing to come upon this archaic notational practice in even most modern of the motets, *Emendemus in melius*. Here all the voices have two flats in the signature except the second tenor, with one—and the alto and first tenor drop the E♭ from the signature in their last lines (beginning at the first and second E♮s in the word 'honorem' respectively).

This phenomenon should warn us against placing too much reliance on signatures as a criterion for determining a composition's mode. H. K. Andrews did so when he assigned both *Libera me* and *Emendemus in melius* to the transposed Aeolian mode, while settling *Libera me Domine et pone me juxta te*, which has two flats in the signature of the second tenor voice but one in all the others, in the transposed Dorian.* Byrd most probably regarded them all as Dorian; they all exhibit about the same amount of fluctuation between the raised and lowered forms of the sixth degree of the scale. Sixteenth-century polyphony inherited this characteristic of the Dorian mode from plainchant. The practice seems to have grown up of adding an extra, 'informal' flat to the signature when it was noticed that a particular piece, voice part, or even single line included more flat sixth degrees than sharp. Thus untransposed Dorian pieces sometimes contain an 'informal' B♭ in the signature, and transposed ones an 'informal' E♭ along with the regular B♭ required by the transposition.

Most of the notational anomalies in the *Cantiones* can be explained in this way, though it will come as no surprise to discover some inconsistencies. These aberrant signatures serve to dramatize an important melodic characteristic of the Dorian mode, the fluidity of treatment of the sixth degree. And this is linked directly to an important harmonic characteristic, the option of making cadences on the fifth degree of this mode either in the

*Andrews, *Byrd's Polyphony*, 19 (table).

Phrygian form, with the bass moving from ♭6 to 5, or in the perfect form, with the bass moving from 2 to 5. The latter are stronger, of course, and can sometimes have a 'dominant' feeling.

The point is worth making if we wish to employ the concept of mode as a means of distinguishing between the actual sound of certain groups of compositions, rather than as a purely taxonomic device. *Libera me Domine de morte aeterna* and *Emendemus in melius* must be aligned with Dorian compositions such as *Libera me Domine et pone me juxta te*, not with Aeolian ones ending on A—of which there are two examples in the *Cantiones* of 1575, *Da mihi auxilium* and *Domine secundum actum meum.** It is a secondary question whether Byrd assented to Glarean's analysis and terminology and would actually have called this music 'Aeolian'. Whatever he called it, the essential point is that in the early and middle years there is a real difference between his motets in A on the one hand, and those in G with signatures of (generally) two flats on the other. Motets in A exhibit none of the flexibility with regard to the sixth degree that characterizes motets in G. They exclude the sharp sixth almost entirely, except in incidental contexts where it is used as local support for the VII triad (F♯–G). As a consequence these motets make cadences on the fifth degree only in the weaker Phrygian form. They eschew the stronger 'modulatory' effect of perfect cadences on the fifth degree.

In Byrd's motets of the middle period the most common 'minor' modes continue to be those based on G and A. The distinction between the two groups is perhaps even sharper than before, though on the other hand motets with a D final are admittedly more ambiguous and sometimes difficult to construe. By the time of the *Gradualia* Byrd's practice had become remarkably consistent. 'Minor' motets in A and G now occur only exceptionally, whereas whole Masses—the Marian Masses in book 1 and Christmas, Epiphany and Easter in book 2—are set in D with very little use of the sharp form of the sixth degree. There are next to no perfect cadences on the dominant A. This music is best understood as Aeolian, then, transposed to D and furnished with a flat in the signature.

In the Lydian mode the 'informal' flat sometimes added to Dorian compositions is supplied all but invariably, making this mode indistinguishable from Glarean's Ionian. Both of the 'major' modes, the Mixolydian and the Lydian or Ionian, allow for perfect cadences on the dominant, though the Mixolydian makes these cadences on the minor dominant. Only the Mixolydian makes subdominant cadences; the Ionian avoids them, featuring the

*According to Benham, the A mode is not previously found in England (*Latin Music*, 174).

submediant instead. To the extent that major-minor tonality depends on a balance of dominant and subdominant pressures, then, the Mixolydian and Dorian modes can be said to come closer to modern practice than the Ionian and the Aeolian. Indeed, we shall see that Byrd's route towards a more tonally-oriented major mode was not by way of adding subdominant cadences in the Ionian mode, but rather by raising the seventh of the Mixolydian mode when it occurs as the third of the dominant.

It is no doubt anachronistic to think about sixteenth-century modality so much in harmonic terms—hard as it may be for the modern listener to do otherwise, especially when he is listening to music such as Byrd's which seems well on the way towards tonal organization. From the contemporary standpoint, melodic considerations were primary. The overall sound of the music—what the Germans can refer to conveniently as its *Klang*—is affected not only by the mode itself but also by the ranges of the various voices in respect to the mode's final. A single note can sometimes make a great deal of difference. For example, if the soprano extends up only to the seventh degree of the mode, its melodic high-points will be heard as over-shooting the fifth degree, descending to it as a point of repose, and often serving to decorate it. But if the soprano extends up to the octave the high-points will have much more of a sense of achievement, even of excitement. Likewise the quality of harmonic support, and with it the overall *Klang*, will be significantly different when the bass extends down to the fifth of the mode to make perfect cadences, and when it goes down one note more to make plagal cadences in addition.

Byrd's Ionian compositions can be heard as belonging to four rather distinct groups characterized by voice ranges extending from the low 3rd of the mode in the bass to the high octave in the soprano, from low tonic to high 6th, from low 6th to high 5th, and from low 4th to high 2nd. These overall ranges correspond to certain particular clef combinations. The normal outer clefs used in the notation of late sixteenth-century polyphony are either soprano and bass or treble and baritone, and the normal positions of the modes are either untransposed or transposed down a fifth. Of the four possible combinations of these factors, one is typically associated with each of the overall ranges given above (see Ex. 3a).*

As for the other modes, Ex. 3b–d shows all the groups that Byrd employs

---

*The third Ionian group is in fact represented by only one motet, *Unam petii* (1605 a 5/27), but compare *Domine secundum multitidinem dolorum meorum* (1589/27) and *Visita quaesumus* (1605 a 4/11). Other examples may be found among the 'pastorals' of the *Psalmes, sonets & songs* of 1588, Nos. 11, 12, 15, 20 and 21.

Ex. 3

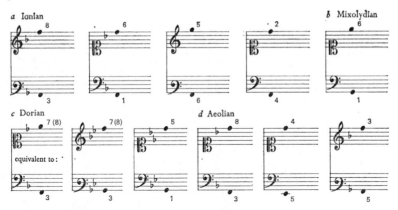

with any regularity. It is hard to account for the existence of two equivalent notations for the first Dorian group.

The late Siegfried Hermelink, in a seminal study of modal treatment in Palestrina, first drew attention to the importance of voice ranges in determining the actual quality of sixteenth-century polyphony, and to the relation of voice ranges to the clef combinations used in the music's notation. Of the twenty combinations that can be obtained from the five modes and the four clef-transposition pairs, Hermelink found sixteen used in Palestrina's *œuvre*, twelve of them with considerable frequency; and for Hermelink each one of these combinations constituted a mode, one constituent of a new *Tonartsystem der Vokalpolyphonie*. Such a classification, he argued, accords more closely to musical realities than does the system of authentic and plagal modes which was carried over from plainchant theory and still maintained by the more modern theorists such as Glarean and Zarlino.* The 'modes' in Hermelink's sense used in Byrd's Latin sacred music are those shown in Ex. 3. But (and this comes as no surprise) Byrd does not hold to his 'modes' as strictly as does Palestrina; for this reason, as well as others, one hesitates to distinguish them as sharply as Hermelink attempts to do for Palestrina. There are also too many oddities in Byrd—such as, for example, his use of the Ionian mode with a final of B♮ and two flats in the signature. Presumably composers regarded this as the Lydian transposed, with a signature consisting of one transposition flat plus one 'informal' one. Byrd used it

*S. Hermelink, *Dispositiones Modorum: Die Tonarten in der Musik Palestrinas und seiner Zeitgenossen* (Münchner Veröffentlichungen zur Musikgeschichte, iv, Tutzing, 1960). For a magisterial defense of the traditional system see, however, B. Meier, *Die Tonarten der klassischen Vokalpolyphonie, nach den Quellen dargestellt* (Utrecht, 1974).

in two monumental early compositions, the archaizing motets *Tribue Domine* (1575/14–16) and *Infelix ego* (1591/24–6).

'What can they possibly do with such a number of flat ♭♭', demands Morley in the *Plaine and Easie Introduction to Practicall Musicke* of 1597, 'which I could not as well bring to pass by pricking the song a note higher?'* It is true that the range of those two archaizing compositions could have been accommodated just as well with the same clefs in C. But it seems Morley was making a mystery for polemic purposes. An answer to his aggrieved rhetorical question emerges without much difficulty from an examination of music employing these special signatures: in Byrd, the Phrygian Lamentations (in D with two flats) and the relatively early Dorian motet *Peccavi* (in C with two flats), as well as the two B♭ Ionian compositions mentioned above. Before Morley's time, composers felt much easier about writing extra flats than extra sharps. Especially in situations where F♯ is used as anything other than a cadential raised leading-note— where it is used as the actual or implied fifth of a B triad or root of an F♯ triad—they preferred to set the whole thing down a step and write E♮ instead of F♯, A and E triads instead of B and F♯.† To Morley, the first English madrigalist, this must have seemed impossibly timid and clumsy. Some contemporary scribes seem to have agreed with him, for Byrd's Ionian motets in B♭ sometimes appear in manuscripts 'a note higher', that is, transposed back up again to C.‡

[4]

At this point it may be helpful to have a few facts and figures about Byrd's cantus firmus motets tabulated for purposes of comparison. The majority of them are responds, following the tradition of Tallis and Sheppard; *Christus resurgens*, a processional antiphon, falls into the same broad category. Table 2 shows the mode, final and range of the plainchants themselves, the

---

*Morley, *Introduction*, 262.

†This preference can also explain the choice of transposition in Byrd's keyboard Pavan and Galliard B♭1 (BK 23) and in the consort songs *O that we woeful wretches* (BE 15/9), *Sith death at last* (BE 15/22), *When first by force* (1589/31) and the famous *Lullaby*, which Byrd transposed up from C minor (Dorian) to D minor for publication in 1588 (see BE 16/25). The explanation does not hold for the two C minor Pavans and Galliards for Keyboard, however.

‡*Gloria Patri* (1575/16), part 3 of *Tribue Domine*, appears in C in Add.30810–6, and *Tribulationes civitatum* (1589/24–6), which begins in B♭ Ionian but ends in G minor, is transposed up a step in the Sadler MS and Tenbury 369–75. *When first by force* (see the previous note) is also transposed up in some MSS.

sections which Byrd composed, their length, and the location of the cantus firmus within the choir. Though this is not consistently indicated in the sources, the three responds that include a setting of the verse should have the *repetendum* (the last section of the respond proper) sung *da capo* after the

TABLE 2: Byrd's Cantus Firmus Responds

		Mode, final and range of cantus firmus	Location of cantus firmus and length of section, in breves		
			RESPOND	VERSE	REPETENDUM
a 4	Christus resurgens (1605 *a* 4/10)	1 (D) C–b♭	T, 58	(*free*, 41)	T, 15
a 5	Libera me Domine (1575/17)	1 *transposed* (G) f–f′	S, 79	—	(S, 14; S, 32*)
	Aspice Domine (1589/18–19)	1 (D, *but partly transposed to* A) C–e, e–b♭′	T, 71	A, 32	T, 28
	Ne perdas (BW 8/12)	2 *transposed* (G) D–d, f–d′	T, 51	S, 31	T, 13
	Omni tempore benedic Deum (BW 8/14)	8 (G) d–d′	S, 57	S, 36	S, 31
a 6	Afflicti pro peccatis nostris (1591/27–8)	8 (G) D–d	T, 91	—	(T, 27)
	Descendit de coelis (1591/21–2)	1 (D) C–b♭	T, 91	—	(T, 36)

verse, according to the liturgical requirement. And the responds lacking verses are nevertheless also composed in such a way that the *repetenda* can be separated off easily. Hence these pieces, too, can be made liturgically complete by adding the verses in chant and then the polyphonic *repetenda*, even though Byrd probably did not expect them to be sung past the respond proper.

Aspice Domine de sede sancta tua, published in the *Cantiones sacrae* (1589/18–19), was circulating in manuscript in the early 1580s and continued to circulate widely (see p. 126f). It is tempting to view this composition as a vigorous reaction to *Libera me Domine*. Energy, variety, clarity and contrast are now the order of the day. The imitative sections are shorter—

*This respond has three verses and two *repetenda*, the second longer than the first.

except for the one ending the respond and the *repetendum*, 'et vide tribulationem nostram', which at 43 semibreves is a good deal longer. Here Byrd
takes hold of his favourite syncopation idea and seems to work it out of his
system; the motive that had wound its way aimlessly through the first and
last sections of *Libera me Domine* now makes a loose ostinato defining no
fewer than ten cadences, in various degrees of strength, on the same tonic, D.
By placing the cantus firmus in an inner voice, Byrd frees the soprano to
make strong melodic climaxes which focus and point up the phrasing. He
had foregone this normal feature of his emerging style in *Libera me Domine*, in
view of the more leisurely though still secure melodic structure of the chant.

The chant *Aspice Domine* lacks such a structure, and Byrd seems to have
determined to inject interest into it by transposition up an octave during the
verse and (much more surprisingly) up a fifth at the beginning. This causes
a partial signature—in 1589!—for the respond, though not for the verse.
The Dorian chant sinks back to its proper range only at the words 'inclina,
Deus meus, aurem tuam'. As word illustration, this recalls the age of Obrecht
rather than the age of Thomas Morley, but as a means of obtaining variety it
certainly succeeds, for the unmistakable A minor profile of the transposed
cantus firmus demands harmonization with a B♮, which is then largely
abandoned in favour of B♭ until the verse. In the verse B♮ returns at a
tremendous Dorian-sounding climax for the words 'et de excelsis'. And if it
is true that in *Libera me* the 'modal' chant *incipit* GFG suggested the vague
harmonic style of Byrd's setting, the mutilation of the chant *Aspice Domine*
can perhaps be explained as another reaction, as a declaration of allegiance to
harmonic clarity. In a change that must have shocked anyone who still
remembered his Sarum antiphonal, Byrd bowdlerized the characteristic
chant *incipit* from the modal-sounding pattern DCFGA to one that offers
no hint of harmonic ambiguity, DFGA. A speeded-up version of Parsons's
type of opening proclaims this pattern in three of the voices, answered at the
upper fifth by the soprano and the tenor cantus firmus—whose aberrant
position is therefore apparent from the very start.

The fact that the imitative motives in *Aspice Domine* are more sharply
characterized than in *Libera me Domine* is partly a reflection of Byrd's
growing maturity; the motives are also more skilfully worked out. But it is
also a change matched to the change in conception from a structure based on
soprano melody to one based on counterpoint and lucid phraseology.
Comparing the two compositions helps us see not only how Byrd's technique
had progressed in the later one, but also how well he had turned his technical
limitations to account in the earlier.

A pair of respond settings, *Omni tempore benedic Deum* and *Ne perdas cum*

impiis Deus animam meam, is preserved in a number of manuscripts.*
Ne perdas cum impiis (BW 8/12) is like a shorter, quieter, smoother
version of *Aspice Domine*, without any wrenching at the chant and with less
energetic climaxes. It seems the later work. As a ferial respond for Lent, the
Ne perdas cum impiis plainchant is short and lies low, in the second mode;
with this dull melody, it was all the more prudent to shift it up an octave
during the verse, a device that had served well in *Aspice Domine*. In **Omni
tempore benedic Deum** (BW 8/14) Byrd placed the cantus firmus in the
soprano, as in *Libera me Domine*, and carried it on all through the verse,
something he had backed away from in the earlier composition. But if this
was a stubborn effort to prove that he could do the impossible, it was also a
circumspect one, for he systematically shortened the chant at the melismas
so as to leave himself with more manageable dimensions. Eleven breves were
saved in this way. Again for the sake of conciseness, perhaps, Byrd abandoned
any kind of imitative beginning in favour of a relatively dramatic gesture: to
accompany the first eleven cantus firmus notes, he devised a short 'cell'
strongly oriented towards a tonic cadence, repeated at once in transposition
up a fourth. Other such cells are used later in the motet to emphasize
appropriate scale degrees.

In spite of all this, however, the meandering cantus firmus in the soprano
too frequently destroys any clear sense of direction. The force of this
criticism becomes clear if *Omni tempore* is compared with **Afflicti pro
peccatis nostris** (1591/27-8), a work in which Byrd's cantus firmus
writing rises to a new level of technical assurance ('a miracle of skill',
according to Collins) and expressive force. *Afflicti* forms with *Descendit de
coelis* another pair of similar responds, for six voices, published in the
Cantiones sacrae of 1591. The point of the comparison is that the two eighth-
mode chants *Omni tempore* and *Afflicti* resemble one another closely and so
Byrd was faced with a similar task in setting them.

Two unusual but related features distinguish Byrd's treatment (or
inspired mistreatment) of the Hypomixolydian mode in this piece: the
prominence of harmony based on the seventh degree, F, and the frequent
flattening of the characteristic Mixolydian third degree, B. At the beginning
Byrd uses B♭ consistently, and occasionally even E♭. He may have done this
mainly in order to establish a more mournful feeling in his opening imitation,

---

*Both are in the same clefs (S A T T B) and have about the same dimensions. Baldwin,
who copied them next to one another in both his MSS, Christ Church 979-83 and
R.M.24.d.2, provided *Omni tempore* with a curious 'precautionary' B♯ signature in all
voices, and *Ne perdas cum impiis* with an even more curious partial signature of B♭ in the
soprano, B♭ and E♭ in the lower voices. This makes better sense in the verse, where the
soprano carries the transposed Hypodorian cantus firmus.

an exquisite expansion of Parsons's type of opening employing a fully developed double point; but B♮ also serves as long-range support for the last of four well-paced cadences in the first cantus firmus phrase—a final cadence in F. From here on, F and G major are skilfully balanced to control the larger harmonic proportions. Progressions up the circle of fifths lead from F to A in the phrases 'quotidie cum lacrimis' and 'expectemus finem nostrum', and from F to the tonic G in the two phrases of the *repetendum*. The last of these phrases, in which a 3-part imitative complex moves up a fifth in free sequence, conveys the incomparable mild accents typical of Byrd's mature essays in the Mixolydian mode. This beautiful passage is shown in skeleton form in Ex. 4.

Ex. 4

The basic harmonic idea of *Afflicti* already shows up in *Omni tempore*, for the earlier piece also begins with B♮s and E♮s and stresses F major harmony in its second phrase.* Thereafter, however, there are too many G major cadences, and some not very convincing D minor ones. Coming back to an unresolved problem, in *Afflicti*, Byrd held on to the F and found the right solution.

Other masterly features of this work are the finely etched motives throughout, the anticipation of the last phrase 'quae innovantur in nobis' by the phrase 'quotidie cum lacrimis', and the very striking homophonic passage at 'Dolor cordis nostri'. Homophonic passages in cantus firmus setting can occasionally be found in the work of older composers, such as Tallis's *Dum transisset sabbatum* and Mundy's *Videte miraculum*,† but they provide no precedent for Byrd's rich workmanship or for the wonderful expressive

---

*In one source, Tenbury 389-James, the beginning of *Omni tempore* is notated with a partial signature. The first alto has two flats in the signature, up to a page turn (BW 8, 124, bar 3), where the flats are abandoned, while the top voice with the cantus firmus has none.

†See TCM 6, 258 and Christ Church 979-83, No. 75.

effect he gets by starting his homophonic passage back on F major, directly after a tense remote cadence on A. **Descendit de coelis**, the companion piece in the *Cantiones sacrae* (1591/21–2), also contain some obvious express-ive and even madrigalian effects (can Byrd possibly have meant those unusual augmented triads to word-paint 'stola purpurea'?). However, this is a less inspired work and in some respects seems a positively careless one: look, for example, at the last few lines of the second tenor voice.*

[5]

Byrd's three remaining cantus firmus motets all count as special cases of one kind or another. **Petrus beatus** (BE 8/16) has already been mentioned on account of its anomalous text (p. 33). Its chant, a hymn of three stanzas plus an Amen,† confronted Byrd with a lengthy melody sung through several times, a melody which is largely syllabic (and partly 'group-wise') in decla-mation and which therefore leaves little space for contrapuntal development. Many of the imitative motives can only appear once in each of the free voices. Years before this, *Similes illis fiant* had posed a similar problem, in an even more exacerbated form; but the present chant introduced its own particular difficulties.

The challenge that hymn setting offered to composers was that of writing variations, of course. Tallis liked to change metre for the later hymn stanzas, and Sheppard used an array of different devices to achieve variety. Byrd had already started developing his own ideas on the subject in hymn settings for consort and keyboard variations. But as a 'theme' for variations, the *Petrus beatus* melody was not happily chosen. Besides going on for 87 semi-breves, far longer than any other hymn set by Byrd, it is resolutely modal, its five constituent lines all ending with melodic cadences moving up a whole-tone step: 7–1 in the first line, 3–4 in the third, and 1–2 in the other three, including the last one! The Amen after stanza 3 finally restores the tonic (in TCM; in BW 8 the Amen is unaccountably dropped and we are left on the dominant). That Byrd saw the problem is pretty clear from his setting. Less certain is the success of his solution.

His idea seems to have been to define the Dorian tonic firmly at the beginning and the end and let nature take its course in the middle. Classic

---

*In the motet as published, the cantus firmus stops with a semibreve on the final, D, one and a half breves before the end of part 1, and gives way to rests (BW 3, 155). The D should be emended to a long pedal note, as at the end of part 2 and as in Mus.Sch.e.423 (a *longa*) and Tenbury 807–11 (a ligature *cum opposita proprietate* with fermata).

†*Hymni . . . secundum morem eccl. Eboracēsis* (Rouen, 1517), fol.44. The present-day form of this hymn is *Miris modis repente liber*.

Dorian accents are established by the tonic and major subdominant cadences early in the piece. Consistent tonic cadences are resumed in stanza 3, where—to mention a few points—lines 2 and 5 conclude with half cadences in D (on A) rather than with A minor perfect cadences as in stanza 1, and line 5 begins with a powerful circle of fifths leading to the tonic in place of the A minor ostinato of stanza 1. In the short space allotted to it, the final motive of this stanza, 'Per infinita saeculorum saecula', manages to repeat itself in a reasonably infinite manner and build excellent climaxes in the alto and bass; the soprano and tenor wait for their climaxes until the Amen—seven breves as smooth as sugar, with one pinch of false-relational spice. But Byrd loses his harmonic bearings in the second stanza, apparently as a result of trying to manipulate an uncomplicated canon between the two upper voices at the fourth, at a time interval of three semibreves. (Again *Similes illis fiant* comes to mind, with its canonic middle stanza of three, though in the present case the canon is illustrative, the words being 'Quodcunque vinclis super terram strinxeris'.) The non-canonic voices fail to imitate strictly, too, and the quality of the melodic material plunges.

A much more successful canon figures in the 6-part cantus firmus motet **Miserere mihi Domine** (1575/13): a shorter contrapuntal exercise by a good proportion, but not really a simpler one, for this is a double canon (4 in 2) at time intervals of one and two semibreves, rather than three as in the hymn. Presumably this learned little motet was written expressly for the *Cantiones* of 1575, where it appears in conjunction with Tallis's canonic monster on a similar text, *Miserere nostri Domine*. Byrd's composition is in effect a small-scale variation work. The *Miserere* chant appears twice, first as a standard long-note cantus firmus in the bass voice, and then a second time in canon between alto and soprano, with the melody ornamented.

In terms of cantus firmus setting, the much-used *Miserere* chant posed its own special problem. The melody is cripplingly short and constrained: 26 semibreves which span no more than a fifth and which are joined only twice by a leap (and only once by an upward leap) as against 23 times by stepwise or unison progressions. Byrd knew the chant of old from his settings of it for consort and for organ and he gauged these limitations shrewdly. Since the melody ranges from the seventh to the fourth degree in the Mixolydian mode, it is more or less doomed to sink into the subdominant. Byrd did not allow this to happen until the end of the first half of the piece, at the cadence ending the bass cantus firmus statement. Then he used his new canon to restore (just barely) Mixolydian stability: by placing one canonic voice at the upper fifth and slipping in some accidentals, he arranged for cadences in the second statement to be heard on A and D, as

well as on G and C (BE 1, 165, bars 25, 29, 34). He also took the opportunity
to stress D at the beginning of the motet, by means of a prominent imitative
entry.

The one upward leap in the chant melody is a leap of a minor third,
reaching up to the climactic fourth degree of the mode. Byrd underlined this
upward third by making it the one melodic fragment in each of the cantus
firmus statements that is imitated by all the other voices. In the first (bass
cantus firmus) statement all the contrapuntal motives—there are only three
of them—are exceptionally striking: the long descending scale figure used to
make the luminous opening; the motive stressing the upward third, with its
majestic augmentation in the soprano;* and the more fluid motive for the
key phrase 'orationem meam', which flares up suddenly in crotchet thirds
and sixths. The first of these motives find a resonance in one of Byrd's most
famous later compositions (see Ex. 5).

Ex. 5

a Miserere mihi Domine   b Five-Part Mass

Christe qui lux es (*Precamur sancte Domine*) (BW 8/9) is a cantus
firmus motet by Byrd which has enjoyed relative popularity in modern
times: though others might be deemed more deserving. This hymn setting is
not only a special case but also a curiosity; its unusual style—strict note-
against-note harmony in plainchant rhythm, notated in black breves—cannot
be duplicated anywhere else in Byrd's writing. Only one source preserves it,
but a very reliable one, Robert Dow's manuscript, Christ Church 984–8.
Dow actually supplied a cross-reference pointing out a setting of the same
hymn by Robert White in the very same unusual style and notation. Other
settings of *Christe qui lux es* by White were followed by Byrd in his many
settings of this hymn for consort (see Vol. III, p. 53f).

In the vocal piece he overhauled White's basic plan in order to obtain
climactic effects of an obvious kind. White, making a liturgical setting, with
stanzas 1, 3, 5 and 7 of the hymn left to be chanted, had placed the cantus
firmus symmetrically in the treble in stanzas 2 and 6 and transposed it down
an octave for the tenor in stanza 4. Byrd set stanzas 2–6, moving the cantus
firmus steadily up from the bass by fifths and fourths through all five voices,

*Notice how the plainchant declamation for the words 'et exaudi', A C BC A, is
changed to the more 'natural' G A C B, etc., in the non-cantus firmus voices.

one stanza at a time.* He also made stanza 6 climactic by including B♭s for the first time in any number, by drawing out the cadence slightly, and by setting the Amen after it. But how insecure his chord progressions and larger patterns sound by comparison with White! His bass lines seldom fall into clearly directed configurations, and they cannot do so because he employs so few chords in first inversion—proportionally only half as many as the older composer. *Christe qui lux es* seems to catch Byrd at an uncomfortable stage, when he has conceived some bright ideas for the larger structure but lacks the technique on a local level to project them. The work is best understood, perhaps, as a beginning study in 5-part writing.

Oliver Neighbour concludes that Byrd's cantus firmus writing for instruments, in the consort hymns and In Nomines, did not extend beyond the mid-1560s (see Vol. III, p. 259). It was mainly after this that he applied the technique to vocal compositions, if exception is made for *Christe qui lux es*, whose genesis is in any case involved in some shadowy way with the early consort hymn settings, and *Christus resurgens*. *Libera me Domine* was presumably written during Parsons's lifetime, or perhaps on the occasion of his untimely death in 1570. (Byrd, as is well known, wrote a moving *tombeau* for Tallis on his death in 1585.) It is natural to assume that *Miserere mihi Domine* was written for the publication project in 1575, but this is so obviously a demonstration piece that one cannot make too confident a stylistic estimate for purposes of establishing a chronology. Of the other cantus firmus compositions only *Petrus beatus* shows signs of a very early date of composition.

That *Aspice Domine* predates the publication of the *Cantiones* in 1575 is unlikely, for a piece that proved to be so popular a few years later would surely not have been left out if it had been available. The style of this motet supports a date in the later 1570s; *Ne perdas cum impiis* and *Omni tempore* should follow it. *Afflicti pro peccatis nostris* and *Descendit de coelis* seem to belong to a still later period, around 1580.† Writing cantus firmus motets in the 1580s can only be understood as an act of conscious archaism, of course, especially in Anglican England; but the same is really true for the

*Transposition up by fourths and fifths would have been more 'normal', but the initial interval of a fifth allowed for cadences on the tonic at the end of the transposed stanzas—as in Byrd's settings of *Te lucis ante terminum* for consort.

†Faint support for this dating is provided by an unusual manuscript source, the heavily glossed copy of the 1575 *Cantiones* once owned by William Rokeby and now in the library of Trinity College, Dublin (see MB 22, 175). Of the twenty-odd polyphonic pieces entered incompletely into this source, two are Byrd motets: *Ne irascaris Domine*, which is dated 1580 and 1581 in other sources, and *Afflicti pro peccatis nostris*. *Afflicti* is preserved only as a fragment of a single voice part, the soprano, with a flat in the signature and several variants in accidentals.

1560s and 1570s. Anyhow Byrd never flinched from archaism. In the 1591 *Cantiones sacrae*, *Afflicti* stands next to *Infelix ego*, another impressive motet which, as we shall see, was also composed relatively late according to another ancient model.

2b

Motets of Praise and Penitence

Laudate pueri Dominum *a 6*	1575/7	Domine secundum actum meum *a 6*	1575/11
Attollite portas *a 6*	1575/5	Da mihi auxilium *a 6*	1575/10
Memento homo *a 6*	1575/8	Peccantem me quotidie *a 5*	1575/3
Laetentur coeli *a 5*	1589/28–9		
In resurrectione tua Domine *a 5*	1589/17	Tribue Domine *a 6*	1575/14–16
		Ad Dominum cum tribularer *a 8*	BW 9/23
		Domine quis habitabit *a 9*	BW 9/25
De lamentatione Hiere-miae prophetae *a 5*	BW 8/1	Siderum rector *a 5*	1575/9
		O lux beata Trinitas *a 6*	1575/6
Libera me Domine et pone me iuxta te *a 5*	1575/2	Diliges Dominum *a 8*	1575/12
		O salutaris hostia *a 6*	BW 9/22
Aspice Domine quia facta est desolata civitas *a 6*	1575/4	Emendemus in melius *a 5*	1575/1

The motet *Decantabat populus* (BW 8/10), if authentic, would have to be construed among the small group of very early motets influenced by the chanson style, such as *Memento homo* and *Laetentur coeli* (see below). But while these could perhaps be said to offer a precedent for the rigidities of *Decantabat populus*, they offer none for its poverty of invention and low level of craft. For much of the time the piece sounds like a string of cadence formulas (see BW 8, p. 69 bars 6, 8, 9, 12, p. 70 bars 1, 2, 4, 6, 8, 11, p. 71 bars 2, 4, 6, 10, etc.). A mechanical feature that speaks against Byrd's authorship is the notation *a note neri*, used by Byrd in his early years only for hymn settings, not for his authentic chanson-like motets. *Decantabat populus* is known from only two manuscripts, and it picks up Byrd's name only in the later and much less reliable of them, Add. 37402–6. Dow's MS transmits it anonymously within a small group of older, non-Byrd pieces.

On Accession Day, 1575, it has been suggested—on November 17 of XVII Elizabeth—Tallis and Byrd presented their seventeen numbers each to Queen Elizabeth in the famous *Cantiones quae ab argumento sacrae vocantur*.* Tallis had engaged in such numerical games before, according to another agreeable suggestion: his 40-part motet *Spem in alium* may have

*The best account of the circumstances surrounding the publication is by Craig Monson in the preface to BE 1.

been offered to the Queen in 1572 for her fortieth birthday.* Inside the patriotic tangle of front and back matter, the musical contents of the *Cantiones* show traces of an organization according to mode and clef combination, as was usual in sixteenth-century publications. The general plan was to lay out the music in groups of three numbers alternating between the two composers. The first three of these groups—two by Tallis, one by Byrd—assemble motets in the Dorian mode, transposed to G and often furnished with aberrant signatures of the kinds discussed above. Byrd's next group is Mixolydian; the three Mixolydian pieces all employ the same clefs, a brilliant combination including two sopranos. His next group is Ionian or Lydian, on F, and his last two groups are made up of music in different modes. Motets by Tallis, the senior partner, open the publication and his fierce 7-part *Miserere* canon brings it to a close.

Obviously the *Cantiones* served Tallis and Byrd in different ways. For the old man it served as a 'retrospective': much of his music goes back to the time of Queen Mary, or even earlier, and only a few items seem on stylistic grounds to have been written for publication in 1575. The young man was launching his London career—and in a sufficiently sensational fashion. Byrd writes three canons to Tallis's two and caps the 7-part *Miserere* with his 8-part *Diliges Dominum*; wherever possible, it seems, he writes for six voices rather than for five. And he had probably produced about half of his pieces very recently, expressly for the publication. It looks as though the publication project supplied the major stimulus for motet composition in the whole of Byrd's early career.

However this may be, the first quality that would have struck an English listener to Byrd's music in the *Cantiones* is its novelty, variety, and intensity of expression. *Emendemus in melius* stands at the head of Byrd's first group in the publication as a manifesto of the new expressive world revealed in the Dorian and Aeolian compositions that follow. The incorporation of a highly inflected affective style into the traditional grand dimensions of the English motet was to be one of Byrd's most distinctive contributions. At the one extreme is this urgent note of pathos, which had never been struck in English music before; at the other is the variegated and equally novel brilliance of motets such as *Attollite portas*, *Tribue Domine* and *O lux beata Trinitas*. Hardly any of the pieces is quiet in sentiment, let alone neutral. 'Revolutionary' is a term we are inclined to use gingerly as a term of approval for English music, but no other term will do for the expressive range of Byrd's motets of 1575.

At the same time, Byrd's motets for the *Cantiones* betray a striking

*Doe, *Tallis*, 41.

technical orientation. This has already been mentioned (p. 32f) in connection with their texts, which appear often to have been chosen not for their own sake but as an abstract accompaniment to certain compositional studies. As though in a spirit of comprehensive experiment, Byrd tried many different kinds of text used for motets in his day—hymns, responds, didactic biblical extracts, psalm selections, prayers—and many styles and forms: cantus firmus setting, continuous homophony, various antiphonal arrangements, and even something resembling the early Tudor votive antiphon form. Many pieces make reference to the work of other composers, such as Tallis, Parsons, Philip van Wilder and especially Alfonso Ferrabosco, in order to adopt a text, a general idea, a groundplan or sometimes a specific musical phrase as model. Symbolic of this technical orientation is the conspicuous group of canons—conspicuous because the authors pointed these out themselves by means of a special index at the end of the partbooks.

Of all Byrd's technical concerns in these years, the first must have been to work out a model or models for imitative motets, motets built in principle entirely of sections in imitative counterpoint. As though to draw attention to this sustained effort, he included two imitative motets in each of four different modes, printing each pair together in one of his groups in the publication. One thinks of the scheme of the pavans at the beginning of My Lady Nevell's Book. In the Dorian mode, on G, there are *Libera me Domine et pone me iuxta te* and *Peccantem me quotidie* (Nos. 2 and 3), in Mixolydian *Aspice Domine quia facta est desolata civitas* and *Attollite portas* (Nos. 4 and 5), in Ionian or Lydian, on F, *Laudate pueri Dominum* and *Memento homo* (Nos. 7 and 8), and in Aeolian *Da mihi auxilium* and *Domine secundum actum meum* (Nos. 10 and 11).

It is clear that Byrd had two quite distinct kinds of contrapuntal writing in mind for the composition of motets. For affective penitential pieces, he evolved a highly fluid style closely accommodated to the text and organized for the most part around rhetorical climaxes. Motives are carefully—sometimes beautifully—moulded to the words and the musical flow is largely unimpeded by schematic elements. Here Byrd had the most to learn from the Continent. For motets of praise and jubilation, on the other hand, he paid less attention to the text, even though on a superficial level melismas and upward figures are likely to be employed in their time-honoured illustrative function. What he required of these motets was brilliance of a fairly generalized nature, and this he obtained by use of strettos, ostinatos, repetitions, and balanced or symmetrical contrapuntal structures of various kinds. These devices have little to do with the words, which are sometimes fitted to the music in a positively nonchalant fashion. More abstract in its impetus,

Byrd's 'brilliant' motet style depends to a large extent on devices of purely musical organization.

In this style Byrd was following in his own selective way the broad lines laid down by mid-century English composers. In their antiphons, psalms and other imitative pieces, whether the texts be cheerful, melancholy, hortatory or (as is often the case) neutral in sentiment, composers such as Tallis, White and Mundy tend to deploy polyphonic phrases by means of symmetrical structures and strict repetitions. Very rarely do they significantly *develop* a contrapuntal idea within the course of a point of imitation. This holds true even for their most monumental and carefully worked points, those with which their compositions begin. Tallis typically constructs his beginning points with an exposition followed by a counter-exposition retracing the exposition exactly, or nearly exactly. He does this in his well-known motet *Salvator mundi*, the first number in the *Cantiones*, and also spaces the five imitative entries in each exposition with typical rigidity: subject—one breve—tonal answer—two breves—subject—one breve—tonal answer—two breves—subject, and then the whole scheme is repeated voice by voice in the counter-exposition. The second number in the *Cantiones*, Tallis's *Absterge Domine*, which also circulated as the anthem *Wipe away my sins*, is built up almost entirely out of little repetitions. The fearful symmetry of White's writing was noticed with some pain by the editors of *Tudor Church Music*, who judged that White composed 'at times . . . by specific, mechanically, even pompously', and who went so far as to single out certain compositions in which 'the formal instinct is shown at its coldest and most calculating'.* It is not infrequently the case, especially in Tallis, for two successive fragments of the text to be adapted to the identical imitative subject. Occasionally one can suggest a symbolic or textual reason for this identity (or a scribal error). More often one has to conclude that the imitation was laid out on purely musical grounds and the text adapted as a secondary consideration.

In Byrd the most extreme—one might almost say, savage—embodiment of these principles is the joyful 'motet' **Laudate pueri Dominum** (1575/7) which he adapted with minor improvements from an early fantasia for viols (Fantasia 6/F, BE 17/11). From one point of view, its *contrafactum* status might seem to put the piece *hors de combat* as far as the present discussion is concerned. From another, however, the fact that Byrd was ready and willing to transform a purely musical construct into a motet of the brilliant variety gives us some telling evidence as to his attitude in the matter. Not to repeat or pre-empt the discussion of this piece in Volume III, p. 62f, we need here

*TCM 5, xv.

Ex. 6

a Laudate pueri Dominum (BE 1, 84f)

6 times

b Attollite portas (BE 1, 55f)

3 times, followed by free entries

c Attollite portas (BE 1, 67f)

7 times, of which two are in free diminution

d Memento homo (BE 1, 99f)

6 times, with melodic variants

e Domine secundum actum meum (BE 1, 138f)

4 times

f Ad Dominum cum tribularer (BW 9, 73f)

3 times; then 3 more times, up a 5th; then 3 more times, up another 5th

g Domine quis habitabit (BW 9, 137f)

4 times

h Domine quis habitabit (BW 9, 151f)

3 times; then 3 more times, up a 4th

i Quis est homo (BW 3, 21f)

Twice; then 4 more times, freely

j Quomodo cantabimus (BW 9, 109f)

or:

or:

4 times, freely

Ex. 6 (Cont.)

k Reges Tharsis (BW 6, 57f)

3 times

l Laudate Dominum omnes gentes (BW 7, 133f)

3 times, with linking entry at (𝄌)

only draw attention to a few of its salient characteristics. One is the systematic adaptation of new words to each of the repeated sections of the original four-section form (AABBCCDD), a process that led to wretched declamation at a number of places. Another is the lockstep imitation in section 1: after an exposition ('Laudate, pueri, Dominum') with the subject and tonal answer alternating on F, C, F, C, F and C, all at the interval of one breve, Byrd takes a gulp of air and then adds a counter-exposition on precisely the same plan ('laudate nomen Domini'), merely reversing the two basses and compressing the initial dactylic rhythm.* Another is the stiff sixfold ostinato in stretto which constitutes section 2, accommodating the two text phrases 'sit nomen Domini benedictum' and 'ex hoc nunc et usque in saeculum'. Ostinatos of this kind are a rather common and peculiar feature of Byrd's writing at this period.

Example 6 attempts to provide an epitome of all these stretto ostinatos. The repetitions indicated at the right of each excerpt all take place at the unison or octave, except in the case of Example 6b, but the material circulates among the various voices and sometimes varies slightly in melodic or rhythmic detail; the time intervals also vary. This archaic procedure recalls the medieval English *rondellus* and *rota* techniques, traces of which survive into the sixteenth century, as Harrison has observed.† In Byrd's distinctive form, which involves a 'real' or 'tonal' stretto at the fifth or fourth, it survives up to the time of the *Gradualia* (see Ex. 6k–l).

The innocent, spirited 6-part motet **Attollite portas** (1575/5) is perhaps even earlier than the fantasia which was turned into *Laudate pueri*. Here the entries in the opening point of imitation come at irregular time intervals on the pitches d, G, d, G, C and G', pitches which make for maximum lucidity

---

*The choice of words from Ps. 112:1 to add to the beginning of the fantasia (followed by Ps. 112:2, 120:2 and part of 124:4) was inspired by Tallis's short psalm-motet *Laudate Dominum*, in which the first two phrases of Ps. 116, 'Laudate Dominum, omnes gentes' and 'laudate eum, omnes populi' are set to almost identical subjects (though there is no strict repetition, as in Byrd). This Tallis motet is often found next to Byrd motets in contemporary manuscripts.

†*Medieval Britain*, esp. 319f (Browne), 414 (Wilkinson), 281f and 332f (Taverner).

in the Mixolydian mode. As soon as the bass begins the sixth of these entries
on low G′, the tenor pounces on it with a stretto on D, at the tight interval
of a semibreve, to initiate the counter-exposition. Now if exception is made
for one addition to the scheme (indicated by italic), the new series of entries
follows the same pitch order as before, and mostly in the same octave: D,
G, d, G, C, *d*, G′ and D. So the exposition and the counter-exposition are
laid out symmetrically as regards pitch, asymmetrically as regards rhythm.

The point as a whole is short-breathed, but at least it has the breath of life
in it, unlike the wooden opening of *Laudate pueri Dominum*. Strettos were
very much at the heart of Byrd's conception here, and to make them work
he was ready to tug and haul at his subject quite relentlessly. 'Lift up your
heads, O ye gates': this bounding subject, with its broken seventh sounding
more like Tallis or White than Byrd, makes for a lively text setting such as
Tallis and White rarely achieved.

As in *Laudate pueri Dominum*, the second point in *Attollite portas* is a
stretto ostinato accommodating two different text phrases, 'et elevamini,
portae aeternales' and 'et introibit Rex gloriae' (Ex. 6b). Since the ostinato
figure itself modulates to the dominant, it is with the deepest lack of conviction that the music twists around to a final cadence in the subdominant, C.
This ingenuous manoeuvre seems to have been conducted so that the next
point may gain brilliance by schematic movement up the circle of fifths from
C to G and D.

This next point and the two remaining ones in the motet employ a
primitive form of a contrapuntal technique that grows important for Byrd
in the later *Cantiones sacrae*. The basis for the polyphony is not so much a
subject or motive as a self-contained 'cell' for several voices, a few breves in
length, first sung in one semichoir and then repeated (strictly or freely) in
others. The cell itself may be homophonic, half-homophonic, fully imitative
or even strictly canonic, but in any case it will always be clearly oriented
to a little cadence at the end. In the present instance, Byrd uses a 2-part
canonic cell in fast crotchet rhythms to set the threefold question 'Quis est
ipse Rex gloriae?'—an unusually dramatic (as well as an unusually early)
application of 'cell' technique. These antiphonal 2-part cells are followed by
3-part cells, to essentially the same music but new words, and then by a
climactic section *a 6*.

The cells with which the motet ends congeal around another stretto
ostinato (Ex. 6c) adapted to various different fragments of the doxology text;
even Tallis must have been surprised by Byrd's lack of concern for any real
relationship between text and motive. But the young composer seems to
have been mainly interested—hypnotized, rather—by the idea of perpetual

stretto. He was so pleased with the tintinabulation of his final 21-breve period that he wrote repeat marks around it, something we see in Tallis but do not see again in Byrd's motets until the time of *Ave verum corpus*.

The short 6-part motet **Memento homo** (1575/8) must be later than *Attollite portas*, though it shares a number of technical features with that composition. It accumulates strettos in the opening point and it incorporates a close repetition within the final point, which is built on a stretto ostinato, once again (Ex. 6d). Byrd's idea here was to write a motet with a fully polyphonic texture dominated by the soprano, or at least by the soprano in conjunction with the bass. This effort finds a parallel in works like *Libera me Domine de morte aeterna*, *Emendemus in melius* and *Siderum rector*, experiments with soprano-dominated motets in various different textures; it is diametrically opposed to the basic idea of *Laudate pueri*, which relies for its structure on counterpoint and clear phraseology. *Memento homo* has the simple songlike structure of a chanson, and also the lucid tonality associated with that genre. The complicated counterpoint tends to blend together and fade away into background accompaniment.

Thus in the opening point, the symmetrical build is crystal clear as we listen to the soprano sing the words twice, the second time with a firm new subdominant support which leads punctually to the cadence. The inner voices, however, make a cat's cradle of strettos scarcely to be untangled into exposition and counter-exposition or any other coherent order.* Apart from F, C and B♭ triads, no prominent harmonies occur in this little motet at all, certainly no affective sonorities to match the text 'Remember, O man, that thou art ash and shall return to ash hereafter' (a versicle sung on Ash Wednesday, the Sarum version). Byrd treated this not as material for affective setting but as a neutral didactic sentence. There is something curiously abstract about the whole exercise.† It is perhaps not accidental that the only other didactic text among the early motets adheres to the highly abstract canon *Diliges Dominum*.

Two other compositions can be brought into this context, though Byrd published them much later, in the *Cantiones sacrae* of 1589. Both are for five voices. **Laetentur coeli** (1589/28-9), a Sarum respond text set without cantus firmus, reads and sounds as archaic in its surroundings as does the

---

*For an effort to untangle them, and to draw a comparison with Tallis's typical practice, see J. Kerman, 'Byrd, Tallis, and the Art of Imitation', *Aspects of Medieval and Renaissance Music*, ed. Jan La Rue (New York, 1966), 519ff.

†Realizing this, perhaps, the person who turned this motet into an anthem made no effort to provide a real translation. Nor did he try to improve the match between music and text: 'O Lord, give ear to the prayer of thy servants, and forgive us our sins, we beseech Thee. Grant this, O Lord, for thy Son's sake Jesus Christ our Lord' (BW 11/12).

actual cantus firmus respond which is also printed there, *Aspice Domine*. Awkward details of melody, dissonance treatment and cadence formation betray an early date of composition, and many features can be matched in the motets we have just been discussing: the abrupt crotchet rhythm at 'et exultet terra', the ostinato—really a free *rota*—at 'Iubilate montes laudem', the repeated section lasting for seven breves within the point 'et pauperum suorum miserebitur', which as the *repetendum* is repeated yet once again after the verse—and more generally, the dull rhythms, square-cut phrases and strictly formal modulations to the dominant reminiscent of the chanson idiom, or of someone's unimaginative interpretation of it. Byrd sets the verse of this respond as a trio for the high voices (presumably a solo trio) to contrast with the 5-voiced choir. This forecasts his regular procedure in the *Gradualia* many years later, and demonstrates the lineage of that procedure with almost Euclidian lucidity. For the style of the 3-part counterpoint is a concise version of the neutral imitative style of the mid-century votive antiphon's semichoir sections—a style which comes up in a few other of Byrd's early motets, too. This verse, 'Orietur in diebus tuis iustitia', gets off on the wrong foot with a clumsy upward scale motive and never recovers. Such comparisons are perhaps too easily made, but we can turn to several verses in the *Gradualia*—in the motets *Tollite portas, Gaudeamus omnes* and *Spiritus Domini* (1605 *a* 5/13, 23 and 1607/31)—to see how ascending motives in 3-part counterpoint are supposed to go.

Byrd may possibly have felt inclined to print *Laetentur coeli* in 1589 on account of the 'political' interpretation that could be placed on its Advent text (see p. 41). However, he may also have had his reservations about the piece, for he re-used portions of its text and music in a shorter and much more impressive composition, one that is still something of a favourite, **In resurrectione tua Domine** (1589/17).* Again, this is a motet with many archaic features: the brevity of the various sections, the exuberance of the cadences, and the aspect of the opening point, which recalls *Attollite portas* and *Memento homo* in the density of its strettos (there are twelve entries in the space of thirteen breves) and the free form of the subject (there are ten distinct shapes). But the treatment of harmony, pacing and rhetoric reveals a quite new mastery; the brief sections sound terse and strong, not pokey. When the initial opening outline of a fourth opens up to an eleventh (see Ex. 7), this extreme expansion is placed in serene relief by a calculated

---

*In the Willmott-Braikenridge manuscripts, copied by a provincial scribe, John Sadler, in 1591, the two pieces are run together without a double bar as though they were sections of a single composition. They do indeed use the same clefs and signature, though they are in different modes (see Fellowes, *W. Byrd*, illustration opposite p. 72).

Ex. 7

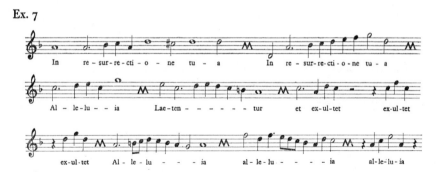

reduction of rhythmic activity in the lower voices, and by the first introduction of an A minor chord. What seems to expand here is not so much the
actual trajectory of the resurrection, but rather our own sense of wonder
at the miracle.

This motet shows no trace of schematic musical organization. Instead
Byrd works with harmonic and motivic means of a more imaginative sort.
The harmonic range is controlled with great care: after D and G minor
chords at the beginning, the first A minor chord makes a fine effect, as has
already been mentioned, followed by the first F major sonorities at BW 2,
p. 135, bar 4, C major at bar 6, B minor and G major at p. 137, bar 2. In the
sequel the Dorian major subdominant gleams gently, and one solid E minor
chord supports the first (and only) authentic cadence in the piece (bars 5–6:
E-A-D).* Meanwhile the motives have been evolving from one another
in a manner reminiscent of Byrd's technique in instrumental fantasias (see
Ex. 7; cf. Vol. III, p. 75f). The 'exultet' idea borrowed from *Laetentur
coeli* is better prepared here, and itself helps prepare the final alleluia motive.†
The bass figure which interrupts the grandiose cadence at p. 137, bar 2
(BCD) sounds like an augmentation of the soprano figure in the cadence at
p. 136, bar 5 (c♯'d'e'), and this motive returns at the final cadence after the
second alleluia—a half close which also links back to the half close after the
first alleluia.

In *In resurrectione* surprisingly archaic features are placed under surprisingly mature control. The second part of the final alleluia section, with

---

*Not strictly authentic; the bass fills in the root progression A–D with a scale. Fellowes
supplied a natural to the D chord; the accidentals in this and other passages of *In resurrectione* are unusually difficult to construe, and all contemporary scribes come up with their
own, generally hopelessly confused, solutions. Byrd himself must have made changes for
the publication. False relations appear to be used structurally at BW 2, 135, bar 5, 136,
bars 1 and 5, as well as at 137, bar 6.

†The 'exultet' motive is imitated by Richard Nicolson at 'exultent' in his motet *Cantate
Domino* (New York Pro Musica Series, No. 24, 1964).

its darting canonic imitations over a slow cantus firmus in the bass, looks back to Byrd's more brilliant In Nomines, while the first part glances ahead to certain suave, melodious alleluias of the *Gradualia* (see Ex. 52). *In resurrectione* also looks forward to the *Gradualia* in terms of form; in this respect, too, it can be seen as complementary to *Laetentur coeli*. The concise layout of the four sections—

In resurrectione	alleluia,	laetentur coeli	alleluia.
tua, Domine,		et exultet terra,	
13 *breves*	4	9	12

is never repeated in the early or middle-period motets but is picked up again exactly in the *Gradualia*. The text of this motet is not quite liturgical, though Byrd put it together from liturgical materials.* In doing so he created a text that is identical in form to dozens of liturgical items that were to face him later in composing the *Gradualia*.

Not to short-circuit our discussion, we can content ourselves for now with the observation that in the period between the composition of *Laetentur coeli* and *In resurrectione* Byrd gave up the simple, relatively abstract style developed in the earliest of his motets of praise and jubilation. He was already moving away from this concept, as we shall see a little later, in some other 'brilliant' motets of the 1575 *Cantiones*.

[2]

From the start Byrd's motets in the expressive, penitential vein reveal an altogether different underlying conception of polyphonic organization. The first phase of his work in this genre is represented by a 5-part setting, preserved in several manuscripts, from one of the two gloomiest of all text sources, the Lamentations of Jeremiah. Settings from the other such source, the Book of Job, followed in due course. Shaky in counterpoint, reckless in dissonance treatment and frequently uncertain in harmonic progression, Byrd's **De lamentatione Hieremiae prophetae** (BW 8/1) has some wonderfully strong passages, too; it is a work of the greatest interest throughout its nearly two hundred breves of unceasing counterpoint, and deserves extended discussion here. The effort was an ambitious one, both in sheer scope and also in the implied challenge to the great Lamentations of Tallis

---

*The closest liturgical model for Byrd's text is an Easter versicle found in the Sarum breviary (not the Roman): 'In resurrectione tua, Christe, coeli et terra laetentur, alleluia' (*Sarum Breviary*, dcccxviii, dcccxxii).

and White. Byrd takes something from his elders, but what stands out is his pointed divergence from them.

Surprisingly, perhaps, he avoids the memorable half-homophonic style used to such fine effect by Tallis.* He also finds no place for the short overlapping phrases that Tallis tends to write in his more polyphonic moments, nor for the characteristic measured, orderly imitative patterns of White. Byrd's imitative entries come at irregular time and pitch intervals. His phrases ebb and flow unpredictably and the cadences between them are often obscured; text phrases overlap, sometimes for as many as five breves during which one voice pursues free counterpoint on an old text fragment while the others are beginning a new one. When he came to compose in the pathetic idiom, Byrd set aside brilliant strettos, ostinatos, schematic repetitions, and all traces of symmetrical structure. His essential aim and his study was to produce extended musical periods of seamless, apparently unpatterned polyphony.

For all its boldness and ambition, the Lamentations was shrewdly chosen as a trying-out ground for this kind of polyphony. The peculiar form of Byrd's text is perhaps indicative in this regard. Readings from Lamentations prescribed for Holy Week always consist of an opening rubric such as 'De lamentatione Hieremiae prophetae', a final appeal 'Hierusalem convertere ad Dominum Deum tuum', and a number of verses from the Book of Lamentations in between, each prefaced by a Hebrew letter. The actual selection of verses seems to have varied considerably from place to place. All the earlier sixteenth-century English settings—by Tallis, White, and the Norwich composer Osbert Parsley—employ one of the selections of verses prescribed in the Sarum rite, or at least something close to these selections. But although very old, Byrd's piece does not date back to the time of the Sarum rite. He picked on the first Good Friday reading in the Roman rite, Lamentations 2:8–11, complete with the traditional rubric, appeal and Hebrew letters—and then cut out the second part of verses 8, 9 and 10 and the whole of verse 11.

This was a text chosen (and mutilated) for strictly technical reasons, as the basis for a calculated study in affective setting. With a more usual motet such as *Attollite portas*, the composer had to tackle five or six continuous text-phrases, and with them the formal problem of how to hold all that music together. The Lamentations text, especially as cut down by Byrd for his own use, offered sections of manageable length separated off from one

*Not that this style failed to impress Byrd. He alludes to it in the motet *Libera me Domine et pone me iuxta te* (1575/2) at the words 'noctem verterunt in diem'—a recollection, surely, of Tallis's haunting phrase 'Plorans ploravit in nocte'.

another by the Hebrew letters. These provided little interludes; English composers traditionally set them as spurts of abstract florid counterpoint. Byrd balanced the sections,* roughly:

		Verse 1		Verse 2		Verse 3	
De lamentatione	HETH	Cogitavit	TETH	Defixae	IOD	Sederunt	Hierusalem
		Dominus		sunt		in terra	convertere
33 *breves*	9	37	9	35	6	37	31

The formal problem was as it were compartmentalized. Byrd could concentrate his attention on a grandiose but isolated opening section, an equally isolated climactic ending section, and compact verses in between, containing no more than three or four text-phrases each.

He designed the inner verses along parallel lines. The beginning phrases he handled concisely: in free stretto—so free that some entries bear only a faint resemblance to others—the voices each sing the words only once before moving on. They may come to a cadence or they may not, as in verse 3, depending on the syntax.

The endings of the verses he set at greater leisure. Motives are maintained more consistently and repeated more frequently. To stabilize and drive home the endings, each verse concludes with a sort of codetta or special cadential phrase built on a short new motive. In verse 1, the words 'a perditione' are kept in reserve for this new motive, which might on that account have given the impression of a new point of departure. But both the syntax ('et non avertit manum suam *a perditione*') and the way Byrd works the phrase in makes it sound like a codetta, and an effective one at that. In verse 2, the weakest in all respects, the new motive is adapted to words ('in gentibus') which have already been set amorphously, that is, they have come several times during the previous phrase ('regem eius et principem *in gentibus*') without ever attaching themselves to distinctive thematic material. In verse 3,

---

*These are the sections transmitted in the earliest sources, Add. 32377 and Baldwin's Partbooks. By the time the piece reached Edward Paston, who had it copied into Tenbury 369–73 after 1605, it had shed the three sections *De lamentatione*, TETH and IOD; and since the Tenbury source is the only one that still has all five partbooks, we lack the full text of these three sections.

Other bits may have come loose in the twenty years or so which must separate the composition of the piece from its first source, Add. 32377 (1584). Perhaps after all Byrd did set CAPH: *Defecerunt prae lacrimis oculis*, the missing verse in the Good Friday reading, between *Sederunt . . . capita sua* and *Hierusalem convertere*. The tonal discontinuity here (between the A major cadence of 'capita sua' and the C major beginning of 'Hierusalem') one would have expected him to smooth over, judging from his setting of the other Hebrew letters.

again, the cadential motive takes over old words, but this time words which have been articulated previously by a fairly clear motive; the cadential motive is not strictly new but an intensified, free inversion of the previous one. This much more integral imitative technique plays into a cadential phrase which is itself better developed. At the impressive stark passage in downward sequence at the words 'capita sua', the piece finally begins to take on powerful emotional colouring.*

And this is intensified in the sequel. For the first time in the Lamentations, homophony of a sort is employed for the invocation 'Hierusalem, Hierusalem'; the delicacy of the variations as the little 'cell' is repeated and transformed suggests a general heightening of Byrd's inspiration as he came to this section. The plainchant Lamentation tone is paraphrased briefly. Then for the appeal 'convertere ad Dominum Deum tuum' Byrd mirrors the downward sequence of 'capita sua' with a more extended upward sequence. The soprano grimly inches up the chromatic scale from e to b♭', the bass following inexorably but irregularly at the twelfth below from A to E♭. False relations fall where they may. At the climax the rhythm eases, as though rocked by the portentous minor sixth with which the soprano breaks the stepwise pattern and reaches its goal with extraordinary emphasis.

This is blunt writing, no doubt, and very intense by the standards of Byrd's older contemporaries; one need only look at the last 'Hierusalem convertere' section in White's 5-part Lamentations, likewise built around a climax approached by chromatic motion and an upward sixth. Most admirable is the way Byrd discharges his blunt climax. The bass, after moving up one further step to a peak on F, descends in a suddenly energetic series of interlocking fourths and fifths. Just before the end, a new motivic idea flickers in the upper voices, retracing the field of action of the previous soprano climax, while the bass drops far down into the hard, blazing texture of the final chord. The distinctive cadence here, employing a *cambiata* figure in the bass, comes from the first Lamentations by Tallis.

In general Byrd paid less attention to White than to Tallis, especially as he came to plan his opening section, 'De lamentatione'. Tallis in each of his two sets of Lamentations treats the rubric 'De lamentatione Hieremiae prophetae' or 'Incipit lamentatio Hieremiae prophetae' as a magisterial single point on a very long subject. And in his first set—the one which is in the Phrygian mode and is in every way the more 'extreme'—Tallis lays out

*Fellowes silently emended the final 'capita sua' in the cadence to this passage from a′a′a′b♭′a′ to a′a′a′d′a′ (BW 8, 18, bars 6–8) in order to avoid parallel octaves; but no such happy solution presents itself for the octaves on the previous page. On the awkward part-writing and cadences of the Lamentations see Kerman, *Chronology and Canon*, 379ff.

this long point not with his usual regularly spaced entries but, unusually, with irregular ones. To tabulate the time intervals between the successive entries in the opening points of these Lamentations is to tell the story:

TALLIS,					*semibreves*						
Lamentations II	5	5	5	5	5	5	5	5	5	*total length:*	28 *breves*
Lamentations I	1	8	2	9	1	3	4	1			22
BYRD	5	6	11	10	5	5	5*	4	4*		33½

Though Byrd's point is less intricate than Tallis's, the scheme he adopted was calculated for even greater breadth and potentiality for climax.

He shows his hand towards the end of the long 'De lamentatione' point. Up to now the subject has been using a scale passage as preparation for its peak note F, the third degree of the Phrygian mode, here transposed to D with two flats in the signature (Ex. 8a). Now in the final bass entry this third degree is stressed by a leap of a fifth, DDCE♭DB♭CDB♭F (Ex. 8b). The next stretto entry (ddcf...) is further modified so as to leap up at once to this same degree, F, rather than to E♭ as expected. The soprano follows with the highest entry yet, a'a'gb♭'... All this makes for a fine crescendo;

Ex. 8

*In these two entries the opening breve is compressed to a semibreve. It should also be borne in mind that the tenor is missing in this section and that the second and sixth entries have been reconstructed.

but how will Byrd arrange for it to subside? We have seen the device he used for this function, involving a new cadential motive, in the three inner verses of the Lamentations. Here he conceived the idea of presenting the last two 'De lamentatione' entries, in the S and A² (contratenor), in a constrained form. The subject no longer reaches up to the third degree, only up to the second—yet in that climactic soprano entry (a′a′gb♭′ . . .) the second is still the very highest note that has been heard so far, b♭′. So it is the affective semitones b♭′a′ (soprano) and e♭d (second alto), echoed by a fine emotional leap of a sixth in the first alto, that remain in the memory as the sombre residue of this remarkable opening.

Incidentally, or not so incidentally, the semitone which moulds the word 'lamentatione' in Byrd's subject is a sufficiently remarkable feature in itself. It is not generally realized, perhaps, how few subjects hinging on affective semitones occur in the earlier English repertory. One is scarcely surprised to come upon a rare exception in Tallis's 'extreme' Lamentations set, at the letter ALEPH; but whereas Tallis conducts his imitation cautiously so that only two semitones emerge, EF and AB♭, Byrd conducts his almost roughly so as to produce three. After several entries of 'De lamentatione' on the tonic and fifth of the transposed Phrygian mode, the first soprano entry bores in on the raised second degree (e♮edfe . . ., after DDCE♭D . . . and AAG′B♭A . . .). Opening subjects that stress affective semitones are an impressive feature of many later motets, starting with the first two phrases of *Peccantem me quotidie* in the *Cantiones* of 1575—'Pec*cantem* me quotidie' and 'et non me poeni*tentem*'. Interior points of this kind are also common: we need look no further than HETH, TETH and 'et non avertit manum suam' in the Lamentations. Sooner or later Byrd always brings in a third semitone which artfully lacerates the modal fabric. HETH actually incorporates a fourth semitone.

[3]

In the music of Byrd's time, a basic tension arose from what may be described as an incipient imbalance between verbal and musical rhetoric. In principle, each syntactic unit of a text was supposed to be handled by a point of imitation employing an appropriate subject. To this end, texts were divided up into short fragments for musical setting—as short as possible, often enough: but even so, some minimal syntactical units still embraced too many syllables to fit in comfortably with a single imitative subject. The pace of Latin prose was not always easily accommodated to the pace of sixteenth-century polyphony. As is generally true in such cases, tension within the medium caused composers trouble and also impelled them to develop solutions of ingenuity and eloquence. The solutions become, in a sense, an index of the vitality of the style in question.

The text-unit 'De lamentatione Hieremiae prophetae' is one of those with too many syllables. Byrd keeps a consistent motivic profile only through the first part of the text; things get vague at the word 'prophetae', though the embryonic motive of a third expands deftly into fourths and fifths near the end. Tallis maintained clear thematic definition triumphantly all the way through such lengthy texts as 'Incipit lamentatio Hieremiae prophetae' and 'Suscipe, quaeso Domine, vocem confitentis', in the great 7-part motet of that title. But he did so only at the price of contrapuntal rigidity. If a composer wanted to work with a whole series of brilliant strettos, as Byrd did in *Attollite portas* and *Memento homo*, he had to treat long text-units of this kind more loosely. Although the opening sections of these motets cover the phrases 'Attollite portas, principes, vestras' and 'Memento, homo, quod cinis es', only the first two words in each case are articulated thematically. The remaining words are sung many times amorphously, without attaching themselves to consistent musical ideas.

The situation is different with the last point of *Memento homo*, 'et in cinerem reverteris'. Here clear thematic definition is achieved both for the words 'et in cinerem' and also for 'reverteris', a descending scale fragment which in due time can be usefully broken away from the 'et in cinerem' fragment to guide in the final cadence. We have seen a variation of the same technique, involving inversion, in the point 'consperserunt cinere capita sua' —another ashen text!—which ends verse 3 of the Lamentations. These are early stages on the way to true double imitation, imitation in which the two parts of a single composite subject are developed flexibly together throughout a point.

We have also seen an even more primitive stage, in the precocious cantus firmus motet *Christus resurgens* (p. 64). Several phrases of this piece employ two subjects simultaneously; but in each case Byrd conceived the subjects as entirely separate, not as separable parts of a single musico-rhetorical unit. They work together, certainly, but the result—by comparison with even slightly later examples, such as those in *Memento homo* and the Lamentations —sounds arbitrary and choppy. In *Christus resurgens* Byrd had hit upon the basic technical idea of double imitation but had not yet linked this with the rhetorical idea. For this very reason, perhaps, imitation of this particular kind remains an isolated experiment in Byrd's earliest writing.

The force of these remarks will become clearer by reference to a mature example of double imitation, at the beginning of the motet *Memento Domine*

Ex. 9

from the *Cantiones sacrae* of 1589. The subject itself is to all intents and purposes another version of the 'De lamentatione' subject (see Exs. 8a and 9a). But it is clearly separable into two halves, and the second of these, 'congregationis tuae', develops into countersubject material by engaging in complex combinations with the first, 'Memento, Domine' (Ex. 9b). From this vantage point, the lack of such countersubject action in the 'De lamentatione' point can be seen as an impoverishment. The two subjects of *Memento Domine* certainly fall together as a single composite unit, with obvious melodic connections; the rhythmic distinction between them suits the natural spoken rhythm of the sentence 'Memento, Domine, congregationis tuae'; and as the point develops we may consider apt the contrast between the sporadic, sober appeal to God and the constantly repeated murmuring insistence on the congregation. At the end, the second subject alone remains to make the cadence. This puts a special rhetorical emphasis on the text, of course, one that was presumably not lost on the composer.

When Byrd had developed double imitation to this stage he had an immensely powerful technique at his disposal. Characteristic of mature double imitation is that the second subject appears early in the point not only in situations where it emerges naturally out of the first subject, but also independently, so that it may combine with the first subject (or with itself) in as fertile a fashion as possible. A typical feature is the short rest between the two subjects, as in *Memento Domine* (see Ex. 9). In the extreme case, a voice will even sing the second subject, not the first, as its initial entry (this happens in the late cantus firmus motet *Afflicti pro peccatis nostris*, at the first alto entry). For Morley, in the *Plaine and Easie Introduction* of 1597, the best way to begin a song was with 'two several points in two several parts at once, or one point foreright and reverted', but preferably the former alternative: 'this way of two or three several points going together is the most artificial kind of composing which hitherto hath been invented either for

Motets or Madrigals, specially when it is mingled with reverts.'* In saying
this, Morley may very well have been reflecting Byrd's teaching; and the
way he says it rather suggests that double imitation was still something of a
novelty to him. The example he gives does not convince that he understood
the matter fully, for although the counterpoint is correct something very
important is omitted and not even mentioned: the words. The technique of
double imitation did not arise from any purely musical impetus, but from
the desire to differentiate, articulate, and contrast successive fragments of a
text-phrase within the unity of a single musical section. Byrd very rarely
used double imitation in instrumental music.

Before Byrd, double imitation was virtually unknown in England. Tallis
seems to use it in only one piece, *Suscipe quaeso Domine.* Byrd himself comes
to it only in his more mature imitative motets, not in the Lamentations,
Laudate pueri Dominum, Attollite portas, Memento homo, Tribue Domine or
the two large psalm-motets *Domine quis habitabit* and *Ad Dominum cum
tribularer.* It took some time before the technique was thoroughly mastered,
to judge from what appear to be his two earliest attempts.

It is a curious fact that both of these involve the effort to incorporate a
third motive into the contrapuntal complex. **Libera me Domine et pone
me iuxta te** (1575/2) is another study in expressive counterpoint, set for
five voices in the Dorian mode to a text from Job (see p. 36). In the concluding point Byrd clearly conceived of the text in three fragments, 'et
rursum/post tenebras/spero lucem.' He starts with a perpetual sequence in
thirds which amused him in several works of this time and which here
quaintly illustrates the word 'rursum', in its meaning 'again and again'
(Ex. 10).

Ex. 10

The first subject moving stiffly in semibreves is typical of Byrd's early work.
The contrapuntal combination of 'et rursum' and 'post tenebras' never
grows very eloquent, the latter motive tends to dissipate in short ostinatos,
and the words 'spero lucem' are at first handled amorphously. But then Byrd

*Morley, *Introduction*, 276.

articulates these words with a distinct new motive, GFb♭a; only this motive remains, and flourishes, during the peroration of the motet, even leading to a somewhat late climax during the cadential prolongation. The hoped-for light emerges unobtrusively and then glows throughout the ending.

This lengthy motet has many antiquated features: the Tallisian homophony at the phrase 'noctem verterunt in diem', the free imitation beginning part 2, the awkward, jerky cadence built into the subject 'dissipatae sunt'— this looks all the way back to the Lamentations—and the bizarre triple-time antics of the second alto at 'transierunt'. No doubt its most modern feature is the suave opening point with its tight tetrachord motive in inversion, a common enough pattern in Continental music which may have reached Byrd by way of one of Alfonso Ferrabosco's motets, *Laboravi in gemitu*.* From this it is clear that *Libera me Domine* was written later than the very earliest motets of the *Cantiones*, mentioned above. In those motets, furthermore, as Craig Monson has pointed out, Byrd had not yet begun to use the typical continental cadence pattern involving a suspended seventh resolving to a 'consonant fourth' ($^{7\,6\,5\,-}_{\;4\,4\,3}$). Monson also observes that in *Libera me Domine* the use of this formula and of other expressive devices, too, is less confident and effective than in the most advanced of the *Cantiones*, such as *Emendemus in melius*.†

The 6-part motet **Aspice Domine quia facta est desolata civitas** (1575/4) was probably written at approximately the same time. It is one of Byrd's more puzzling compositions. Though the text tells of the destruction of the City—a model for many motet texts of the later period—he sets it in the Mixolydian mode with little reference to the language he was developing for affective writing. A stretto figure which provides a brilliant conclusion for its Mixolydian neighbour in the publication, *Attollite portas*, provides a featureless one for *Aspice Domine*.‡ As in *Libera me Domine*, but less

---

*Which Ferrabosco in turn took from Lassus, from the verse *Laboravi* in the 1st Penitential Psalm. The beginning of Alfonso's piece (Egerton 3665 (Tregian), No. 9) is cited in NOHM 4, 496f, with a mistaken attribution (following Arkwright) to the younger Alfonso Ferrabosco. Many motets, madrigals and chansons by Alfonso senior are modelled on Lassus (see Kerman, *Elizabethan Motet*, 302).

†C. Monson, 'William Byrd and the 1575 Cantiones sacrae', *Musical Times*, cxvi (1975), 1089ff and cxvii (1976), 65ff.

‡Monson (loc. cit.) notes the similarity between the two endings, and goes on to draw up a detailed schedule of parallels between the two motets. This seems somewhat forced, as does also his argument that Byrd wrote *Attollite portas* after *Aspice Domine* in an effort to use the same devices more effectively. To speak only of the ending points: whereas 'Sicut erat in principio' (*Attollite portas*) depends on blunt textural contrast and incessantly repeated chiming effects, 'nisi tu Deus' (*Aspice Domine*) builds up gradually in texture and establishes a solid melodic climax (affirmed, to be sure, in a disappointingly mechanical fashion). The point in *Aspice Domine* works according to a more sophisticated principle,

successfully, Byrd experiments with triple imitation in order to deal with another awkwardly long text unit, 'Aspice, Domine,/quia facta est/desolata civitas'. By starting with a subject that leaps down a third, the point can make its climax with an inverted entry that spurts upward (an inversion in free diminution; and this climax is underlined rather self-consciously with the first subdominant chord to be heard in the piece so far).* But the original subject moves creakily and the climax lacks force, partly because the other soprano voice has been singing higher and partly because the discourse evaporates into ineffectual 3-part cells. Later there is a curious homophonic section in jerky fast rhythms which puts an almost sardonic interpretation on the words 'non est qui consoletur eam'.

What is interesting about *Libera me Domine* is to see Byrd attempting to cope with the formal problems posed by the very long text by means of extra attention to individual words. There is the striking declamatory setting of 'noctem verterunt in diem' and what seems to be word illustration at 'verterunt' (again: an abrupt harmonic change), 'transierunt', 'dissipatae', 'torquentes', 'et rursum' and (most poetically) 'spero lucem'. No such guiding principle can be detected in the present composition. The respond text *Aspice Domine* was a great favourite abroad, and settings of it by Jachet of Mantua and Philip van Wilder were among the few Continental motets known to have circulated in England during Byrd's youth.† Possibly his setting was conceived of as an exercise, a first essay in the Continental manner. For the phrase 'plena divitiis' he took over a familiar Netherlandish idea used by Wilder for another phrase of the text, 'sedet in tristitia'; seeing Wilder repeat the canon exactly with the addition of an extra voice, the bass (Ex. 11a, bars 6–8), Byrd goes a step further in the repetition by cramming in strettos of the kind we have seen in several other early motets (Ex. 11b, bars 5–8)—and then repeats the canon once again, including a seventh entry.

[4]

His later essays of this sort were carried out with the music of Alfonso Ferrabosco in his ear. From Morley's *Introduction* we learn that Byrd and

even though we may judge it less successful in the realization. Indeed the style is more advanced point by point in *Aspice Domine*.

*There is a similar motive for 'Sed tu, Domine' in *Levemus corda* (1591/16).

†On Jachet's piece, the one Continental motet in the early Peterhouse MS, see L. Lockwood, 'A Continental Mass and Motet in a Tudor Manuscript', *Music & Letters*, xlii (1961), 336ff. For the many sources of the Wilder, see J. Noble, 'La répertoire instrumentale anglais: 1550–1585', in *La Musique instrumentale de la Renaissance*, ed. J. Jacquot (Paris, 1955), 103.

Ex. 11

'Master Alfonso' vied together in working out canons on the *Miserere* plainsong—collegial behaviour which Morley contrasts with the backbiting he detected everywhere in late Elizabethan musical life.* Another 'friendly æmulation', in Henry Peacham's famous phrase, can be inferred from Byrd's setting of the poems of two Ferrabosco chansons, themselves emulated from Lassus, *Susanne un jour* and *Le rossignol*. The friendship must have flourished between 1572, when Byrd settled in London, and 1578, when the Italian left Queen Elizabeth's service and her realm for good. But even before 1572 Byrd had modelled two of his In Nomines on examples by Alfonso (see Vol. III, p. 43f). This is one of several small signs that in his Lincoln days Byrd kept clear lines of communication with London and probably spent some time there. The two composers may well have been acquainted in the 1560s.

In another, more surprising context, Morley appoints Alfonso the first of two main 'guides' for the composition of madrigals, the second being Marenzio.† This was wide of the mark; as a madrigalist Alfonso was a negligible figure, and in the 1590s his madrigal style was too antiquated to serve as a serious guide for the young English madrigal development. One reason for the routine quality of his madrigal writing, perhaps, is that at heart he was a composer of motets, some fifty of which are preserved in

*Morley, *Introduction*, 202 *et passim*. For information on Alfonso, see p. 31n.
†Ibid., 294.

English libraries. Although Alfonso has received some praise as a composer of motets, these have not been fully investigated, and it cannot be said that his stylistic allegiances *vis-à-vis* the various Continental schools of composition are clearly understood. What is clear is that he presented his English friends with motet models which were in touch with recent Continental developments, and that he exerted a far greater influence on Byrd in the years around 1570 than he could ever have done on Morley and the other madrigalists of the 1590s. If Tallis in his imitative phase sounds like a contemporary of Clemens, and Byrd sounds like a contemporary of Lassus, the difference must in good measure be due to the young Italian musician and secret agent who slipped back and forth between England and the Continent, and whose motets were copied over and again into the manuscripts of Elizabethan collectors. The progress of English music in these years owes much to Master Alfonso's guidance.

In the matter of double imitation, Byrd's own progress appears with special clarity in the 6-part motet **Domine secundum actum meum** (1575/11). This is the first really distinguished imitative motet of his early maturity. Its first point, a point in double imitation, is modelled directly on the corresponding section of Alfonso's 6-part motet *Domine non secundum peccata nostra.** The text, the nature of the double subject, the overall dimensions, the general lay-out, the tonal plan—all are strikingly similar. The contrapuntal technique is now well advanced. In Byrd's hands the second subject 'secundum actum meum' becomes infinitely flexible countersubject material and contributes to a wonderful new richness of texture. The contratenor (second alto) voice, like Alfonso's alto and soprano, makes its initial entry not with the first subject but with the second; and the latter comes about sixteen times in situations where it does not follow automatically from the first subject (plus one 'revert' for Morley to admire: the inversion in the first alto, BE 1, pp. 132–3, bars 6–7).

Alfonso's subject, with its 'chiselled' monotone declamation for 'Domine' and its tendency to appear in stretto pairs, belongs to a type that Byrd knew well (see Ex. 12). It may have been the flexible shape, involving sometimes a semitone and sometimes a third, that interested him particularly. But at

---

*Sambrooke MS (Tregian), No. 15, without words and with the half-erroneous *incipit* 'Domine non secundum *iniquitates*'. The words 'Domine, non secundum peccata nostra necque secundum iniquitates nostras retribuas nobis [cf. Tract, Ash Wednesday]; parce mihi, Domine, quia benignus et pius est' are found in Tenbury 389–James. The Requiem respond set by Byrd reads 'Domine, secundum actum meum noli me iudicare: nihil dignum in conspectu tuo egi: ideo deprecor maiestatem tuam, ut tu Deus deleas iniquitatem meam'. The beginning of Alfonso's point is cited in J. Kerman, 'Byrd, Tallis, and the Art of Imitation', p. 530.

Ex. 12

every point Byrd is more arresting. His subject harps on the semitone more insistently, his basic stretto pair brings the subject in this affective form not once but twice, and he turns the flexible shape into an expressive resource, carefully saving the expanded form, with the semitone for 'secundum' changed to a third, until late in the day. As the final entry, the bass brings the subject in its new craggy form stretching over a sixth rather than a fourth as support for a fine soprano climax swept up in developing crotchet figures.

This climax, incidentally, leaves the sopranos gasping oddly on high e', with a breve rest during the cadence itself. Here too we may discern an intention to improve upon Alfonso, this time in the matter of rhetoric. The opening points of both motets set text phrases that fall short of a true syntactical unit; to patch over this, Byrd gives the sopranos a conspicuous rest, like a stylized rhetorical pause, before they attack the words required to complete the syntax, 'noli me iudicare', while the cadence is still sounding.

Most impressive of all, both in its own terms and also by comparison with Alfonso, is the control of the large-scale harmonic action in this lengthy opening point. Thanks to its insistent semitones, the stretto pair acts like an unstable dominant pedal, and so by starting well over on the dominant side, with Phrygian entries on E and B, Byrd can swing slowly and inexorably round to the subdominant. A half-cadence in the subdominant, D, provides a brief resting place between the exposition and the counter-exposition. How can the tonal balance be restored? One way would be to remove one of the semitones and obtain a stable, neutral relation between subject and answer—as in Alfonso. At the counter-exposition, then, Byrd has a strictly technical reason as well as an expressive one for the introduction of thirds into the subject. The rising energy towards the end—a result of Byrd's control over the modification of the subject, in both melodic and harmonic terms—is perfectly discharged into the sombre, urgent homophony of the ensuing supplication 'noli me iudicare'.

More double points end both *partes* of the motet. At the end of part 1, the first subject 'nihil dignum' begins as a free ostinato (Ex. 6e) and then fades away after 14 breves, leaving the field for 16 more breves to the second subject (which belongs, incidentally, to the early category exemplified by Ex. 2). Byrd allows the counterpoint to grow diffuse before he focuses it sharply by means of three successive deceptive cadences prior to the full

Ex. 13

close. The end of part 2 follows a similar plan: first a loose long-note ostinato for the words 'ut tu, Deus', then a short passage that digresses (here by means of a fluid *cambiata* figure generated by the second subject) and then a sequential device to focus the cadence. The passage deserves to be quoted, at least in a skeleton form, to show Byrd's way of managing large-scale structure during this period (Ex. 13). The splendid cluster of dissonances at the last appearance of 'ut tu, Deus', starting from a 'consonant seventh', is there to solidify the cadence, which is then extended by strettos on the second subject: weight enough for a Mass or a symphony, let alone a motet.

Earlier in part 2 there is a setting of the words 'maiestatem tuam' which is highly condensed by Byrd's standards of this time: close strettos lasting for six breves on a figure moving up from D to A, followed by another six moving up from A to F, F at the very top of the soprano and tenor tessitura. The rhythmic relaxation and harmonic underpinning of the astonishing soprano climax here is very fine indeed. Much more stiffly, the same imitation occurs in the point 'iubilate monte laudem' in the 'brilliant' motet *Laetentur coeli*.

Domine secundum actum meum and its Aeolian neighbour in the publication, **Da mihi auxilium** (1575/10), are similar in style. They have the same six voices in the same clefs, so that the ranges are nearly identical, and also the same general proportions. A chart giving the length in breves of their various periods suggests that Byrd conceived an ideal shape and size for a motet at this period, and a similar chart for Ferrabosco's *Domine non secundum peccata nostra* suggests a likely origin for this ideal:*

BYRD, Domine secundum actum meum	32_i	$10\frac{1}{2}_i$	31_i			$22\frac{1}{2}_{iv}$	32_i
Da mihi auxilium		31_i		23_{iv}		21_i	45_i
FERRABOSCO, Domine non secundum		33		20	6	20	25

Both motets served Byrd as advanced studies in double imitation, and both conclude with rather ponderous double points employing a first subject in semibreves. At the beginning of *Da mihi auxilium* Byrd once again used a subject that changes shape: first the initial interval of the subject, a minor third, expands to an expressive minor sixth, then it contracts to an equally expressive semitone. Equally, or more so: for in the final, climactic entry, at the very top of the tenor range, the high f that forms the melodic semitone

---

*In charts of this kind in this book, roman numerals refer to the degrees of the mode on which the cadences are made, as in the analysis of the tonal music of later times. The symbols '½ i' and '½ iv' refer to half closes *in* i and iv, i.e., *on* major chords a fourth below those degrees (here, the half closes A–E and D–A).

ef also forms a piercing clash with E in the bass. This is rude but powerful, and it lends sufficient emphasis to the word 'mihi'—the significant first person singular substituted for 'nobis' in the psalm, as we have observed (p. 36f).

Perhaps the most impressive of all the imitative motets of the *Cantiones* is **Peccantem me quotidie** (1575/3). As compared to the 6-part Aeolian motets, this work gives an impression of greater flexibility, perhaps because Byrd was working in a texture of five voice parts and in the Dorian mode. The Dorian mode encompasses all the possibilities of the Aeolian plus some others of its own; for example, it allows semitones to be built on successive scale degrees, such as (in the transposed form) DE♭ and E♮F. Byrd saw how this resource could enrich the expressive language he was developing, and made use of it in both of the linked points that constitute the opening period of this motet, 'Peccantem me quotidie' and 'et non me poenitentem'. (He also threw in a third semitone, the Phrygian semitone GA♭, here and elsewhere in the piece.) The four large sections are well characterized and contrasted, and the final one, 'Miserere mei, Deus, et salva me', shows how the technique of double imitation could be used in a more plastic, eloquent way than in the 6-part compositions. This is a very long point which perhaps does not quite maintain its sense of direction all the way through. But its climax on the characteristic Dorian semitone E♮f, followed by a pungent, expressive false relation, is beautifully planned in itself and also with reference to the climax of the first point (see Ex. 14).

Ex. 14

As a literary construct—a direct appeal to God, with a vocative—this final phrase 'Miserere mei, Deus, et salva me' is a prototype for many final phrases in the motets of Byrd's later years. 'O Domine, libera anima mea',

'Domine, ne moreris', 'sed tu, Domine, miserere nostri', 'O Iesu, fili Mariae, miserere mei' and the archetypal 'Domine, miserere': these stand out as some of Byrd's most memorable utterances. But he never again set texts of this kind as double points. While double imitation worked powerfully for Byrd in the service of musical architecture and rhetoric, to achieve the greatest emphasis he moved on to freer structures involving declamatory and homophonic writing. We shall see the first of these in *Levemus corda nostra* (1591/16), a motet written not long after the publication of the *Cantiones* (p. 137f).

[5]

Some interesting light on Byrd's apprenticeship in the art of imitative polyphony is shed by the longest of his early pieces, the 6-part motet **Tribue Domine/Te deprecor/Gloria Patri** (1575/14–16). This massive work is earlier than those that have just been discussed, and it is not continuously polyphonic in texture. If in most of the motets in the *Cantiones* we see Byrd working over single stylistic ideas, one at a time, with the tenacity of a young bulldog, in *Tribue Domine* we catch him squirrel-like bringing together anything available in order to create maximum interest during an inordinately long exercise in text setting. The guiding compositional principle was, quite simply, variety and contrast. There are sizeable sections in homophony, near-homophony, antiphonal writing and in 2-, 3-, 5- and 6-part polyphony of various sorts. Strong and surprising measures were adopted in an effort to bring the manifold contrasts under some modicum of control.

One such measure appears in the five large blocks of imitative polyphony placed at strategic junctures to bear the main weight of the form ('unum Deum omnipotentem', 'semper in fide stabiles et in opere efficaces', 'ad vitam, te miserante, perveniamus aeternam', 'cuius opera inseparabilia sunt, cuius imperium sine fine manet' and 'in saecula saeculorum. Amen'). In each of these sections, the soprano attains its highest note, f', shortly before the cadence, to be echoed almost at once by the first contratenor (alto) voice* staking out its own climax on f, an octave lower. Though the actual cadences of the five blocks come on different degrees—B♭, half close on D, G, G, B♭—the twin peaks always come on the same pitches and come couched in rather similar harmonies. As though possessed of a sudden insight into melodic climax as a means of organizing polyphony, Byrd seems to have laid down a schematic plan for the climaxes before starting work on the actual counterpoint.

*Or the second contratenor (first tenor), in the second of these passages.

And perhaps the insight was indeed new to him at the time of *Tribue Domine*, for in spite of the plan nearly all the climaxes seem curiously ineffectual. The point 'et in opere efficaces', a loose ostinato, harps on the pitch D, perhaps as a way of stabilizing the main modal change of the motet from Ionian (B♭) to Aeolian (G). After more than twenty semibreves sounding D, however, the climax on F is not broadly prepared and fails to exert a real influence on the cadence. The last point in the motet, 'in saecula saeculorum. Amen', also disappoints. In its construction it forecasts many aspects of the 'cell' technique of Byrd's later years: four short semichoir cells, overlapping and building tension, generate a longer period which expands the basic cell by means of a full-choir stretto on a new crotchet figure, for the words 'saeculorum. Amen.' But although things now seem to be well prepared for the prefabricated climax, once again the melodic peaks flicker up and down in a hasty, preoccupied way as though the composer were quite busy enough with the brilliant strettos and the big plagal cadence to come. The whole apparatus winds down in a way that is merely strenuous, not strong. The point 'unum Deum omnipotentem' suffers from the reverse trouble. After preparing the soprano high f′ carefully, indeed laboriously, Byrd holds to the plateau too inflexibly, keeping the bass fixed and reducing the upper voices to repetitive triad patterns. The unsubtle harmonic approach to the climax sets up high tension that is never properly discharged.

And yet one point in *Tribue Domine*, or one pair of linked points, succeeds marvellously well. In 'ad vitam, te miserante, perveniamus aeternam', at the end of part 2, the counterpoint, instead of straggling, falls quietly into place below a perfectly moulded soprano line. Closer analysis shows how the harmony and the imitations play in to the clear, essentially linear organization, and assure that here for once the climax sounds like an inevitable outcome and focus of the musical thought.*

This beautiful passage serves, in fact, as a salutary warning against quick critical generalizations. In many respects the level of technique in *Tribue Domine* is elementary. Double imitation is not found, there are some thoroughly archaic contrapuntal configurations and cadences, and certain passages clearly recall passages in the early motet *Attollite portas*. Yet this technique allowed for the pure construction and rhetoric of the 'ad vitam' point. In a similar way, one might not have thought that the composer of the halting verse 'Defixae sunt' in the Lamentations was also capable of the fine opening and closing sections in that early work.

The three *partes* of *Tribue Domine* were printed successively in the

---

*See J. Kerman, 'Old and New in Byrd's Cantiones sacrae', *Essays . . . in Honour of Sir Jack Westrup*, ed. F. W. Sternfeld *et al.* (Oxford, 1975), 25ff.

Cantiones but without any indication that they go together. *Prima facie* textual evidence for this is confirmed by musical evidence: for example, a homophonic passage from part 1 is heard again when similar words recur in part 3 ('sanctam et individuam Trinitatem', 'summae et individuae Trinitati'). Furthermore, the three parts of the motet begin in the same distinctive manner: the initial text-phrase (or phrases) is always sung by a 3-voice semichoir (or by several successive semichoirs) before the full choir of six voices enters with new words at a later point in the text. Part 1 begins with one such phrase, part 2 with two, and part 3—the doxology of this trisectional Trinitarian collect—with three. These semichoir sections employ essentially the same archaic cadence formula to make the first serious cadence in each part of the motet. In part 1 the cadence comes on B♭, in part 2 on C, and in part 3 on D.

This all seems very odd indeed until we realize that Byrd's formal model for *Tribue Domine* was the votive antiphon, whose proliferating sectional layout of semichoir and 'full' sections served the early Tudor composers as their main means of attaining breadth and grandeur. Many of the old antiphons remained popular after the liturgical context for them had lapsed, and the form itself was still used into the 1560s for long texts of various kinds—psalms, mainly, but also Lamentations and prayers.* Byrd's text is a prayer. He evokes the style of the votive antiphon only in the 3-part semichoir sections, with their stiff imitations, minimal word repetitions, and archaic cadences reminiscent of *Similes illis fiant* and *Alleluia. Confitemini Domino*, not in the other sections of the motet. We have seen such 3-part writing before, in the verse section of *Laetentur coeli* (p. 90).

It could have been predicted, perhaps, that a composer who at one time or another experimented with all the other motet forms of his youth—the cantus firmus hymn and respond and the large-scale psalm setting—would not neglect the most monumental of them all, the votive antiphon. By 1575, to be sure, Byrd must have found the form too ponderous for current taste and he broke it up for publication. But he also wrote two more 6-part motets on the same model, and one of them, *Infelix ego*, is not much shorter than *Tribue Domine*. (We shall discuss the striking similarities in lay-out between these two pieces later.) Byrd published *Infelix ego* in the *Cantiones sacrae* of 1591 as a single long piece in three parts, without apology.

This may be the occasion for a backward glance at two rather amazing early compositions which show Byrd's interpretation of another ancient

---

*See for example EECM 2/6, 8, 10 and 11 (psalms by Mundy), White's 6-part Lamentations (TCM 5, 35ff), and Tye's prayer *Peccavimus cum patribus* (*Latin Church Music*, ed. John Satterfield, ii (Madison, 1972), 73ff).

form, the psalm-motet. **Ad Dominum cum tribularer** (BW 9/23), for eight voices, and **Domine quis habitabit** (BW 9/25), for nine, are preserved only in manuscript, each uniquely. Like *Tribue Domine*, these are highly ambitious works—overweeningly so, one is inclined to say, with respect to the latter. For while *Ad Dominum cum tribularer* was not a psalm much set by English composers, *Domine quis habitabit* was the one they set most frequently of all. Byrd must have been courting comparison with the 5-part versions of Tallis and Parsons (Parsons set only the first half of the psalm) and the 6-part versions of Mundy and White—who actually set the whole text three times in three very different styles.

No doubt Byrd's opening in stretto pairs was suggested by some of these other pieces (see Ex. 12). It also looks forward to the stretto pairs in Ferrabosco's *Domine non secundum peccata nostra* and his own *Domine secundum actum meum* in 1575 (Ex. 12). But even apart from the poor declamation, the upward sixth sounds much too excited for the prosy question which opens this most didactic of psalms, 'Lord, who shall abide in thy tabernacle?', just as the sonorous half-homophonic *tutti* used for 'Ad nihilum deductus est in conspectu eius malignus' (and used nowhere else in these two motets) sounds too portentous for that dry segment of text. To be sure, Byrd adopted this style here essentially on formal grounds. He was evoking the style of the oldest psalm-motets, a style close to that of the votive antiphon, by reducing the number of voice parts in the choir for the prior passage 'Nec fecit proximo suo malum...' and then starting up again at 'Ad nihilum' with the full choir in quasi-homophony. But in White's oldest setting of *Domine quis habitabit* (II), the composer managed to juggle formalities so that his massive homophonic statements coincide with text-fragments of a more resounding nature ('Qui loquitur veritatem in corde suo', 'Qui facit haec, non movebitur in aeternum'). Byrd's planning was also not of the best when he chose the phrase beginning 'Nec...' to demarcate his reduced-voice section.

Clearly what interested Byrd in these psalm-motets was mass, mass above all. Even so, it is remarkable how consistently he holds to the full-choir texture (the voice-reduction in the middle of *Domine quis habitabit* still leaves him with a clutch of seven). Each motet contains about fifteen phrases, scarcely any of which employ homophony, quasi-homophony, antiphonal work or 'cell' technique. Such as it is, the cell technique reveals a primitive stage of workmanship, and there is no double imitation whatsoever; in many points of imitation the last words dissolve into amorphous counterpoint, in the manner we have examined in the opening 'De lamentatione' section of Byrd's Lamentations. These psalm-motets are essentially extended studies in old-fashioned English imitative polyphony, studies made more pointed by Byrd's insistence on manipulating choirs of a size almost unknown in earlier Tudor music.

Some of the points are dense, apparently aimless accumulations like 'cuius opera inseparabilia sunt . . .' in *Tribue Domine*. (Subjects very much like that of 'cuius opera' appear in both psalms.) In other points, Byrd makes use of the two sopranos in his choirs to organize the web of imitations into repetitive patterns controlled by the top melodic line. For example, the point 'aut quis requiescat in monte sancto tuo' in *Domine quis habitabit* is built on a twofold statement of the motive in the sopranos, each of which trails essentially the same complex of imitations below it ($A^1S^1T^2B^1A^2B^3$ and $B^1S^2–A^1B^2A^2$).* Repetitive structures of this kind blend easily into the characteristic stretto ostinato points that we have observed in many motets of this period. Among the numerous examples here (see Ex. 6f–h), 'timentes autem Dominum glorificat', running for twenty-one breves, is perhaps the most intricate that Byrd ever fashioned.

In effect, repetitions and ostinatos take the place of soprano climaxes as the basic means of organization in this music. None the less, Byrd developed a climactic plan for *Domine quis habitabit* as a whole which recalls that of *Tribue Domine* in its schematic quality. During the first half of the piece, the soprano climax is c' (though a single d' appears at BW 9, p. 139, bar 1); d' comes as the climax in the later phrases, and e' is reserved for the very last one, just six breves from the end. A similar plan can be discerned in *Ad Dominum cum tribularer*. Byrd also laid out the last forty or fifty breves of the two pieces according to the same groundplan. In each, an unusually lively point of imitation with a subject containing prominent crotchets ('cum his, qui oderunt pacem', 'et munera su*per inno*centem') is followed by an unusually short phrase, and then by a long final phrase; and each of these final phrases has a motive with the interval of a seventh expanding to an octave, which settles into a powerful ostinato and hammers home the new soprano climax note. In *Ad Dominum cum tribularer* this ostinato is a fourfold repetition of a soprano-tenor idea, doubled (roughly) at the lower sixth (BW 9, p. 97f). In *Domine quis habitabit* the basses engage in a double threefold pattern, first on the pitches CBAG'FEDC at intervals of five semibreves, and then lower on the pitches AG'F'E'EDCB—doubled at the tenth above—at intervals of six (p. 165ff). The extraordinary disposition of the choir including three basses finally explains itself. Meanwhile the sopranos reach up first to d', then to e', as the passage sinks into a Phrygian cadence of magnificent solemnity.

---

*There is an error in BW 9, 135; the last five notes of the third bass should read a third higher (cf. TCM 9, 225).

Byrd succeeded less well with the beginnings of the motets. The stretto pairs are deployed less rigidly than in the other psalm-motets cited in Example 12, but much less imaginatively than in Byrd's own *Domine secundum actum meum*. In *Ad Domine cum tribularer*, it was surely incautious to bring the dull opening subject twice in each of the eight voices, always on the same scale degrees (except for a customary reversal of the two basses), and doubly incautious to have followed the same general plan to launch the *secunda pars*. However, the point 'Heu mihi, quia incolatus meus prolongatus est' is furnished with a more expressive subject (the minor sixth makes much better sense here than in *Domine quis habitabit*) and with a useful rhythmic variant when, as it appears,* the next text-fragment 'habitavi cum habit-antibus Cedar' is sung to the same subject and counter subject. This pro-cedure, unusual for Byrd, recalls *Laudate pueri Dominum* and *Attollite portas*.

Coming from Byrd's early psalm-motets, we can appreciate more keenly the need he felt to marshal every resource of textural variety in his next really monumental composition, *Tribue Domine*. The extreme harmonic plan of *Tribue Domine* can also be understood as a reaction—perhaps an over-reaction—to the entirely level one of *Ad Dominum cum tribularer*. In this and other respects, *Domine quis habitabit* manifests considerably more variety. While not significantly advanced in style, this psalm is far better designed and so presumably a little later. These two remarkable works, with their dense texture stirring with ceaseless imitations, their cadences softened by overlapping phrases, their sudden spurts of soaring melody and their *al fresco* treatment of dissonance, constitute Byrd's most impressive evocation of the ancient sound-ideal of Taverner and early Tallis.

*Underlay is far from certain, for since both motets are preserved as *unica* without text (*Ad Dominum* occurs in the instrumental source Add. 31390 and *Domine quis* is one of the scores—mostly textless—in Baldwin's 'Commonplace Book'), the words have to be adapted from the psalms. Generally this goes smoothly—but not always. In *Ad Dominum* no text is available for the short penultimate phrase (BW 9, 91f); where the TCM editors threw up their hands and simply left the text out, Fellowes reached back and supplied a couple of words from earlier in the psalm. Byrd really cannot have meant this. But it is hard to know what other course of action to take. To improve the awkward declamation in the following phrase, furthermore, the TCM editors added a non-biblical 'sed' before 'cum loquebar illis impugnabant me gratis'. In *Domine quis habitabit* they were able to make the words fit only after altering Baldwin's rhythmicization in about thirty places (starting in bar 3 with the alto crotchets). In the phrase 'et opprobrium non accepit . . .', either Byrd left out the word 'et' or Baldwin ironed out the two crotchets in the subject with unaccustomed thoroughness (see TCM 9, 229f, notes).

[6]

We have traced the sometimes wavering course of Byrd's work in forging viable models for the imitative motet, a process to be observed in about a dozen motets in the *Cantiones* and elsewhere. This was his main technical concern as a motet composer in the years up to and around 1575, but not his only one. In the remaining motets of the *Cantiones*, he pursued other technical problems: cantus firmus setting—in *Libera me Domine de morte aeterna* and *Miserere mihi Domine*, as we have seen—canon, affective homophony, and the development of a light antiphonal style suitable for the setting of poetic texts.

The latter takes place in the two pieces labelled 'Hymnus', in *Siderum rector* and in the first two stanzas (of three) of *O lux beata Trinitas.** Clearly among the most modern motets in the collection, these are concise, schematic works featuring lively syllabic declamation in homophony or half-homophony. Each of the two stanzas of *Siderum rector* is sung through by a semichoir and then repeated by the full choir. Each line of *O lux* is sung twice in succession by antiphonal semichoirs. Byrd derived both of these schemes from Ferrabosco, once again, from a pair of hymns *Ecce iam noctis* and *Aurora diem nuntiat.*† Byrd's lucid, consonant harmony also derives from Alfonso, who is at his most Italian—and at his least Netherlandish—in these pieces. Even his notation is Alfonso's *a note neri*, in a basic crotchet pulse, adopted to match rhythms that are certainly more dance-like than ecclesiastical.‡

For both composers, the basic idea was to hold to a simple metrical pattern for the declamation of the repeated verses. Byrd had observed this method of setting Latin poetry in the hymns of Tallis, and would retain a fondness for it throughout his lifetime. In *Ecce iam noctis*, a 5-part setting of a hymn in Sapphic stanzas, Alfonso employed the pattern:

$$— \cup \cup — — \cup \cup \cup \cup — —$$
$$— \cup \cup — — \cup \cup \cup \cup — —$$
$$— \cup \cup — — \cup \cup \cup \cup — —$$
$$— \cup \cup — —$$

*The Trinity hymn *O lux* was one of the most popular in the Sarum repertory for musical setting, but *Siderum rector* is thoroughly obscure. Except for the first two words, it is identical with *Huius obtentu*, an unimportant hymn for the Common of Holy Women in Sarum and Roman rites. No explanation is forthcoming for the two altered words.

†Egerton 3665 (Tregian), Nos. 26 and 27.

‡In BW 1 Fellowes's unfortunate selective policy of note reduction confused the issue, and indeed also confused Fellowes, who stated that he had reduced note values in *Siderum rector* when in fact he had not. All is well in BE 1.

which for all its wildly unclassical implications was traditional in Continental settings of Sapphics. Alfonso picked it up from Lassus.* Stanza 1 has a bright little soprano tune on this pattern, harmonized throughout *a 3*, which goes down to the tenor for a slightly reharmonized repetition *a 5*.† A new tune is treated in the same fashion for stanza 2, this time moving from tenor to soprano, while the texture grows more polyphonic. Byrd uses the same traditional metrical pattern in stanza 1 of **Siderum rector** (1575/9), another 5-part Sapphic hymn, but holds to the pattern less strictly and drops it entirely in stanza 2. He takes over Alfonso's formal scheme, too, with only small differences: in stanza 2 the opening tune builds up from 3- to 4-part texture, and the coda after the full-choir repetition is shorter. *Siderum rector* is not an important work, but it is deft enough and less mindless than its model. It served Byrd as a technical practice ground both in the matter of satin-smooth counterpoint and also for slipping out of homophony into polyphony of various stages of density.

Alfonso's *Aurora diem nuntiat*, a more complicated piece, seems to have made a particularly vivid impression on his friend (see also Ex. 27). The second stanza again employs a metrical pattern, this time — — ∪ — ∪ ∪ ∪ — for iambic tetrameter. Juxtaposing the beginning of this stanza and the beginning of stanza 2 of **O lux beata Trinitas** (1575/6) shows the extent of Byrd's indebtedness, and also shows Byrd providing just that much extra contrapuntal interest:

Ex. 15

*Alfonso's *Nuntium vobis* (Egerton 3665, No. 20) is modelled on the famous setting by Lassus, published in 1571. Both works set two stanzas of the 3-stanza Epiphany hymn and both employ the Sapphic formula shown.

†This whole section is published in NOHM 4, 493ff.

Most of the lines are not, in fact, set homophonically but as facile polyphonic 'cells' two, three or four breves in length guided to clear little cadences, sung by one semichoir and repeated by another. For the climactic lines at the ends of stanzas 1 and 2, Byrd treats the cell in the slightly more ample way that we have already encountered in earlier 'brilliant' motets such as *Attollite portas* and *Tribue Domine*. After repeating the cell in three lower voices, he confirms the cadence by adding a further version of the cell expanded in texture, length, and contrapuntal density (Ex. 16). 'Cell'

Ex. 16

technique is being used to make a climax, as happens increasingly in Byrd's music of the 1580s; it is striking to see the music at the end of stanza 2 (Ex. 16) recur almost note for note in two of the greatest motets of the later period, *Ne irascaris Domine* (1589/20) and *Laudibus in sanctis* (1591/1). The rich style of *Laudibus in sanctis*, indeed, one of the most popular of Byrd's motets, is best understood as an imaginative development of the simple antiphonal style of these early hymns *alla Ferrabosco*.

The third stanza of *O lux beata Trinitas* is a canon, and as such is conspicuously entered in a special index in the *Cantiones*, along with Tallis's canons and Byrd's *Miserere mihi Domine* and **Diliges Dominum** (1575/12)— a *tour de force* of little artistic merit consisting of twenty-two breves of consonant 8-part writing read forwards and then backwards to new words.

Special interest attaches to the *O lux* canon because it shows Byrd reapplying and refining a plan he had evolved for an earlier canonic hymn, **O salutaris hostia** (BW 9/22), which is preserved in manuscript. Both works are in the Mixolydian mode. The plan involves a 3-part canon, with soprano and tenor at the octave and alto at the fourth or fifth, plus three freely imitative voices. Canons of this general description are also incorporated in two 6-part motets by Ferrabosco, *Cantabo Domino* and a setting of the very same stanza of *O lux beata Trinitas*.* (As a 3-stanza hymn to the Trinity, *O lux* seems to have driven composers inevitably into 3-part canon when they came to its third, doxology stanza.) Evidently some 'friendly æmulation' was involved, but setting Byrd's piece next to Alfonso's reveals less of interest than does a comparison of the two by Byrd (see Table 3).

TABLE 3: Canons in Motets by Byrd and Ferrabosco

			OCTAVE			
FERRABOSCO Cantabo Domino		T	*3 breves*	S	*1 breve*	A
						5th down
				OCTAVE		
O lux beata Trinitas		S	*2 breves*	A	*1 breve*	T
				5th down		
					OCTAVE	
BYRD O salutaris hostia		A	*1 breve*	S	*1½ breves*	T
		5th down				
					OCTAVE	
O lux beata Trinitas		A	*1 semibreve*†	T	*2½ semibreves*	S
		4th down				
			OCTAVE		UNISON	
Quomodo cantabimus		B	*3 breves*	A	*3 breves*	A
(see p. 180f)						*inverted*

Cantabo Domine (Sambrooke MS (Tregian), No. 17) is the final section of the huge psalm-motet *Benedic anima mea Domino* (Ps. 103); we know Byrd knew this work because he modelled *Emendemus in melius* on another section of it, *Qui fundasti terram. O lux* was one of the few Ferrabosco motets to be published, in Lechner's *Harmoniae miscellae cantionum sacrarum*, 1583², and one of the few which did not circulate in English manuscripts.

†Unlike the other canons, Byrd's *O lux* is notated *a note neri*, in a basic crotchet pulse.

Table 3 shows the different disposition of the canonic voices in these four motets, as to time and pitch intervals. (Also tabulated is a fifth canonic motet, *Quomodo cantabimus*, which will be discussed later.) All the changes in plan between Byrd's two canons work in the direction of system and lucidity. In *O lux* he obtained a more climactic arrangement by moving the soprano into the last position. He also allowed himself a little more leeway by extending the time interval, a change that tends to produce an uncomplicated series of short phrases repeated at the octave between tenor and soprano—a clear analogy with the antiphonal structure of stanzas 1 and 2 of the hymn. Even Byrd's *O salutaris hostia*, it will be seen, has a less abstract, more purposeful and focused canonic plan that either of Alfonso's pieces.

In both Byrd motets the canonic voices sing the four hymn lines (*O salutaris hostia* and *O lux beata Trinitas* have the same verse form) largely in syllabic declamation.* Between the lines come clear punctuating rests. In Table 4, the signs ×1 and ×2 show which lines are sung once or twice. In the later piece systematic repetitions and transpositions of lines replace the free transpositions of the earlier one. The effect of climax in the fourth and final line is stressed in several ways: by the slow build-up of the four statements, by the strong sequence provided by the exact upward transposition, and by the avoidance of any diversion such as the long, florid, archaic three-fold Amen in *O salutaris hostia*. Unlike *O salutaris hostia*, *O*

TABLE 4: The Canonic Voices in *O Salutaris Hostia* and *O Lux Beata Trinitas*

O salutaris hostia	O lux beata Trinitas
line 1 × 1	× 1
line 2 × 1	× 1
line 3 × 2 No.2 is a free transposition of No.1, down a step	× 2 No.2 is an exact repetition of No.1
line 4 × 2 No.2 is a free transposition of No.1, up a step	× 4 No.4 is an exact sequential transposition of No.3, up a step
Amen × 3 No.2 is a free transposition of No.1, down a fourth No.3 is a free transposition of No.1, down a step	× 1

*In declamation, too, *O lux* is the more systematic work; the canonic voices adhere fairly closely to the metrical pattern established in the earlier stanzas. The declamation in *O salutaris hostia* is less strictly organized, and in fact better adapted to the natural word accent.

lux beata Trinitas has the more 'modern' texture including two sopranos in the choir. The second soprano further stresses the climax by vaulting up over the canon.

The harmonic scheme in *O lux* is much clearer, too. In *O salutaris hostia* the canonic soprano and tenor do not even conclude line 4 on the tonic, though of course this is accomplished ultimately by the long Amen. The most glaring difference, however, is in the counterpoint and dissonance treatment. *O salutaris hostia* must be about the most dissonant composition Byrd ever wrote. Even if we apply greater charity with the accidentals than did the scribes of any of its sources,* it makes a ceaseless racket of false relations and resolutions sounding simultaneously (at pitch) with syncope suspensions. The piece has the air of an exercise that would scarcely survive actual performance. Perhaps Byrd wrote *O lux beata Trinitas* to assure Alfonso (and himself) that he could write a canon of much the same sort in correct counterpoint. All three stanzas of *O lux* are so conspicuously smooth, in fact, that a small cadential impropriety such as that shown in Ex. 16 stands out like Eliza Doolittle's innocent expletive.

[7]

Emendemus in melius (1575/1), the essay in affective homophony which Byrd placed first among his contributions to the *Cantiones*, though far from the most elaborate among them shows more clearly than any of the others the strides he had taken and the artistry which was now within his reach.†
It is possible to view the piece as a kind of summary of all or most of the technical investigations carried out in this extraordinary group of motets. Only Byrd's studies in cantus firmus and canonic work are not involved; yet probably the grave, entirely assured homophonic style of part 1 of *Emendemus in melius* could not have assumed the form it did without the

---

*Add. 31390, Tenbury 389-James and Baldwin's Partbooks.

†*Emendemus in melius* evidently made its impact. Byrd himself took advantage of some of its features in the anthem *O God whom our offences* (BW 11/6), and the motet was more widely copied—that is, copied by more collectors—than any other of the 1575 motets (*Laudate pueri* and *Attollite portas* out-top it only if their anthem versions are counted).

Generally speaking, the 1575 motets were not much copied, probably because scribes were disinclined to duplicate music that was available in print and musicians preferred the more modern motets by Byrd that started circulating quite soon after 1575. Even Paston, who never balked at copying printed music and who included motets from the 1575 *Cantiones* in eleven of his surviving manuscripts, chose only five of the twelve 6-part numbers and only one of the five 5-part ones. The 5-part piece was *Emendemus in melius* (Add. 18936-9, Tenbury 341-4 and 369-73. Tenbury 341 has a curious bowdlerization in the soprano at BE 1, 6, bar 41: minim d', dotted minim d', crotchet c', semibreve c'.)

regime of smooth consonant writing undertaken in the canons *O lux beata Trinitas* and *Diliges Dominum*. And if we take the consistent smoothness of these pieces as in some sense a reaction to the consistent roughness of earlier ones such as *O salutaris hostia* and *Attollite portas*, we can see a further stage represented by *Emendemus in melius* in which smoothness and roughness are applied selectively for expressive reasons. In the relatively subdued first part of the motet, Byrd handles dissonance with almost Palestrinian reticence, but in the more emotional second part he spikes the middle cadences with clashes of a quite un-Continental kind. At the climax on the words 'propter honorem nominis tuis' dissonance is compounded by extreme harmonic effects, by a juxtaposition of F and D major chords followed by an E minor chord (in a G Dorian context). Then Palestrinian orthodoxy returns in the concluding phrase 'libera nos', with its suave Continental cadence involving a suspended seventh and a 'consonant fourth'. 'If ther happen to be any iarre or dissonāce, blame not the Printer', Byrd remarks dryly in the preface to his 1588 songbook. He knew his writing was dissonant; he had been manipulating dissonance for its expressive value at least since the motets of 1575.

Byrd's exercises in syllabic declamation in the hymns *Siderum rector* and *O lux beata Trinitas*, and his studies in affective writing in the Requiem responds and other Dorian and Aeolian compositions, come together in *Emendemus in melius*. The terse opening phrase with its two semitones and its outline of a diminished fourth must have jolted English ears in 1575. The affective semi tone E♭D for the word 'Emendemus' returns for 'praeoccupati', 'poenitentiae' and 'peccavimus', to be capped by the characteristic second Dorian semitone FE♮ when the phrase 'quia peccavimus tibi' is repeated, so tensely, at the end of part 1 of the motet. At the climax in part 2, the free upward sequence traced by the soprano and bass in twelfths is invigorated by a powerful leap of a minor sixth (D♭♭: BE 1, 6, bar 47); this retraces the action of the 'convertere' passage in the Lamentations in a more urgent, condensed form. Under the pressure of this affective vocabulary, the syllabic declamation in part 1 of *Emendemus in melius* has to be rhythmically much freer than that of the hymns. Prose, in any case, did not invite the patterning appropriate to poetry. Byrd's declamatory rhythms follow every nuance of the text to project a remarkable sense of controlled anxiety.

Is it far-fetched also to see in *Emendemus in melius*—in the one contrapuntal phrase in it, the final phrase 'libera nos'—a culmination of Byrd's extensive studies in imitative polyphony? This cannot be said to be far-fetched in a literal sense, for the tetrachord motive in inversion for 'libera nos' was distilled from the beginning of the next motet in the publication, *Libera me Domine et pone me iuxta te*; and perhaps not in a more general sense, either, for this miniature point of imitation has the quality of something simple but exquisite emerging from an enormously sophisticated machine. The way Byrd makes this imitative phrase emerge naturally from the homophonic writing is doubly impressive by comparison with the motet by Ferrabosco on which *Emendemus in melius* is so closely modelled, *Qui fundasti terram** (see Ex. 17). For whereas Alfonso plies the same homo-

Ex. 17

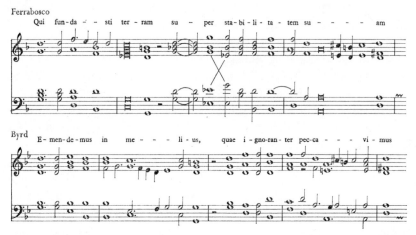

phonic style throughout, Byrd does not; he seems to have discerned in it a compositional problem of some subtlety. This might be formulated as the problem of moulding an individual phrase (or a total composition) in terms of texture. In part 1 and increasingly in part 2, one can observe Byrd easing the accompaniment texture from block chords at the phrase beginnings to some kind of contrapuntal activity and then back again at the cadences. Thus the conditions are set for the appearance of the fully imitative final phrase 'libera nos', like a delicate unravelling of the homophonic statement in which these words and their tetrachord motive are first presented. There is no such phrase in Alfonso.

All currents, finally, can be seen to play in to a superbly coherent expressive reading of the text:

---

*Egerton 3665 (Tregian), No. 34; part of the psalm-motet *Benedic anima mea* (Ps. 103). For details of this comparison, and on the Byrd piece in general, see J. Kerman, 'On William Byrd's *Emendemus in melius*', *Musical Quarterly*, xliv (1963), 431ff. Andrews's suggestion that *Emendemus in melius* might be performed liturgically, with a *da capo* of the respond, should be firmly rejected (*Byrd's Polyphony*, 260f).

Emendemus in melius, quae ignoranter peccavimus: ne subito praeoccupati die mortis quaeramus spatium poenitentiae et invenire non possumus. Attende, Domine, et miserere, quia peccavimus tibi. *2ᵃ pars* Adiuva nos, Deus salutaris noster, et propter honorem nominis tuis libera nos [Roman respond, 1st Sunday in Lent].

The declamation and the affective intervallic structure provide maximum excruciation at the repeated confession of sin, 'quia peccavimus tibi.' Byrd saw the climax of the text at the invocation of God's name, 'propter honorem nominis tuis', rather than at the appeals 'miserere', 'adiuva' or 'libera'; it was the doctrinal aspect of the text that interested him, not the personal. And after this, the imitative counterpoint spells serene liberation. This is a way of 'expressing' a text that exists on quite another plane than bounding subjects for 'Attollite', perpetual sequences for 'rursum', and 3-part canons for the Trinity.

Many years later, in the dedication to the *Gradualia*, Byrd wrote very beautifully about words and music: 'There is such a profound and hidden power in sacred words, as I have learned by trial, that to one thinking upon things divine and earnestly and diligently pondering them, the most suitable of all musical measures occur (I know not how) as of themselves and suggest themselves spontaneously to the mind that is not indolent and inert.' In this area *Emendemus in melius* stands out as Byrd's most brilliant early trial.

3
The Middle Period

Nearly fifty motets are known from the middle period of Byrd's career, from 1575 to around 1590, many of them large works in two or even more parts. Thirty-seven appeared in the two volumes of *Cantiones sacrae* issued in 1589 and 1591 as part of the composer's general programme of assembling and ordering his work in various genres. In the dedication of the 1589 book to Worcester Byrd wrote:

> When some people, close to me and of solid reputation, realized very recently that certain songs of mine had, through the carelessness of scribes in making the copies, suffered some impairment, which had certainly not come from our Museolus in the autographs: they implored me and finally got me to submit the autographs to the press, though not before I had first polished and disciplined them further. But so great was their number and confusion that I thought it better to divide the collection (as my leisure permitted) into several books, and publish each at its time.

Perhaps this was a conventional excuse or pretext for publication. A good many early manuscript copies of the middle-period motets have survived (as is not the case with the 1575 *Cantiones*) and these survivors cannot be said to be notably faulty. Admittedly, the scribes tended to adopt a casual attitude towards accidentals, text underlay, and minor rhythmic adjustments to do with underlay. On the other hand, errors in pitch and essential rhythm seldom occur; when manuscripts diverge in pitch and rhythm from the texts printed in 1589 and 1591 they are nearly always preserving distinct earlier versions of the motets.* However, the fact is that with one or two exceptions the manuscript and printed versions differ only in relatively unimportant details. Byrd 'polished and disciplined' some of the pieces for publication, especially some of the earlier ones. But he never seems to have felt a need to make substantial changes, not even as substantial as the small improve-

---

*Account will be taken of these early versions in the forthcoming volumes 2 and 3 of BE. Thurston Dart's revision of BW 2 and 3 in 1966 did little more than correct most of the several dozen errors in Fellowes's transcription (most, but by no means all: four errors remain in *Ne irascaris*, for example, as well as the appalling octave misplacement of the second alto in *Circumdederunt me*, bars 1–8). Dart and his assistant did not consult manuscripts.

ments applied to Fantasia 6/F when it was made over into the motet *Laudate pueri Dominum* (see Vol. III, p. 65).

Analysis of the early sources, then, does not tell us too much of interest about Byrd's compositional second thoughts. It does shed some light on the order of composition of these middle-period motets and also on their relative popularity. Several of the manuscripts in question are dated; others which are not can still be made to yield some chronological information. The discussion below is supplemented by Table 5.*

Add. 47844. This small motet collection, from which only the contratenor part survives, can be viewed with some satisfaction as the first manuscript source to give over the lion's share of its contents to Byrd. Next to copies of four numbers from the 1575 *Cantiones*, it transmits the motets *Ne irascaris Domine* and *Peccavi super numerum arenae maris* (all six without words). *Ne irascaris* and several other pieces are marked '1581', evidently the date of copying.

Christ Church 984–8. Robert Dow's manuscript has been mentioned previously (p. 46). It is a large and very elegant source containing only 5-part music, arranged in an orderly fashion. Dow first copied 8 motets by Robert White, then 5 by Byrd, then 16 miscellaneous motets, then a second group of 5 by Byrd, then 16 more miscellaneous ones; after which he added a sort of exemplary pair of compositions by 'Alfonso Ferabosco Italus' and 'Gulielmus Birde Anglus' before going on to nearly a hundred anthems, songs and instrumental pieces. He took his time. The front page of the manuscript is inscribed '1581', yet No. 43 carries an annotation recording the day and the month of Tallis's death in 1585 and his place of burial, and Nos. 60–1 are Byrd's 'funeral songs' for Sir Philip Sidney, killed in 1586. This tells us with fair certainty that the second Byrd group in Dow was copied by November 1585 and that the first group was copied in, or a little later than, 1581. 1581 is also the date attached to *Ne irascaris*, Dow's opening number, in Add. 47844.

Three numbers in Dow's first group, *Ne irascaris*, *Tribulationes civitatum* and *Domine praestolamur*, formed together with the cantus firmus respond *Aspice Domine de sede sancta tua* (see p. 73f) a specially favoured group. These four are found again and again in manuscripts of the period, often in

---

*For complete inventories of some of these manuscripts, see G. E. P. Arkwright, *Catalogue of Music in the Library of Christ Church, Oxford* (London, 1915–23), E. H. Fellowes, *The Catalogue of Manuscripts in the Library of St. Michael's College, Tenbury* (Paris, 1934), A. Hughes-Hughes, *Catalogue of Manuscript Music in the British Museum* London, 1906–9), and the TCM Appendix (for the Willmott-Braikenridge and Petre MSS). There are no published inventories for Add. 47844 nor for the Bodleian or RCM MSS.

TABLE 5: Byrd Motets in Contemporary Manuscripts

NOTE: Motets are provided with 'real' numbers, not necessarily corresponding with those in the sources themselves. All motets are for five voices except when marked *a 6*. For the sources marked with an asterisk, the table shows all the Byrd motets contained in them; for other sources, the table shows only selections, as indicated.

(a)   Major Sources

CHRIST CHURCH 984–8 (Dow)*

first Byrd group (1581)
- 9 Ne irascaris Domine
- 10 Tribulationes civitatum
- 11 O Domina adiuva me
- 12 Domine exaudi
- 13 Domine praestolamur

first miscellaneous group
- 27 Tribulatio proxima est

second Byrd group (1581–5)
- 30 O quam gloriosum
- 31 Tristitia et anxietas
- 32 Apparebit in finem
- 33 Audivi vocem
- 34 In resurrectione tua

second miscellaneous group (1585)
- 36 Fac cum servo tuo
- 39 Deus venerunt gentes
- 40 Domine tu iurasti
- 41 Exsurge quare obdormis Domine
- 45 Christe qui lux es
- 46 Laetentur coeli

'exemplary pair'
- 51 Mirabile misterium 'Alfonso Ferrabosco Italus'
- 52 Miserere mei Deus 'Gulielmus Birde Anglus'

BODLEIAN MUS. SCH.e.423

first Byrd group
- 43 Aspice Domine
- 44 Ne irascaris Domine
- 45 Domine praestolamur
- 46 Levemus corda nostra
- 47 Ne perdas cum impiis
- 49 O Domine adiuva me
- 50 Memento Domine
- 51 Omni tempore
- 52 Tristitia et anxietas
- 53 Domine exaudi
- 55 Peccavi
- 56 Tribulationes civitatum

CHRIST CHURCH 979–83 (Baldwin)

first Byrd group
- 8 Domine Deus omnipotens
- 9 O quam gloriosum
- 10 Apparebit in finem
- [11 Dum transisset *attribution changed from Byrd to Jo. Strabridge*]
- 12 Audivi vocem
- 13 Levemus corda nostra
- 14 Peccavi
- 15 Memento Domine
- 16 O Domine adiuva me
- 17 Domine exaudi
- 18 Omni tempore
- 19 Ne perdas cum impiis
- [20 Noctis recolitur *spurious: see p. 58*]

(b)   Secondary Sources

BL ADD. 47844 (1581)*

    4 Laudate pueri *a 6*
    5 Ne irascaris '1581'
  15 Libera me Domine
      et pone
  16 Peccavi
  20 Da mihi auxilium *a 6*
  22 O lux beata Trinitas
     a 6

BL ADD. 32377 (1584–5)*

  46 Ne irascaris Domine
  47 Cunctis diebus *a 6*
  57 Lamentations
  76 Domine praestolamur

TENBURY 389-JAMES

first group { 1 Aspice Domine
           2 Ne irascaris Domine
           3 Domine praestolamur

BODLEIAN MUS. SCH.e.1–5
(Sadler, 1585)*

  32 Attollite portas *a 6*
  35 Ne irascaris '1580'
  37 Tribulationes
     civitatum

later   { 1 Aspice Domine
additions { 2 Domine praestolamur

TENBURY 341–4 (Paston)

end of the { 24 Tribulationes
Byrd group {   civitatum
         { 25 Ne irascaris Domine

PETRE MS (Paston)

end of the { 31 Tribulationes
Byrd group {   civitatum
         { 32 Ne irascaris Domine

WILLMOTT-BRAIKENRIDGE
(Sadler, 1591)*

    { 4 Ne irascaris Domine
    { 5 Tribulationes
      civitatum
  10 Infelix ego *a 6*
  11 Deus venerunt gentes
  13 Petrus beatus
  12 Cunctis diebus *a 6*
  16 O quam gloriosum
  26 In resurrectione tua
  27 Laetentur coeli

RCM 2089 (Paston)

end of the { 53 Tribulationes
main Byrd {   civitatum
group   { 54 Ne irascaris Domine

TENBURY 369–73 (Paston)

final Byrd   52 Defecit in dolore
group   53 Salve Regina
         54 Quis est homo
         55 O quam gloriosum

nests of two or three placed at the beginning of the partbooks or at the beginning or end of Byrd cells. This information is summarized in Table 5. The Sadler Manuscript of 1585, which originally found room for only three pieces by Byrd, included two of these favourites among them; here *Ne irascaris* is dated 1580. And Sadler added the two other favourites later, at the head of the partbooks.

Bodleian Mus. Sch.e.423. The largest and most single-minded of Byrd anthologies is not dated, but can be placed in the middle or late 1580s.* Once again the contratenor part alone survives, containing songs and motets for five and six voices. Byrd has the place of honour at the head of the motet section of this manuscript, which launches at once into a set of twelve of his 5-part pieces, with one by William Mundy and one by Ferrabosco tucked in.

This, it appears, was the basic early corpus from which Dow made his initial selection, or something very close to that corpus. All the members of Dow's first group of five are here, together with (a) three cantus firmus responds, which are presumably early—*Aspice Domine*, *Ne perdas cum impiis* and *Omni tempore*, (b) *Peccavi*, a motet known also from Add. 47844, which is dated 1581, and (c) three other motets, *Levemus corda nostra*, *Memento Domine* and *Tristitia et anxietas*. One of these, *Tristitia et anxietas*, Dow copied into his second Byrd group (he also picked up the Mundy and Ferrabosco pieces). Some further evidence on the dating of this Bodleian set of twelve will be mentioned in a moment.

There is less to be learned from the subsequent Byrd cells in this manuscript, obviously, for even if we believe that the scribe was writing later there was nothing to prevent him for copying old music along with new. Nevertheless the last Byrd group, consisting of *Miserere mei Deus*, *Vigilate*, *Quis est homo* and *Salve Regina*, includes three pieces (the last three) which are not found in the other early sources and which seem on stylistic grounds to belong with the latest of the middle-period motets. After copying this group, the Bodleian scribe had actually assembled thirty-two of Byrd's 5-part motets of this period. Which known motets did he miss? Not many; and among them are *Defecit in dolore* and *Laudibus in sanctis*, which as the first numbers of the two volumes of *Cantiones sacrae* of 1589 and 1591 were most likely composed expressly for the publication. They do not appear in any manuscripts before 1600.

The Bodleian scribe did less well with music for six parts. He copied Byrd's cantus firmus responds *Descendit de coelis* and *Afflicti pro peccatis nostris* and his archaizing compositions in votive antiphon form, *Cunctis*

*See W. A. Edwards, *The Sources of Elizabethan Consort Music* (unpublished dissertation, Cambridge, 1974), i, 111.

diebus and *Infelix ego*; the latter two circulated fairly widely, as Table 5b suggests. But he missed a few older compositions which had never been printed—*O salutaris hostia* and *Domine ante te*—and many newer ones: *Deus in adiutorium, Circumpsice Hierusalem*, and four motets in an advanced style published in 1591: *Cantate Domino, Haec Dies, Domine non sum dignus* and *Domine salva nos*. These four, again, were evidently 'very rare and newly composed', as Byrd remarks of certain pieces in the *Psalmes, sonets & songs* of 1588. They do not figure in any of the manuscript sources we have been discussing.

Christ Church 979–83. Baldwin's Partbooks, a huge retrospective collection, incorporates the second largest Byrd anthology that is known, exceeded only by Mus. Sch.e.423. Baldwin started his first Byrd group with a somewhat haphazard selection of five motets, including a *unicum* and a spurious item which he himself reattributed. Next come seven pieces which are concordant with the early set of twelve in e.423. Another four from that set—the four favourites mentioned above—turn up as a special cell elsewhere in the partbooks (Nos. 58–61). That makes eleven; the twelfth, *Tristitia et anxietas*, turns up later, after a few more pages (No. 69). Since in Dow, too, this fine motet does not occur until the second group, we may regard it as a somewhat later addition by the scribe of e.423 to a basic early corpus of eleven.

Some sources of a slightly later period also contain good-sized collections of Byrd motets. Among them are four manuscripts written for Edward Paston, the so-called Petre Manuscript (Essex County Record Office D/DP.Z.6/1), Tenbury 341–4, 369–73 and RCM 2089, a lute manuscript. Paston's scribes seem often to have copied motets directly from the printed partbooks; yet sometimes they also seem to reflect habits of the 1580s in the way they select and order material (see Table 5b). Thus in Tenbury 369–73, after copying 14 middle-period Byrd motets and 21 items from the 1605 *Gradualia*, the scribe added a group of four more middle-period motets, *Defecit in dolore, Salve Regina, Quis est homo* and *O quam gloriosum*—three late pieces, on the evidence of e.423, plus an earlier one. It is also interesting to go through the Paston manuscripts (the four mentioned above with large Byrd holdings, as well as others which include only a few Byrd motets) and see which 5-part motets are consistently left out. Missing are *Laudibus in sanctis*, once again, and several from the early set of twelve: *Peccavi, Domine exaudi, Omni tempore* and *O Domine adiuva me*.

Finally, Table 6 shows how Byrd went about correcting the 'farrago' of early copies which he deplored in his dedication to Worcester. All the favourite items of the 5-part repertory appear in the 1589 book, and so do

TABLE 6: Contents of the *Cantiones sacrae*, Books 1 and 2, 1589 and 1591

			signature	initial/final
		Liber primus		
a 5	1–2	Defecit in dolore		A
	3–4	Domine praestolamur		A
	5	O Domine adiuva me		A
	6–7	Tristitia et anxietas		A
	8	Memento Domine	♭	A
	9–10	Vide Domine afflictionem nostram	♭	D
	11–14	Deus venerunt gentes	♭	D
	15	Domine tu iurasti		D–A
	16	Vigilate	♭	D
	17	In resurrectione tua Domine	♭	D–A
	18–19	Aspice Domine de sede sancta tua	(♮)(♭)	D–F(–D)
	20–1	Ne irascaris Domine	♭	F
	22–3	O quam gloriosum est regnum	♭	F
	24–6	Tribulationes civitatum	♭♭	B♭–G
	27	Domine secundum multitudinem dolorum meorum		C
	28–9	Laetentur coeli	♭	F
		Liber secundus		
a 5	1–2	Laudibus in sanctis		C
	3–4	Quis est homo	♭	F
	5	Fac cum servo tuo	♭	F
	6–7	Salve Regina		A
	8–9	Tribulatio proxima est		A
	10–11	Domine exaudi orationem meam		A
	12	Apparebit in finem		D–A
	13–14	Haec dicit Dominus	♭	D
	15	Circumdederunt me		D
	16	Levemus corda nostra	♭♭	G
	17–18	Recordare Domine	♭♭	G
	19	Exsurge quare obdormis Domine	♭♭	G
	20	Miserere mei Deus	♭♭	G
a 6	21–2	Descendit de coelis	♭	D
	23	Domine non sum dignus	♭	D
	24–6	Infelix ego	♭♭	B♭
	27–8	Afflicti pro peccatis nostris		G
	29	Cantate Domino	♭♭	G
	30	Cunctis diebus	♭♭	G
	31	Domine salva nos		C
	32	Haec dies	♭	F

most of the earlier pieces, though there are some exceptions. The music is ordered by mode or by final. Thus the 1589 book can be seen to begin with five motets on A (the last of them having a B♭ in the signature) and to end with five motets in the Ionian or Lydian mode (on F, C or B♭). In between come five motets on D, with or without a B♭ in the signature, plus a sixth which is eccentric as to mode: *Aspice Domine de sede*, the one cantus firmus composition and the one piece with a partial signature. As we have already seen, here the *prima pars* (the respond) starts with the cantus firmus transposed up to A before dropping down to D, and the *secunda pars* (the verse) ends on F! The placement can hardly be accidental. Ordering by mode or final is also evident in the 1591 *Cantiones sacrae*, especially in the 5–part section, where, in addition, motets with the soprano(s) written in the treble (G) clef are placed last within each group.*

It does not take more than a cursory overview of Byrd's middle-period motets to reveal that with few exceptions they derive stylistically from the various motet models worked out in the 1575 *Cantiones*. The affective homophony of *Emendemus in melius*, the lively antiphonal style developed for the hymns, the evocation of the votive antiphon in *Tribue Domine*—all of these can be traced directly in the music of the middle period. However, as is well known, Byrd now worked mostly within the tradition of the imitative motet, the establishment of which had been the main study of his early years. Continuously imitative in texture, at least in principle, with balanced phrases and even rhythms, leisurely in pace and characteristically 'minor' in mode, this is the model presented by the Dorian and Aeolian motet-pairs of 1575, by *Libera me*, *Peccantem me*, *Da mihi auxilium* and *Domine secundum actum meum*. Byrd plies this style again and again in the following years, albeit with many modifications and developments and admixtures.

In the first section of this chapter we shall trace the course of his writing within this basic tradition. The other motets, a smaller but much more miscellaneous group, will be treated in the second section. This will make a workable framework for discussion, though it goes without saying that imitative techniques are also used in the second group of motets—as was the case in *Emendemus in melius* with its luminous final point of imitation—and that sooner or later the distinction between 'basically imitative' and 'basically non-imitative' motets is bound to break down. The way a motet begins, however, is generally indicative. Motets that begin with a full imitative exposition establish certain implications for the total polyphonic development;

*Nos. 3–5, 12, and 20—and it is worth noting that No. 19, which uses the soprano C1-clef, really ought to have used the treble clef instead in order to accommodate the soprano range d–f′.

those that do not are less predictable, more 'open'. For Byrd at this period, and for his listeners, the motets of the second group were all in some sense special or radical. The continuously imitative style was the norm. Its endless refinement still occupied the artistic centre of his work.

3a

Motets in the Central Imitative Tradition

Domine ante te *a 6*	BW 9/21	Vigilate	1589/16
Domine exaudi orationem		Circumspice	
meam	1591/10–11	Hierusalem *a 6*	BW 9/19
Domine praestolamur			
adventum tuum	1589/3–4	Exsurge quare	
Memento Domine	1589/8	obdormis Domine	1591/19
Levemus corda nostra	1591/16	Defecit in dolore	1589/1–2
Peccavi	BW 8/15	O quam gloriosum	
Tristitia et anxietas	1589/6–7	est regnum	1589/22–3
Deus venerunt gentes	1589/11–14	Ad punctum in	
		modico	BW 16, 122f
Domine tu iurasti	1589/15	Recordare Domine	1591/17–18
Apparebit in finem	1591/12	Audivi vocem de	
Domine exaudi . . . et		coelo	BW 8/7
clamor meus	BW 16, 127	Benigne fac Domine	BW 8/8
Fac cum servo tuo	1591/5	Plorans plorabit	1605 *a 5*/28
Domine secundum multitu-			
dinem dolorum meorum			
	1589/27		
Quis est homo	1591/3–4		

In the years after 1575 Byrd turned away from 6-part writing. He composed only a few English pieces in six parts (and several of these, such as *Christ rising* and *Who made thee Hob forsake the plough?*, can usefully be viewed as adjuncts to the 5-part repertory since they consist of a duet or dialogue with four parts accompanying). He produced Masses for three, four and five voices but none for six. The norm becomes 5-part texture, and it can be seen that already in the 1575 *Cantiones*, where Byrd limits himself to five voices in only a third of the contents, these include the most modern in style. There are no more than two 6–part motets which fall into the main category of Byrd's middle period, the category of motets in continuous or at least predominant imitation.

One of these, **Domine ante te** (BW 9/21), may date back to a time before Byrd had entirely formed his new habits. He never published the piece. The tenor part has not been preserved,* but a good deal of what remains looks

*Reconstruction of such missing parts is more precarious than is usually acknowledged; compare the two very different results in BW 9/21 and TCM 9, 208f. TCM is clearly

early: the straggling first point of imitation, with its rather inexplicable melismas for the word 'ante', the stiff long-note subject for 'Cor meum', the homophonic setting of 'derelinquit me virtus mea' starting with a hectic climax, and the conceit whereby the text-phrase 'a te non est absconditus' is omitted entirely (hidden, 'absconded') from some of the voice parts. There are also features that look later. The first point has only seven entries, rather than an exposition of six followed by six more as counter-exposition, and the final point, with its freely repeated sequential structure (geared to the soprano high c's and d's at BW 9, 45 bar 6, 46, bar 4, 47 bars 1 and 4), shows a growing fluency of technique. Unfortunately the motives here lack character, and the final cadence lacks conviction. A composer with long experience in writing motets would not choose to end with words like 'et ipsum non est mecum', and if the choice were forced, would not highlight them in double imitation.

Stylistically *Domine ante te* occupies a middle ground between the *Cantiones sacrae* of 1589–91 and the *Cantiones* of 1575, between a closely matched pair of 5-part motets, **Domine exaudi orationem meam** (1591/10–11) and **Domine praestolamur adventum tuum** (1589/3–4), and a 6-part pair which may be regarded as their model, *Domine secundum actum meum* and *Da mihi auxilium* (see pp. 104ff: for the text of *Domine praestolamur*, see p. 41). All this is music in the Aeolian mode, written in the same outer clefs, bass and soprano, so that the range is in principle from the low fifth of the mode (E) to the high fourth (d'); this high fourth is typically treated as an upper neighbouring note to the more stable third degree. (See Ex. 3d. The 6-part pieces occasionally go up to the fifth and even to the sixth.) The 5-part motets, both of which figure in the early group circulating by 1581, give the impression of successive expeditions into the same quarry. *Domine exaudi* is presumably the earlier of the two and certainly the poorer, and one could understand Byrd's reluctance to print it in the 1589 *Cantiones sacrae* next to the popular *Domine praestolamur*. When he did come to publish it, two years later, he 'disciplined' it rather more than usual.*

---

wrong in its opening imitation starting on the sixth degree (!), but Fellowes in BW 9 was also wrong not to fit in the 'omne desiderium' motive. TCM puts it in bar 11. It goes even more naturally into Fellowes's bars 15–16.

*The early version is preserved in Dow's MS (complete), Baldwin's Partbooks (lacking the tenor) and Mus. Sch.e.423 (first alto part only). The following collation has been adjusted to apply to BW 3. *Soprano* p. 71, bar 7: A♭, not A♮. 74/8–9: *longa* in Dow (!); minim C, minim rest, *longa* C in Baldwin (his emendation?). 77/5: dotted crotchet C ('ser-'), quaver B♭ ('-vo-') instead of A♭C. 78/4: F, not F♯. 81/3: two minims A♭F. 82/6–7: dotted minim C, crotchet C instead of CDE♭B♭. *First alto* 68/8: A♮, not A♭. 73/9: the bar begins with quavers E♭DD, the E♭ tied to the previous bar. 74/7: rest in place of F; the word 'et' is missing. *Second alto* 71/9: F, not F♯. 82/1–3: minim G instead

These two motets are still leisurely, even monumental compositions, and we shall begin our examination of the middle period with works of this scale, written in the years between 1575 and around 1580. They are laid out in approximately the same ample dimensions—

Domine exaudi	22_i	21_i	25_i		24_i	44_i	
			12 15			19 28	
Domine praestolamur	21_i	15_i	34_i		23_i	26_i	22_i

—though comparison with the chart on page 107 will show that Byrd's 'ideal' length for a long point of imitation is shrinking somewhat. Double imitation is now handled more loosely, even in the most formal points, those with which motets begin. Instead of a full-scale counter exposition, as in most of the earlier motets, *Domine exaudi* (like *Domine ante te*) has no more than a single entry after the original group. *Domine praestolamur* has a more original arrangement, involving an exposition of four entries only, followed by an imaginative, fast stretto introducing another four.

The third phase in *Domine exaudi*, 'in veritate tua', consists of 4-part cells repeated four times in a sort of loose ostinato. This resembles 'et gemitus meus' in *Domine ante te*. But otherwise imitative style prevails throughout these 5-part motets, and there can be no doubt that the constant imitations, in conjunction with the restriction of the main cadences to the tonic and the use of melodic material hewing closely to modal formulae (see Ex. 18), makes for a relentless homogeneity of effect. *Domine exaudi* drones on and on, and Byrd only saves *Domine praestolamur* by means of very superior workmanship in the different kinds of imitative writing.

For example, *Domine exaudi* ends with a lengthy double point containing one subject in long notes, as in many of the 1575 motets (see Exs. 10 and 13). The analogous point in *Domine praestolamur* (which ends part 1, instead) has the semibreves always rhythmicized so as to create a somewhat less ponderous impression (Ex. 18a). Each motet includes a point based on a long, plodding subject which moves up through a sixth and is treated as a sort of loose ostinato (Ex. 18b)—a device prefigured in *Da mihi auxilium* by the point 'quia vana salus hominis'. Whereas in *Domine exaudi* the subject reaches all its peaks on C and F, in a space of 19 breves, in *Domine praestola-mur* it also overshoots C and F to D and G, in 24 breves, making a longer

of two crotchet Gs—words 'omnis vivens'. 82/3–4: slightly different declamation in each source. *Tenor* 73/1 B♮, not B♭. 82/1–3: words 'in conspectu tuo'. *Bass* 74/3: first note minim E♭; the word 'et' is missing. 77/4–5: melisma A♭GCF for 'tu-'. 78/8–79/1: 'om[G]nis[FE♭] vi[CD]vens'. BW 3 is in error at 71/10: the first note in the first alto is E♭.

Ex. 18

point but also a more interesting one. For the end of part 2 of *Domine praestolamur*, Byrd took over the relatively lively subject at the end of *Domine exaudi* (Ex. 18c). The subject is made more emphatic, and the contrapuntal development much more exciting: a swinging ostinato evolves during which the subject repeatedly peaks on C, or else climactic c's are thrown up by free melismas in the soprano (BW 2, 27, bars 1–6).* The last subject entry in this passage, a forceful bass entry reaching up to high c, is capped by an expected but still very effective soprano entry touching high d', following a vivid little stretto. In general Byrd now wants to give his motets rather more vigorous conclusions than can be provided by full-scale double points.

The spread in quality between the two motets stands out most clearly in two very similar points of imitation—double points, once again: those at the beginning of *Domine praestolamur*, part 1, and *Domine exaudi*, part 2 ('Et non intres in iudicium'). The first shows how far Byrd had progressed in flexibility and subtlety of style since the 1575 *Cantiones*; the draughtmanship and rhetoric are equally admirable.† The second shows him working well below the level of craft he had set for himself in that prize collection. A detailed comparison of the contrapuntal writing is instructive, but cannot be carried out here; the upshot, however, could almost be predicted from

---

*In bar 7 the soprano challenges us to insert B♮ . . . The scribe of Add. 32377 seems to have recoiled from this, for he rewrote the beginning of bar 8 to read crotchet rest, crotchet g.

†See J. Kerman, 'Byrd, Tallis, and the Art of Imitation', *Aspects of Medieval and Renaissance Music*, ed. Jan LaRue (New York, 1966), 533ff.

the subjects themselves (Ex. 18d). In *Domine exaudi* the subject limps, returns too insistently to E, and fits the words much less beautifully (Byrd may have found little beauty, to be sure, in the words 'iustitia', 'iudicium' and 'iustificabitur' in this text). That the subject beginning part 1 of this motet, too, keeps returning to E is certainly no coincidence; the whole piece must have been designed to stay rooted in the tonic, without any cadences on other degrees and without so much as a single added B♭. *Domine praestolamur* ranges further afield, though again all the main cadences hold to the tonic. Numerous F♯s at the end of part 1 are balanced by an expressive B♭ at the beginning of part 2.

Byrd worked with a much more various harmonic palette in some other motets of the same period. **Memento Domine** (1589/8) comprises four balanced imitative phrases lasting from 22 to 25 breves in the A Phrygian, D Dorian, D Aeolian and A Phrygian modes respectively. The characteristic Dorian colouration of phrase 2 comes from the systematic alternation of B♭s and B♮s; in phrase 4 the modality of the opening is re-asserted with the help of four cadences on A, three of them Phrygian and one (the final one) plagal. Byrd aimed for modal variety here, combining and balancing his modal effects with considerable sophistication. *Memento Domine* is an unusually subdued piece, no doubt on account of the glum text (see p. 41). Since it works within a smaller range than the Aeolian motets discussed above, from low F' to high c', the soprano climaxes make less of an impression and the bass never reaches down to the striking half closes on E' which help characterize the sonorous world of those compositions.

Levemus corda nostra (1591/16), another of the earliest group of middle-period motets, makes strong cadences on the first, third, fourth and fifth degrees of the Dorian mode. The antiquated opening point 'Levemus corda nostra' recalls that of *Attollite portas* and actually out-tops it in motivic saturation, fitting 13 regular entries and 3 free ones (some of them in stretto at the semibreve or minim) into a span of 18 breves. Of the following points, 'cum manibus ad Dominum in coelos' resembles a pair noted in *Domine exaudi* and *Domine praestolamur*, built ostinato-fashion on long subjects moving up through a sixth (Ex. 18a), and 'et ad iracundiam provocavimus' employs double imitation to little effect.

More interesting is the last phrase, 'Sed tu, Domine, miserere nostri', a direct appeal to God, including a vocative. Byrd sets it in an impressive half-declamatory, half-homophonic style. That this was the first of his many passages of the same kind is suggested both by a certain stiffness of execution, and also by the aspect of the piece as a whole, with the passage in question following on four rigorously contrapuntal phrases; in later motets featuring these appeals, Byrd takes care to have the half-homophonic ending emerge from textures that are less consistently polyphonic. (These motets are therefore left for discussion until the next part of this chapter.) In *Levemus corda nostra* the motives for the two text-fragments 'Sed tu, Domine' and 'miserere nostri' never engage significantly. After the first of these motives has made its dramatic entrance in block-chord homophony, it returns twice as a 3-part canon—each time essentially the same canon, which seems oddly unenterprising for Byrd, though the second time a fifth higher, which seems oddly abrupt as a way of establishing a climax. However, a forceful modulation to the dominant is engineered by the transposition of the canon, and the expansion of the motive in the final 'miserere nostri' section is excellently managed.

Another early Dorian motet, **Peccavi super numerum arenae maris** (BW 8/15), Byrd left aside when he came to publish the *Cantiones sacrae*. It may be that he had grown dissatisfied with the piece. It features some extreme or eccentric harmonic effects: a cadence on the second degree (albeit deceptive: BW 8, 136, bars 6–7),* a very long section on the seventh degree, and a most uncomfortable lurch to the subdominant in an effort to stabilize the tonic at the conclusion. Byrd may also have had second thoughts about the points 'videre altitudinem coeli' and 'prae multitudine iniquitatis meae', which are based on similar subjects, both rooted in B♭ and both treated as octave canons at the time interval of a semibreve. Starting at BW 8, 138, bar 6, one hears a succession of similar canons all chiming around the pitches F, G, B♭ and D after 15, 8, 9, 11, 3 and 13 semibreves. The subjects themselves sound less like Byrd than White, who has much the same subjects in the same order in the 'Omnis populus eius' section of the 6-part Lamentations.

Peccavi was quite popular, all the same; it is known from several manuscripts, the first of them dated 1581.† The opening point is the most interesting and successful. The 'Peccavi' subject features an affective semitone, but instead of buttressing this with other semitones, as usual, Byrd adds a second subject for the same word, a procedure that becomes common in his writing only at the time of the *Gradualia* (Ex. 19). The two subjects form intense suspensions with one another but do not modulate, and when after a somewhat indistinct setting of 'super numerum' Byrd comes to the words 'arenae maris', he holds them strictly to the tonic C minor also. The

---

*It was this cadence, presumably, that caused Byrd to employ the unusual double transposition to C, with the two-flat signature that so exasperated Morley: see p. 72.

†Add. 47844 (see Table 5). The text, a curtailed respond for the 1st Sunday after Trinity, suggests an even earlier date: but compare *Recordare Domine*, p. 156f.

Ex. 19

sins which are as the sands of the sea are sung to an eightfold ostinato peaking on E♭; the last six times E♭ is despondently underpinned by C. Only when the sins are spread even further ('et multiplicata sunt peccata mea') does the harmony expand, A♭ gives way to A♮ and cadences form on G as well as on C.

Byrd shelved *Peccavi* but took over a number of its features in other motets. The 'prae multitudine' canon appears in *Exsurge quare obdormis Domine* (1591/19) as the germ of a forceful point which could not sound less like White. The little homophonic echoes of 'peccata mea' appear in *Infelix ego* (1591/24) to illustrate the words 'non audeo'. Doubtless both works date from the later 1570s. And the rather pointless crotchet *echappée* figure at 'iniquitatis' (BW 8, 143) turns up as a magnificent detail near the beginning of **Tristitia et anxietas** (1589/6–7)—the diminution first heard in the tenor at bar 12 (Ex. 20). Once again, as in *Peccavi*, Byrd falls under

Ex. 20

the spell of a single word, 'Tristitia', but the result—it sounds almost like Rore—is much more original and haunting.

Tristitia et anxietas, which appears to be a little later than the imitative motets we have discussed, is also the masterpiece among them. It contains other very moving homophonic or half-homophonic phrases: 'propter nomen sanctum tuum', with its reminiscences (musical and textural) of *Emendemus in melius*, and 'in dolore', where a distant echo from Tallis's Lamentations is developed in Byrd's own incomparable way. Nevertheless this long motet leaves a final impression of predominant imitative polyphony, an impression that grows on us during the three solemn double points incorporated in the *prima pars*. It is interesting that Byrd should have juxtaposed two points as similar as 'et contenebrati sunt oculi mei' and 'Vae mihi, quia peccavi'. Their first subjects hinge on lamenting semitones and their second subjects interlock descending fourths and fifths, in White's manner, once again. Both points start on the subdominant side of the Aeolian mode, employing B♭s, before settling into old-fashioned free ostinatos focused on the pitch A. And both conclude with heavy cadential passages built on their second subjects. The 'Vae mihi' point, which ends the *prima pars*, comes to a very decided stop, but so does the preceding point 'et contenebrati sunt'—so decided, that one looks hard to see whether 'Vae mihi' might have been added as an afterthought when the rest of the piece was done. Another strange formal junction arises when yet another double point, 'occupaverunt interiora mea', comes to a full stop in a texture of four voices only, the soprano having stayed silent during the previous five breves.

As in several other impressive motet texts of this period, after a first part dwelling upon the soul's anguish the second brings a clear message of consolation. This is depicted in various ways: by the initial light texture permeated by intervals of a sixth, by major 6–5 progressions in the motive 'sperantes in te', and by a striking sonority of a diminished fifth first built on F♯, a relatively fresh note (BW 2, 48, bar 4: the sonority is repeated a fifth lower at 49, bar 1). The harmony continues to brighten, and at the word 'consolare' the rhythm spurts forward in an enthusiastic, awkward, and curiously affecting way. Byrd's special accomplishment in this motet was to have maintained so earnest and intense a response to the long succession of text fragments—this in addition to his altogether inspired writing in the opening and closing phrases.

'Cell' technique, as we have seen, was evolved in several of the motets published in the 1575 *Cantiones* (pp. 88, 110, 117). The closing point of *Tristitia et anxietas*, 'et miserere mei', shows how perfectly Byrd had learned to manipulate this technique a few years later (Ex. 21).

The plan remains as simple as ever. A semichoir cell ending with a distinct cadence is first repeated by another semichoir, then taken up by the full choir and expanded to prepare the final cadence. Here a cell moving in slow duple metre (as determined by the octave imitation and the cadence

Ex. 21

point) is repeated a fifth lower with the B, T and A¹ voices transposed
almost exactly from the original T, A¹ and S parts. An extra entry (A²)
serves to link these cells rhythmically and harmonically, by overlapping the
cadence in bar 4 and making it deceptive. The subtlety here is that this

extra entry—also at the octave—comes three semibreves after the last entry heard, not two, and so begins to suggest large triple rhythms; yet at the same time it initiates the new series of duple-metre entries carried on in the second cell (A², B, T, bars 3–5). When the linking voice returns at the end of the second cell (A², bars 6–7) it establishes triple metre as the basic means of organization for the richer contrapuntal action that is now to follow.

The S entry in bar 8 seems to be starting all over again, as though from bars 1–2. But this time it trails a new stretto at the lower fourth, in the A¹; the stretto pair recurs after three semibreves in the B and T. And at this point Byrd moves very quietly towards a melodic climax in each one of the voices. The motive is moulded again and again, always with a superb expressive effect, from the basic form ga′b′c′ (S, bar 8) to Gabd (A², bar 11), gb′c′d′ (S, bar 13: soaring high above the lower voices' inversion), Ebcd (T, bar 15) and finally a′b′c′d′ (S, bar 17). After d′ has come twice as the high note in the S, the altos gently silhouette e, a seventh below, as the peak of the motive bcde in a new unison stretto (bars 14 and 18).

As for the very striking 'sprung' entry with which the T moves up to *its* high note, d, in bars 15–16 (Ebcd), this feels at first like an expansive cadential gesture but is soon revealed as the beginning of a powerfully heightened repetition. The T entry parallels the A² entry of bars 11–12. The texture strains, the harmony stiffens, and strettos curl up the circle of fifths from d–g (A²), a′–d′ (S), E–a (B) and b–e (A¹ and A²)—the last pair 'recapturing', as it were, the altos' b–e entries of bar 14. Just before this, the A² and B voices, too, have reached their peaks on g and a respectively. Not to be outdone, the other alto pulls g out of the air at the last moment, before the voices regroup elegantly on lower ground to make the final cadence.

The crotchet *echappée* figure that evolves so beautifully as a diminution near the beginning of *Tristitia et anxietas* (see Ex. 20) also occurs in **Deus venerunt gentes** (1589/11–14), the longest by far of Byrd's imitative motets. Once again the figure evolves as a diminution (though not, alas, so beautifully: 'et non erat qui sepeliret', BW 2, 98). This technical detail seems distinctive enough to associate the two motets in date, as they also appear to be associated in basic technical impulse, the impulse to push the leisurely imitative style that Byrd had developed in the late 1570s as far (or at least for as long) as it would go. At the heart of this style was the technique of double imitation, which he had adapted from Ferrabosco to provide the basic breakthrough of his own style of the early 1570s. One has the feeling that in these two exhaustive compositions of around 1581 Byrd finally worked double imitation out of his system. In any case, the technique served his purposes less and less in the more concise imitative motets that he wrote in the middle 1580s.

Like *Tristitia et anxietas*, *Deus venerunt gentes* opens with a phrase that is not imitative, an urgent, half-homophonic cry of alarm which flares up and subsides in eleven breves: 'Deus, venerunt gentes in haereditatem tuam.' After this, however, no fewer than thirteen phrases follow without interruption by homophony or half-homophony of any sort. Contrast is provided on a rhythmic level, by a large number of phrases moving in faster rhythms for purposes of word illustration—a matter to which we shall need to return later (p. 149f). Most of the other phrases, which are set as double points,* lack the melodic and expressive distinction of those in *Tristitia et anxietas*. The part writing and harmonic progressions of *Deus venerunt gentes* are not always smooth, and the cadential treatment is not always easy to understand. Byrd is just as ready to use—or, rather, overuse—the modern continental consonant-fourth pattern as to reach back to his and to Tallis's Lamentations for an archaic cadence (at the end of part 1) with a *cambiata* figure in the bass.

Also puzzling is Byrd's general strategy of composition, as best we can reconstruct it. The text (see p. 42) is long but not exceptionally so; what is exceptional is the diffuse way in which he sets it, and given the dimensions that result from this diffuseness, the lack of textural and especially harmonic interest. Written in D with B♭ in the signature, the motet must be construed in the transposed Aeolian mode rather than the Dorian, for never once in its 266 breves does it venture as far as a perfect or even a deceptive cadence in the dominant, A. Nor is a single E♭ inserted after the first thirty-odd breves. In other very long motets, such as *Tribue Domine* (1575) and *Infelix ego* (1591), Byrd always capitalized systematically on resources of harmonic and textural variety.

Deus venerunt gentes was written in response to the martyrdom of Edmund Campion and his companions in 1581: a strong speculative case, at least, can be built to support this idea on external evidence. One piece of internal evidence is the extreme length (39 breves) of Byrd's setting of the key words 'carnes sanctorum tuorum bestiis terrae' in the *secunda pars*. It is

---

*A rare example of a triple point, with three independent subjects worked out simultaneously, is afforded by the phrase 'Facti sumus opprobrium vicinis nostris' at the beginning of part 4. Is it entirely by coincidence that these words recall the words from I Cor. 4:9 with which Campion began his speech from the scaffold, 'Spectaculum facti sumus Deo, angelis, et hominibus'? (see R. Simpson, *Edmund Campion, A Biography* (London, 1866, 2/1896), 450). 'A pacient spectacle was presented then,/In sight of God, of angels, saints, and men', according to a contemporary poet (see L. I. Guiney, *Recusant Poets*, i (London, 1939), 179).

tempting to speculate further that the composer may have been impelled to produce this enormous, drawn-out motet of outrage in a very great hurry. Here we are whistling in the dark, of course; but one feels the need for some such explanation for the rather disappointing quality of this obviously very seriously considered work.

[2]

In another group of imitative motets—motets which are still entirely imitative in style, or predominantly so—Byrd pursued a more concise ideal. In general, no doubt, these motets were composed later than the large-scale compositions that have been discussed above. (However, it is clear that later he occasionally went back to a sober gait and leisurely dimensions when a text evoked for him the spirit of the late 1570s.) Phrase diagrams drawn up for these more concise motets now grow cumbersome, for a number of reasons. Their tonal schemes are more varied and subtle, employing many half closes, and Byrd writes more phrases which do not come to clear cadences, but instead run imperceptibly into other phrases, forming with them larger periods comprising several different musical ideas. Some of the motets are as long as ever, but they are made up of shorter elements:

Domine tu iurasti* 15_i 10_v 16_v $5_{\frac12 i}$ $19_{\frac12 i}$ 14_{III} 18_v
                                               $\underline{7\quad 15}$ $\underline{9\quad 7}$

Apparebit in finem* 17_i $8_{\frac12 i}$ $10_{\frac12 iv}$ 15_{iv} 13_i 5_i

Domine secundum multitudinem $33_{\frac12 I}$ 15_v 17_I
                       $\underline{13\quad 14\quad 13}$

Fac cum servo tuo 12_v 18_v 12_v 7_I 13_{vi} $10_{\frac12 vi}$ 20_I

Quis est homo 11_I 12_v 16_{vi} 18_{vi}

2ª pars Diverte a malo 9_v 5_v 15_I 20_{ii} 10_{vi} 23_I
                                        $\underline{5\quad 9\quad 9}$ $\underline{5\quad 7}$

*Domine tu iurasti is analyzed in D, Apparebit in finem in A; see below.

The texts of **Domine tu iurasti** (1589/15) and **Apparebit in finem** (1591/12) have been cited among the 'political' motet texts on page 41. At first glance (though only at first glance) the two motets appear similar enough so that Byrd may have thought it just as well not to publish them in the same book. Written in the same clefs, with no flats in the signature, both begin with imitations on E and A and both end in A, yet both tilt dangerously towards D at many points in between. In fact the two pieces toy with modal ambiguity from opposite standpoints.*

Ex. 22

In *Domine tu iurasti* the initial subject (Ex. 22a) moves from E directly to D, where Byrd brings the first strong cadence, after which many Dorian pages follow. As frequently happens in motets of this period, the penultimate phrase comes to a firm cadence on a somewhat remote scale degree; the degree in question here, F, actually confirms the Dorian feeling, for F is not a usual cadence point in the Aeolian mode. However, the final phrase veers off to A in a surprisingly decisive fashion, even though the sense of 'modulation' is weakened by the high A in the bass of the final chord. (The whole bass part is pitched unusually high.) In *Apparebit in finem* the initial subject (Ex. 22b) stays in A and this is where the first phrase makes its cadence, despite a strong bias towards D. All the phrases end with A or D cadences, but the penultimate phrase includes one solid cadence on C, which works in support of the Aeolian modality. So does the low A at the final Aeolian cadence—the first low A in the entire bass part.

As one would expect, the Dorian composition is the more brilliant and extrovert of the two, with its very effective homophonic phrases, the first of them vehement, the second intense and harmonically audacious. *Apparebit in finem* lives on the characteristic Aeolian semitone FE, which is already at the heart of the opening subject. Typically enough, FE is always† reflected by two other semitones, CB and B♭A: something that happens in only one phrase in *Domine tu iurasti*, 'terram fluentem lacte et melle'. And these

*Byrd's own classification of the modes of these motets can be inferred only partially from the ordering of the publications (Table 6). He placed *Domine tu iurasti* within the group of motets with a D final, *Apparebit in finem* in between groups with A and D finals.

†The first note in the first alto in a BW 3, 84, bar 6 should be sung as B♭, as indicated in Tenbury 342. *Apparebit in finem* is another motet that was considerably touched up for publication; the original version is preserved in Tenbury 341–4, Dow's MS and Mus. Sch.e.342. Most of the changes provided for more rhythmic activity. Thus at BW 3, 86, bars 1–4, the syncopated setting of 'expecta' in the two altos is new; at bar 5, the first alto originally had a dotted semibreve; and at 88, bars 5–6, the soprano originally had minims EAB etc.

words provide a perfect gloss for the unusually plastic quality that this semi-tonal style promotes all the way through the other motet. As though exhausted by its own consistency, at the very end *Apparebit in finem* explodes in a sudden flurry of crotchet imitations using a free diminution of the last motive 'et non tardabit'. There are few places in Byrd where the larger rhythm is distorted so seriously—or so surprisingly, in view of the level discourse up to this point—for reasons of word illustration.

Byrd never repeated this particular effect, but in his more concise motets of this period he often arranged to bring in faster rhythms near the end. The acceleration performs a purely musical function, whether or not it is instigated by the text, and it is typically followed by a cadential deceleration (which does *not* happen in *Apparebit in finem*). Motives involving some crotchet declamation occur in the last phrases of *Domine secundum multitudinum dolorum meorum* ('*laetifi*caverunt a*nimam* meam') and *Quis est homo* ('ut per*det de* terra'); one thinks also of the beautiful phrase ending the verse of the late cantus firmus respond *Afflicti pro peccatis nostris* and the coda of *Ne irascaris Domine* (see Exs. 4 and 29a). The last phrase of **Domine exaudi . . . et clamor meus** (BW 16, 127) absorbs crotchet and even quaver declamation ('*Velociter exaudi* me'), as is sufficiently clear from the three parts that survive of this short motet.* A subtler kind of rhythmic acceleration was contrived for the close of **Fac cum servo tuo** (1591/5).

This motet is one of Byrd's masterpieces of quiet rhetoric. The text, to judge from the very personal quality of the setting, was his own choice, not that of a patron; in any case, it sits strangely among the penitential and 'political' motets of this period:

Fac cum servo tuo secundum misericordiam tuam et iustificationes tuas doce me. Servus tuus ego sum; da mihi intellectum, ut sciam testimonia tua [Ps. 119:124–5].

What is also strange is that the opening phrase consists of a single, not a double point. This meant that Byrd could set in place as many as ten subject entries in the relatively short span of twelve breves; and there is none of the strain or confusion that had attended such stretto exercises in works such as *Memento homo* in the 1575 *Cantiones*. The subject itself hovers as though

---

*Soprano and alto in Tenbury 389-James, tenor on a single manuscript sheet tipped into a bound volume of Marenzio madrigal editions in the Bodleian Library, Mus. Sch.e.526. The text of this motet is abbreviated from Psalm 101:2–3; the similar text of *Domine exaudi orationem meam* (1591/10–11) is paraphrased from Psalm 142:1–2, with reference also to Psalm 87:7. The Penitential Psalms 101 and 142 figure prominently in the Roman funeral services.

meditating on the tonic F, dipping twice to the dominant: FCDCFC. (A similar configuration at the beginning of *Domine exaudi orationem meam* makes little effect because it is overshadowed by the more active second half of the double subject.) As most of the entries begin on F, the tonic sonority is constantly gleaming through the texture; this pellucid point of imitation establishes at once a reigning mood of quietude. At the end the music turns quickly to the dominant, C, a frequent gesture in Ionian compositions which becomes a positive structural feature in this one.

The second phrase, 'secundum misericordiam tuam', has less individuality, as is often the case with phrases in cell construction. The second cell swerves rather heavily towards E♭—the only E♭ in the piece—and the sharp rhythmic and textural break between phrases 1 and 2 seems a puzzling response to the syntax of the psalm, especially by contrast with the wonderfully eloquent treatment of phrases 3 and 4. In phrase 3, a free ostinato on a subject very much like 'Fac cum servo tuo', Byrd again saturates the texture impeccably with crystalline tonic sounds. When once again the phrase turns to the dominant at the end, this cadence is immediately caught up in a half-homophonic setting of the words required to complete the meaning ('et iustificationes tuas *doce me*'). The soprano, moving in its own slow triple metre, and the bass intone 'doce me' four times around the F major chord, joining with the other voices to produce a fivefold duple-metre ostinato. An exquisite cadential detail, involving a crotchet *echappée*, echoes the note A in the ostinato figure CAC. The urgency of this appeal for divine instruction is evident, but the supplicant does not raise his voice, and the cadence—a tonic cadence, now—leaves him in a frame of mind more pensive than insistent.

The next phrase 'Servus tuus ego sum' resumes the melodic contour of phrases 1 and 3 and the texture of phrase 2. But 'da mihi intellectum' expands beautifully towards new rhythmic and tonal horizons. When the bass takes over the lowest line of the basic cell, moving up to high f (a full fourth higher than it has sung before) and then straining to hold e, the fifth of the half close on the tenor's high a, the motet vibrates with new quiet fervour. The last phrase 'ut sciam testimonia tua' is built from a basic 3-part cell, once again, and in its own muted way it is as fine as the concluding phrase of *Tristitia et anxietas* (Ex. 21). The looping, intertwining dotted-note figures, prepared in the phrase 'da mihi auxilium', are now moulded into ever-new half-sequential patterns. The soprano ascends to high g' and the bass descends to low B♭, both for the first time, but both in the most tranquil fashion possible. The bass also promotes a final gesture towards the dominant as well as several delicate recollections of the scale degree emphasized by the two preceding main cadences, the submediant D.

The difference in tone between *Fac cum servo tuo* and the general run of Byrd's motets incorporating appeals is as striking as it is obvious. When praying from the condition of grief and affliction, which follows upon sin, as the motet texts often make explicit, Byrd does not presume very far on God's Grace. 'Domine, ne moreris', 'O Domine, libera animam meam', 'Miserere mei, Deus, et salva me': anxiety as much as anguish informs the great waves of supplication which conclude so many motets of this period. The answer to the prayer must always be in doubt. In *Fac cum servo tuo* Byrd assumes another posture. The appeal for illumination rather than mercy rests on a conviction that man is capable of understanding God's ways. Understanding will not come about without divine assistance, of course; but there is no reasonable doubt that this assistance, devoutly prayed for, will be forthcoming.

One motet which brings up the subject of affliction, and then does not become overwhelmed by it, is **Domine secundum multitudinem dolorum meorum** (1589/27). Although the brief text leaves room for few shadows—

Domine, secundum multitudinem dolorum meorum in corde meo, consolationes tuae laetificaverunt animam meam [cf. Ps. 93:19].*

these are deepened in Byrd's setting. The superb opening period works smoothly without sharp cadential articulation through three distinct text fragments. The first of them inspired one of Byrd's most gracious melodic ideas, in the Ionian mode; this modality is then clouded, faintly, by the next phrase with its expressive gapped subject for 'dolorum', touching on minor harmonies; but in a remarkably subtle conception, Byrd allows minor harmonies to dominate only at the most 'inward' words, 'in corde meo'. As usual, the crotchet rhythms of the motet's final phrase are prepared in the penultimate one. There are, in fact, two slightly different forms of the basic motives of these phrases: the second 'consolationes tuae' is wonderfully limpid, and the second 'laetificaverunt' flows like silk into yet another fast-moving motive, involving a *cambiata* figure, for 'animam meam'. This motet is a flawless gem, unless we conceive of a positive excess of smoothness as some sort of flaw. The final cadence, for example, which treats the *cambiata* figure canonically, amounts to an elegant variation of a standard trope; it

---

*This is the same psalm from which Byrd took consolatory words at the end of *Defecit in dolore* (see p. 154), where however the musical setting accentuates the long catalogue of afflictions more than the consolation. The motive 'et anni mei' in *Defecit in dolorem* recalls 'dolorum' in the present motet.

does not, perhaps, touch as deeply as the more original *cambiata* figure in the final point of *Fac cum servo tuo*.

The text of **Quis est homo** (1591/3–4) comes once again from the psalter. These five didactic verses from Psalm 33 must have reminded Byrd of Psalm 14, *Domine quis habitabit*, which he had set for a massive 9-voiced choir in his Lincoln days. The words 'prohibe linguam tuam a malo, et labia tua ne loquantur dolum' in Psalm 33 and 'qui loquitur veritatem in corde suo, qui non egit dolum in lingua sua' in Psalm 14 would have had a special meaning for English Catholics, who now, under Elizabeth's recusancy laws, had a great deal to fear from paid informers and blackmailers. Byrd's setting of 'et labia tua . . .' at the end of part 1 of his motet looks back to an earlier style, that of his psalm-motets. The relatively long phrase begins with a free stretto ostinato of the early variety (Ex. 6i) and continues with a second ostinato on a faster subject.

No doubt didactic texts are better served by the brisk Ionian accents of *Quis est homo* than by the Phrygian semitones and minor sixths of *Domine quis habitabit*. But the piece cannot be counted as one of Byrd's happiest efforts. Was it the spitting words 'Quis est homo qui vult vitam' that caused the extremely concise—even nervous—opening point of imitation, or was it an uneasy eye to the long text that lay ahead? A melismatic crotchet rhythm, turning upwards for the question 'Quis est homo?', is at once intensified by a dotted rhythm for 'vitam', and then by a quaver pair—all within an 11-breve double point which admits only four entries, in effect, inasmuch as the second soprano and alto sing in parallel thirds. Such rhythmic agitation duly permeates the rest of the motet. There may be too many short intense phrases; by the time we reach the end, at 'ut perdet de terra . . .', the customary crotchet rhythms seem prepared only too well. The piece contains many features of technical interest, however, and some very lively details of word illustration: a motive in inversion for 'Diverte', a conspicuous canon for 'persequere', and a prohibited upward auxiliary figure (which promotes the only high g's in the soprano parts) for 'prohibe'.

[3]

Word illustration or 'word painting' is another major technique of Renaissance music that entered the main stream of English music through Byrd. It is used only sporadically and self-consciously, though sometimes very impressively, in the work of older composers. Every student of this repertory will have his favourite examples, but they are few and far between and the illustration is of a straightforward kind. The words 'et ascendit in coelum' in the Credo of Taverner's *Missa Gloria tibi Trinitas* are painted by long upward lines. At the word 'dormitationem' in Tye's *In pace* the music moves in slow, staggered breves tracing quiet melodic lines and consonant harmony.

Even in Byrd's earliest motets, from which only a handful of cases can be gleaned, the cases tend to assume a new imaginative quality. One thinks of the upward lines at 'maiestatem tuum' in *Domine secundum actum meum*, the grand full sonority at 'plena divitiis' in *Aspice Domine* and the unique semi-breve A♭ triad at 'timor mortis' in *Peccantem me quotidie*—a forecast of the greatly admired setting of 'Sion deserta facta est', in *Ne irascaris Domine*, and other such purple patches. The period following 1575 saw Byrd's experiments in this area grow more frequent, more subtle, and more assured, especially in motets of the more vigorous, concise variety. So by the time the madrigal fashion began to spread in England, in the late 1580s, the madrigal's illustrative techniques were already quite familiar through Byrd's more recent motets. As though to drive the point home, Byrd opened his 1591 *Cantiones* with a motet displaying not only the illustrative techniques of the madrigal but also its characteristic rhythmic and textural style, *Laudibus in sanctis* (see p. 171).

The term experiment carries with it the implication of something tentative and potentially unsuccessful in the outcome; we may indeed find ourselves questioning the aesthetic outcome of Byrd's word illustration in a number of his compositions. We have already done so in *Libera me Domine et pone me iuxta te*, the motet which applies the technique more consistently than any others in the 1575 *Cantiones* (p. 100f). Word painting bears, in any case, only an ambiguous relationship to the great Renaissance ideal of music that will be 'framed to the life of the words', as the title-page of the *Psalmes, songs and sonnets* of 1611 puts it. 'To one thinking on things divine and diligently and earnestly pondering them, all the most appropriate musical measures occur as of themselves': Byrd in his famous statement in the *Gradualia* is describing a very different sort of process from that of watching for key words and fitting them to certain conventional tropes, however elegantly this is done. And it is not always done very elegantly. Apart from this, the aesthetic problem stems from the natural tendency of the tropes to disrupt the prevailing musical discourse. To rationalize the disruption is usually easy enough when the word illustration is a matter of pitch, but gets harder when harmony, rhythm and especially metre are involved. At the end of *Apparebit in finem* Byrd was content to leave the listener with a sense of paradox, of breathlessness. It is not that the tropes must always be adjusted in such a way as to fit imperceptibly into the prevailing musical matrix. But when this is disturbed by some clash or contrast, the contrast itself has to be treated in a musically coherent fashion.

It was perhaps predictable that sooner or later Byrd would grasp this general problem, tackle it and solve it. He evaded it, rather, in the first of his motets that employ word illustration in a systematic way—motets in which one might say word illustration becomes a stylistic determinant. In *Laetentur coeli* (see p. 89f) the curiously stiff chanson-like style accommodates four* illustrative phrases (out of a total of eight) in an unprepossessing way. At the words 'coeli', 'montes' and 'Orietur' the melodic lines mechanically rise; at 'exultet' an excited three-crotchet figure moves in sequence and stretto. Byrd had only to make sure that the crotchet figure did not disturb the prevailing rhythm: which he did by enlivening the previous phrase, too, with crotchet melismas ('Laetentur') and a cadential crotchet syncopation.

The unusually long motet *Deus venerunt gentes* includes an unusual number of illustrative phrases, as has already been noted. They enliven but do not altogether justify the heavy, discursive structure. The essential function of the motives for 'volatilibus coeli,' 'bestiis terrae,' 'tanquam aquam,' 'in circuitu Hierusalem,' 'subsannatio et illusio his' and 'qui in circuitu nostro sunt' seems to be that of providing rhythmic contrast, but it is hard to feel that this contrast is rationalized over the motet as a whole. The word illustration itself feels distinctly laboured—with the exception, perhaps, of the fast mocking sequential thirds for 'et illusio his'—and the use of matching motives for the two 'circuitu' phrases seem less aesthetically significant than absent-minded.

Byrd had this style much better in hand when he came to compose **Vigilate** (1589/16: the vivid text is given on p. 41). This motet is a great favourite with commentators, if not with choirmasters. A spirited ascending figure crows cheerfully at 'an galli cantu'; a madrigalian descending scale seems to beckon the sun down at 'sero'; and the exclamation 'omnibus dico' towards the end brings out all five voices in block chords for the first time in the piece, making excellent rhetoric as well as conventionally apt word illustration. Crotchet rhythms (more intricate than those that had brought the motet *Apparebit in finem* to its quizzical conclusion) set the repeated word 'repente'. But here the implied metrical diminution is balanced by a fine slow-down in the next phrase, 'inveniat vos dormientes'. This phrase, the longest in the motet because the sleepiest, is worked out as a beautifully moulded double period, a mode of construction which occurs elsewhere in *Vigilate* and which looks ahead to the *Gradualia*.

---

*A fifth, possibly, is 'abundantia pacis', where the upward leap may reflect the idea of abundance. Other less-than-obvious words that seem to have inspired Byrd to upward- or downward-moving lines are 'maiestatem' (*Domine secundum actum meum*), 'aedificantur' (*Benigne fac*), 'perimus' (*Domine salva nos*) and 'sero' (*Vigilate*).

The setting of 'inveniat vos' in crotchets and quavers serves as a rhythmic transition to the proliferating slow suspensions at 'dormientes'.* In the first statement (Ex. 23a) the 'inveniat vos' motive appears seven times, moving

Ex. 23

down by thirds before returning to its original point of departure, C. There is a dramatic jolt when this C is followed by the low pedal A which supports the snoring suspensions. In the second statement (Ex. 23b) 'inveniat vos' goes through only three steps, C–A–F–D, for now the 'dormientes' figure seeps in early, and more pervasively. When after a momentary prolongation in the bass the D moves down smoothly to the same low pedal A, this sounds unexceptional and the passage can work itself out naturally at greater length.

One ingredient of Byrd's recipe for success in *Vigilate* was simply the fact that he could now work within the more concise style developed in the period just following that of *Deus venerunt gentes*. But in addition, what he now saw clearly was that all the many contrasts promoted by word illustration needed to be held together. This appears from the way he returns to the music of the opening exhortation 'Vigilate' when the word itself returns so dramatically at the very end of the motet. The opening 'Vigilate' phrase

*Part of the point is lost if the two-crotchet form of the 'inveniat vos' motive is always accommodated to the dotted form, as in BW 3. It is worth noting that for the expressive suspensions at 'dormientes' Byrd never once employs the stereotyped continental consonant-fourth pattern which he had used for a cadential function as early as in the 1575 *Cantiones* (see p. 101).

is set as a double period, once again, of a kind that we shall discuss later (p. 164): a short solemn call like a cantus firmus, sung twice with some intensification the second time, is accompanied by a faster, flowing motive—which indeed sounds vigilant or at least alert as it repeatedly curls higher and higher in strettos. And it is an expanded version of this same flowing motive, built into stretto pairs, that accommodates the word 'vigilate' at the end of the motet. Originally heard as a shadowy, stirring accompanimental figure, the motive now takes the centre stage in a series of brilliant flourishes. Five breves before the end, a single soprano cry of 'vigilate' (b♭′b♭′a′d) adds a splendid touch of iron; and this detail vividly recalls yet another musical phrase set to the word 'vigilate', one which comes at dead centre of this remarkable motet. The central 'vigilate' in this text was added by Byrd; only the opening and concluding ones are to be found in St. Luke.

Another concise motet that makes much of word illustration is **Circumspice Hierusalem** (BW 9/19). This too is an excellent piece, and Byrd's decision not to publish it can presumably be laid to the text (see p. 42) rather than to any qualms about the musical quality. In the loose imitation at the start, the fast circling figure for 'Circumspice' resembles those applied to circling words in *Deus venerunt gentes* (twice) and *Circumdederunt me* (1591/15); the words 'iucunditatem' and 'gaudentes' also summon up conventional tropes, and a few scattered octave leaps do service for 'dispersos'. At the beginning of the *secunda pars*, can it be that the unprecedented strict canon in diminution illustrates the words 'Ecce enim veniunt filii tui'? If so, the invertible counterpoint at the twelfth still remains to be decoded . . . Other unusual features of this motet are the Mixolydian mode, which for some reason Byrd used in no other motets of this period, and of course the 6-voiced texture, which adds further brilliance to this lively composition. The texture never becomes homophonic, and never needs to; especially at the ends of the two *partes*, Byrd builds grand textures that are fully polyphonic. One judges, unfortunately, without the two middle voice parts, whose reconstruction with the aid of a contemporary lute version is rather less certain than Fellowes gave reason to believe.

[4]

Not all Byrd's imitative motets of the middle period fall easily into the two primary groups we have tried to isolate—the older group of evenly-paced, large-scale works, and the newer one developing the style that may be thought to culminate in that conspicuous essay in brilliance, *Vigilate*. Other motets, again evidently of a somewhat later period, move in a distinctly more supple way than those of the first group while eschewing the concise, vigorous treatment of the second.

Exsurge quare obdormis Domine (1591/19) slips easily into a chronological slot between two of the works we have just been discussing. The opening imitation recalls but vastly improves on that of *Laetentur coeli*, especially through its use of light countersubject material and its lucid texture and harmony; one can hardly compare the two passages without recognizing the influence of the madrigal style. In another way, *Exsurge* looks like a preparatory study for *Vigilate*. A key word, 'exsurge', excited Byrd's imagination and he determined to have it come at the beginning, middle and end of the composition. The psalm provided the first and second of these *desiderata* (see p. 41) but it was Byrd who added 'exsurge, Domine' to the end. The word is always set to rising lines, of course, and it can be no accident that this motet also employs such a wide range (F$\sharp'$ to f') and moves towards its melodic climaxes so emphatically. Yet the relation between the three statements of 'exsurge' is not made into an expressive feature, and there is something faceless about the piece as a whole, despite a number of 'extreme' details which are unquestionably striking in themselves. What one remembers most vividly from this motet, perhaps, is the augmented fifth rasping against the last 'exsurge' motive in the codetta, then the tense spread texture of the final chord.

Defecit in dolore (1589/1–2) is one of the few motets of the *Cantiones sacrae* which has not survived in earlier manuscript copies. The text reads like a shorter and slightly less anguished paraphrase of *Tristitia et anxietas*, but the setting is on the whole darker. *Defecit in dolore* employs the range A to c', little more than two octaves; and as Byrd treats the high c' unequivocally as the *repercussio* or reciting note of the Hypoaeolian mode, this note recurs frequently in the two upper voices and produces no effect of climax whatsoever. Furthermore, many of the subjects focus on the pitch C and the bass moves up to its own high note, middle c, only when taking part in ostinato-like imitations on these subjects. The literary construction of the text is matched in its intricacy by the musical technique used in the setting:

Defecit in dolore vita mea, et anni mei in gemitibus; infirmata in paupertate virtus mea [Ps. 30:11], et dolor meus renovatus est [Ps. 38:3]. *2ᵃ pars* Sed tu, Domine, refugium factus es mihi [cf. Ps. 93:22], et misericordia tua consolatus sum.

Both external and internal evidence suggest that *Defecit in dolore* is a later work in which Byrd reached back to the spirit of sobriety that had produced the Aeolian motets of the 1575 *Cantiones* and works such as *Domine praestola-mur* and *Tristitia et anxietas* in the next period. This is not the last retro-spective composition of this kind that we shall encounter.

One modern feature is the presence of two equal-range upper voices in the choir, a texture found in only four of the 5-part motets of this period. Byrd had used two sopranos in some earlier 6-part music, but only now does he deploy them in such a way as to produce systematic echoes which play a major role in structuring the phrases. This technique can replace the more usual type of organization around soprano climaxes, as Byrd had discovered in his early psalm-motets for eight and nine voices (see p. 112f). The counter-point has grown wonderfully supple. There are no drawn-out double points, not even at the opening, where a subject in stretto and inversion glides through three separate text fragments, allowing all the voices to speak or mutter them in tiny phrases which are always telling yet always unobtrusive. Indeed for much of the time in this piece the setting proceeds almost word by word—'Defecit', 'in dolore', 'vita mea', 'et anni mei', 'in gemitibus', 'infirmata', 'in paupertate', 'virtus mea', 'misericordia', 'consolatus'—though the phrasing is still in larger units. The end of the last phrase of part 2 is especially fine: the dissonant articulation of the 'consolatus' figure over a thoroughly disconsolate plagal cadence (BW 2, 12, bar 2), and its diminution into sombre madrigalian scales which focus and accelerate the gathering crotchet rhythms. Especially in the bass, these scales clearly echo the end of part 1 of this unusual and distinguished composition.

To move from *Defecit in dolore* to the Ionian motet **O quam gloriosum est regnum** (1589/22–3)—a much better-known work, and an equally distinguished one—is to move into a very different atmosphere, almost a different world: like stepping into a clear garden from a dark Elizabethan room walled with tapestries. The atmosphere gleams with lucid major triads and major 6–5 progressions and repeated murmuring feints at dominant modulation. Yet in technical terms the two motets have a good deal in common, starting with the two sopranos in the 5-voiced choir; it is an even, suffused light that informs *O quam gloriosum* and not the sharper brightness that comes with a texture conducive to soprano climaxes. The two motets also share the same basic formal plan. A relatively strong contrasting cadence in one of the mediants ends the penultimate phrase, and the final phrase clearly echoes the opening one. In the Ionian piece the penultimate cadence comes on the submediant, D; as always in this mode, subdominant cadences are avoided. However, subdominant sounds are used to link the outer phrases, each of which contains one glowing soprano E♭ and a number of perfectly placed bass B♭s. In the opening phrase the E♭ makes a very memorable 6–5 progression; in the final phrase this burgeons into a typically English thicket of these (BW 2, 179, bars 1–3). The texture is artfully congealed for a few bars, then rarefied as madrigalian scale-motives, anticipated in the previous passage, celebrate the final tonic pedal. This procedure too finds it parallel in *Defecit in dolore*.

The text runs as follows:

O quam gloriosum est regnum in quo cum Christo gaudent omnes sancti! Amicti stolis albis, sequuntur Agnum quocunque ierit [*Magnificat* Antiphon, All Saints], laudentes Deum et dicentes:

    2ᵃ pars Benedictio et claritas, et sapientia, et gratiarum actio, honor virtus et fortitudo Deo nostro, in saecula saeculorum. Amen [Chapter at None, All Saints; from Rev. 7:12].*

The first phrase, a quiet *tour de force* encompassing the entire opening sentence in twenty-two breves, works its way effortlessly from word to word with the perfect, natural 'framing' that Byrd achieves when he is writing at the height of his inspiration. At the beginning of the second part, the series of brief acclamations invited more concise cell-like phrases, some lasting no longer than three breves. These phrases feature dotted rhythms for the first time and move restlessly through various cadence degrees; everything is calculated so as to contrast with the stable, measured gait of the first part of the motet. Byrd had set the words 'in saecula saeculorum. Amen' as a well-developed cell structure once before, at the end of *Tribue Domine*. A comparison of the two passages (the subjects are not dissimilar) makes graphic the new mastery of contrapuntal technique and rhetoric that has been gained since the period of the 1575 *Cantiones*.†

Vague clues, and too many of them, confuse the issue of dating the motet **Recordare Domine** (1591/17–18). The fact that the text comes from a Sarum respond suggests an early date—though the fact that the liturgical text is abbreviated irregularly gives pause: a respond, furthermore, belonging

---

*Although these All Saints texts were familiar sources for motet texts, Byrd's particular combination has not been traced elsewhere. The word 'dicentes' appears in Rev. 7:12; the words 'laudentes Deum' seem to be a free addition. Byrd had set some of these phrases before in *Tribue Domine*.

†*O quam gloriosum*, *Defecit in dolore* and *Quis est homo* (also *Salve Regina*: see p. 173) are motets employing two equal-range upper voices in the 5-part choir. We know that Byrd also experimented with a 5-voiced texture including two bass voices. He did this in **Ad punctum in modico** (BW 16, 122f), an Aeolian motet evidently in his grandest manner, of which only the two bass parts survive, one in Mus. Sch.e.423 and the other in the Petre MS. The basses echo one another systematically much in the way that the sopranos do in the motets just discussed.

to the same service as *Peccavi*, which Byrd also abbreviated (in a different way) in his unpublished motet found in a manuscript dated 1581. However, part of the same text also served as the introit for Masses *pro vitanda mortalitate vel tempore pestilentiae*; might not Byrd have set it in one of the plague years 1582 or 1583? The scant circulation of the motet suggests a later date; only two contemporary copies are known.* Stylistic evidence supports the later dating. *Recordare Domine* is an understated work and on first hearing, perhaps, an unremarkable one, but many fine points reveal themselves on closer acquaintance.

The contour of the final subject, 'ut non desoletur terra', may bring to mind that of an earlier Dorian motet, *Peccantem me quotidie* (see Ex. 14b). But the smoothness of the part writing is new, and so is the lucidity of the formal plan. In a brief first exposition the soprano subject gdef♯ga′bb′a′ moves down a fourth to d and then up a fifth to a′, as though butting up against repeated dissonances on the syllables 'deso*letur terr*a'. In the second exposition (BW 3, 130, bar 6ff) the dissonances evaporate, and after three entries on g and G the entry at the fifth (da . . .) is replaced by a tonal answer (dG . . .). And at the end the original subject is for the first time resolved melodically to its initial note, g or G. This elegant phrase sets the abbreviated *repetendum* of the respond when it comes at the end of part 2. The same words are provided with different music at the end of part 1; strangely, where close musical kinship exists it is not between the two 'ut non desoletur terra' phrases but between the first of them and a different phrase in part 2, 'et a civitate sancta tua' (compare especially BW 3, 125, bars 3–4 and 129, bars 1–2). But the cadence of 'et a civitate sancta tua' (129, bar 4) also links forward to the climax of the second 'ut non desoletur terra' (131, bar 4).

Byrd seldom repeated himself in points of imitation, especially in points at the beginnings of pieces. The idea of beginning a work with strettos on a scale figure of a fourth or fifth in inversion must, then, have exerted a special fascination on him. He picked up this idea from Ferrabosco and used it to construct the opening point of *Libera me Domine et pone me iuxta te* in the 1575 *Cantiones*—a point which echoes unforgettably at the end of *Emendemus in melius* (see p. 122). He returned to it from another standpoint in *Recordare Domine* and in a pair of short manuscript motets of about the same period, **Audivi vocem de coelo** and **Benigne fac Domine** (BW 8/7 and 8). In two very different works published in the *Psalmes, songs, and sonnets* of 1611,

*In Mus. Sch.e.423 the text is identical with that of the publication, at least throughout the one voice part that survives in this source. The copy in RCM 2089 is a lute arrangement.

the 3-part madrigal *Who looks may leap* and the great 6-part anthem *Turn our captivity O Lord*, he had his final say on the matter.

Byrd's manipulation of the stretto subject at the beginning of *Recordare Domine*, though characteristically unspectacular, is much more skilful than in *Libera me*, where the harmony seems by comparison static and uninventive and the rhythm lame. In the two short motets the same subject is developed along rather surprisingly similar lines. The treatment is thoroughly relaxed, with little attention paid to the inversion (*Audivi vocem* abandons it after a single entry) and with the *recto* led into similar melismatic continuations. The two compositions diverge after their opening points, to the great advantage of *Audivi vocem*, which in the 1580s circulated widely;* it ends with a wonderful (and unusual) train of suspensions for the words 'qui moriuntur in Domino'. However, Byrd published neither of these motets, perhaps because he had worked the opening subject so much more intricately in *Recordare Domine*.

But his richest treatment of a subject of this kind comes at the beginning of **Plorans plorabit** (1605 *a* 5/28), the last of Byrd's great laments of captivity, or at least the last in Latin (for the text see p. 42). The subject and the inversion are now expanded from fourths or fifths to minor sixths, the *recto* statements outlining Ge♭ and db♭' or cb♭', and the inversions b♭D, dF and E♭G' (the last bass entry moves down in two stages from b♭D to E♭G'). The polarity of G and E♭ impresses particularly, not only as a melodic outline but also as the basis of the first harmonic event in the piece. A deep G minor chord spreads itself out slowly after an initial E♭ triad has been traced in the middle register—this by the opening subject entry which starts, exceptionally, on the third degree of the transposed Dorian mode, b♭ (Ex. 24). The subject itself is moulded rhythmically in

Ex."24

Plo - - rans   plo - ra - - bit ...

half a dozen different ways and imitates itself in ever-fresh stretto combinations. It surges and sinks in a magnificent free flux of lamentation.

*Though it is only fair to say that *Benigne fac* has to be judged without its tenor part, missing from the only known sources, Baldwin's Partbooks and Mus. Sch.e.423. It seems to be the earlier of the two motets. *Audivi vocem* appears in those two MSS and also in Dow's MS, the Petre MS, RCM 2089, Tenbury 341–4, 389-James and 369–74, usually in close conjunction with *Apparebit in finem* (cf. Table 5a).

Everything is magnificent in this motet: the threefold invocation 'Dic regi', recalling Tallis imprecisely by way of many such passages in Byrd; the expressive transformation of White's favourite octave stretto idea in the final point 'corona gloriae vestrae'; the sardonic move to the dominant at 'et dominatrici'; the relentless low Gs at 'humiliamini, sedete';* and most magnificent of all, the indescribable bleak fervour of Byrd's setting of 'captus est grex Domini', which must have stood out in his mind as the key words of this fragment from Jeremiah. His mastery of affective counterpoint is evident everywhere, for example in so unobtrusive a detail as the modification of the basic stretto pair in 'corona gloriae vestrae'. The considerable dissonance built into this stretto pair—a seventh and a diminished fifth—dissolves after three appearances with the advent of a new bass line (Ex. 25).

Ex. 25

New and newly powerful: the bass reaches up through a seventh, something it does nowhere else in the piece, and its new minim figure moving to F prefigures the tenor's crotchet figure moving to c ('gloriae vestrae')—a fragment of the subject which is always heard as its climax, even though it does not touch on the highest note. (One does not miss the relationship between the two figures. When previously the crotchets of the original subject came in the bass, they moved up to this same F.) Under the 'climactic' tenor c, and under the soprano c' just beforehand, there is now for the first time an emphatic F major triad: and against this, as the cadence unwinds

*The soprano's first statement of the word 'humiliamini' (BW 4, 170, bars 2–3; TCM 7, 95, bar 1) should probaly be emended to bb'ggggg or bb'gebggg to avoid the parallel octaves (cf. Andrews, *Byrd's Polyphony*, 90).

with a beautifully (and integrally) decorated version of the Continental consonant-fourth formula, the D major dominant triad stings in the traditional English fashion.

Published in the *Gradualia* of 1605, *Plorans plorabit* cannot have been written much earlier, not if we take seriously the text's reference to a king and queen. Composing this motet, Byrd looked back past such works as the Masses, *Laudibus in sanctis* and *Vigilate* to the austere, slowly-paced music of the late 1570s. He evoked a style which he had already once resumed after a ten-year period, when planning *Defecit in dolore* as a suitable opening number for the 1589 *Cantiones sacrae*. One hesitates to affirm that any of the phrases of *Plorans plorabit* could actually have been written in Byrd's middle years, but with the exception of 'captus est grex Domini', all of them are at least within the conceptual frame of reference of that period.

In fact Byrd looked back farther than that, back forty years to his early setting of the Lamentations of Jeremiah and to the Lamentations of Tallis and White which had inspired that precocious act of composition. These were models that haunted Byrd, and consequently also haunt the student of his work. Leafing through the hundred-odd motets of the *Gradualia*, almost all of them motets of acclamation or devotion, one might think that their composer had now exorcized the memory of those great landmarks of Tudor gravity. But like some other composers as they grow old, Byrd did not forget and found himself returning, always from a new standpoint, to the visions of his past. Then as now, the words 'plorans plorabit' must have reminded English musicians inevitably of one particular composition, the first Lamentations of Tallis. Byrd's *Plorans plorabit*, his masterpiece in the affective imitative style pioneered in his own Lamentations and now superbly developed, is also a superb final tribute to his former master and colleague.

3b

Motets in Other Styles

Tribulationes civitatum	1589/24–6	Infelix ego *a 6*	1591/24–6
Ne irascaris Domine	1589/20–1	Cunctis diebus *a 6*	1591/30
Vide Domine afflictionem		Quomodo cantabimus *a 8*	BW 9/24
nostram	1589/9–10		
O Domine adiuva me	1589/5	Cantate Domino *a 6*	1591/29
Miserere mei Deus	1591/20	Haec dies *a 6*	1591/32
Haec dicit Dominus	1591/13–14	Domine non sum	
		dignus *a 6*	1591/23
Laudibus in sanctis	1591/1–2	Domine salva nos *a 6*	1591/31
Circumdederunt me	1591/15		
Salve Regina	1591/6–7		
Tribulatio proxima est	1591/8–9		
Deus in adiutorium *a 6*	BW 9/20		
Domine Deus omnipotens	BW 8/11		

Vide Domine quoniam tribulor (BW 8/18) is a very interesting motet which is not infrequently heard in performance today. Even Fellowes expressed doubt as to its authenticity on stylistic grounds (*W. Byrd*, 109ff), but he trusted the ascription in the one contemporary source known to him, the partbook Tenbury 389. (The motet as a whole is preserved in Add. 23624, an eighteenth-century score made from Tenbury 389-James and the three partbooks which have since been lost.) Fellowes took this to be a specially good Byrd source because Tenbury 389 bears the initials 'W.B.' and 'T.E.' (Thomas East?) and because of indications that the lost partbooks contained glosses due to Byrd himself (see p. 45n). On the other hand, the fact that the manuscript mutilates the sectional motet *Deus venerunt gentes* and ascribes several spurious works to Byrd—the play-songs *Guichardo* and *Abradad* and the isorhythmic *Sponsus amat sponsam* (see p. 57)—argues that it was never in the hands of Byrd or anyone close to him.

However this may be, the concise treatment of the text in *Vide Domine* would be unprecedented in Byrd's writing at the period indicated by the manuscript, and the sensuous harmonic idiom of the music unmatched at any period. Chromaticism is applied not principally in order to illustrate individual words and concepts, but rather to enrich the harmony in a general way. Byrd was never much attracted to chromaticism and his few extended essays in this direction, such as *O quam suavis est* (1607/18) and the seemingly parodistic *Come woeful Orpheus* (1611), were written late in life and are nowhere as extreme as the present motet It is probably by a younger contemporary of Byrd, experimenting all out in the Italian manner.

An *Ave Regina coelorum* is attributed to Byrd in the Paston lutebook RCM 2089; it also appears in a closely associated set of five partbooks, Tenbury 369–73, in which no composers' names are given. Despite the authority which one is inclined to accord the Paston ascription, this cannot be right, for the colourless and regular imitative writing is unlike that of Byrd at any point of his career. Two voice parts of this piece can be seen in TCM Appendix, 36f, ascribed for no discernible reason to Taverner. As for the 4-part *Salve Regina* published as Byrd's by Thurston Dart (Stainer & Bell Church Choir Library, No. 577, 1955), that is preserved anonymously and incompletely in another Paston MS, Folger Shakespeare Library V.a.405 (formerly 460328). Dart never divulged his grounds for the ascription and there is no reason to credit it.

Byrd's systematic programme of assembling, ordering and issuing his music in the late 1580s began with the *Psalmes, sonets & songs* of 1588 and the first *Cantiones sacrae* of 1589. Of all his publications these are the two most homogeneous. The motet book is dominated by one musical technique, imitative polyphony. It is true, as we have seen, that some of the pieces are more concise or more vivid than others, and that occasionally the steady 5-part counterpoint is interrupted by a phrase in some sort of homophonic texture. Yet even the unforgettable block-chord opening of *Tristitia et anxietas* does not, in the end, disturb the overriding impression of polyphonic discourse. For Byrd at this period, imitative polyphony was the normal stylistic field which he worked repeatedly and with ever increasing subtlety.

Three motets stand out from this fertile but level landscape, the three 'Jerusalem' motets *Tribulationes civitatum, Ne irascaris Domine* and *Vide Domine afflictionem nostram*. Their texts have been discussed on page 40f. God is implored to forgive his people, who have sinned and who lament their affliction in the City made desolate; the hidden reference to the situation of the English Catholics is inescapable when these statements and sentiments are considered in the total context of Byrd's text repertory. It may well be, then, that with these 'political' texts Byrd made a special effort to impress. He succeeded well. *Tribulationes civitatum* and *Ne irascaris* circulated very widely in manuscripts from around 1580 on, and they were also among the few motets of this period to penetrate the Anglican Church as anthems. *Bow thine ear*, the second part of the anthem version of *Ne irascaris* printed in Barnard's *Selected Church Musick* of 1641, has remained a favourite to the present day. As though to collect some of Byrd's debts to his father, the younger Alfonso Ferrabosco chose the beginning of *Tribulationes civitatum* to imitate or parody in a motet of his own with a similar incipit.*

Tribulationem et dolorem inveni (Sambrooke MS (Tregian), 103ff). On the manuscript circulation, see Table 5. As to the anthems, *O Lord turn Thy wrath/Bow thine ear* (*Ne irascaris Domine/Civitas sancti tui*) is found in many sources, but *Let not our prayers be rejected* (*Nos enim pro peccatis nostris*, part 3 of *Tribulationes*) only in the Southwell Minster

Tribulationes civitatum (1589/24–6) is a long and to us a rather strange piece of work. Byrd worked with 'cell' technique more single-mindedly here than in any other composition, employing it for no fewer than five text phrases, and in a particularly deliberate way: the phrases tend to be long and to have unusually distinct cadences, and they all make use of the same semi-choirs, selected for maximum contrast: SAT^1, T^1T^2B. With one exception, these and the other phrases of the motet do not flow smoothly by means of overlaps from prior phrases. Instead they start up after sharp breaks—always after the same time interval, what is more, a dotted semibreve (or else after a *pars* ending).

The music often moves haltingly or stiffly, then; perhaps Byrd meant it to sound glum. And perhaps he considered that an extreme harmonic plan would help stave off dullness. The *prima pars* begins with an entire section in the Ionian mode, transposed to B♭, but ends in the Aeolian G minor. The *secunda pars* opens abruptly in E♭ but closes in C, with rich major-mode inflections extending back several bars from the *tierce de Picardie*. Only the *tertia pars* settles down at last, holding to half cadences on G and D and full cadences on G. The underlying structure can be construed as a pair of parallel progressions up the circle of fifths, the second of them broader in scope: B♭–(F)–C–G | E♭–B♭–F–C–G–(D)–G (see Ex. 26). The Aeolian

Ex. 26

centre is kept in mind during some of the more distant sections: in the opening, for example, where the 'Tribulationes' motive dwells on G as well as B♭ and F, and in the E♭ section, 'Timor et hebitudo mentis', which is the first of only two strictly imitative points in the motet. Here a striking entry on the third degree, G, leads strongly towards C, though in the event the cadence is diverted and the point ultimately moves to the dominant.

Tenor Partbook, Tenbury 1382, dated 1617. *Ne irascaris* also circulated as *Behold I bring you glad tidings*, as *Let not Thy wrath* and as *Be not wroth* (part 2 only, much mutilated). The other Byrd motets that were made into anthems are *Attollite portas* (*Lift up your heads*; another translation in the Southwell MS, *Let us arise*), *Laudate pueri* (*Behold now praise the Lord*), *Memento homo* (*O Lord give ear*), *Exsurge quare obdormis Domine* (*Arise O Lord why sleepest Thou*) and *Tribulatio proxima est* (*Blessed art thou O Lord*). See BW 11/12, 16 138f, 142f and R. T. Daniel and P. Le Huray, *The Sources of English Church Music, 1549–1660*, EECM Supplementary Vol. I.

The false relation between the fifth Eb–Bb beginning part 2 and the G major chord ending part 1 is quite out of the ordinary; *secondae partes* of Byrd compositions regularly pick up the root or the fifth of the previous cadence chord. This extreme effect must have been designed to introduce the words 'Timor et hebitudo mentis'—though the serene progress of the point itself would seem to allay anxiety rather than depict it. For that matter, the gentle 'Tribulationes' cells at the beginning of the motet hardly strike the expected note of distress. This comes to the fore only in the lengthy, intense concluding point 'et vide afflictionem nostram'; the cry 'afflictionem' rises higher and higher, until in the last few bars several of the voices find themselves singing a third higher than at any previous point in the composition; and then all five voices sink down suddenly, as though exhausted, through a sixth or an octave into the final cadence. But despite this show of power the point (and hence the motet as a whole) fails finally in eloquence, mainly because the descending step which echoes within the subject ('et *vide affl*ictionem') is developed too exhaustively.

In Byrd's motets direct appeals to God are generally set in some sort of massed homophony or half-homophony, as we have seen (p. 137f). Very affecting are the phrases 'Domine, miserere' and 'Aperi oculos tuos, Domine' in this piece (especially, perhaps, the beginning of the first of them, and the end of the second). What strikes one immediately about **Ne irascaris Domine** (1589/20–1) is that the opening appeal is *not* set in this way. Instead Byrd employs a peculiar sort of 3-part cell which he seems to have picked up from Ferrabosco (the elder) and which he also used at the beginning of half a dozen other motets of the *Cantiones sacrae* and the *Gradualia* (Ex. 27).* We have seen an example in *Vigilate* (p. 153). A cantus firmus-like fragment is accompanied by two other voices in busy, rather neutral counterpoint, forming a cell which is designed not for development but simply for repetition in another semichoir or in the full choir, with no extension and little variation. The variations in *Ne irascaris* are exquisite but minimal. The melody voice never moves out of its very limited range of a fourth, F–Bb, escaping only at the end of the next phrase and escaping downwards, to E supported by an unanticipated A major chord. The threefold opening appeal has lacked the customary urgency, to say the least. Now the supplicant sinks down in positive self-abasement.

Ne irascaris is one of Byrd's quiet masterpieces, and the continuous popularity of its *secunda pars*, as the anthem *Bow thine ear*, says something about the taste of Anglican choirmasters over four centuries. It says they have handsomely appreciated the motet's expressive qualities but not—since

*The Ferrabosco motets appear in Egerton 3665 (Tregian), Nos. 27 and 4.

Ex. 27

the *prima pars* has been discarded—its beauty of form. Like *Tribulationes*, *Ne irascaris* has an underlying harmonic structure of two parallel progressions, with the second more intense than the first; but the plan here is simpler, firmer, more clearly effective. Each of the two parts of the motet begins and ends solidly in F, and the middle of each part digresses tonally. The middle section of part 1, 'Ecce, respice', reaches out to C and D minor and G major sonorities and feints at a cadence on B♭ (irregular in the Ionian–Lydian mode). In part 2 the motive 'facta est deserta' embarks on an uneasy search for cadence points, even trying Phrygian ones on A and E, before stopping on a D major triad. At this point the famous block chords for 'Sion deserta facta est' start up in F, once again—one thinks of the false relation at part 2 of *Tribulationes*—but in a momentary Mixolydian F encompassing rich, sombre E♭ triads.

The tonal organization is reinforced by melodic and motivic parallels. There is a general similarity between the upward melodic thrust in the outer sections of part 1, and the motives in the outer sections of part 2—downward motives—correspond almost exactly. Moreover in part 2 the key word 'deserta' in the two central phrases comes repeatedly on the same notes, AB♭A, even though one phrase employs polyphonic texture, the other

Ex. 28

homophonic; and the *second* motive for 'Hierusalem *desolata est*' is taken (complete with its contrapuntal fixtures) from the *second* motive for 'respice' in part I (Ex. 28). Indeed, it is hard to think of any reason for the presence of this second 'respice' motive except to provide Byrd with an explicit thematic link.

Over such remarkably firm structural underpinnings Byrd spread a musical surface that is just as remarkable for its gentle iridescent quality. The part writing is controlled with great subtlety, starting with the little variations in the opening cells and the melancholy mild 6–5 sounds in the succeeding phrase 'iniquitatis nostrae'. At the end of part I the section 'populus tuus omnes nos' emerges from supple cells to become one of Byrd's most beautiful points, a distinction it shares with 'Timor et hebitudo mentis' in the companion-piece *Tribulationes civitatum*. At its calm climax the imitations coalesce in thirds and tenths and move warmly to the dominant, following a hint that has already been given several times in the motet; then a murmuring cadential stretto on a crotchet figure moves back to F. The mood of this passage was not lost on the contemporary translator who rendered

Ex. 29

'populus tuus omnes nos' as 'we be Thy people and Thy pasture sheep', from the Jubilate. And there is another luminous cadence at the end of part 2, with its crotchet figure for 'desolata est'—the fourth distinct motive for this phrase—recalling not only the 'omnes nos' stretto in part 1 but also even earlier motives for 'satis' and 'respice' (Ex. 29a).

Part 2, *Civitas sancti tui*, is one of Byrd's most beloved compositions, so it comes as something of a shock to find that it is modelled on the work of another composer. Recently David Humphreys has observed that the opening phrase, 'Civitas sancti tui', takes its inspiration from that of Philip van Wilder's *Aspice Domine*—a motet which Byrd had already drawn on for his own setting of the same words in 1575 (see p. 102f). Not surprisingly, he completely rethought Wilder's original point, even while adopting much of its detail, and some further connections between the two motets are slighter, though unmistakable. But the modelling helps explain why Byrd set so gloomy a text in one of the major modes: Wilder's piece is in the Mixolydian mode, Byrd's in the F Ionian.

The third and most intense of the 'Jerusalem' motets did not circulate so early or so widely as its companions. **Vide Domine afflictionem nostram** (1589/9–10) looks back to the affective homophonic style of *Emendemus in melius* in the 1575 *Cantiones*, and is best considered along with other motets of a similar stylistic inclination: *O Domine adiuva me*, which figures in the earliest layer of the middle-period repertory, and *Miserere mei Deus* and *Haec di-it Dominus*, later works which were printed in 1591. This music shows that as compared with the polyphonic style of 1575, the homophonic style caused Byrd rather more trouble when he tried to adapt it to his maturing vision of the 1580s.

Although the very terse, breathless chordal style that he took over from Alfonso worked brilliantly for him in *Emendemus in melius*, Byrd was never one to repeat himself when he had already carried off a *tour de force*. That terseness, as he must have come to see, really went against his basic inclinations as an artist. The text phrases of *Emendemus* are sharply demarcated; the homophonic texture is nearly always clear-cut; words are never repeated for rhetorical effect, only for the purpose of formal closure at the ends of the two parts. By instinct Byrd preferred to blur phrases together, to unravel block-chord textures, to dwell a little for emphasis on key sentiments.

So whereas the words 'Emendemus in melius' had only been sung once, the *incipits* of the later motets are always repeated and the leading words underlined by small but always effective melodic expansions (as at the opening of *Tristitia et anxietas*, Ex. 17). In *Vide Domine*, furthermore, although Byrd set five of the text phrases in block-chord homophony—with one or two voices slightly awry, perhaps—he set twice that number in a much looser texture which he tried out in *Emendemus* only once, at the words 'Deus, salutaris noster'. In phrases of this kind things are more than slightly awry: below what sounds clearly enough like the main melody, the other voices are staggered, some of them interrelated by strict, free or 'rhythmic' imitation, others not. The impression is of a textural grey area, on a shifting spectrum between genuine polyphony and animated homophonic writing.

O Domine adiuva me (1589/5) makes heavy use of this amorphous texture and no use at all of block chords. It is with some relief that we come to the fine sturdy point of imitation at the close—for all these motets follow *Emendemus* in turning to polyphonic writing as preparation for the final cadence. But Byrd never tried to recapture the concise, practically aphoristic effect of the 'libera nos' phrase which ends the early piece in a span of no more than eight breves. In *O Domine adiuva me* the ending imitative phrase is backed up by another that is also imitative, amounting to 22 breves of polyphony in all. In Miserere mei Deus (1591/20) the concluding point looms larger yet. This suave but rather facile short motet alternates just two homophonic and two polyphonic phrases, lasting for 10, 13, 9 and 22 breves*.

To return to *Vide Domine*: here the concluding polyphonic section accounts for 38 of the total 135 breves and covers several text phrases. The text in question, 'et miserere populi tui gementis et flentis, Domine Deus noster', is actually one of those appeals that Byrd tends to set in an impressive half-homophonic style. Clearly the idea of closing with polyphony answered a purely musical need. Byrd seems to have sensed the paradox, for in the beautiful setting of 'Domine Deus noster' at the very end he made the four statements grow more and more homophonic.

Example 29b shows the last 'Domine Deus noster' with its highly inflected cadence, harsh yet both powerfully affective and logical—logical because E♭D and B♭A semitones have also been prominent earlier in the piece.† Placed next to the ending cadence of *Ne irascaris*, the cadence of *Vide Domine* seems to epitomize the special character of the motet as a whole. This is a work composed with rare passion, uniquely intense and sometimes

---

*The 4-part *Miserere mei Deus* (BW 8/4) which Fellowes reconstructed from a later organ score, Add. 21403, is a clumsy and most curious recomposition of Byrd's 5-part motet in which the motives, gestures and dimensions are all slavishly imitated while the mode is changed from G minor to C major. Byrd cannot have been responsible for this (though in a sense he deserves the attribution). The organ score sometimes goes into five or even six parts; it must have been conceived as a free accompaniment to a 5-part piece, not as a strict reduction of a 4-part one. On Add. 21403, see BK 27, 169.

†Cadences with a suspended minor sixth resolving under a *tierce de Picardie* occur in some earlier Byrd motets, but never treated so consciously. See BW 8, 4f and BW 3, 213.

contorted in expression. At the words 'Plusquam Hierusalem facta est desolata', Byrd strove to outdo the strong harmonic effect at 'Sion deserta, deserta . . .' in *Ne irascaris* and overreached himself: the soprano intones 'desolata' first on the notes fga′g and then on fgab′g, with an Ab triad under the third note and an astonishing Db *echappée* in an inner voice. The mode shifts restlessly as the composer turns from one extreme affective setting to the next. Though the music is Dorian, with an 'informal' Bb in the signature, it inclines strongly towards the Phrygian, importing Ebs liberally; most of the tonic cadences are plagal (as in Ex. 29b). But as expected in the Dorian mode, there are also some authentic cadences in the dominant supported by E major triads. These and the Ab triad mentioned above span a harmonic range even greater than that of *Emendemus in melius*.

Most extraordinary of all is the illustrative treatment of the parallel clauses ending part 1, 'gaudium cordis nostri conversum est in luctum, et iocunditas nostra in amaritudinem conversa est'. 'Gaudium' and 'iocunditas' call forth hasty chanson-like motives, featuring dotted minims and crotchets, in close stretto; then the conversions take place very abruptly, after 7 and 11 semibreves respectively, when slow pathetic subjects intervene and the Bhs and F♯s of the cheerful phrases are cancelled in favour of Ebs. Seldom in English music does one encounter a passage as hectic—as manneristic, one is almost inclined to say—as this one.

Haec dicit Dominus (1591/13-14) is probably the greatest of all Byrd's homophonic compositions. There is no actual reference to captivity or to the City in its text (see p. 42), but this comes from Jeremiah and everyone at the time would have recognized it as another 'Jerusalem' motet. It must have been some years after *Vide Domine* that Byrd returned to this theme, for he now found a musical realization for it that is newly powerful and moving. Within essentially the same style the musical material and the part writing are much more distinguished, and so is the sense of control, both technical and emotional. He also returned to the same Phrygian-coloured Dorian mode and to the same distinctive clef combination.*

One could hardly call *Haec dicit Dominus* less bold than *Vide Domine*; consider the unresolved sevenths built into the stretto at 'in novissimis tuis', and the mere six breves between perfectly situated B minor and Eb major triads which demarcate the harmonic range. But nothing here sounds eccentric, forced or uneasy. The overpowering severity of style is not relaxed until the words 'et est spes in novissimis tuis', where a glint of F major (Ionian and later Mixolydian) cuts through the minor-mode sonorities

---

*The combination bass, baritone, tenor, alto, mezzo-soprano is used by Byrd in these two motets only.

for a time. The return of D minor accents for the obligatory concluding section in polyphony, 'et revertentur filii ad terminos suos', makes better musical than rhetorical sense, perhaps (unless Byrd was punning harmonically as well as melodically: the 'ad terminos suos' motive clearly inverts 'et revertentur'). 'Ad terminos suos' comes five times as an ostinato peaking on B♭, then eight or nine times peaking on F. The soprano's final utterance recalls the B♮ peak, and with it half a dozen earlier phrases in the motet which have been built around the B♮A semitone.

Fellowes was not a critic who delved deeply or strayed far from conventional paths, but his appreciation of Byrd's motets in *William Byrd* is on the whole just and sensitive. There are some surprises, though, among his brief remarks on these 'Jerusalem' motets. After observing that *Ne irascaris* is 'perhaps to be regarded as the finest piece in the [1589] set' he went on to characterize the concluding 'Hierusalem desolata est' section as a 'plaint . . . reaching its climax in a state of exhausted grief at the final cadence': which could conceivably be said of Byrd's setting of very similar words in *Vide Domine* (another passage that Fellowes cites with great approval) but not of the smooth Ionian ostinato chiming on the word 'Hierusalem' in *Ne irascaris* or the sequel (see Ex. 28). This misinterpretation speaks worlds for the style of Byrd performance in the early (and later) part of the twentieth century.* On the other hand Fellowes finely singled out the passage 'Rachel plorantis filios' in *Haec dicit Dominus*, describing it as 'an example of Byrd's power of tender expression and pathos such as has, perhaps, never been surpassed by any composer'.† One would also wish to mention the superb sequential ending of part 1 of this motet, and the way it mirrors the sequential opening; the Tallisian echoes at the words 'a ploratu, et oculi tui'; and the exceedingly original setting of 'et est spes', with its new tonality and newly deliberate harmonic rhythm, investing the moment with a unique combination of relief, inevitability, austerity, drama. Fellowes might have settled on *Haec dicit Dominus* as the finest piece in the 1591 set, one feels—if that set did not also happen to include *Laudibus in sanctis*.

*Fellowes, *W. Byrd*, 70. Styles are perhaps changing: Peter Le Huray says that an anthem version of *Ne irascaris*, *Behold I bring you glad tidings*, 'serves as a salutary reminder that a great deal of Byrd's early work . . . has no very pronounced emotive character of its own. Absurd as it may seem to replace so stern a text as "Ne Irascaris" with a joyful Christmas narrative, the adaptation does not in practice seem particularly incongruous' (*Music and the Reformation in England, 1549–1660* (London, 1967), 241).

†Fellowes, *W. Byrd*, 73.

[2]

The second volume of *Cantiones sacrae* differs from the first as the second English songbook—the appositely named *Songs of sundrie natures*—differs from the *Psalmes, sonets & songs*. The material that Byrd was able to bring together for these later books was less homogeneous in style, texture, date of composition and also in musical quality. The remaining 5-part motets of the 1591 *Cantiones sacrae* offer a varied picture.

Laudibus in sanctis (1591/1–2) is one of a kind. Presumably written in 1591, specially for the publication, its stylistic lineage can be traced back to the homophonic experiments of 1575—not to the affective Dorian homophony of *Emendemus in melius*, of course, but rather to the bright Ionian or Mixolydian homophony of the antiphonal hymns *Siderum rector* and *O lux beata Trinitas*. Like the hymns it is written *a note neri*, in a basic crotchet pulse. This style and this notation were associated in Byrd's mind with Latin poetic texts. However, since *Laudibus in sanctis* is in elegiacs—it is an anonymous humanistic paraphrase of Psalm 150—there is no question of a fixed metrical pattern, as in the hymns. Instead there is a much greater flexibility of rhythm, matched to the same conciseness of phraseology and a much wider range of textural variety: a style, in short, designed to dazzle Morley and his admirers in the 1590s, as well as the twentieth-century generation that had come to Tudor and Elizabethan music by way of the English Madrigal School.

Byrd engages in a good deal of 'madrigalism', too. He was more ready to slip into quavers for words like 'cantate', 'agili', 'laeta chorea' and 'canat' than to illustrate the psalmist's instrumentarium (the lyre gets lost almost entirely). What he was after was a battery of very lively contrasted rhythms, and it is worth noting that he chose many of them in order to pair with others: 'agili' with 'laeta chorea', for example, and 'cymbala dulcisona lauda' —a tricky syncopated idea coolly explicated in augmentation—with 'omne quod aethereis in mundo'. Towards the end of the motet half a dozen text phrases start with the same dotted-note figure, a madrigalian rhythm which indeed tends to dominate the whole piece. Just as in the affective homophonic motets, a strong dose of polyphony serves as peroration, with a characteristic 'Halleluia' section and an almost Handelian slow-down at 'tempus in omne Deo'. The Ionian mode as usual makes dominant and submediant cadences, not subdominant ones. Byrd takes advantage of this harmonic pecularity to get an effect of special airy exhilaration at the end of this greatly admired, and greatly admirable, composition.*

*Which has seldom been sung in correct rhythm in modern times. After the word 'laudet' in part 3 (BW 3, 9) the old Fellowes edition has an erroneous crotchet rest (cor-

Whether in a brilliant or an affective style, homophony for Byrd seems to have been a technique to be concentrated in certain motets, while others—the majority—held fast to polyphony. He did not often balance the two techniques so carefully and so beautifully as in **Circumdederunt me** (1591/15), another of his most impressive compositions. The first two phrases may be said to rewrite the first two in *Haec dicit Dominus* in a more pliant version; and it is perhaps already indicative that the half-homophonic repeated *incipit* admits of more contrapuntal stirrings, as the main melody for 'Circumdederunt me' moves from the tenor to the soprano and finds smooth, darkening new harmonies. Three lucid imitative phrases follow, though a short section of dramatic exclamations in block chords (or something close enough to block chords) intervenes for the words 'et pericula inferni *invenerunt me*'. The imitative phrase 'Tribulationem et dolorem inveni' goes back to one of the most successful early motets, *Domine praestolamur*. Picking up the lengthy motive 'et dissolvas iugum captivitatis nostrae', Byrd wonderfully realized a detail suggested there but left unexploited, the expressive interval between the two halves of the motive.

The concluding appeal 'O Domine, libera animam meam' is less impassioned but no less urgent than similar appeals in *Vide Domine* and in the early motet *Levemus corda nostra*, which in some respects it resembles the most closely (see p. 137f. *Levemus corda* comes next in the publication, with *Haec dicit Dominus* one before.) The appeal as a whole is issued only twice, starting each time with the words 'O Domine' in slow homophony;* the words 'libera animam meam', first set half-homophonically with elegantly contrasting rhythms, blossom at their next appearance into multiple minim strettos. Byrd found the motive itself in *Domine praestolamur*, once again, in the concluding ostinato phrase 'et libera populum tuum' (Ex. 18c). But the treatment is very different, smoother and more concise, two sections 4 and 13 breves in length standing in place of the single 23-breve period of the early motet. As a further point of sophistication, the characteristic triple metre and

rected to a minim rest in Dart's revised edition of 1966) and then reduces note values in the following section, 'laeta chorea pede', without the slightest indication that the original is notated in triple metre. Dart transmits the original notation not quite accurately and implies the wrong proportion; it should be $o = \d$. See the thorough discussion in Andrews, *Byrd's Polyphony*, ch. 3.

The consistent declamation 'Hal-le-lu-i-a' in Dart's revised edition of BW 3 is generalized from the syllabification 'Hallelu-y-a' which is found but once in the partbooks, at the first appearance of the word in the alto—where the line ending after 'Hallelu-' may well have thrown the compositor off. At its dozen or so other appearances in the partbooks the word is always written 'Hallelui-a' or 'Halleluy-a'.

*The second time the soprano sings the tenor's melody reharmonized—a subtle textural and harmonic echo of the beginning of the composition.

dotted notes of 'libera animam' have been explicitly prepared in the preceding phrase 'et nomen Domini invocavi'.

Like *Haec dicit Dominus*, *Circumdederunt me* stands out as one of Byrd's greatest works in the mournful vein. If it is less austere in mood and less extreme in technique, that may in the last analysis reflect Byrd's mature response to the two main types of text which called for this kind of expression, one political, the other personal. Though both motets count technically as Dorian, *Circumdederunt me* employs a more limited harmonic range, never extending to the Phrygian E♭ that colours *Haec dicit Dominus* (and *Vide Domine*) so vividly. The music is almost programmatically Dorian. The B♭s introduced near the beginning yield to B♮s before the first large cadence, which reaches the dominant with the help of a low E′ in the bass (a note never touched on in the other motet, though otherwise its overall pitch range corresponds closely). And when decisive B♮s return near the end, they prepare the two strong statements of the appeal in the major subdominant, another characteristic Dorian sonority.

Two motets placed next to one another in the 1591 *Cantiones sacrae* commence oddly with short isolated sections for a 3-part semichoir. Other semichoirs do not then pick up this material, according to the norm of 'cell' technique; when the other voices enter they do so with new words and new music, as in the old votive antiphon form. Indeed, in their wooden style the opening ten breves of **Tribulatio proxima est** (1591/8–9) resemble nothing so much as the opening of *Tribue Domine*, the *grande machine* of the 1575 *Cantiones* in which Byrd paid his respects to the venerable tradition. In **Salve Regina** (1591/6–7) the opening section is more fluid in style and more interesting in concept. The melismatic setting of the word 'Salve' (actually sung by only two of the voices, S² and T¹; T² enters with the word 'Mater') is resumed and expanded when extra 'Salve's' are inserted to round out the little section. Then later, at the very end of the motet, this kind of writing returns. One particularly graceful melisma does service for the two acclamations 'O clemens' (sung by S²T¹T² only, once again) and 'o pia', and another ornaments the name of Mary.

Meanwhile the words '*o dulcis Virgo* Maria' are set to a gentle semibreve figure in interlocking thirds which transforms an early cliché (compare Exs. 10 and 30). This works together with the melismatic figure for 'Maria' as a double point, one of Byrd's most original and inspired. The semibreve sequence CABG CABG...DBCA DBCA between S² and S¹ is all harmonized in the Mixolydian mode, even though we are practically arrived at the end of an orthodox Aeolian motet; Byrd manages the transition back to A perfectly, first by leaning on F and A minor triads and fading the 'o

Ex. 30

dulcis' figure into a diminution, then closing down the melismas on 'Maria'. This was his individual contribution to the stock of familiar tropes inspired by Marian devotion—a theme, incidentally, which is distinctly surprising to meet in a book published only three years after the Armada. Unfortunately what comes in between the workable beginning of this motet and its superb conclusion is writing of a relatively routine character, and a long stretch of it.*

In *Tribulatio proxima est* it is the beginning that disappoints. Neutral 3-part counterpoint seems an inadequate response to the first sentence of the text:

Tribulatio proxima est et non est qui adiuvet. Sed tu, Domine, defensor vitae meae vindica me. *2ᵃ pars* Contumelias et terrores passus sum ab eis [pastiche of several Lenten responds]. Adiutor et protector meus es tu: Domine, ne moreris [cf. Ps. 69:6].

But as the piece continues and picks up musical interest, we can perhaps grasp Byrd's strategy. Both parts of the concise, balanced text proceed from laments to appeals, and Byrd chose to downplay both of the former so that the latter would stand out more dramatically. The 'Tribulatio' motive, in any case, though utterly plain, is far from inexpressive. The phrase 'defensor vitae meae' is set with mounting fervour—so is the parallel phrase 'et protector meus es tu' in part 2—and 'vindica me' whips around the circle of fifths to cut short part 1 of the motet after only forty breves. Especially

---

*The early version of *Salve Regina*, preserved only in the contratenor partbook Mus. Sch.e.423, provides a surprise. Byrd originally designed the piece in a single part, and added three semibreves when he split it into two *partes* for publication. (At BW 3, 50, bars 9–10 and 51/1, the first tenor originally read semibreve b, crotchet rest, crotchet e.) E.423 also supplies some preferable word underlay for the tenor at the end of the motet: 'Maria' at 55/6–7 and 57/2–3. The early MS sources do not offer an alternative for the bad part writing at 54/7 (for another unusually bad place, see BW 2, 74/5–7, in *Vide Domine*).

fine is the appeal 'Domine, ne moreris' at the end of part 2. The simple 3-part cell which generates it begins with a monotone soprano e answered at the lower fifth; this low cry of 'Domine' is destined to move up very strongly to g, a' and b'. Whereupon two delayed entries at the lower twelfth, E, pierce through the increasingly intricate web spun by the 'ne moreris' motive and usher in the eloquent Aeolian cadence, which incidentally echoes the ending cadence of part 1. In concept, though not of course in technique, this passage recalls the 'convertere' section in the Lamentations.

The words of the appeal were borrowed from Psalm 69, the whole of which Byrd set as a large sectional psalm-motet for six voices. **Deus in adiutorium** (BW 9/20) is a very interesting composition which was not published; and unfortunately the tenor part is lost.* The five sections count as relatively short by Byrd's standards, employing (at least in principle) different styles and textures. Evidently he was looking for a more modern format for psalm composition than that of the votive antiphon, which he had taken over from White and Mundy to frame his early settings of Psalms 14 and 119 for eight and nine voices. Models lay readily at hand in the Penitential Psalms of Lassus, even in Ferrabosco's enormous setting of Psalm 103.† Yet one whole section in Byrd's piece, 'Ego vero egenus', in part 5, is written in the archaic and abstract semi-choir polyphony of the votive antiphon. Part 3 of the piece is for five voices only. Part 1 and the ending of part 5 (after the semi-choir passage) contain blocks of massed homophony.

The twin opening phrases 'Deus in adiutorium...' and 'Domine ad adiuvandum me...' summoned up Byrd's grandest style. In the first the soprano presides over solemn intonations of an imitative subject rising steadily from e to a'; in the second the texture, already thickening, grows more homophonic as the soprano moves the line up to b', which is underpinned by the first G major chord in this Phrygian composition. B♮ cancels B♭s which had just been imported for a burnished cadence on the word 'intende'.

---

*The sources are Baldwin's Partbooks and Tenbury 389-James. For some reason the TCM editors made no effort to supply the missing part, and Fellowes's reconstruction in BW 9 is a lapse from his usual standard. In bar 4, G must be supplied by the tenor, entering (like the first alto) with the word 'Meum'. The whole beginning of part 5 must be completed *a 3*. At BW 9, 23, bar 1, one could perhaps echo the bass inversion in the tenor, resting it in bar 3 and the first half of bar 4, and at 27, bar 3, there is no reason not to raise the third of the chord. The odd soprano quavers in bar 8 occur in both sources, but perhaps they should read a third lower.

†See p. 118n. The Ferrabosco seems much less likely as a model, since each of the eleven parts is really a full-scale motet, longer than Byrd's parts and containing more text. Yet part 6, *Saturabuntur ligna campi*, is a systematic study in inversion, like Byrd's part 2.

Part 2 of the motet seems to have brought out the schematic side of Byrd's nature. The phrases are scaled in a suspiciously orderly way—

Avertantur	et erube-	qui volunt	avertantur	erube-	qui dicunt mihi:
retrorsum	scant	mihi mala,	statim	scentes	Euge, euge!
9	10				
16 *breves*		16	8	4	17

and not only do the words 'Avertantur retrorsum' promote a subject imitated in stretto inversion, but much the same stretto pair *inverted* serves for the other 'avertantur' phrase. While he was at it Byrd wrote inversions in 'qui volunt mihi mala' and 'erubescentes' too. In part 3 'those that seek Thee' seek in three little homophonic statements reaching out by a second, a third, a fourth ('qui quaerunt te'). In part 4 the perpetual sequence in thirds that had illustrated the word 'rursum' in *Libera me Domine* (Ex. 12) illustrates 'Et dicant semper'.

As part 5 begins with old-fashioned 3-voiced writing the musical interest plummets. Was it this passage that gave Byrd the idea of beginning the motet *Tribulatio proxima est* with writing of the same kind? He would have thought of the one work while composing the other, for in the last forty breves or so of each he found himself setting the same words (with one small difference). The settings are similar in style and both are very impressive, but *Tribulatio* reveals a significant deepening of Byrd's conception. In *Deus in adiutorium* the surging motive for 'Domine, ne moreris' is reiterated relatively simply to make a solemn, massive climax. In *Tribulatio* Byrd obtains a more subtle effect by using a bleak, hopeless motive which nevertheless rises to even greater eloquence as a result of more intricate development. What is more directly intense in the 6-part motet, and more despairing, is the preliminary double invocation 'Adiutor meus et liberator meus es tu'.

A relatively long homophonic appeal is probably the most memorable feature of **Domine Deus omnipotens** (BW 8/11), a 5-part manuscript motet from which the tenor is lost, once again.* In itself, however, the 'miserere' passage seems like no more than a pale reflection of appeals such as those in *Deus in adiutorium*, *Miserere mei Deus*, and so on. This whole motet, from the bland opening phrase onward—what other Byrd motet opens as unimpressively as this?—makes an uncharacteristically subdued effect. It

---

*The source, again, is Baldwin's Partbooks (see Table 5); the text is from a motet by Cornelius Canis in Susato's *Liber quintus ecclesiasticorum cantionum quinque vocum*, 1553[12]. The short passage beginning at BW 8, 81, bar 8 must be read in three parts.

also has its share of pedestrian writing. Yet there is something appealing about the many unassertive upward scale motives and their attendant trains of gently striving ascending sixth chords; and the last of the phrases in question, 'exspecto liberationem', attains a certain distinction.

[3]

It probably was a reservation concerning the length of *Deus in adiutorium*, not its quality, that caused Byrd to omit it from the 6-part section of the 1591 *Cantiones sacrae*. Or perhaps it would not quite fit into the scheme he had decided on for the selection of motets for this section—a scheme whose almost exaggerated neatness is somewhat obscured by the ordering by mode or final (see Table 6). The eight 6-part compositions break down into two times four and four times two. As though he had the idea of rationalizing the thoroughly miscellaneous character of this motet collection, Byrd included four pieces in archaic styles and four in distinctly modern ones: two cantus firmus responds, two motets in a form derived from the votive antiphon, two brilliant motets of jubilation and two intimate motets of prayer. The latter clearly constitute a matched pair, both employing brief texts taken from Roman *Magnificat* antiphons. The two jubilant motets are both notated *a note neri* and both change to triple metre in their central sections.

We have discussed the cantus firmus responds *Afflicti pro peccatis nostris* and *Descendit de coelis* on page 75ff. The motets in votive antiphon form, *Cunctis diebus* and *Infelix ego*, enjoyed a modest circulation around the same time as the early 5-part group of middle-period motets (see Table 5). They also circulated in a mutilated form: starting with Thomas Mulliner of the famous organ book, the Elizabethans liked to anthologize semichoir sections snipped out of their favourite old Masses, votive antiphons and other large compositions. The two by Byrd were the last such works to be accorded this dubious compliment.*

There are some stylistic points of contact between **Infelix ego** (1591/24-6) and one of the early 5-part motets, *Tribulationes civitatum*.† However nothing as delicate as the point 'Timor et hebitudo mentis' from *Tribulationes* occurs in *Infelix ego*, and the essential orientation of this piece is not contemporary but retrospective. In form it hews so closely to *Tribue Domine* from the 1575

*In Christ Church 45 (containing *Infelix ego* as a later addition in Baldwin's hand), Baldwin's 'Commonplace Book', Tenbury 342-4, Add. 29246, RCM 2035 and 2036. Paston also authologized 3-part introit verses excerpted from the *Gradualia*: see p. 232n.

†The descending stepwise motives and their attendant harmonies in the opening 3-part sections, the C major cadences at BW 3, 169, and BW 2, 191 (there transposed to E), and perhaps also the aspect of the cells at BW 3, 173, and BW 2, 189.

Cantiones that it can only be regarded as an effort to fill an exceedingly intricate old mould with new matter.

Byrd's procedure is curious enough to be worth illustrating in detail with the help of a diagram:

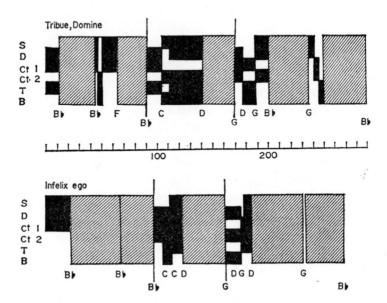

The motets employ the same clefs (see p. 180n) and the same unusual modal transposition, Lydian or Ionian in B♭. The dimensions are similar and the sectionalization broadly analogous. Both works are trisectional, and *Infelix ego* mirrors the opening 3-part semichoir sections in each part of *Tribue Domine* and also the 5-part interlude in part 2. Closer still are the large-scale harmonic parallels, which extend not only to the part-endings, but even to the schematic feature mentioned on page 111, the successive use of cadences in B♭, C and D in the three initial semichoir sections.

Like the older work, the newer one takes over the actual style of the votive antiphon only in the semichoir sections; the 'full' sections once again sample the entire range of styles, techniques and textures that Byrd was developing at the time. *Infelix ego* offers a regular compendium of block-chord homophony, half-homophony, single and double points, and 'cell' constructions of various kinds. But while the contrapuntal technique is up to date, the harmonic idiom, especially in the 6-part polyphonic stretches, remains close to that of the earlier period. The final page is a good example, with its rough, exuberant part writing, its characteristic 6–5 progressions in sequence, its plunging bass lines and chords spaced in an almost Stravinskian mannar.

As for the new matter poured into the old mould, that is even more curious. The Tudor votive antiphon—archaic, monumental, decorative, impersonal—accommodates a Continental text which stands out as the most dramatic and anguished of all Byrd's expressions of personal penitence:

Infelix ego, omnium auxilio destitutus, qui coelum terramque offendi. Quo ibo? quo me vertam? ad quem confugiam? quis mei miserebitur? Ad coelum levare oculos non audeo, quia ei graviter peccavi; in terra refugium non invenio, quia ei scandalum fui. *2ª pars* Quid igitur faciam? desperabo? Absit. Misericors est Deus, pius est salvator meus. Solus igitur Deus refugium meum; ipse non despiciet opus suum, non repellet imaginem suam. *3ª pars* Ad te igitur, piissime Deus, tristis ac moerens venio, quoniam tu solus spes mea, tu solus refugium meum. Quid autem dicam tibi, cum oculos levare non audeo? verba doloris effundam, misericordiam tuam implorabo, et dicam:

Miserere mei, Deus, secundum magnam misericordiam tuam [Ps. 50:1].

With a text as long as this, it would appear, Byrd simply saw no other way to go. He most likely took it from Lassus's *Sacrae Cantiones* of 1566; it was also set in whole or in part by Willaert, Rore, Clemens, Vicentino and no doubt others.*

And what is perhaps most curious of all is how well the piece works. It must be one of Byrd's strangest successes. Even the neutral 3-part beginning makes a certain artistic sense as a contrasting background for the string of desperate questions which follows—'Quo ibo?' and 'quo me vertam?', set to the same music, mounting dramatically up a third and an octave; 'ad quem confugiam?' with its prophetic turn towards G; and 'quis mei miserebitur?', which by broadening the phrase lengths restores a measure of calm. For the next phrase, 'Ad coelum levare oculos non audeo', Byrd devised a rapid and original double point in which the 'non audeo' motive forms itself (after one neat augmentation) into a series of sighing antiphonal echoes. This makes for a very affecting setting of these words, though it is not altogether easy to say why.

Other points, such as the straggling 'quia ei scandalum fui', betray technical problems; here the first tenor pitches in to the imitations only at the last minute, as though by oversight. The 'miserere' section at the end appears to be one of the earliest of Byrd's half-homophonic concluding appeals,

*See Edward E. Lowinsky, *Secret Chromatic Art in the Netherlands Motet* (New York, 1946), 116. At the beginning of the *tertia pars* the original publication and modern editions have 'ipsissime'. Early manuscript versions have the correct word.

simpler than that in *Deus in adiutorium* and much more heavy-footed than the later setting of the same words from Psalm 50, in *Miserere mei Deus* (1591/20). Yet as the six voices come together after a portentous halt, bringing yet a new resource—an A♭ chord—to the petition for divine mercy, and then diverge into the old-fashioned solemn cascading of that last page, it is impossible not to be swayed by the seriousness and dignity of Byrd's response. This quality is sensed only dimly in the more sophisticated late motet.

In **Cunctis diebus** (1591/30) the votive antiphon form, telescoped down, amounts to no more than four sections, for three, six, four and six voices respectively. The speaker faces a death without redemption:

Cunctis diebus, quibus nunc milito, expecto donec veniat immutatio mea [Job 14:14]. Dimitte me ergo, ut plangam paululum dolorem meum, antequam vadam ut non revertar ad terram miseriae ubi est nullus ordo, sed sempiternus horror inhabitat [cf. Job 10:20–2].

It is hard to understand why Byrd would have set a relatively short text in this unwieldy form unless he was setting it as a pair with *Infelix ego.** If anything the piece looks even older. The point 'dolorem meum' recalls 'et rursum' in another Job setting, Byrd's early 5-part motet *Libera me Domine et pone me iuxta te* (1575/2: see Ex. 10). The brief semichoir section 'ut non revertar . . .' is laid out in schematic patterns, and the following 'full' section concludes with a single point, 'sed sempiternus horror inhabitat', which drones on as endlessly as the words suggest. It cannot quite make up its mind to plump for an ostinato; there is no clear climax, and when a new motive emerges for the cadential passage, it stresses the word 'inhabitat' and therefore makes no rhetorical point. One feels a sense of routine throughout *Cunctis diebus*, quite unlike *Infelix ego*. And indeed, what is still hard to understand is the attraction of these deathly texts to a young composer who in the later 1570s was just feeling out his true powers. Were they perhaps given to Byrd as a package by a patron advanced in years, still loyal to the musical fashions of his youth?

The great 8-part canonic motet **Quomodo cantabimus** (BW 9/24) was written in 1584 in response to a motet by Philippe de Monte; the story

---

Cunctis diebus uses the same clefs as *Infelix ego* and *Tribue Domine*, C clef on each of the five lines of the staff and the standard bass (F) clef—a symmetrical combination used by Byrd in these three motets only. *Cunctis diebus* is in G minor moving strongly to B♭; the other two are in B♭ moving strongly to G minor. *Tribulationes civitatum*, it may be recalled, starts in B♭ and ends in G minor.

has been told and the texts given on page 44. The work obviously occupies a special place in Byrd's output. He followed Monte only in the number of voices, not in the mode (Byrd writes in the F Ionian, Monte in the G Dorian) nor in the characteristic Continental deployment of the forces as two anti-phonal SATB choirs. Byrd's 3-part canon between the bass and the two altos effectively ruled this out, although in the motet's non-canonic second part the phrases 'Memor esto, Domine' and 'filiorum Edom' do indeed form antiphonal SATTB cells, with the tenors working overtime.

The canon itself is appreciably simpler than those in the early canonic hymns *O salutaris hostia* and *O lux beata Trinitas* (see Table 3). The entries all come at the octave or unison at a leisurely time interval of three breves. The second *comes* inverts the *dux*, but when (as is usually the case) the canonic voices sing their text phrases and motives only once, Byrd does not generally build a full-scale point of imitation in inversion around the single inverted entry. Instead he turns a blind eye as this dies, buried in the counterpoint, for lack of a helping hand from the free voices.

Exceptions come, as might be expected, in the canon's opening phrase and in the penultimate and most interesting one, 'si non meminero tui'. These all-important words are indeed repeated by the canonic voices. The *dux* actually inverts the expressive motive at its last statement, and the free voices take up both the *recto* and inverted version. Byrd contrived to turn this canonic point into the most learned of all the stretto ostinato passages that we have traced throughout the early motet repertory (Ex. 6j). For the first time in the piece (except for an inordinately broad hint six breves before) the harmony swings powerfully towards D minor, invigorated by systematic 6–5 sounds, in place of the steady bland F major aura of the early phrases. This steady F major seems to emerge from meandering bass lines which respond to the canon in inversion by stressing the subdominant much more than usual in the Lydian-Ionian mode.

Part 2 of the motet, freed from the canon, moves more flexibly in harmony as well as in texture. Byrd introduces C major cadences—entirely absent from part 1—and balances the total structure with another strong turn to D minor near the end, in the antiphonal section prior to the sonorous con-clusion 'in die Hierusalem', with its grand periods of five breves. Both here and at 'si non meminero tui' he must have been remembering not only Jerusalem but also the votive antiphon style, once again, the style he had used years earlier for another 8-part setting of another psalm, *Ad Dominum cum tribularer*. Religious conservatism, for English Catholics, went hand in hand with musical nostalgia.

[4]

Of the four 6-part compositions in the *Cantiones sacrae* in a more modern style, the two jubilant motets are naturally the more glamorous, and hence better known, though the two intimate ones are no less important. The pairing between **Cantate Domino** (1591/29) and **Haec dies** (1591/32) can be quickly shown by a chart of their main sections. The central sections of each motet change to triple metre after a full stop and a *General pause*:

Cantate Domino canticum novum, laus eius in ecclesia sanctorum.	Laetetur Israel in eo qui fecit eum,	et filiae Sion exultet rege suo [Ps. 149:1–2].	
33 *semibreves*	19*	26	=77

Haec dies, quam fecit Dominus:	exultemus et laetemur in ea.	Alleluia [cf. Easter Gradual].	
22	20*	38	=80

Like *Laudibus in sanctis*, which also features a section in triple metre, the 6-part motets are written in a basic crotchet pulse, and in their triple-metre sections they catch something of the rhythmic virtuosity of that brilliant madrigalian exercise *in nuce*. To which they add brilliant devices of their own. A major difference between them comes, of course, in the amount of text they cover. The outer sections of *Cantate Domino* contain several musical ideas, of which the very first is the most distinguished: cells of the same type as those at the beginning of *Ne irascaris* but treated more intricately, with the countersubjects inverted at the twelfth as the original 3-part cell (with the slow melody in the alto) is filled out *a 6* for bass and soprano statements. This cell starts in G minor but shifts at once to B♭—and by missing a beat at its third appearance, it abandons even its original *pro forma* Dorian sonority to the insistent Ionian jubilation. We shall see Byrd copy this distinctive point more than once in the *Gradualia*.

The outer sections of *Haec dies* contain only one point of imitation apiece (though the first of them is a double point). Both are quite different from anything Byrd had ever written, at least in a motet. If one makes a chart of the voice entries in the 'Haec dies' point leaving little gaps where the entries do not overlap closely—S^1A $S^2S^1T^2$ $BT^1S^1S^2$ T^2T^1AB—one sees

---

*These are triple-metre bars equivalent in length to the duple-metre ones. Again the modern editors have got this wrong. Fellowes reduced note values in the passages at BW 3, 206 and 230; the correct proportion is not ♩ = ♩ (Fellowes) or 𝅗𝅥 = ♩ (Dart) but o = 𝅗𝅥. See the thorough discussion in Andrews, *Byrd's Polyphony*, ch. 3.

a more or less straightforward 6-part exposition and counter-exposition spaced in such a way as to form increasingly dense groups of chiming strettos—chiming, because apart from two tonal answers (shown in the chart by italics) the madrigalian motive simply winds its way up the F major triad again and again. The second half of the double subject, 'quam fecit Dominus', comes into its own during the gaps. It ends the duple-metre section with canzonet strettos written more dutifully 'after the Italian vaine' than anything in *Laudibus in sanctis*.

Byrd never designed a grander alleluia than the one in this motet. It runs two or three times as long as any of the alleluias in the *Gradualia*. The main motive is doubled in thirds by an unusual, plastic figure which adds a dotted-note rhythm and a quaver *echappée* by way of rhythmic and contrapuntal spicing. This powerful cadential combination heads initially towards F and B♭; but the latter cadence is aborted by a repetition in which the harmony is shunted around to D minor—the standard Ionian ploy. The next implied B♭ cadence (Ex. 31, bars 1–2) is interrupted by an entry a tone higher,

Ex. 31

leading to three cadences on c, c′ and c (deceptive). Then, in a roughly sequential passage, entries a tone higher yet—and for the bass this is very high indeed—make four cadences on d′, D, d and D, the last a magnificent plagal affair coming after the phrase length has been drawn out to six semibreves. That *echappée* has played itself out with some satisfaction (as shown in brackets in Ex. 31, bar 4), but the dotted-note figure now returns to cement the D minor cadences and take firm hold after the last of them, during the final period. It does not take much imagination to discover some Shepherds and Nymphs of Diana assisting at this particular Easter service, fresh from their secular Lauds. And many obvious points of contact appear between *Haec dies* and Byrd's own madrigals in praise of Queen Elizabeth published a year earlier, in Watson's *Italian Madrigals Englished*, 1590, the 4- and especially the 6-part versions of *This sweet and merry month of May*.

The pairing between **Domine non sum dignus** (1591/23) and **Domine salva nos** (1591/31) is a matter of the general proportions, once again—

Domine non sum dignus	19_{III}	11_{iv}	7_i	15_i
Domine salva nos	19_I	$11_{\frac{1}{2}vi}$	$4_{\frac{1}{2}vi}$	21_I

and also of the clef combination* and the choice of texts from Roman *Magnificat* antiphons. Both are intimate prayers: one more general, for God's saving Grace and His gift of peace, the other more specific, a father's plea for a dying child (see p. 48). Writing these pieces, Byrd seems to have been struck for the first time by the possibilities of the 6–part choir for intimate chamber-music effects. His early 6–part music had inclined to the grandiose; it is no accident that the older of the two models we have discerned for the 1591 motets is the monumental votive antiphon, and the more recent the *al fresco* celebratory madrigal. Byrd now manipulates the 6-part texture with quite new delicacy, following an equally new ideal of concise expression. The texture is less melismatic and more motivic, the motives sharper, the phrases shorter.

Set to three notes, the word 'impera' in *Domine salva nos* explodes (or implodes) sixteen times in the space of four breves. This is only the most extreme of many instances that could be cited. Even the quite traditional ideas for the vocative 'Domine' in each motet, which in earlier years Byrd would inevitably have made the basis for discursive double points†, he now handles almost aphoristically. In *Domine non sum dignus* the monotone

---

*Bass, two tenors, alto, two sopranos. In *Domine non sum dignus* Fellowes designated the second soprano as an alto, since its range is G–c′ (A–d′ in his transposition). It should however be paired with the first soprano (range c–c′) rather than with the alto (F–a′); the upper part of the range is critical, and in any case the voice goes above a′ on eight occasions, below c on only two.

†The monotone figure of *Domine non sum dignus* had been used in *Domine secundum actum meum*, etc. (see Ex. 12), and the descending steps of *Domine salve nos* in *Domine secundum multitudinem dolorum meorum* (1589/27).

figure for 'Domine' is joined to another subject for the same words—a technique prefigured in the early manuscript motet *Peccavi* (Ex. 14)—and separated off from the more polyphonic 'non sum dignus' point; the voices whisper 'Domine' twenty times in succession in the first nine breves. In *Domine salva nos* the motives for 'Domine' and 'salva nos' do indeed combine, though not along the familiar lines of double imitation. 'Domine' is first uttered as an isolated statement in affective homophony *a 3*, and when this is repeated *a 6* (Ex. 32, bars 6–7), Byrd achieves a startling effect of muted drama which could hardly emerge from a traditional imitative context.

Ex. 32

In all this we are bound to detect the influence of what German writers call the 'chiselled' style of the Italian *madrigale arioso*. Madrigal style and process is evident on many levels in this pair of motets. For example, Byrd uses rapid descending scale figures interlocking in triadic patterns at the end of the 'non sum dignus' point in the first motet and at 'perimus' in the second. The device is not simply imported, as madrigal ideas are imported in *Haec dies* and *This sweet and merry month of May*; it is quietly worked into two different but equally individual modes of expression. The jolting change from a basic minim to a crotchet pulse in *Domine non sum dignus* (this is comparable to the change to triple metre in *Cantate Domino* and *Haec dies*)

recalls a favourite effect of the Italian *alla breve* madrigal, one that would
soon be popularized in England by Thomas Weelkes. Somewhat similar
accelerandi occur in some of Byrd's 5-part motets, such as *Apparebit in
finem* and *Domine exaudi . . . et clamor meus*, but they always occur quite
briefly at the ends of the pieces; here the change comes in the middle and
extends to two separate text phrases, 'sed tantum dic verbum' and 'et
sanabitur puer meus'. To be sure, the latter concludes with an admirable
rallentando using a strict augmentation of the basic polyphonic cell.*

Also madrigalian is the haunting chromatic colouration at the beginning
of *Domine salva nos* (see Ex. 32). Translating a quintessentially Italian
effect into something entirely personal, once again, Byrd investigates third-
related chords once removed (C and A major, G and E) in five different
manifestations, while the sopranos brood repeatedly on the same interval,
a′e (sometimes ge). How beautiful that the last G♯ should emerge as the
resolution of a suspension; but even more so that G♯s and C♯s should be
dropped altogether in the second half of the phrase, as the motives are
developed polyphonically. Here the sopranos trace and retrace a fourth
lying higher in their range, c′g, while the bass carries the main 'Domine'
motive, involving another fourth, far down in sequence. It brings with it a
rich contrapuntal complex which has grown up gradually since the motive
was first heard. And beautiful again the spontaneous new upward scale
figure at the very end of the phrase, by which the lower soprano prepares
both motives that are used for the word 'perimus' a moment later.

It remains to say that each of these short motets contains some music of a
more traditional cast, the ostinato-like phrase 'ut intres sub tectum meum' in
Domine non sum dignus and the double point 'et fac, Deus, tranquillitatem' at
the end of *Domine salva nos*. Yet there is also something novel about the
latter point, the heightened contrast between the two parts of the subject,

Ex. 33

*The last two phrases of this motet should not really be tallied as 7+15 breves, as in the
chart above, but as 13+17 semibreves +7 breves (the augmentation section).

achieved by the fast, dotted-crotchet rhythm in 'tranquillitatem'—an almost Monteverdian touch (Ex. 33; cf. Ex. 9). The arresting declamation of this word; the augmentation of the dotted rhythm built in to the subject from the start; the progressive expansion of 'et fac, Deus' in melodic range; the sequential resolution of 'tranquillitatem' in, principally, the alto and second soprano—these cannot be called novel, for Byrd had long been capable of craftsmanship on this level. Not novel, just exceptionally fine. This combination of old and new looks forward to the style of the *Gradualia*, although paradoxically, and a little sadly, all the 6-part motets in the later collection return in their own way to the more impersonal monumental ideal. But there were good reasons for this, as we shall see. *Domine non sum dignus* and *Domine salva nos* are the most advanced of all Byrd's earlier motets, and the clearest stylistic link between the *Cantiones sacrae* and the *Gradualia*.

4

The Masses

Byrd's three settings of the Ordinary of the Mass were published as separate small editions of six or eight pages each per partbook. They lack title-pages and hence any indication of a date or identification of a printer (though Byrd's name as author is coolly entered at the top of every page). Over the years there has been much speculation as to the date of this music. Edward Rimbault, writing in 1841 when Byrd's birthdate was not known, along with many other things, confidently placed them in Queen Mary's reign, as Hawkins had done. Fellowes speculated that they were issued as companion publications to the *Gradualia* of 1605. H. C. Collins placed only the Five-Part Mass in that period, the others around 1590.

The question was resolved in 1966 as a result of a close examination of all the surviving partbooks by Peter Clulow.* Clulow made the elementary observation (as it now seems) that there were two different editions of the Three- and Four-Part Masses, and the more sophisticated discovery that the printer (who was Thomas East) owned only single woodblocks for the ornamental initial letters K[*yrie*], E[*t in terra*], P[*atrem omnipotentem*], S[*anctus*] and A[*gnus Dei*], and that traces of deterioration of these blocks can afford a means of placing the Masses chronologically among East's other publications. The Four-Part Mass was issued in 1592–3 (probably early in the period), the Three-Part Mass in 1593–4 (probably late in the period), and the Five-Part Mass in 1594–5. The second editions of the Three- and Four-Part masses can be dated around 1599.

Whether the music was actually written at the time it was issued is of course another question, and one which Harrison and others have approached with proper scholarly caution.† The three Masses might be older works whose publication was delayed until a propitious moment; the Five-Part Mass might have been left till last not because it was the last composed but because it was the least practical for undercover services. Indeed, in so improbable a publishing situation almost any argument can be made, and

---

*See P. Clulow, 'Publication Dates for Byrd's Latin Masses', *Music & Letters*, xlvii (1966), 1ff, H. K. Andrews, 'The Printed Part-Books of Byrd's Vocal Music', *The Library*, 5th series, xix (1964), 9f, also the editions of the three Masses by Frederick Hudson (Edition Eulenburg, Nos. 997–9).

†See NOHM 4, 486.

almost any argument must be admitted; it is hard to know how to gauge probabilities. However, such actual evidence as can be adduced is consistent not only with a date of composition for the Masses in the period following 1592–3, but also with the order of composition indicated by the publishing history. The simplest answer to the question has, after all, a good deal to recommend it.

The strongest arguments that can be made in this connection speak to the order of composition. The Four-Part Mass must have been written before the others; the internal evidence for this—a matter of form, style and tone—will be set forth at some length later in the course of this chapter. As to the period itself, there is a general stylistic point to be made, and also a circumstantial biographical one. The Masses are obviously written much more concisely than most of the *Cantiones sacrae*. One could argue that Byrd, who in the 1580s cultivated distinct styles for Latin motets, English songs and English liturgical music, also developed a distinct style for secret Latin liturgical music at the same time. The texts of the Mass demand concise settings; he would have had to come to terms with this whenever he wrote Masses, whether late or early. The Catholic historian Philip Caraman winningly proposed that 'one or more' of the Masses was sung in 1586 at Byrd's famous meeting with the Jesuit Fathers Weston, Southern and Garnet.*

But apart from the question why the two Latin styles did not continue side by side into the 1590s, arguments and speculations of this kind cannot easily survive the application of Occam's razor. They introduce a complication that is unnecessary, for a single stylistic progression fits the facts much more simply. Increasing conciseness of style can be traced more or less continuously from Byrd's motets published in 1575 to those of 1589 and 1591 to the Masses of 1592–5 and then to the *Gradualia* of 1605 and 1607. In a stylistic continuum the Masses follow smoothly upon some of the latest works of the 1591 *Cantiones*, particularly the 6-part motets *Domine salva nos* and *Domine non sum dignus*.

As we have seen in Chapter 1, on approaching fifty Byrd gives the appearance of winding up one stage of his career. He publishes four collections of his songs and motets, some of them dating back over a considerable period, in 1588, 1589 and 1591, and in the latter year also supervises a retrospective anthology of his keyboard music, My Lady Nevell's Book. In 1593 he moves from Harlington to Stondon Massey, where, it has been suggested, he entered increasingly into the life of the Catholic community under the aegis of his old patron and new neighbour Sir John Petre. It seems reasonable to

*P. Caraman, *Henry Garnett, 1555–1606, and the Gunpowder Plot* (London, 1964), 33.

associate this major change of life with a change in patterns of composition. Certainly Byrd turned away from penitential and 'political' motets at this time; it was probably at this same time that he turned towards music for use in the Catholic liturgy. This impetus reached a climax in that astonishingly comprehensive liturgical project, the *Gradualia*, with its more than a hundred pieces, mostly items for the Proper of the Mass for the main feasts of the Church year. In this broad view of Byrd's composing career, the three settings of the Ordinary of the Mass can be seen as his first essays within a new concept of Catholic activity or activism.

The specialist is not likely to quarrel with received opinion which places the Masses at the pinnacle of Byrd's work, though he may allow himself to wonder how far this opinion has been influenced by the simple fact that these works are longer than any others by the composer, and therefore more immediately impressive. The care and seriousness with which Byrd went about the composition of this music is perfectly evident. As the first of his new strictly liturgical projects, and as settings of the central element of Catholic ritual, the Masses must obviously have held a special importance for him. His regard for them is shown most graphically by the fact that he arranged for their publication: which must have been a very risky action. And we are very lucky indeed that he undertook it, for only two of the Masses seem to survive in independent manuscript copies of the time.* As compared with Byrd's motets of the 1580s, the liturgical music of the 1590s and 1600s circulated much less widely in contemporary manuscript collections.

[2]

One's first instinct in approaching Byrd's Masses is to look around for models, such as can be found for his motets and most other musical genres that he began composing early in his career: though 1592 is not early in Byrd's career, and by this time he could certainly not be considered to be in need of guidance. The musical style and form of the Masses themselves give the impression—hard to substantiate, but strong nonetheless—of having emerged as a highly individual synthesis of the composer's own experience and imagination. In any case, Mass models were a good deal harder to come by in England in 1592 than motets and other shorter com-

*Baldwin's copy of the Three-Part Mass in R.M.24.d.2 and Hamond's copy of the Four-Part Mass (not that of the Three-Part) in Mus.f.16–19. That the former is independent appears from the collation given in Hudson's edition, though Hudson states that Baldwin copied from the first edition. Hamond's copy of the Four-Part Mass contains a substantial variant in the alto voice at the second Osanna, BW 1, 61, bar 6 and 62, bar 1: dotted minim A♭, quavers GF, minims GG, semibreve G, minims A♭B♭.

positions. For obvious reasons, Masses do not appear at all frequently in Elizabethan manuscripts.

Of the few that do appear, fewer yet are Continental. It is interesting that a manuscript owned by Petre includes a handful of 6-part Osanna and Agnus Dei sections excerpted from Masses by Clemens non Papa, printed in the 1550s. Presumably Byrd knew this manuscript. Later Edward Paston had his scribes copy out numerous sections from Victoria Masses published in 1576 and 1583, and later still the whole of the same composer's *Missarum liber secundus* of 1592. But this was long after Byrd had written his own Masses—indeed, after he had written the *Gradualia* of 1605 and 1607, excerpts from which appear next to Victoria in the same Paston manuscripts. Another of Byrd's patrons, Lord Lumley, had a copy of Palestrina's widely-circulated *Missarum liber quintus* of 1590 in his library, but again this was probably acquired after 1600.*

If memory needed jogging, English Masses were more readily available in copies than Continental ones, and would surely have meant more to Byrd. He had no need for models in a technical, compositional sense. But his new commitment to music for the Catholic life brought him closer than ever before to issues of traditionalism in music as well as in religion; an urgent tenet of Elizabethan Catholicism was its continuity with the past. By returning to liturgical composition, Byrd was asserting a similar continuity, and in this endeavour music of the Sarum rite may well have offered him inspiration in the broadest, most literal meaning of the term.

In order to see and perhaps to sing specific Masses of the past Byrd could have turned, for example, to his friend John Baldwin, who is known to have had access to a great variety of old English music (Baldwin actually completed or recopied part of the Forest-Heyther manuscript, a major source of Tudor Masses). Byrd would have been less interested in the central

*Petre's MS is Essex County Record Office D/DP.Z.6/2 (the only complete Mass it contains, however, is English—Fayrfax's *Missa Sponsus amat sponsam*). Fragments of Victoria Masses of 1576 and 1583 appear in Add. 41556, RCM 2035 and 2036; the 1592 book is copied into Add. 18936-9. See also Tenbury 359-63 and RCM 2041. The Palestrina is the last item in the Lumley catalogue of 1609, following several numbers after Byrd's 'kyries' and *Gradualia*: see *The Lumley Library: The Catalogue of 1609*, ed. S. Jayne and F. R. Johnson (London, 1956), 248ff. (The entry actually says 'manuscript 1591', but the editors assume that the second edition of 1591 is meant.)

Information about the Victoria copies in Add. 18936-9 has been kindly communicated by Davitt Moroney, who notes that the *Liber secundus* is a liturgical collection covering the Church year. It contains the Masses *O magnum misterium* for Christmastide, the *Missa Quarti toni* appropriate to Lent, *Trahe me post te* for Eastertide, *Ascendens Christus* for Ascensiontide, *Vidi Speciosam* for the Assumption and *Salve Regina* for the summer season, plus a Requiem Mass and the *Asperges* and *Vidi aquam*. But Paston's scribe jumbles the music thoroughly and arranges it according to the number of voice parts.

tradition of huge festal Masses, exemplified by Taverner's 6-part *Gloria tibi Trinitas* and in another way by Tallis's 7-part *Puer natus est nobis*, than in the simpler, shorter compositions for four voices which seem to have become popular from around the middle of Henry VIII's reign. Taverner's *Mean* Mass (for five voices, but with very extensive sections for four) was perhaps the most powerful single stimulus for this development.* And Philip Brett has observed that the Sanctus of Byrd's first Mass, the Four-Part Mass, is closely modelled on the Sanctus of the *Mean* Mass. Taverner's Sanctus is indeed one of the four-part sections, developing the 'head theme' which opens all four movements. In halved note values, Taverner's motive is taken over by Byrd, as well as a cardinal feature of Taverner's treatment of it in the Sanctus (and Agnus, though not in the Gloria or Credo): namely the expansion of the upward scale line from a fifth to a sixth to a seventh. Byrd even quotes the memorable half close that Taverner writes in the middle of his 'head theme' sections—and writes twice in the Sanctus, with a striking modification the second time.

At a number of other points in the Four-part Mass Byrd's reference to Taverner's composition is apparent. Of all the many instances in which Byrd can be seen to have derived his work from that of another composer, this is perhaps the most remarkable, and also the most paradoxical. Byrd's instinct was to look to the past, the Catholic past. He looked back past the Masses of Sheppard and Tallis to pay homage to the greatest of his predecessors. Yet Taverner's musical style and his whole stance towards Mass composition are so remote from Byrd's that comparison simply points up the chasm between them. It is impossible to feel that Byrd 'learned' from Taverner, as in earlier years he had learned from Tallis, Parsons and Ferrabosco. One thinks of certain mature Brahms pieces which adopt a tonal strategy from Beethoven: the derivation may be clear, but the musical gesture is completely independent and individual.

In addition to this specific modelling on Taverner, there are other respects in which Byrd's inspiration for the composition of Masses was English. In the Four-Part Mass, he seems to have experienced some uncertainty as to the right place to make the second division in the Credo; this was exactly the point at which English composers habitually made cuts in the Credo text, and could therefore not have provided any guidance. It may also be significant, in view of the traditional omission of the Kyrie from English Mass settings, that the Kyrie of the Four-Part Mass is the most consistently imitative—the most Continental, in a sense—of all Byrd's Mass movements, and that on the other hand the Kyrie of the Three-Part Mass employs a

*See Benham, *Latin Music*, p. 138f. *et passim*.

stark litany style unlike anything else in the rest of that composition. More important is the native precedent for Byrd's use of short sections for a reduced number of voices at the beginnings of movements and major sections of movements. Here he was looking back not to the repertory of smaller Masses (or at least, not to what we know of this thanks to Gyffard), but rather to the festal repertory, whose traditions in this respect he completely reinterpreted for his own use in a very different context. The semi-choir sections are whittled down and their exuberance tamed. Yet an archaic flavour remains—in their insistent free canonic writing, in their harmonic idiom coloured by 6–5 progressions, and in their not infrequent medieval-sounding cadences.

Elsewhere, of course, Byrd's writing is much more modern, and many passages in the Gloria and Credo movements of the Four- and Five-Part Masses are scarcely to be distinguished in style from parallel passages in Continental Masses of the time. But while a foreign musician might have approved and indeed admired many passages in these works, two features about them in particular would have astonished him. First, all of them are freely composed. Not one of them is derived from a polyphonic model such as a motet, nor from a simple Gregorian melody as in the category popularized by Palestrina of small-scale Masses based on hymn tunes. Apart from the lack of external reference, this means that Byrd's Masses also lack the intensive web of thematic repetitions and cross-references that results from the derivation (or 'parody') technique. They use the same or similar material to open most of the movements: 'head themes' link the Kyrie, Gloria, Credo and Agnus Dei of the Four-Part Mass (the Sanctus is modelled on Taverner, as we have seen), the same four movements of the Five-Part Mass, and the Kyrie, Gloria and Credo of the Three-Part Mass, in which, additionally, the Agnus Dei is thematically linked to the Benedictus. Beyond this the Byrd Masses display only a few internal thematic interrelationships.*

The other glaring feature that distinguishes Byrd as a composer of Masses is his refusal to spin out the shorter Mass texts into musical passages of some amplitude and independent musical development. He sets the phrase of the Kyrie, Benedictus and Agnus Dei at no greater length—with no more word repetition—than many phrases of the long Gloria and Credo texts. In this Byrd stands apart as sharply from his English forbears as from his Continental contemporaries. The Benedictus of Taverner's *Mean* Mass is its most expansive (and perhaps its most beautiful) moment. Even in Palestrina's very short Masses such as *Aeterna Christi munera* and

*For a somewhat different account, see Andrews, *Byrd's Polyphony*, 267ff.

Iste confessor in the *Liber quintus*, where he rattles through the Gloria and Credo in from 25 to 50 percent less time than Byrd takes, he invariably grants much more leisurely treatment to the Kyrie, Agnus Dei and especially the Benedictus.

These two peculiarities (as a foreign musician would have regarded them) point to the special seriousness with which Byrd embarked on the composition of the Masses. His concise treatment of the shorter texts seems to bespeak a determination not to be diverted by purely musical considerations, a determination to concentrate on irreducible liturgical requirements. If musical ornamentation is wanted, Byrd seems to be saying, this can be accomplished in other compositional genres without impinging on the most solemn rite of the Church. His point of view is unassailable, though in skimping on the Benedictus, in particular, one can feel that he was carrying seriousness to the point of austerity, if not positive asceticism. Also austere is his apparent rejection of the derivation technique, which was universal on the Continent and well known in England, where it had been adopted by Taverner and Tallis among others. For almost all Catholic composers except Byrd, the composition of Masses was an exercise many times repeated, sometimes very many times. It was carried out within one tradition or another that provided certain ready aids for a task that without them would have been onerous indeed. Byrd availed himself of none of these aids. When he came to compose the Four-Part Mass, he thought through his response to every portion of the text, every relationship, every point of balance, every formal problem afresh, from the ground up. And he did the same with each of the others, except insofar as the Four-Part Mass served as a model—an incipient individual tradition—for the later works.

The unusual seriousness of Byrd's attitude in this matter is explained directly enough by the actual circumstances in which his Masses were composed, in England in the 1590s. It must itself explain, though no doubt less directly, why in spite of their notable restraint, these works seem to many listeners to emanate an unusual integrity and special fervour. It is completely impossible, even somehow shocking, to think of Byrd as the author of a hundred Masses like Palestrina, or sixty like Lassus, or twenty like Victoria, or even eight like Taverner.

[3]

For Byrd and all other composers the movements of the Mass that cause problems are the Gloria and the Credo. The first decision is always how to sectionalize these lengthy texts. In the Four-Part Mass Byrd established the divisions that he holds to, with one exception, in both later compositions. There are two major divisions in the Gloria and three in the Credo, and further semichoir reductions as shown in Table 7. In the semichoir sections, the words are sung only by the semichoir and skipped entirely by the other voices. (There are, of course, also some shorter passages for a reduced choir which are always answered by other passages bringing the words in the remaining voices.)

TABLE 7: Sectionalization of Byrd's Gloria and Credo Movements

| | Sections for Reduced Voices | | |
	Four-Part Mass	Three-Part Mass	Five-Part Mass
GLORIA			
Et in terra	a 2		a 3
Laudamus te			
Domine Deus			a 4
Domine fili			
Domine Deus	a 3	a 2	a 3
Qui tollis	a 3		a 3
Qui tollis	a 3		a 3
Qui sedes			a 4
Quoniam			
CREDO			
Patrem omnipotentem	a 2		a 3
Visibilium			
Et ex patre	a 3		
Deum de Deo			
Qui propter	a 3		a 3
Et incarnatus			a 3
Crucifixus	a 3		a 3
Et resurrexit			
Et in spiritum		a 2	a 3
Qui cum patre			a 3
Et unam sanctam			
Confiteor			a 4
Et exspecto			

These divisions are somewhat idiosyncratic. Byrd divides the Gloria not at 'Qui tollis', as is customary, but one phrase earlier, with the result that the three-fold prayer of the 'Qui tollis' opens with the three-fold apostrophe

'Domine Deus, agnus Dei, filius patris' which also serves as antecedent for the 'qui'. One wonders whether he did this for syntactic reasons to reflect the way he had been taught to read and punctuate the Gloria text.* On the other hand he might have decided on this division in order to highlight the previous words 'Iesu Christe'. In the Four-Part Mass these words are repeated several times to make an impressive cadence, and the setting of the next 'Iesu Christe' a little later highlights the words even further by referring back to the original music:

. . . Domine fili unigenite *Iesu Christe.*|Domine Deus, agnus Dei, filius patris. Qui tollis peccata mundi, miserere nobis. Qui tollis peccata mundi, suscipe deprecationem nostram. Qui sedes ad dexteram patris, miserere nobis. Quoniam tu solus sanctus, tu solus Dominus, tu solus altissimus, *Iesu Christe* . . .

As for the Credo, Byrd perhaps had logic on his side in making the first break at 'Qui propter nos homines et propter nostram salutem descendit de coelis', rather than at the next phrase 'Et incarnatus est'. But most composers have been sufficiently struck by the concept of the incarnation to make the division at the later point. In the Four-Part Mass, indeed, Byrd works his way through these words as though they left him relatively unmoved. In the later compositions he sets the 'Et incarnatus' in a more expressive way, but he still holds to the same early division.

The Credo of the Four-Part Mass has a second irregular division, at the phrase 'Et unam sanctam catholicam et apostolicam ecclesiam':

. . . cuius regni non erit finis. Et in Spiritum Sanctum Dominum, et vivifi-cantem, qui ex patre filioque procedit. Qui cum patre et filio simul adoratur, et conglorificatur, qui locutus est per prophetas.|Et unam sanctam catho-licam et apostolicam ecclesiam. Confiteor unum baptisma in remissionem peccatorum, et exspecto resurrectionem mortuorum, et vitam venturi saeculi. Amen.

There seem to have been two reasons for this. Byrd had the quaint idea of illustrating the words 'non erit finis' by means of a conspicuously incon-clusive cadence, which effectively ruled out the customary break at 'Et in Spiritum Sanctum' (Ex. 34). Also he obviously wanted to emphasize as strongly as possible the article of belief in a holy Catholic Church. In the

*One thinks also of the Masses of Schubert.

Ex. 34

original partbooks of all three Masses, the words 'Catholicam', 'Apostolicam' and 'Eccelesiam' are always printed with initial capital letters.

This division has two obvious disadvantages, however. It leaves a rather uncomfortably short final section for the Credo text, and it slights the Holy Spirit—or, if that puts the case too strongly, at least it obscures the effect obtained by the division at 'Et in Spiritum Sanctum' of three sections in the Credo devoted principally to the Father, the Son and the Holy Ghost. In any case, things worked out awkwardly on account of the similar and (as it seems here) redundant homophonic or half-homophonic style employed for the phrases 'Et in Spiritum Sanctum', 'Qui cum patre et filio', 'qui locutus est' and 'Et unam sanctam . . .' In the later Masses Byrd reverted to the traditional division at 'Et in Spiritum Sanctum' and found other ways to underline the concept of the holy and apostolic Catholic Church.

Byrd evidently thought better of his treatment of several aspects of the Four-Part Mass, in tone as well as in form. He had mismanaged the end of the Credo at his first try, and it is to the correction of this mistake that we can attribute the most important change he made in the dimensions, or proportions, of the Four-Part Mass when he came to plan the Five-Part composition. The section from 'Et in Spiritum Sanctum' to the end is now 20 percent longer: which is the main reason why the Credo as a whole is some 10 percent longer. Yet Byrd's general tendency in both later Masses was to compress his original dimensions, not expand them. With the Three-Part Mass, no doubt, his hand was forced, but with the Five-Part Mass he certainly made a deliberate compositional choice. While keeping the Sanctus and Agnus Dei movements roughly the same size as before, he set the Kyrie and Gloria much more concisely.

Byrd's setting of these movements seems to represent an austere reaction to purely musical indulgences of the earlier composition—where, for example, the three-fold prayer of the Kyrie is set to three points of imitation of increasing length and density, with a natural climax on the last of them. In the Five-Part Mass, on the contrary, the contrapuntal elaboration decreases, section by section; the final Kyrie, set as a relatively brief and simple ostinato, can almost be experienced as an exaggerated cadence to the Christe, rather than as a third new idea. The result, in any case, is a movement that is shorter by almost a third, 25 breves rather than 37. As for the Gloria, here Byrd cut down ruthlessly on what he must have regarded as the excessive word-repetitions of the Four-Part Mass, particularly at 'Deus pater omnipotens' and 'Iesu Christe' and in the trios beginning the second section. The compression here amounts to about 15 percent.

Byrd's use of sections for a reduced number of voices has already been mentioned. The archaic style manifest to some degree in almost all this music makes it stand out all the more from the 'full' texture. The device of voice reduction is always applied for purposes of contrast, of course; but passages in which contrast seems to be desired on general or expressive grounds are worth distinguishing from those in which it serves an essentially formal function. Passages of the latter kind, in particular, might well be sung by soloists. And in respect to these 'formal' duos, trios and quartets, Byrd once again established in the Four-Part Mass the general plan that he would follow later. Semichoir sections begin the Gloria, Credo and Agnus Dei. The 'Pleni' is set as a trio. The Agnus Dei increases the number of voices from two to three to four in Agnus I, II and III.

The Five-Part Mass does much the same. Furthermore, it can be seen to systematize the somewhat haphazard use of semichoir sections to mark the sectionalization of the Gloria and Credo in the earlier composition (see Table 7). There Byrd sets off the break in the Gloria (at 'Domine Deus') by means of three successive trios, but does not carry out this scheme in the Credo; while the Credo also contains three trios, only one of them is placed at one of the breaks ('Qui propter nos homines') and the others occur elsewhere (at 'Et ex patre natum' and 'Crucifixus'—presumably for expressive reasons). Planning the Five-Part Mass, he analyzed the Gloria text more carefully and placed *four* reduced-voice sections at the break, the point being that after 'Domine Deus' there comes the three-fold prayer 'Qui tollis . . .', so it is more logical to keep the reduced texture for the four sections, rather than three. Then in the Credo both of the divisions (at 'Qui propter' and 'Et in Spiritum Sanctum') are demarcated symmetrically by means of pairs of trios. The Three-Part Mass makes little use of voice reduction, bringing duos at 'Domine Deus', 'Et in Spiritum Sanctum' and Agnus II only.

[4]

Of Byrd's three settings of the Ordinary of the Mass, the Four-Part Mass is the most intense, personal, and highly coloured. An immediate indication of this is its mode, the Dorian with a range extending from the low third in the bass to the high seventh in the soprano, which Byrd had reserved for some of his most expressive motets in the *Cantiones sacrae*, such as *Vide Domine afflictionem nostram*, *Haec dicit Dominus* and *Circumdederunt me* (see Ex. 3c). In each of these compositions the soprano touches the high octave only once—in the Mass, at the words 'ascendit in coelum'. The transposition to G is used, with E♭ added to the signature since as usual the frequent lowering of the sixth degree inclines the music towards the Aeolian. But there are many clearly Dorian details involving E♮, and Byrd provides each of the movements except the Agnus Dei with one almost self-consciously prominent cadence in D, the characteristic Dorian dominant cadence.* In the Gloria and Credo these cadences seem to emphasize certain key text phrases—'tu solus *altissimus*, Iesu Christe' and 'Crucifixus etiam *pro nobis*'. For the rest, the Four-Part Mass like the others seems deliberately restrained in harmonic range. Subdominant cadences are even scarcer than dominant ones; almost all harmonic shifts are to B♭ or F.

Another indication of intensity is the presence of a number of striking dissonant passages, striking not only in themselves but also because they appear in a matrix that in general remains consonant. There is a quality of high relief in the Four-Part Mass that the others do not share. The listener first becomes aware of this at the end of the Christe, perhaps, when an unexpected upward-sixth leap to f in the tenor clashes with a suspended e♮ in the alto, causing a 2–3 progression, or 9–8 in respect to the bass note D. Then Kyrie II builds on a brief 2-part cell, lasting for only two breves and deriving its main energy from its cadential 7–6 progression. Again the suspension dissonance is typically a piercing major seventh.

This cell is in fact an unusual one for Byrd. It is true that in the familiar 'cell' technique of the 1580s cells depend on dissonances to make the cadences that give them their definition; but since the cells are relatively long and (usually) relatively bland, the dissonances seem merely formal. The terseness of the configuration in the Kyrie forces attention onto its cadential dissonance and its expressive potential, a potential that is realized magnificently at its last appearance, as the bass and alto draw apart from a tenth to a fifteenth (see Ex. 35, bars 4–5). Byrd had seldom used cells of this kind before because he had seldom worked on so concise a scale. And such examples as can be found earlier are mostly examples in the pathetic vein, such as the phrase 'Peccavi' in the manuscript motet of the same name (see Ex. 19) and 'in paupertate/virtus mea' in *Defecit in dolore* (1589/1). This dissonant second Kyrie is recalled several times by dissonant passages later in the Four-Part Mass.

*These are perfect cadences except for a half close in the Gloria.

Ex. 35

The imitations in Kyrie I generally proceed by a stretto interval of two semibreves and outline only tonic, dominant, and subdominant harmonies. The Christe is arranged as a more involved and tighter stretto, making a strong cadence in the dominant. Kyrie II begins by imitating its cell after three semibreves—only to close up this time interval in the sequel, unravel the two parts of the cell so as to supply a whole array of even closer strettos, and introduce a diminution and two free off-beat entries for good measure. The music is more highly organized, around two parallel sequences by thirds, which provide clear intimations of the tonal areas of B♭ and F. This beautifully constructed second Kyrie caps a movement which as a whole beggars superlatives. It seems both a miracle of compression and a classic demonstration, in its small scope, of the principles of imitative polyphony and harmonic organization.

In Byrd's earlier music it would be hard to find anything of comparable contrapuntal intricacy and elegance worked out over so short a span. The first Kyrie is 10 breves long, the Christe 12, the second Kyrie 16. The story of Byrd's evolution as a motet composer from *Domine secundum actum meum* and *Da mihi auxilium* in 1575 to *Domine non sum dignus* and *Domine salva nos* in 1591 is one of increasing conciseness of expression; still, something like a quantum leap seems to have taken place at the point where he had to contemplate complete settings of the Mass text. Byrd's new phase as a composer of Catholic sacred music, determined by a change in attitude towards liturgical composition, was in technical terms a phase embodying new agility, pithiness and flexibility.

This may have had something to do with his decision to write Masses first for three and four voices, rather than for his customary choir of five or six. His main consideration might have been the reduced forces available at the clandestine services held in the country houses of the English Catholic gentry; but he might also have considered that it would be easier, at least at first, to achieve the necessary new conciseness working with leaner musical textures.

Kyrie I, Christe and Kyrie II each use a motive which is a variation of a falling fourth or fifth, and the Gloria opens with a bland canonic duo which is another such variation. (The Credo will open with yet another, and the Agnus Dei with exactly the same duo as the Gloria, up to the first rest.) 'Laudamus te' turns strongly for the first time to the subdominant, with a fine effect. The series of curt antiphonal duos here is made more vigorous by the same crotchet declamation (*bene*dicimus te, *ado*ramus te . . . *glori*am tuam'); both features are characteristic of this Mass and not of the others, but while the duos are easily explained as a response to the 4-part texture, the crotchet declamation must have been less technical than expressive in impetus, stemming from the work's special aura of intensity.* The first half of the Gloria concludes with a relatively long, dissonant setting of the words 'Iesu Christe' recalling the harmonic colouration of the second Kyrie, and a solemn half close.

Though the phrase 'Deus pater omnipotens' had turned briefly towards B♭ and F, the main harmonic contrast of this lucidly organized movement is not asserted until the advent of the trios beginning the second half. 'Domine Deus' moves sharply from G minor to F and both 'Qui tollis' trios end in B♭. Perhaps, indeed, Byrd's overriding concern in the trios was with textural and harmonic contrast, for in melodic or contrapuntal terms they make no particular impression. There is more real musical profile to the half-homophonic 'Qui sedes', which is still in F, and to the 'Quoniam', where brilliant antiphonal duos are resumed and the music works its way back to a second solemn half close in G minor at the echoing words 'Iesu Christe'. Then the movement is over in thirteen breves overlapping a small 'Amen' which develops material from the preceding 'in gloria Dei patris'.

As has already been indicated, the Credo of the Four-Part Mass presents more than an expansion of the ideas introduced in the Gloria. For example, the first full-choir section starting at 'visibilium omnium' in the Credo has no precedent in the Gloria. Despite the presence of free stretto imitations, the music of this short phrase sounds more like animated homophony, and the same is really true of the longer one which soon follows, 'Et in unum Dominum Iesum Christum', despite the strict and strong canon between outer voices. Then 'filium Dei unigenitum' is organized as a series of resolving suspensions and appoggiaturas over a line in the bass that plunges down from e♭ to D. The insistent 6–5 progressions give this passage an impressive archaic

---

*All three Masses use declamation on two or more successive crotchets in all voices for the words 'et ascendit', 'vivificantem' and 'resurrectionem' in the Credo. The Three-Part Mass adds 'consubstantialem', 'secundum scripturas' and 'et vitam venturae'—all still from the Credo. The Four-Part Mass adds half a dozen more phrases, from the Gloria, Credo and Agnus Dei.

character, though the distinctive sonority does not seem to have been chosen to bring out the words or to play a clear role in the composition as a whole.

The Credo also differs from the Gloria in its trios. Those in the Gloria are more traditional, each treating two successive themes in free canon and spacing the voices almost always at the time interval of a breve or more. Of the trios in the Credo 'Et ex patre' is essentially homophonic and 'Crucifixus' strictly so, at least for four breves; both sections begin with chords in close position and continue in open position with tenths between outer voices. And although the 'Qui propter nos' trio is freely canonic, the effect is again more homophonic than polyphonic because the canon involves only two voices, its time interval is a tight semibreve, and the third voice doubles the first strictly in tenths. The sound of the tenths in these homophonic trios stands out as a new sonorous resource which Byrd was to make special use of later.

For the phrase 'consubstantialem patri' a motive is combined with its diminution and also with its augmentation—a contrapuntal artifice not often encountered in the Masses or, for that matter, in Byrd's other work. He may have intended this as an illustration of the words; though if so it would seem that his understanding of consubstantiality was not of something very exact. He probably also intended the half close at the end of the first large section of the Credo ('per quem omnia facta sunt') to echo that in the Gloria ('Iesu Christe'), for the same distinctive 9–8 suspension occurs in both.

After the restrained phrases beginning the second section, 'Qui propter nos homines', 'Et incarnatus est' and 'Crucifixus', the next text sequence is set with the greatest energy and variety. 'Et resurrexit' marches up the scale and 'et ascendit in coelum' takes wing until the voices are well past their normal ranges. 'Ad dexteram patris' develops a splendid polyphonic flurry. When the swinging motive for 'et iterum venturus est' is transformed into the one for 'cum gloria iudicare', a duple-time ostinato hammering away at F conflicts artfully with the motive's basic triple metre.

Like other composers of Masses, Byrd found more to stimulate his imagination in these vivid descriptive phrases than in the doctrinal articles of faith that follow; here his evident concern to enunciate everything clearly led to a rather faceless result. The awkward division at 'Et unam sanctam' has already been commented on. The last section of the Credo parallels that of the Gloria; 'et vitam venturi' is of about the same length and character as 'in gloria Dei patris', and the two 'Amen' cadences are constructed similarly. (This is also the case, as has just been mentioned, with the central half closes of the two movements at 'Iesu Christe' and 'per quem omnia facta sunt'.)

In harmonic terms, the Credo is shaped less clearly than the Gloria, perhaps because the text was too long to be divided up so simply; in any case the individual phrases are less clearly organized around a harmonic centre. The tonal plan of the Sanctus, on the other hand, could not be more lucid:

Sanctus	Domine Deus	Pleni	Osanna I		Benedictus	Osanna II
(i) (i) v	i	III	$\frac{1}{2}$i		iv	i

A *da capo* of the Osanna would not fit into this plan, and Byrd instead recomposed the second Osanna using much the same material as in the first. This allowed him to treat Osanna II as the climactic element of the movement—a typical gesture for the Four-Part Mass which he would not repeat in the others. Osanna II is anticlimactic in the Three-Part Mass and exactly balanced in the Five-Part.

The final cadence of the movement echoes the striking Dorian colouration of the early cadence after the word 'Sanctus'. The initial three-fold 'Sanctus' acclamation had been set by three simple strettos on a rising scale figure, taken from Taverner. As the figure expands from a fifth to a sixth to a seventh, the Aeolian lowered sixth degree opens up inevitably to the Dorian raised sixth and thence to a dominant cadence. The harmonic quality of this cadence, in conjunction with its low pitch relative to the previous melodic peaks and preliminary cadences, makes for a remarkable mood, a quiet intensity of awe. Of all the trios in this Mass, the 'Pleni' is the most archaic. Next to it the motive for 'qui venit' in the Benedictus seems almost startlingly modern.

And then the famous Agnus Dei: a movement which exposes the high relief of the Four-Part Mass to the sharpest possible illumination. The harmony is almost purely consonant up to the concluding 'dona nobis pacem' point. The duo that constitutes Agnus I extends its bland gestures much farther than the parallel duos at the beginning of the Gloria and Credo; but Agnus II, a trio, grows more expressive, especially with the unusual repeated-note motive (CB♭B♭A, etc.) for 'miserere nobis'. A strangely affecting dotted-crotchet figure, sung sequentially by the bass alone, leads the music to a cadence in B♭ with the help of the first A♭ heard since early in the Gloria. The opening of Agnus III is more expressive yet; a beautifully crafted imitative sequence *a 4* makes this last approach to the Lamb the most emotional. For the words 'qui tollis peccata mundi' a rather stern passage, freely repeated, returns the music to G minor.

But none of this prepares the listener or the communicant for the 'dona nobis pacem', which as the last phrase of the entire Mass is also the most extended. If it seems to last even longer than its sixteen breves, that is probably because of its pedal structure and its ostinato rhythm, features that work with the unique harmonic style to create one of Byrd's darkest and most unforgettable pages. In principle each of the thirty-one semibreves prior to the cadence carries a suspension dissonance, and each of these suspensions (till the last) resolves to a minor chord. Five of the dissonances involve a major seventh, another five the even more piercing minor second or ninth. This recalls the feeling of the second Kyrie in a most powerful way, and intensifies it. Simply in formal—to say nothing of expressive—terms the conception is quite remarkable for the period, for of course there is no direct thematic recall: though Byrd again uses a very short 2-part cell constructed so as to pile up dissonances, the new cell differs from the old in its canonic form as well as in its actual melodic content. At the last moment the heavy minor-mode sonorities are dispelled by a major dominant chord and a *tierce de Picardie*, like a ray of light cutting through the darkness. The effect is practically baroque.

Seldom indeed do settings of the Mass text, in Byrd's time or any other, end with so deeply troubled an appeal for spiritual peace. One hesitates to read into it the state of mind of a composer who lived four hundred years ago; yet this is music that speaks with an unaccustomed personal intensity. In terms of dissonance, certainly, Byrd had never written anything so extreme, nor would he do so again in later years. The closest precedents, in the motets of the 1580s, are passages such as 'conversum est in luctum' from *Vide Domine afflictionem nostram* (1589/9), 'gementes et flentes' from *Salve Regina* (1591/6), and 'qui in Domino moriuntur' from the funeral motet *Audivi vocem de coelo* (BW 8/7).

[5]

One particular texture in the Four-Part Mass appears to have provided its composer with a point of departure for what was presumably his next essay in the form. He needed to draw on all his experience, for it was a sufficiently tricky essay that he had assigned himself—or, as is more likely, had had assigned to him by one of his patrons, probably Petre, someone who fancied a polyphonic Mass from Byrd's hand designed for the most modest of musical forces. Setting the entire Mass text for three voices required much more art—though inevitably art of the kind that conceals art—than setting it for four or five.

Wherever possible he adapted ideas from the earlier composition. First, a sonority: a 3-part texture defined by parallel tenths between the outer voices, with the inner voice proceeding either homophonically (as in the 'Et ex patre natum' and 'Crucifixus' trios of the Four-Part Credo) or else in close canon (as in 'Qui propter nos homines'). This sonority controls the slight Kyrie of the Three-Part Mass; and the 'head theme' of the piece is not so much a melodic element as a textural one (Ex. 36; cf. also Ex. 39). Beyond

Ex. 36

Ky - ri - e   e - lei - - son.   Pa - trem om - ni - po - ten - tem,

direct recurrences of this complex, at 'Et in terra pax' and 'Patrem omni-potentem' and perhaps elsewhere, harmonic textures determined by parallel tenths figure very prominently in the Gloria, still prominently in the Credo, and only somewhat less so in the later movements.

Besides establishing this characteristic sonority, the Kyrie accomplishes very little, for Byrd did not afford it even the mildest contrapuntal elabor-ation, using instead the rock-bottom chordal style of his 4-part setting of the Litany of All Saints in the *Gradualia* (1605 *a* 4/16). (The Litany of All Saints begins and ends with the words 'Kyrie eleison. Christe eleison. Kyrie eleison'.) Unlike the *Gradualia* piece, the Kyrie of the Mass is apparently not based on a litany plainchant, even though it positively flaunts the tell-tale marks of the genre. Each of the three prayers is set only once (should they not perhaps be repeated, in the manner of litanies, to obtain the full number of statements required by the liturgy?); the melody of Kyrie I is repeated for the Christe; and that of Kyrie II sinks down to a low cadence a fourth below the level of the rest of the melody, as at the end of the Litany of All Saints plainchant.

This low cadence, a half close in D minor only eight breves from the opening in F, colours the whole work. More than any other Ionian com-position by Byrd, the Three-Part Mass favours the submediant at the expense of the dominant. The plan of the Sanctus reflects this bias, for example (compare the situation in the Four-Part Mass, p. 203):

Sanctus	Domine Deus	Pleni	Osanna I		Benedictus	Osanna II
(I) (ii) I	$\frac{1}{2}$ii	$\frac{1}{2}$vi	I		vi	I

Strong cadences on D occur as early as twenty-three breves into the Gloria and eighteen breves into the Credo (both of these cadences, incidentally, having been prepared even earlier by weaker ones in the same general harmonic area). Then in the Agnus Dei Byrd finely withholds submediant harmonies until the 'dona nobis pacem'. As in the Four-Part Mass, this phrase is the longest in the entire composition; the motives breathe and expand and combine and reflect on one another with a sense of leisure such as Byrd had up to now never allowed himself. In this stylistic context the three submediant cadences sound wonderfully rich as well as recapitulatory.

The difficult movements, as always, were the Gloria and the Credo, and it is with these that Byrd accomplished one of his most impressive *tours de force*, if perhaps also one of his most self-effacing. Everything is conducted with the greatest naturalness, plasticity and cogency; the music seems always transparent, alert, calm—calm even during the extremely effective illustrative passages in which the voices soar up to the heights. The means are those of the Four-Part Mass, of necessity applied even more concisely. There are many stretto imitations *a 3*, and others pitting one voice against two ranged in thirds or sixths, alternating with some homophonic fragments and an occasional antiphonal pair. At 'descendit de coelis' Byrd actually borrowed material from the Credo of the Four-Part Mass; but elsewhere he reconsidered his earlier treatment. Thus the 'Et incarnatus' is now largely homophonic and makes its effect by means of subdominant harmony suffused by E♭s—almost the only ones in the entire composition. And Byrd now writes a rich and rather mysterious low cadence at 'in remissionem peccatorum' which serves as a foil for the obligatory fireworks at 'et exspecto resurrectionem mortuorum', directly afterwards.

What gives these movements their special cogency, however, is a new attitude towards the text. This was Byrd's compensation for the obvious limitations of the 3-part texture. It is not a question of word-illustration— that is something that is handled more dramatically in the Four-Part Mass— but rather of a rhetorical shaping of entire sentences. The music links words and phrases that belong together in sense or syntax. In the Gloria, for example, the identical motive is used for the successive phrases 'Quoniam tu solus sanctus' and 'tu solus Dominus' (as well as 'cum Sancto Spiritu'), and the same is true of the three separate but parallel statements 'Domine Deus, rex coelestis', 'Domine fili' and 'Domine Deus, agnus Dei'. There are also more subtle cases. The motive for 'unigenite' expands into that for the next words 'Iesu Christe', and since this is the final point of the first half of the movement, there is time for the latter motive to grow even further and expand beautifully a second time prior to the cadence.

One of the best portions of this Mass is the ending of the Credo, starting at 'Et in Spiritum Sanctum'. After a passage in block chords for 'Qui cum patre et filio', with a faintly madrigalian touch of triple metre in reference to the Trinity, the words 'adoratur' and 'conglorificatur' are freely moulded together in melody and rhythm to bring out their parallelism (in sound, as well as in meaning). Byrd makes a rousing climax at the key phrase 'Et unam sanctam catholicam et apostolicam ecclesiam'; one has the illusion of many more than three voices as the bass marches with the soprano in tenths and the tenor responds sounding like an antiphonal choir. This is a splendid realization of the texture first used at 'Qui propter nos homines' in the Four-Part Mass.* Then 'ecclesiam' is trumpeted out in a passage which owes something to Byrd's ancient and now largely abandoned ostinato technique, arriving symmetrically three times on the dominant (Ex. 37). But in addition

Ex. 37

to emphasis and brilliance there is rhetorical unification here; the motives for the words 'unam', 'sanctam', 'catholicam' and 'apostolicam' evolve from one another in a smooth succession. The next phrases cleave together as a result of their common focus on the notes A and B♭ ('Confiteor unum baptisma' and 'in remissionem peccatorum'). Even the final sentence, 'et exspecto resurrectionem mortuorum, et vitam venturi saeculi', is held together as a sense unit more clearly than in the Four-Part Mass, despite the great similarity of the motives involved (Ex. 38). There the special excitement

Ex. 38

that infuses the piece as a whole erupts in reference to the resurrection of the dead. Here the second part of the thought, the life eternal, develops from the first more logically and—as the motive span of a fifth gives way to a sixth—in essence more triumphantly.

In the Sanctus, some ideas taken over from the Four-Part Mass are developed more quietly (at 'Sanctus' and 'Dominus Deus Sabaoth'). With

*It is also used, less effectively, at the start of the present Credo.

the 'Pleni' the listener is likely to feel, and not for the first time, that the composer has fallen back on routine—but only for a moment: a sudden rapid sequence for 'gloria tua' generates what is perhaps the only moment of genuine excitement anywhere in the whole composition. This merges into a feeling of genuine power at Osanna I. The motive expands brilliantly in range and rhythm, and an exhilarating canon guides in the cadence. This is another place where the grandeur of effect seems to belie the modest 3-part texture.

It is hard not to hear the Benedictus as a preliminary draft for the first Agnus of the Agnus Dei. They both open with exactly the same music, a luminous meditation for four breves on the chord of F major; this is a distinctive idea for Byrd, however simple it may look on the page. But the 'in nomine', at five breves, falls uncomfortably between two stools, between the epigrammatic terseness of so many of Byrd's settings of text fragments in the Gloria and Credo, and the slightly greater amplitude he needed to make a real musical point. So at least it seems by comparison with the 'miserere nobis' point following Agnus I, which is able to fit seven imitative entries into its span of eight breves. The gradual expansion of the motive, its subtly placed entries on and off the beat at intervals of five minims, the introduction of E♮s, and the dotted-minim figure interlocking in the strettos—these are the familiar but always fresh signs of Byrd's richest polyphonic writing, deployed here on a jewel-like scale.

Agnus II is a duo in which the tenor, starting with an augmentation of the dotted-minim figure, always moves more freely (that is to say, through larger intervals) than the bass which imitates it. The quieter bass version of the opening motive is picked up by the soprano for Agnus III, and then repeated in a light melodic variation graced by some exquisite unprepared dissonances (Ex. 39). In this passage Byrd must surely have meant to dilate

Ex. 39

further on the F major meditation of Agnus I; the feeling is even more intensely personal. And the 'dona nobis pacem' motive resumes the dotted-minim figure of the first 'miserere' motive, as well as the expressive expansion technique by which it was developed.

The technique of motivic unification here extends to the entire three-fold prayer that constitutes the Agnus Dei. Without much doubt this is the finest movement of the Three-Part Mass. It is hard to think of a more distinguished piece of 3-part writing in the whole of Byrd's output.

[6]

This may be a convenient place to mention two puzzles, one of them directly related to the Three-Part Mass, the other only tenuously.

Reference has already been made to the class of Elizabethan manuscripts that transmits a repertory of 3-part (and occasionally 4-part) fragments extracted from larger compositions, mostly Masses, *Magnificats* and votive antiphons from the reigns of Henry VIII and Mary. The earliest of these manuscripts, Christ Church 45, dating from the 1580s, contains a 3-part Sanctus ascribed to Byrd (BW 8/3). Only the word 'Sanctus' is set; the final cadence comes soon enough, after eighteen breves. What seems to be the *raison d'être* of the piece is a less than inspiring demonstration of how the same free canon on a descending scale figure can be fitted in at various points of a tenor cantus firmus, one that starts in *longae* but ends in the same note values (indeed with the same motive) as the canonic voices. Is this composition a fragment—perhaps the semichoir beginning of a complete Sanctus for a larger number of voices, itself part of a complete Mass that is otherwise lost? And is it really by Byrd?

The music is old-fashioned and devoid of character, recalling the canonic exercises on a plainchant recommended by Morley in the *Introduction* and issued in great numbers by lesser pedagogues like Farmer and Bathe.* If Byrd really wrote it he must have done so early on. It might well have been an isolated exercise, then, and not part of any larger complex. But the real puzzle is the cantus firmus, which corresponds fairly well with a Sanctus melody recorded only in Italian sources of the eleventh and twelfth centuries, and certainly *not* enshrined in the Sarum Gradual.† In the chart below, parentheses enclose cantus firmus notes which are not *longae*:

chant:	G A B C B	G A B C B A G F G A B A A G
	San — — — ctus	————————————
cantus firmus:	G A B C B (G A) G (A	C B A G F♯ G D G F♯) G
	San — — — — — —	— — — — — — — ctus

*Morley, *Introduction*, 179–86, John Farmer, *Forty Several Ways of Two Parts in One made upon a Playne Song* (1591), William Bathe, *A Briefe Introduction to the Skill of Song* (1596?).

†P. J. Thannabaur, *Das einstimmige Sanctus* . . . (Erlangen Arbeiten zur Musikwissenschaft, i, Munich, 1962), *Melodie 60*.

The other puzzle is the Kyrie of the Three-Part Mass. What is the meaning of its unusual setting in litany style? This style seems never to have been used in other sixteenth-century compositions of the Kyrie of the Mass, not even in those made to satisfy the strictest theories mooted at the Council of Trent, and not even in those made for the simplest or most severe occasions, ferial Masses or Masses for the dead. Yet there is a certain grand appropriateness to Byrd's idea, for historically speaking the Kyrie is in fact a vestigial litany. A relic of very early practice remains in the Paschal Vigil on Holy Saturday. After the Benediction of the Font the Litany of All Saints is sung, up to its concluding words 'Kyrie eleison, Christe eleison, Kyrie eleison', which are taken over as the beginning of Mass. The possibility suggests itself that Byrd might have written the Three-Part Mass for this very service.

This is a very attractive hypothesis, for at least two reasons. Byrd seems to have been drawn to the Paschal Vigil at several points in his lifetime: for this service he wrote *Alleluia. Confitemini Domino* in his early years and *Alleluia. Vespere autem sabbati* in the *Gradualia*. And more broadly, the *Gradualia* includes a whole set of 3-part Easter pieces (including the last named) set in the same mode and voice ranges as the Three-Part Mass. Might all this music have been written together as part of a single liturgical programme?

It is possible; but at least three cautions must be taken into account. The Mass on Holy Saturday is a special one, omitting both the Credo and the Agnus Dei. So if Byrd wrote the Three-Part Mass for this occasion, a second hypothesis becomes necessary: in its original form the piece must have comprised only the litany-like Kyrie, the Gloria and the Sanctus, and the other movements must have been added later to make the Mass more generally serviceable. One would be happier with this new hypothesis if the Three-Part Mass showed any signs of such joinery—and one is happier yet to see that it shows none. Second, the 3-part Easter music of the *Gradualia* does not, after all, employ the same style as the Mass, as we shall see, despite its similarity in certain external characteristics. Third, there is the inconclusive situation with the litany plainchant. This is *not* present in the Mass, though it *is* present in Byrd's 4-part litany setting in the *Gradualia*. He was under no obligation to be consistent in this matter, of course; the *Gradualia* piece may date from a later period when he had a different compositional idea in mind; and perhaps he hesitated to allow the Phrygian mode of the litany chant to dictate the mode of so large a composition as the Mass, especially in view of the season. Still, since Byrd employed only the litany style and not the litany chant itself, clear evidence is lacking of an actual connection between his Mass and the litany. And lacking this, we cannot say

confidently that the Three-Part Mass was actually composed for Holy
Saturday.

[7]

One turns with some sense of paradox to the Five-Part Mass, in which Byrd
drew for the first time on the full choral and contrapuntal resources that
produced his greatest music in other genres, to find a more reserved and
distant work than the Four-Part Mass. In certain ways it is more austere
even than the Three-Part Mass: in modal treatment, for example. The
linking of D and A minor chords by way of B♮ at the opening of the Kyrie
defines the Dorian mode unforgettably, especially after the auxiliary-note B♭
in the Kyrie motive itself. One would have expected to hear this B♮ again
when the motive is re-used to launch later movements, for as compared with
'head themes' that Byrd had used before—the homophonic texture in tenths
of the Three-Part Mass, and the neutral-sounding duo of the Four-Part
Mass, with its archaic English flavour—the one in this Mass is more significant, a tensile imitation on a motive whose expressive semitone inflection
seems more Continental than native. But Byrd removes the B♮ from the 'head
theme' in the Gloria and Credo, restoring it only in the Agnus Dei. And
prior to the Agnus Dei there is but a single cadence in the dominant—at the
words 'lumen de lumine' in the Credo. Harmonic illumination, apparently,
was to be kept to a minimum in this composition. It is written almost
throughout in the quiet, orderly D Aeolian mode which comes so strongly
to the fore in the *Gradualia*, with a range from the low fifth in the bass to the
high third in the soprano (see Ex. 3d).

Byrd's retrenchment from the full-scale imitative unfolding that he had
lavished on the 4-part Kyrie has been mentioned above. The harmonic
balance of the 5-part Kyrie, however, is no less finely calculated than in the
earlier composition. The prominent chords in Kyrie I, preparing the
cadence in D, are D and A minor and (perhaps) F major; the Christe adds
B♭ and G minor—this section ends in G—and Kyrie II subtracts A minor,
B♭ and F, so that the only remaining chords that count are G and D minor,
prior to the concluding half close.

As in the Three-Part Mass, many successive phrases of the Gloria and the
Credo are linked by their music into cogent rhetorical units. There is a
beautiful case in the Gloria at the phrase 'Quoniam tu solus sanctus', the
music of which echoes at 'tu solus Dominus' and then expands upwards at 'tu
solus altissimus'; and perhaps the graceful melismatic sequence ending the
latter phrase is itself echoed by the soprano at 'Iesu Christe'. Characteristically, the upward motion at 'altissimus' brings the soprano and alto to the

normal top of their ranges (f' and c') but no further. Unlike the other two Masses, the Five-Part Mass is never tempted by heady text fragments into any breach of registral proprieties.*

Also exceptionally fine is the text sequence in the Credo beginning with 'Et incarnatus'. This section itself, a trio for soprano and both tenors, opens with the tenors in canon at an unusual interval, the upper second. Out of this canon emerges an E♭, which is only the second to be heard in the entire composition; though not repeated—though, in fact, sharply contradicted—it serves nonetheless as a signal ahead to the subdominant shading of the 'Crucifixus'. In the phrase 'et homo factus est' the very surprising little melisma at the end of the motive, with its strange declamation, its regularity, and its slight awkwardness of contour, strikes an unmistakable and touching note of naive enthusiasm. More subtle is the sudden impression of muted grief conveyed by the particular level of placement of the homophonic 'Crucifixus' following the cadence to this phrase—grief contemplated at a distance but still actively felt. The harmonic progression, a B♭ sonority following a D major chord, recalls the progression that comes earlier in the Mass at the first mention of the Crucified, at the words 'Christe eleison' following the cadence of Kyrie I. The simple series of triads moving up the scale at 'passus et sepultus est' also makes its point with the greatest restraint and eloquence.

Once again, the doctrinal phrase 'Et unam sanctam catholicam et aposto-licam ecclesiam' receives special emphasis. The means could scarcely be more direct: solid homophony is employed throughout, for eleven breves, and this section for full choir is placed in between two for semichoir (see Table 7). After this Byrd seems reluctant to abandon homophony; even the grand descending-scale motive for 'in remissionem peccatorum' blends into fauxbourdon-like sonorities. The final phrase of the Credo, however, reverts to polyphony of a traditional kind in a concise phrase employing his charac-teristic 'cell' technique of the 1580s ('et vitam venturi saeculi'). In fact Byrd returned to a cell he had used twice before to wind up compositions ending with doxologies, the motets *Tribue Domine* (1575/16) and *O quam gloriosum* (1589/23).

'Cell' technique depends on a texture of five or more voices, and so does the special brilliance of this passage. But it is only in the Sanctus, one feels,

---

*In the Three- and Four-Part Masses, some of the voices overshoot their normal ranges at 'descendit de coelis', 'et ascendit in coelis' and 'et exspecto resurrectionem mortuorum' in the Credo, and all voices do so at 'tu solus altissimus' in the Gloria (also at the first 'Osanna in excelsis' in the Three-Part Mass). At all these places in the Five-Part Mass the voices certainly tend to move to the top of their ranges, but never past them.

that Byrd finally unleashes the full forces at his disposal, in his superb
settings of the opening acclamations and of the repeated Osanna. The
homophonic treatment of the words 'Domine Deus Sabaoth', too, seems
definitive, though he had worked effectively enough with the same basic
idea in both earlier Masses. At the words 'in nomine Domini' in the Benedictus, a quotation from Taverner's famous In Nomine may perhaps be
detected.* For all the magnificence of this movement, a certain note of
severity is added by the restriction of all the main cadences (and all or most
of the lesser ones) to full or half closes in D.

As in the other Masses, the Agnus Dei resumes and can be said to resolve
certain purely musical issues raised earlier in the composition. In Agnus I,
for three voices, the expressive 'head theme' of the Mass returns to its
original clearly Dorian colouration, coming indeed to a striking half close on
an E major chord; in Agnus II, for four voices, this is balanced by a repeated
cadence in G minor (Ex. 40). A similar but less sharply articulated harmonic

Ex. 40

plan underpins the Kyrie. An elegiac quality informs the two 'miserere'
points, the first with its long descending scale motive (a traditional idea that
Byrd used for his earliest setting of this word: see Ex. 5), the second with its
wonderful nostalgic dissonance arising from the augmentation (Ex. 40).
The mood is shattered by the beginning of Agnus III, by a 5-part homophonic exclamation which gives the last of the three appeals an immediacy
and vehemence unexpected in this composition. As the appeal begins in the
subdominant, G minor, a sequential repetition up a fifth can follow naturally
and achieve even greater intensity.

The characteristic mood of distance and reserve returns at the close of
the Mass, more palpable than ever after the previous outcry. The 'dona
nobis' motive—it is derived from the bass of the cadence on 'peccata mundi'
—first forms itself into a clear phrase but then seems to dissolve into a grey
mist of strettos. In this shadowy point a clear motive never emerges for
'pacem', and the final cadence, which is perfectly firm, is arrived at not by
means of strong dominant harmony but by repeated emphasis on modal

*See *Musical Times*, cxvii (1976), 739.

formulae. There is an extraordinary meditative quality to this quiet passage—
almost a timeless quality, one feels, though it lasts for only fourteen breves,
four of them taken up with the plagal codetta following upon the main
cadence. Thus Byrd depicts the spiritual peace for which the Lamb is
importuned. It is the first time in the Masses that he had attempted to do so.

[8]

'There is such a profound and hidden power in sacred words, as I have
learned by trial, that to one thinking upon things divine and earnestly and
diligently pondering them, the most suitable of all musical measures occur
(I know not how) as of themselves and suggest themselves spontaneously
to the mind that is not indolent and inert.' How are we to understand the
situation at the end of the Four- and Five-Part Masses, where the very same
sacred words—'Agnus Dei, qui tollis peccata mundi, dona nobis pacem'—
suggested such very different music? The context is about as conspicuous as
could be imagined. That the composer's mind was indolent or inert on one
occasion or the other is not a proposition that will be entertained by anyone
who knows the music. The pages in question are some of the most incandescent he ever wrote. One must conclude, rather, that on two different
occasions the mind was disposed very differently.

Speculation on Byrd's state of mind is obviously a delicate, even a danger-
ous undertaking, as it must be for any relatively undocumented figure of his
era. Shakespeare is another such figure. From the facts of his life we can
form a superficial idea of his personality, but he left no personal letters or
memoirs to help us fill this out, let alone any explicit autobiographical or
confessional statements. And the statements made by poets and composers
in their work require cautious interpretation. Shakespeare spoke on behalf
of the characters in his plays, and Byrd perhaps sang on behalf of his patrons
or his priests.

But there are moments in the work of both men when one is certain that
one hears a personal voice, and these two Agnus Dei movements are among
them. The first appeared in 1592–3, after a decade in which Byrd had
returned again and again in his sacred music to professions of guilt and
despair, and prayers for mercy and deliverance. In the Four-Part Mass the
ending prayer for peace is deeply clouded; and if at the very last moment it
seems to be answered, Byrd's marvellous resolution to the *tierce de Picardie*
seems the result of a miracle, as unexpected psychologically as technically
it is unprepared. In 1593 Byrd moved to Stondon Massey, presumably to
join the Catholic community presided over by the Petres. The Five-Part

Mass emerged two years or so later; and now the prayer for peace is calm and confident, its outcome never in doubt. The strange shadowy treatment of the 'dona nobis pacem' motive creates as nearly mystical an effect as Byrd ever achieved. Yet just before this prayer, the third invocation to the Lamb erupts like a great outcry. Was this a last sudden recollection on Byrd's part of the passions of the 1580s?

A Continental composer of the time would have been as astonished by the outcry in the Five-Part Mass as by the clouded, lamenting passage in the Four-Part. To recall the general aspect of contemporary Mass composition is to feel even more certain of the personal quality of Byrd's response. The Agnus Dei was simply not a movement to set expressively; dozens of Masses by Palestrina, Victoria, Lassus and others bear witness to this. Working outside the Continental tradition, and cut off in essentials from the older English tradition, Byrd responded to certain parts of the Mass text in an entirely individual way, and sometimes in different individual ways on different occasions. Only in the Three-Part Mass did he follow general practice and treat the Agnus Dei text as an abstract hieratic unit. That was of course a special technical exercise, and incidentally one with little contemporary precedent abroad. In the Four- and Five-Part Masses he was not so occupied with the technical problem as to preclude the kind of expressive commitment he made habitually in his greatest music. The Agnus Dei movements of these works make different theological statements, and it is hard not to believe that they represent distinct stages in Byrd's own developing spiritual life.

5

The *Gradualia*

The *Gradualia* with its hundred and nine items is by far the largest of the collections Byrd ever made of his music, and surely the most intricately arranged. To obtain even a general overview of its contents and understanding of its organization is no simple matter. We should begin with the composer's own words in the preface 'To the True Lovers of Music' in book 1 and the dedicatory letter in book 2:

> For you, most high-minded and righteous, who delight at times to sing to God in hymns and spiritual songs, are here set forth for your exercising the Offices for the whole year which are proper to the chief Feasts of the Blessed Virgin Mary and of All Saints; moreover others in five voices with their words drawn from the fountain of Holy Writ; also the Office at the Feast of Corpus Christi, with the more customary antiphons of the same Blessed Virgin and other songs in four voices of the same kind; also all the hymns composed in honour of the Virgin; finally, various songs in three voices sung at the Feast of Easter.

> I have attempted, out of devotion to the divine worship, myself unworthy and unequal, to affix notes, to serve as a garland, to certain pious and honeyed praises of the Christian rite to be sung by four, five or six voices. These are adapted to the glorious Nativity of Christ our Saviour, the Epiphany, the Resurrection, the Ascension, and finally to the Feast of Saints Peter and Paul.*

For some reason he forgot Whitsun in this list of book 2 feasts. This was not his only error or inconsistency, as we shall see.

Book 1 includes several liturgical units of a more or less informal nature, as Byrd specifies with some care: settings of the compline antiphons to the Blessed Virgin Mary, the set of Marian Hymns, and a group of miscellaneous pieces for the Easter season. But half of the contents of book 1 and practically the whole of book 2 are given over to what was clearly at the heart of Byrd's scheme, the provision of a formal schedule of 'offices' for the main

---

*Translations of the prefatory matter of both books of the *Gradualia* appear in O. Strunk, *Source Readings in Music History* (New York, 1952), 327ff.

feasts of the Church year. What he meant by 'office' in this connection appears most clearly from the later portions of book 2, headed by the rubrics 'In tempore Paschali', 'In Ascensione Domini', 'In festo Pentecostes' and 'In festo SS. Petri et Pauli'. In principle each feast is furnished with music for the main Proper texts at Mass—the introit, gradual, alleluia or tract, offertory and communion. Byrd also sets the sequence for most of the Masses that include this liturgical item, and adds one or more of the major Office texts, starting with the antiphon for the *Magnificat* at first or second Vespers. These Office texts were probably intended as much for general use as for a specifically liturgical function.

This, then, is the basic liturgical framework of the *Gradualia*. But one notices at once that there are some elements missing from the scheme, and others superfluous to it. For example, the last two pieces in book 2, *Laudate Dominum* and *Venite exultemus Domino*, have nothing to do with Sts. Peter and Paul under whose rubric they are found. They fall into the category of miscellaneous non-liturgical motets 'with words drawn from the fountain of Holy Writ' (from Psalms 116 and 94, to be precise) which Byrd dutifully accounts for in the book 1 preface. The motet *Solve iubente Deo* also appears under this rubric and also stands outside the scheme, or appears to. This text is the alleluia for St. Peter's Chains, a relatively minor feast celebrated on 1 August. Since this Mass is identical in all its other main parts to that of Sts. Peter and Paul, by providing *Solve iubente Deo* Byrd was in effect providing an extra 'office' which is not rubricated. He did the same for two other services, both associated with Corpus Christi: the Benediction of the Blessed Sacrament (1605 *a* 4/5–8*) and the Votive Mass of the Blessed Sacrament (1607/13–14 and 16). Probably Byrd omitted rubrics for these services not by oversight but simply because he saw them as significantly less important than the others.

Armed with this information, we can give a prospectus of the entire contents of the *Gradualia* as Table 8. The feasts or services in Byrd's basic scheme are indicated by capitals; those for which he provided music but no rubrics are enclosed in square brackets. In between come some non-liturgical motets and some less formal liturgical units. This table also gives the mode, key signature, and clef combination under each of the main rubrics. For it is a principle in the *Gradualia* that these basic musical elements remain constant throughout any specific feast or service. The principle is breached

---

*In book 1 (but not in book 2) Byrd established separate numerations for the 5-, 4- and 3-part fascicles. This abbreviation refers to Nos. 5–8 in the 4-part fascicle of book 1. From the binding of certain extant copies, incidentally, it appears that the three fascicles were clearly separated from one another.

only very rarely. The mode used most frequently is Aeolian transposed to D
with one flat in the signature, followed by Lydian or Ionian on F or C, then
by Mixolydian; only three or four of the miscellaneous pieces use the Dorian
or Phyrgian.

(Since in the later portions of this chapter the *Gradualia* Masses will not
be taken up in their order of publication, a column has been added to Table 8
indicating the pages on which discussions of the various items may be found.
The table, then, can serve as an index to all the material on the *Gradualia*
distributed throughout this book.)

TABLE 8: Summary Contents of the *Gradualia*, Books 1 and 2, 1605 and 1607

NOTE Numeration as in the original. Rubrics in capitals are adapted and translated
from those in the original partbooks, except as enclosed in square brackets. The
mode, key signature and clef combination is given for each of the main services
and groups of compositions.

Liber primus

a 5	1–25	[THE MARIAN MASSES:] PURIFICATION, NATIVITY, VOTIVE MASSES THROUGH THE YEAR, ANNUNCIATION, ASSUMPTION	(D,♭, ♮MATBar) *see* p.	250
	26	Adoramus te Christe		320
	27	Unam petii a Domino		320
	28	Plorans plorabit		158
	29–32	ALL SAINTS Nov.	(F,♭, ♮♮MABar)	241
a 4	1–8	CORPUS CHRISTI, [BENEDICTION OF THE BLESSED SACRAMENT]	(G, SATB)	285
	9	Ecce quam bonum		321
	10	Christus resurgens (Easter)		62
	11	Visita quaesumus Domine		322
	12–14	Three Marian Compline antiphons	(G, SATB)	323
	15	In manus tuas Domine		321
	16	Litany of All Saints		326
	17	Salve sola Dei Genitrix		327
	18–19	Two Magnificat antiphons (Purification)	(D,♭, SATB)	328
	20	Deo gratias		328
a 3	1–4	Four Marian hymns		329
	5	Regina coeli (Compline antiphon in P.T.)		331
	6–10	Five miscellaneous texts for the Easter season	(F,♭, SAT)	332
	11	Adorna thalamum tuum (Purification)		335

Liber secundus

It has been mentioned that certain elements are missing from Byrd's liturgical scheme. Taking the Mass of Sts. Peter and Paul as an example, once again, we find under the rubric of this feast the introit, two alleluias, three antiphons and what looks like the gradual, but no offertory or communion. A glance at the Roman Missal in use in Byrd's time will explain this apparent anomaly. The text of the offertory is identical to that of the gradual, *Constitues eos principes*, plus one extra phrase 'in omni progenie et generatione', and the text of the communion is that of the alleluia verse, *Tu es Petrus*, up to the concluding words 'alleluia'. Under the gradual Byrd set *all* the words including 'in omni progenie et generatione' which belong only to the offertory. He marked the cadence preceding this phrase with a *signum* and a barline, and in the alleluia verse he inserted a barline just before the terminal alleluia, as a way of indicating that in certain liturgical contexts the music is to be sung only up to these points. As James L. Jackman put it, in a fundamental article on the *Gradualia*,* there is a 'principle of economy' at work here. Where the same text occurs in two different liturgical situations, Byrd does not generally recompose it or print the music twice. The music is to be transferred from some other point in the partbooks and resung. This is occasionally indicated by means of specific rubrics, more frequently by the use of signs and barlines which otherwise make no sense.

*Jackman, *Gradualia*, 21.

TABLE 9: The Marian Masses of the *Gradualia*

NOTE Numeration as in the original 5-part fascicle. Rubrics are those provided by Byrd, except as enclosed in square brackets. Angle brackets enclose numbers or sections of numbers (indicated by three dots) which have to be transferred to fill out the liturgical scheme; transfers indicated by Byrd himself are marked with a superscript 'B'. Sections given in italics are for a reduced choir, generally consisting of three voices.

Byrd's usual practice with the alleluias is to detach the opening word 'alleluia' and include it at the end of the previous number (the gradual); see p. 236f.

In Festo Purificationis [2 February]

INTROIT	1	Suscepimus Deus ℣ *Magnus Dominus*. Gloria Patri. ⟨ Suscepimus Deus⟩
GRADUAL	⟨ 1	Suscepimus Deus . . .⟩ 2 ℣ *Sicut audivimus*. Alleluia
+ ALLELUIA	3	℣ Senex puerum portabat. Alleluia
after LXXᵐᵃ:		
GRADUAL	⟨ 1	Suscepimus Deus . . .⟩ 2 ℣ *Sicut audivimus* (without alleluia)
+ TRACT	4	Nunc dimittis ℣ *Quia viderunt* ℣ *Quod parasti* ℣ Lumen ad revelationem
OFFERTORY	⟨22	Diffusa est gratia . . .*⟩
COMMUNION	5	Responsum accepit Simeon

In Nativitate S. Mariae Virginis [8 September]

INTROIT	6	Salve sancta Parens (without alleluia) ℣ *Eructavit*. Gloria Patri. ⟨Salve sancta Parens⟩
GRADUAL	7	Benedicta et venerabilis 8 ℣ Virgo Dei Genitrix. Alleluia
+ ALLELUIA	9	℣ Felix es sacra Virgo. Alleluia*
OFFERTORY	10	Beata es Virgo Maria (without alleluia)
COMMUNION	11	Beata viscera (without alleluia)

[Missa Votiva de Sancta Maria:] Pro Adventum

INTROIT	12	Rorate coeli ℣ *Benedixisti Domine*. Gloria Patri. ⟨Rorate coeliᴮ⟩
GRADUAL	13	Tollite portas ℣ *Qui ascendit in montem Domini*. Alleluia
+ ALLELUIA	14	℣ Ave Maria . . . fructis ventris tui. Alleluia*
OFFERTORY	⟨14	Ave Maria . . . fructis ventris tuiᴮ (without alleluia)⟩
COMMUNION	15	Ecce Virgo concipiet (without alleluia)

Post Nativitatem [Domini usque ad Purificationem]

INTROIT	16	Vultum tuum (without alleluia) ⟨6 . . . ℣ *Eructavit*.^B Gloria Patri.^B Vultum tuum⟩

INTROIT 16 Vultum tuum (without alleluia) ⟨6 . . . ℣ *Eructavit*.B Gloria Patri.B Vultum tuum⟩

GRADUAL 17 Speciosus forma ⟨6 . . . ℣ *Eructavit*B . . . ⟩ *Lingua*. Alleluia

+ ALLELUIA† 18 ℣ Post partum. Alleluia

OFFERTORY 19 Felix namque es

COMMUNION ⟨11 Beata viscera^B (without alleluia)⟩

[Post Purificationem usque ad Adventum Domini]‡

INTROIT ⟨ 6 Salve sancta Parens (in P.T.: Alleluia) ℣ *Eructavit*. Gloria Patri. Salve sancta Parens⟩

GRADUAL ⟨ 7 Benedicta et venerabilis 8 ℣ Virgo Dei Genitrix. Alleluia⟩

+ ALLELUIA 20 . . . ℣ Virga Iesse. Alleluia

after LXX^{ma}:

GRADUAL ⟨ 7 Benedicta 8 ℣ Virgo Dei Genitrix (without alleluia)⟩

+ TRACT 21 *Gaude Maria Virgo* ℣ Quae Gabrielis ℣ Dum Virgo ℣ Dei Genitrix

OFFERTORY ⟨19 Felix namque es⟩

in P.T.:

ALLELUIA 20 ⟨Alleluia. ℣ Ave Maria . . . in mulieribus. Alleluia. ℣ Virga Iesse. Alleluia* ⟩

OFFERTORY 10 ⟨Beata es Virgo Maria. Alleluia⟩

from Pentecost to Advent:

ALLELUIA ⟨18 ℣ Post partum. Alleluia⟩

OFFERTORY ⟨14 Ave Maria (without alleluia)⟩

COMMUNION ⟨11 Beata viscera (in P.T.: Alleluia)⟩

In Annunciatione B. Mariae Virginis [25 March]

INTROIT ⟨16 Vultum tuum (in P.T.: Alleluia) 6 . . . ℣ *Eructavit*.B Gloria Patri.B Vultum tuum⟩

GRADUAL 22 Diffusa est gratia ℣ *Propter veritatem.*

+ TRACT Audi filia (without alleluia) ℣ *Vultum tuum* ℣ *Adducentur regi* ℣ Adducentur in laetitia

in P.T.:

ALLELUIA ⟨20 Alleluia. ℣ Ave Maria . . . in mulieribus. Alleluia. ℣ Virga Iesse. Alleluia⟩

OFFERTORY ⟨14 Ave Maria . . . fructis ventris tui (in P.T.: Alleluia)⟩

COMMUNION ⟨15 Ecce Virgo concipiet (in P.T.: Alleluia)⟩

In Assumptione B. Mariae Virginis [15 August]

INTROIT	23	Gaudeamus omnes...* ⟨6 ... ℣ *Eructavit.* Gloria Patri. Gaudeamus omnes⟩
GRADUAL	⟨22	... *Propter veritatem* ℣ Audi filia. Alleluia ...⟩
+ ALLELUIA	23	... ℣ *Assumpta est Maria ... angelorum.* Alleluia
OFFERTORY	24	Assumpta est Maria ... Dominum. Alleluia
COMMUNION	25	Optimam partem elegit

*Liturgical errors: No. 9, *Felix es sacra Virgo*: lacks the concluding words 'Christus Deus noster.' No. 14, *Ave maria ... fructus ventris tui*: the correct text here is *Ave Maria ... mulieribus* (as in No. 20; but *Ave Maria ... fructus ventris tui* is correct for the offertory). No. 20, *Alleluia. Ave Maria ... in mulieribus. Alleluia. Virga Iesse*: on this occasion the verses *Ave Maria* and *Virga Iesse* should be reversed; Byrd's order is correct for the Annunciation. No. 22, *Diffusa est gratia*: if it is to be used as the Purification offertory, this section lacks the concluding words 'et in saecula saeculi.' No. 23, *Gaudeamus omnes*: this introit is printed so as to run directly into the alleluia verse.

†In years when Easter (and hence Septuagesima Sunday) is early, it occasionally happens that a Saturday comes after Septuagesima and still before the Purification. The alleluia *Post partum* is omitted and the tract *Gaude Maria* (No. 21) is sung.

‡In liturgical books this is broken down into three parts: from Purification to Easter, Paschal Time, and from Pentecost to Advent. The most compressed form is given here; Byrd provided no rubrics at all in this whole season (save for an erroneous and puzzling 'Post Septuagesima' prior to the greater alleluia *Alleluia. Ave Maria*, No. 20; the motet that this rubric fits is the tract *Gaude Maria*, No. 21).

Analysis of the liturgical context is required to fill out the scheme. It should be said that musical transfers of this kind are required only in certain Masses—Sts. Peter and Paul, the Votive Mass of the Blessed Sacrament, and especially the large group of Marian Masses at the beginning of book 1—and that they almost always cause musical problems. In the Marian group, the liturgical situation is thoroughly tangled, and further confused by errors on the part of Byrd and his printer or editor, who seem to have got rather out of their depth. Table 9 is an attempt to sort out and spell out all the Marian Masses for which Byrd provided music, and the necessary transfers, in as simple a form as possible (which is, unfortunately, none too simple).

Not one of these Marian Masses can be read off directly from the part-books. Generally there is not enough music. In the very first Mass, the Purification, the gradual has to be patched together right away by repeating part of the preceding number, No. 1, before singing the verse, No. 2, and the offertory has to be made up (not quite accurately) by picking a section out of No. 22. Byrd says nothing about these operations. He gives rubrics directing similar ones only in the first two of the Votive Masses.* Sometimes there is

*See p. 260n.

actually too much music. The alleluias provided with the Nativity motets *Salve sancta Parens*, *Beata es Virgo Maria* and *Beata viscera* are not to be sung on that feast, but only when these texts are employed again for the Lady Mass in Paschal Time (see Table 9, under 'Post Purificationem usque ad Adventum Domini'). The presence of the alleluias, introduced after a full cadence and a barline so that they can easily be separated off, shows conclusively that Byrd had the Easter Mass in mind, though he provided no rubric for it. And since he had the Easter Mass in mind, we must assume that he meant the greater alleluia for the Annunciation, *Alleluia. Ave Maria. Alleluia. Virga Iesse*, No. 20, to serve here, even though in this position the two verses are in the wrong order.

[2]

The scheme that has just been described seems so highly individual, not to say quirky, that one would be very surprised indeed to find any model for it in some earlier, presumably Continental publication. Indeed a survey of the field serves only to underline the unique position of the *Gradualia* in the music of its time. Byrd was following precedent only in the broadest, most general sense that liturgical music is composed systematically for the Church year. This was a venerable principle which he knew from sources of the old Sarum repertory (such as the Gyffard Partbooks) and which had been accorded new emphasis on the Continent in the wake of the Council of Trent. The last decades of the century witnessed the publication of yearly cycles of hymns, responds, *Magnificat* antiphons and other liturgical categories in increasing numbers. This music was inspired by the Counter-Reformation, and the Jesuits were active in its promulgation. As has been suggested in chapter 1, it seems quite likely that Byrd's advisers in the *Gradualia* project were drawn from his friends in the Jesuit order.

If however we speak not of liturgical cycles in general but of actual yearly cycles of complete (or nearly complete) Propers, the *Gradualia* begins to look much more special. In early sixteenth-century Britain, Proper items (with the exception of alleluias) were very rarely set to music, let alone assembled into systematic collections. Even on the Continent at this time, such collections were prepared only occasionally, and almost always by composers in the German orbit. The greatest example, Isaac's *Choralis constantinus*, was composed in 1507–9 and published by Senfl in 1550–5; others by Johannes Knöfel appeared in 1575, by Franz Sale in 1594–6, and by Christian Erbach in 1604–6. In this tradition, the music is still closely bound to the plainchant. Furthermore, these cycles generally omit the offertory—the very item which was to become a favourite for musical setting in later centuries. Walter Lipphardt, in his rather hasty *Geschichte des mehrstimmigen Proprium missae*, sees a decisive turning point in the offertory cycles for the Church year written by Lassus (*c.* 1580) and Palestrina (1593), cycles which are entirely free of the plainchant. So, of course, are Byrd's offertories and all his other Proper settings. According to Lipphardt, the *Gradualia* is 'the first complete Mass cycle to apply the free principle of the new offertory compositions to the totality of songs of a Proper.'*

There is much to admire, then, in the originality and comprehensive sweep of Byrd's undertaking. Admiration turns to wonder when we recall that the project was realized at a time when Catholic services were illegal, and that the composer actually managed to get out a second edition, or at least a re-issue, of both books in 1610.† It scarcely detracts from Byrd's accomplishment to note that the *Gradualia* is less than perfectly integrated— that although the two books form a coherent single scheme, this emerges with full clarity only in book 2.

Reference to Table 8 will quickly show that the two books are not quite parallel in contents and arrangement. Several features mark book 1 (1605) as the more 'popular' of the two, starting with the division into 3-, 4- and 5-part fascicles according to the model of the madrigal publications of the 1590s. It is mainly in book 1 that some non-liturgical motets and liturgical items outside the main scheme are added at the ends of the fascicles (or in the case of the 5-part fascicle, near the end). Byrd, who had never had the occasion to publish any motets for three or four voices before, took the opportunity to broadcast a number of older pieces which he seems to have remembered fondly. With the non-liturgical pieces for five parts, too, Nos. 26–8, he forged a link with the past. *Adoramus te Christe* is a consort song for mean voice and viols of the sort published (with or without words

---

*W. Lipphardt, *Die Geschichte des mehrstimmigen Proprium missae* (Heidelberg, 1950), 66. Lipphardt had some understanding of the liturgical organization of the *Gradualia* and of Byrd's 'principle of economy', though it is clear from some of his remarks that he did not comprehend the system fully.

†They were issued under the imprint of Richard Redmer, who was evidently not a printer but a bookseller, and appear to employ the sheets from the first edition (though on the new title-pages they are mendaciously described as 'Editio Secunda, priore emendiator' and 'Ex Nova & accuratissima Authoris recognitione'). See H. K. Andrews, 'The Printed Part-Books of Byrd's Vocal Music', *The Library*, 5th series, xix (1964), 9f. Since in the one surviving copy of the first edition (at York Minster) book 1 lacks the introductory matter, Andrews concluded that the re-issue involved 'new title-leaves and, in the case of book I, new introductory matter and dedication'. It seems more likely that the preliminaries were simply discarded from the York copy, which shows other signs of tampering, as Andrews pointed out ('the indexes are displaced in most of the books', p. 9).

in all voices) in the 1588 and 1589 songbooks, and *Unam petii a Domino* and *Plorans plorabit* (see pp. 42 and 158f) are non-liturgical 'political' motets in the old tradition. *Unam petii* speaks out in the bluntest language:

Unam petii a Domino, hanc requiram, ut inhabitem in domino Domini omnibus diebus vitae meae. *2ª pars* Ut videam voluntatem* Domini et visitem templum eius [Ps. 26:4].

Book 1, then, could well be the accumulation of several years' work. In addition, it certainly contains at least a few considerably older items. Did any of its music circulate prior to publication? The manuscript evidence for this is quickly related, for as compared to the *Cantiones sacrae* of 1589 and 1591 there survive disappointingly few contemporary manuscript copies of the *Gradualia*. Most of them stem from the busy scriptorium of Byrd's friend Edward Paston, who seems always to have worked from the printed part-books of 1605 and 1607 (or the second editions of 1610). The only trace of variant readings comes up in one of the sets of parts copied by the Suffolk amateur Thomas Hamond in the 1630s, Mus.f.16–19.† The 4-part section of this manuscript includes the famous *Ave verum corpus* and *Ecce quam bonum* from book 1 (Nos. 5 and 9) and then nine pieces from book 2. The latter are identical with and were copied from the printed partbooks; most of them are inscribed 'Gradualia', 'Gradualia, Lib. secundus. 1610' and so on. But the two book 1 copies are not so inscribed and turn out to preserve slightly different texts of the motets, evidently earlier ones.‡

That these particular motets predate the main body of book 1 comes as no surprise. *Ave verum corpus* is a G Dorian composition placed among the

---

*The psalm reads 'voluptatem'.

†The main Paston MSS in question are Tenbury 349–53 and 369–73. On Hamond, see M. C. Crum, 'A Seventeenth-Century Collection of Music Belonging to Thomas Hamond, a Suffolk Landowner', *Bodleian Library Record*, vi (1957), 373ff. On Hamond's copy of the Three-Part Mass in this MS, see p. 190n. He copied another *Gradualia* piece, the 3-part St. John Passion, into another MS that he came to own, Add. 30480–4, this time working from the printed partbooks.

‡*Ave verum corpus* is notated with one flat in the signature, rather than two, as in the publication—a seemingly trivial difference; but since there are more E♭s in the piece than E♮s, it is hard to envisage a scribe with the printed partbooks in front of him arbitrarily removing the E♭ in the signature. The only difference in actual notes (the soprano partbook is lost) comes with the auxiliary E♭ on the word 'Virginis', which in Hamond lacks an accidental. The main variants in *Ecce quam bonum*: alto, BW 5, 54, bar 2: crotchets CA for minim C. Tenor, 56/2: E for C; 58/1: the first B is flatted; 61/1: both Gs are sharped; 63/3: C for D. Bass, 57/5–6: dotted minim G for minim G, crotchet rest. Hamond's tenor is garbled at 58/7.

Mixolydian pieces for the Blessed Sacrament—an almost unique example of modal mismatch in the *Gradualia*. *Ecce quam bonum* is a non-liturgical psalm setting found in the miscellaneous 4-part group which also includes at least two other earlier pieces: *Christus resurgens*, the youthful cantus firmus exercise based on the Sarum plainchant (see p. 62f), and *In manus tuas*, an adaptation of a string fantasy which is dated on internal grounds in the 1570s or 80s (Fantasia 4/G; see Vol. III, p. 92).

Book 1 was only partly planned, then, and partly put together from what the composer happened to have ready. The distribution of the main Propers may also lead us to the same conclusion. At the head of the collection stands the large Marian group. The members of this group are not arranged in correct liturgical order, however (more about this later), and as for All Saints and Corpus Christi, there is no discernible liturgical reason why these particular Masses should have been added. They may again represent what the composer had ready, or they may reflect an entirely different principle of organization. For it is tempting to believe that the book 1 Propers were chosen for political reasons, that is, on account of their special interest to the English Catholics. Marian devotion and transubstantiation were central doctrinal issues, and All Saints would have been applied immediately to the memory of recently martyred priests.

One cannot be sure. But for whatever reason, book 2 is organized much more uniformly than book 1, strictly along liturgical lines. There is only one rather dramatic disturbance to the scheme. Byrd carefully fills in feasts so that now all the most important ones are covered,* sets them in an ascending order of voices, and orders them correctly.

The disturbance mentioned above comes at Epiphany, a 4-part Mass which is unfortunately garbled.† At this point the publication offers a few

---

*Except for Michaelmas; for the Catholics, Sts. Peter and Paul was definitely one of the most important. See p. 306 and J. Bossy, *The English Catholic Community, 1570–1850* (London, 1975), 118. There may be a special reason for Byrd's inclusion of the relatively minor Votive Mass of the Blessed Sacrament. A practice had grown up over the centuries of singing this and other Votive Masses regularly in place of proper Masses throughout the year (see P. Cavanaugh, 'Early Sixteenth-Century Mass Propers—An Evolutionary Process or the Result of Liturgical Reform?', *Acta Musicologica*, xlviii (1976), 151ff). While the Tridentine reform aimed to stamp out this practice, it might well have recommended itself to priests and missionaries working under difficult conditions.

†Missing is the gradual *Omnes de Saba venient* and the alleluia verse *Vidimus stellam*— and for the latter all Byrd needed to do was add a detachable alleluia to the end of his setting of the communion, which has the same words up to the alleluia. There is also no Epiphany antiphon setting. Furthermore the ostensible gradual verse, No. 15, uses not the correct liturgical text 'Surge, et illuminare Hierusalem: quia gloria Domini super te orta est' but the scriptural verse from which it is derived (and which occurs elsewhere in the Epiphany Mass), 'Surge, illuminare, Hierusalem: quia venit lumen tuum, et gloria

more odds and ends for four voices before turning to 5-part music. Included are two antiphons for Corpus Christi matching in mode and texture the other music for this feast in book 1. From this it appears that the idea of including antiphons integrated with the 'office' only crystallized out after the publication of book 1,* and that Byrd was now making a retrospective effort to tidy things up. It is true that book 1 includes a *Magnificat* antiphon for Corpus Christi (*O sacrum convivium*) and two expressly rubricated for the Purification (*Senex puerum portabat* and *Hodie beata Virgo*), though it has none for All Saints or any of the other Marian feasts; and one could argue that Byrd omitted an All Saints antiphon because he had already set words very similar to the second *Magnificat* antiphon for that feast in *O quam gloriosum est regnum* in 1589—using the same mode and clef combination as the Mass items—and that he omitted antiphons for the other Marian feasts because he considered them less important than the Purification. On the other hand, *O sacrum convivium* may owe its inclusion not to its role as a *Magnificat* antiphon but to its other role as a familiar processional piece, and even with the Purification, the antiphons included with book 1 are not integrated with the rest of the music. The Mass is for five voices and the antiphons for four (and the processional antiphon *Adorna thalamum tuum* for three—in a different mode). All in all book 2 can be seen to have completed the scheme begun somewhat unsystematically in book 1, and to have completed it in a newly systematic fashion.

There is evidence that the bulk of the contents of book 2 was composed rather rapidly in 1605. (Exception must be made, however, for portions of the large 6-part Mass of Sts. Peter and Paul, as will be explained later.) In his dedication of book 2 to Lord Petre, dated 3 April, 1607, Byrd writes: 'These songs, most illustrious Sir, long since completed by me and committed to the press (*iamdudum á me peractas, ac Prelo commissas*), deserve to be dedicated to you . . .' The subordinate phrase here reads like an oblique complaint directed towards the printer, Thomas East. It would not have been fair for Byrd to have written in this way if book 2 had been 'committed to the press' after 5 November, 1605; that is the date of the Gunpowder Plot, and one could scarcely blame East for holding back on ostentatiously Catholic matter after that debacle. A Jesuit was arrested at this time in possession of copies of book 1.† However, if Byrd had submitted his

Domini super te orta est' [Isa. 60:1]. Since Byrd added a terminal alleluia to this, it is probable that he was indeed thinking of the gradual verse, but the piece is misplaced among motets of the Blessed Sacrament. Did a setting by Byrd of *Omnes de Saba venient* get lost at the printing house?

*Also, it seems, the idea of including integrated settings of the sequences. See p. 281n.
†Fellowes, *W. Byrd*, 43.

manuscript at some earlier point in 1605, a few months delay caused by the unlucky East would have been extended by political circumstances into a period of one and a half to two years. Longer than this, however, Byrd did not have to wait. For when East brought out book 1 at the beginning of 1605* he did not have book 2 in hand. This appears from the contents of the two books and also from the fact that book 1 was not published (or registered) with the words 'liber primus' in the title—as was the case, for example, with the first volume of *Cantiones sacrae* in 1589. When book 1 was published book 2 was not yet decided on. The words 'liber primus' were added only in the second edition of 1610.

Byrd's complaint still seems rather intemperate, perhaps. It is to political events in the new reign that we must turn for a possible explanation of his impatience in this matter. At first the atmosphere seemed to be clearing for the Catholics, and no doubt Byrd also thought it was a good time to renew some of his ties with London. The dedicatee of book 1 was Henry Howard, son of the poet Surrey, who had been made Earl of Northampton in March 1604; deeply implicated with Mary Queen of Scots, he saw the Wheel of Fortune swing sharply for him under James I. Despite 'a stupendous want of principle', as his biographer puts it, Northampton was 'reputed the most learned nobleman of his time' and counted music among his attainments; Byrd says more specifically than in any of his other dedications that this dedicatee was a connoisseur of his music. In an effusive memorial of 5 December, 1604, in the Cheque-Book of the Chapel Royal, one of the few signed by Byrd in these years, Northampton is thanked for helping persuade James to raise the stipend of the Gentlemen of the Chapel for the first time since the reign of Edward III.† Byrd's dedication refers to this action so warmly as to make one rather suspect that he would have liked to dedicate the book to the King himself, as he and Tallis had dedicated their *Cantiones* to Queen Elizabeth thirty years earlier.

Book 2 was dedicated to Sir John Petre, Byrd's main patron, whom he had known since at least the early 1580s and who had been made Baron Petre of Writtle in July 1603. If Byrd planned to commemorate this event, somewhat late, in 1605, his embarrassment at the publishing delay becomes more understandable. It has been mentioned above (pp. 51, 189) that when the composer moved to Stondon Massey in 1593 he presumably joined the

---

*It was registered in January; registration before publication was a requirement of the Stationers' Company. The book itself is not dated as to the month, but it must have been set up and presumably issued before 24 February, when the dedicatee Northampton received the Garter, for there is no mention of this in the list of his honours in the dedication.

†E. F. Rimbault, *The Old Cheque-Book of the Chapel Royal* (London, 1872), 60f.

Catholic community under the aegis of the Petre family at nearby Ingatestone and Thorndon Halls. Certainly the dedication to book 2 makes it clear that the music was written in the first instance for services there. So no doubt this music—and also the music of book 1—deserved to be dedicated to Petre. Perhaps the situation was made even more delicate by the general disenchantment of English Catholics with Northampton's actions in the aftermath of the Gunpowder Plot.

[3]

In principle, as we have seen, Byrd set five distinct texts for each Mass. From the standpoint of the listener to the services, however, the music presents itself initially not in five but in two broad categories. There are musical units that are relatively short and homogeneous, and others that are long and sharply sectionalized in various different ways.

The short ones are settings of the *offertory*, following the Credo, and the *communion*, towards the end of Mass. These texts consist of only one or two sentences, usually, perhaps with a terminal alleluia. Byrd often sets offertories and communions very concisely indeed, and sometimes achieves an epigrammatic perfection that would scarcely have been expected from the composer of the monumental, leisurely *Cantiones sacrae*.

The long sectional text units appear, first, at the beginning of Mass, where the *introit* is followed by a psalm verse and the doxology (Gloria Patri), after which the introit is sung again; and secondly, at the large musical interlude after the Epistle. What is prescribed here in the liturgy for most of the year is a *gradual*, followed by its verse, followed directly by an *alleluia*: which consists of the word 'alleluia' sung twice, another verse (the alleluia verse), and then 'alleluia' twice more. In Lent and in Paschal Time substitutions are made for the alleluia and the gradual respectively, and on some specially solemn occasions the post-Epistle music is augmented by a long sectional *sequence*. This amounts to a considerable variety of composite sectional texts which call urgently for some clear corresponding system of musical sectionalization.

Byrd employed two main techniques for this, one new and one retrospective. The 3-part style of the *Gradualia* verses can be matched, though only approximately, in the semichoir sections found in Byrd's work at various points of his career—in the Four- and Five-Part Masses and in motets such as *Tribue Domine* (1575/14–16), *Laetentur coeli* (1589/29) and *Salve Regina* (1591/6). From *Tribue Domine* the line of derivation runs smoothly back to the Tudor Mass and votive antiphon. It is a brisk, dry

Ex. 41

Ex. 41 (Cont.)

style best characterized as 'freely canonic' rather than imitative; as the lines are seldom spun out far beyond the imitated notes themselves, the canonic quality stands out in a very obvious way. Strict canon, too, is not infrequent, though it never lasts through an entire verse.* Many of the text phrases are sung only once in each voice; broadly speaking, indeed, word repetitions point to a loosening of the basic style, as does also the presence of non-imitative voice entries, entries doubled at the third or sixth, and crisp motives in crotchet declamation. But whether Byrd stays close to the old style or modifies it, he seems always to reject the conspicuous smoothness of the 3-part writing of the Mass Ordinaries in favour of something spikier. He tends, for example, to extend the final phrases of the *Gradualia* verses into passages of rhythmic ostinato and to end them with florid cadences—rather abruptly florid, in many cases.

The stylistic range of the 3-part writing in the *Gradualia* can be gauged very conveniently by comparing two settings of 'Domine probasti me' (Psalm 138:1–2) for use as the verse in the introits for Easter (*Resurrexi*, in the D Aeolian mode: 1607/20) and Sts. Peter and Paul (*Nunc scio vere*, in the C Ionian: 1607/38). The dimensions, the actual motives, and even what may be called the form are all so similar that it seems clear Byrd used one piece as a template when composing the other (see Ex. 41). But the differences in harmony, harmonic flow and phraseology are so enormous that the two pieces might almost come from separate worlds. It would perhaps be labouring the obvious to spell out the stylistic comparison; at every point the *Resurrexi* verse is more tensile, swift, smooth, directional and highly organized.

*The strictest canons occur in 'Eia ergo' (1605 *a* 4/12), 'Eructavit cor meum' and 'Adducentur regi' (1605 *a* 5/6 and 16).

It can accommodate elegant details unknown to *Nunc scio vere*, such as the expansion of the motive for 'probasti me' to a sixth in bar 3, the suggestion of augmentation in the bass in bar 15, and the crotchet anacruses in the first and last phrases. On the other hand its neat, darting climax at 'et resurrectionem meam' is no match for the powerful action at the end of *Nunc scio vere*, where the music presses forward as though in a trance to a great promontory just two bars from the end, and wakes with the static shudder of the final cadential ornamentation. *Resurrexi* employs the same sort of ornamentation in its own typically directional way.

In the *Nunc scio vere* verse, it is perhaps only the presence of the two dotted-crotchet-quaver motives that would prevent us from placing it years earlier in Byrd's output. But the two pieces were published with their graduals in the same volume of the *Gradualia* in 1607, and the difficulties attendant on an hypothesis of an appreciable chronological spread between them are overwhelming. What we must conclude is that on occasion Byrd deliberately assumed an archaic style in 3-part writing. It may be that at the beginning of the *Gradualia* project he consciously sought to make a link with the past by this means, and that later new stylistic impulses began to take over. We know that the archaic 3-part style retained its popularity throughout the sixteenth century; the evidence comes from the class of manuscripts made up of 3-part fragments carved from old Tudor Masses and votive antiphons. Byrd's own *Infelix ego* and *Cunctis diebus* were regularly beheaded to provide items for these 'fragment' collections, the last of which also include some verses* and other 3-part numbers from book 1 of the *Gradualia*.

If the 3-part sections of the *Gradualia* can be described as relatively long formal elements of low musical density, the opposite is true of the alleluia sections. They are relatively short (8 to 10 breves, on average) and built around one or, more frequently, two brief, arresting motives moulded to the word 'alleluia'. The treatment may be homophonic, sometimes markedly so, or polyphonic, with tight, intricate motivic work reminiscent of abstract instrumental writing. But in either case the phraseology is always curt and sharply patterned, with repetitions of short sections, sequences, antecedent-consequent constructions, and the like. This special alleluia style is the most obvious novelty in the *Gradualia*, and it provided Byrd with a type of musical section that forms a clear contrast with musical blocks composed in his

---

*'Magnus Dominus', 'Eructavit cor meum', 'Benedixisti Dominus', 'Propter veritatem', 'Adducentur regi' and 'Inquirentes' (from 1605 *a* 5/1, 6, 12, 22, 22, 30) are found in three manuscripts copied for Edward Paston, Add. 41156–8, RCM 2035 and 2036. The latter also includes the 3-part verse 'Orietur in diebus nostris' from the early respond-motet *Laetentur coeli* (1589/29).

normal, looser imitative or homophonic styles on the one hand, or in 3-part texture on the other. As the liturgy throws up alleluia sections on very many occasions—not only twice in each alleluia, but also again and again in Paschal Time—Byrd got a chance to employ this new resource liberally.

There is no such thing as a 'typical' *Gradualia* alleluia, but the one at the end of *Ego sum panis vivus* (1607/17) shows many characteristic features (Ex. 42). The S voice leads two successive sequences on different motives

Ex. 42

for the word 'alleluia'. In the first, the A is bound closely to the S as a minim canon, and when the B enters in bar 2 it doubles the S in tenths—or does it really introduce its own stretto? Both, no doubt; in its role as a doubling entry, its solid position on the beat charmingly points up the wayward syncopation in the S, and in its role as a stretto, its third motivic statement extends into bar 4, even though by this time the other voices have abandoned the motive in question. The T, which begins in bar 1 as though bound to the B as firmly as the S is to the A, continues with some agreeably absent-minded roulades before pulling itself together and supervising the cadence in bars 5–6. At this point the second sequence in the S moves up to touch high e′—how beautifully the texture opens up here—and establishes a pattern for loose ostinato imitations in the A (doubled by the B), T and B during the prolongation of the tonic harmony following the cadence. The high Es in the S and T, incidentally, are the only ones in the entire composition.

Alleluias provided Byrd with a means both for the articulation and for the termination of larger forms. In particular, with motets that end with alleluias, the brilliance of the alleluia relieved him of the necessity of making the final point weighty or impressive. He took advantage of this especially in the setting of certain long *Magnificat* antiphons which end with the word 'alleluia'.

[4]

It was with the help of these special stylistic resources that Byrd met a major problem posed by the *Gradualia*, that of finding clear forms for the long sectional units specified in the various Masses. To detail them all here, though this will require a somewhat tedious array of small diagrams, will have the virtue of making graphic the scope and variety of his solutions.

Most characteristic is the form of the introits, all thirteen of which follow exactly the same plan. The introit proper is set for the full choir of four, five or six voices, the verse is invariably set for three, and the doxology returns to the full choir, after which the introit must be sung *da capo*. In the following diagrams italicized sections are those set for a reduced number of voices:

introit – *verse* – doxology – introit

Some other conventions that Byrd followed in composing introits will be discussed on page 242f.

The twenty-odd post-Epistle groups will obviously exhibit much more variety. Half of them are gradual-alleluia combinations. These are usually set in a form which approximates that of the introits:

gradual – *verse* – alleluia – verse – alleluia (most Lady Masses, Sts. Peter
and Paul, St. Peter's Chains)

It is interesting that Byrd never writes identical music for the two alleluias in these groups, though from the liturgical point of view this would be the most natural thing to do. He prefers to make the second alleluia more impressive than the first, in one way or another. Perhaps the simplest way is to vary the scheme slightly by keeping the first alleluia in 3-part texture:

gradual – *verse* – *alleluia* – verse – alleluia (All Saints, Christmas)
gradual – *verse* – *alleluia* – *verse, pt. 1* – verse, pt. 2 – alleluia
(Corpus Christi)

(The arrangement at Corpus Christi is a response to the problem caused by an exceptionally long alleluia verse.) Omitting the voice reduction entirely was also a possibility—and in the setting of the Paschal alleluia pairs, the so-called greater alleluias, a probability:

gradual – verse – alleluia – verse . . . (Easter)
gradual – verse – alleluia – verse – alleluia (Nativity of the B.V.M.)

alleluia – verse – alleluia – verse – alleluia (Annunciation in P.T.,
                                                              Ascension)
alleluia – verse – alleluia – verse . . . (Whitsun)

Two of these 'full' settings are parts of even larger groupings, augmented by a
sequence, those at Easter and Whitsun*; and the Easter sequence *Victimae
paschali laudes* itself consists of a series of alternating 'full' and reduced-voice
sections.

The situation with the Lenten gradual-tract combinations is less regular,
though in two of the Marian Masses Byrd followed the identical plan:

gradual – *verse* – tract – *verse 2 – verse 3* – verse 4 (Purification,
                                                              Annunciation)
gradual – verse – *tract* – verse 2 – verse 3 – verse 4 (Lady Mass in Lent)
gradual – *verse* – tract – verse 2 – verse 3 (Votive Mass of the Blessed
                                                              Sacrament in Lent)

Finally some special arrangements come up as a result of transfers:

gradual – verse – alleluia – *verse* – alleluia (Assumption)
alleluia – verse – alleluia – *verse, pt. 1* – verse, pt. 2 – alleluia (Votive Mass
                                                 of the Blessed Sacrament in P.T.)

There are half a dozen cases in which Byrd runs all the elements of these
composite forms together as a single number, showing conclusively that he
regarded the post-Epistle music as a single unit. Frequently, however, he
presents it as two or even more numbers which are ostensibly distinct. In
this matter he seems to have been following a rule derived from the 'principle
of economy' discussed above. When the composite number does not have to
be divided up for transfer purposes (as at the Annunciation in P.T.†,

*Though Byrd seems to have made provision for omitting the sequence at Whitsun;
see p. 281n.

†Although in fact transfers are necessary in connection with the greater alleluia for this
Mass, *Alleluia. Ave Maria . . . fructum ventris tui. Alleluia. Virga Iesse*, Byrd seems not to
have taken them into account. When this piece is used in the Lady Mass in P.T., the two
verses should be sung in the reverse order, but the way he composed the music makes this
impossible. Byrd also really needed the separate section *Ave Maria . . . fructis ventris tui*
for use in the Advent Lady Mass, but erroneously specified the similar text *Ave Maria . . . in
mulieribus*; and he really needed the separate section *Virga Iesse* for the Lady Mass from
the Purification to Quadragesima, but specified nothing there at all.

As for the Mass of the Annunciation in Lent: Byrd's setting of the gradual-tract group
Diffusa est gratia ℣ *Propter veritatem. Audi filia* ℣ *Vultum tuum* ℣ *Adducentur regi* ℣
Adducentur in laetitia is involved in a transfer of the most involved sort. The interior
sections 'Propter veritatem' and 'Audi filia' have to be pulled out and joined to an extra
alleluia to construct the gradual for the Assumption. This operation would not be facili-
tated by anything as simple as splitting a number up, as in the case of the other Marian

All Saints, Corpus Christi, the Votive Mass of the Blessed Sacrament, and Easter), its elements are run together. But they are presented as separate numbers when they do have to be transferred (as with most of the Marian Masses, Sts. Peter and Paul, and St. Peter's Chains).

This was only common sense. Some apprehension about the transfer process can be read into Byrd's remarks in the book 1 preface: 'Further, to the end that [the various songs] may be ordered each in its own place in the various parts of the service, I have added a special index at the end of the book; here all that are proper to the same feasts may easily be found grouped together, though differing in the number of voices.' In fact connecting up motets for different numbers of voices is only the first of the problems that comes up with the Marian Mass transfers, in particular, which would have been well-nigh impossible to work out if the individual elements had not been numbered separately. (And a survey of the later portions of the *Gradualia* —the 4- and 5-part music of book 2—suggests that Byrd had given up on the whole system of transfers. He could have saved himself the trouble of composing the Christmas communion and the Ascension offertory by indicating transfers from the Christmas gradual and the Ascension greater alleluia but did not do so, instead composing the texts over again. Nor did he write a detachable alleluia after the Epiphany communion, by which means he could have supplied the Epiphany alleluia. The only transfers in book 2 come in the 6-part Mass of Sts. Peter and Paul, which for this and other reasons appears to be earlier, as has already been mentioned.) In any case, it emerges that the reason there are more Masses with separate number-ings for the post-Epistle music is that in the *Gradualia* as a whole there are more Masses involving transfers than not.

When dividing up the post-Epistle music for transfer purposes, Byrd always elides one of the alleluia sections in the greater alleluias for Paschal Time:

alleluia – verse – alleluia | verse – alleluia

(*rather than* alleluia – verse – alleluia | alleluia – verse – alleluia)

and he splits up the gradual–alleluia combination in a way that really runs counter to the liturgy:

gradual – *verse* – alleluia | verse – alleluia

(*rather than* gradual – *verse* | alleluia – verse – alleluia)

Masses and Sts. Peter and Paul, and Byrd seems to have thrown up his hands and merely run all the material needed on both occasions together as No. 23: *Diffusa est gratia. Propter veritatem. Audi filia. Alleluia. Vultum tuum. Adducentur regi. Adducentur in laetitia.* Observe that this number is never to be sung through exactly as printed, as Jackman first pointed out. (See Table 8.)

Here a second rule is in operation, a rule that was evidently powerful enough to override the liturgical consideration: never end a number with a section for a reduced number of voices. As the gradual verses are nearly always set *a 3*, Byrd caps them with an alleluia section for the full choir so as to conclude the number with what he regards as a seemly texture.*

There are fewer exceptions to these rules than may at first appear. The greater alleluias for the Ascension and Whitsun have separately numbered elements even though nothing is ever transferred and nothing is set for reduced voices. The Christmas gradual and alleluia, which never transfer either, are also numbered separately, and what is more the gradual *Viderunt omnes* ends with a 3-part verse and a 3-part alleluia. This sectionalization, however, must have resulted from an error by the printer, for after the 3-part alleluia he added an unusual rubric, 'Chorus sequitur', which seems to do its best to minimize the division and assure the puzzled singers that they are all to start singing again at once, with the next number, the alleluia verse *Dies sanctificatus*. This is the only rubric of this sort in the *Gradualia*. The word 'chorus', incidentally, confirms something we would have suspected in any case on stylistic grounds, namely that the reduced-voice sections were intended for solo singers.†

*It is worth noting that he allows himself to continue the 3-part texture of gradual verse into the central alleluia section only in cases where the gradual and alleluia are written as a single number (Corpus Christi, All Saints).

†See Jackman, *Gradualia*, 28f, with a note on Fellowes's persistent misinterpretation of the rubric (in *W. Byrd*, 90 and BW 6, 15).

5a

All Saints, the Marian Masses, Easter, Ascension, Whitsun

One's first impression on turning to the actual music of the *Gradualia*—on turning, let us say, from the *Cantiones sacrae* of 1589 to the 5-part motets of 1605 and 1607—is likely to be that of entering a new musical world. With the sectional pieces and groups that were discussed at the end of the previous section, there is of course a radical difference of form; but there is also a decisive difference of style to be observed in all the music—in the homogeneous, non-sectional pieces as well as the sectional ones. Some general observations were made in Chapter 1 about the impact on the *Gradualia* motets of the new milieu and function for which they were designed. When music is composed for actual services, the liturgical role of a text may be as important as its intrinsic meaning, and the particular conditions under which these services were held required simplicities of certain kinds. Byrd was alive to these new requirements, and they all entered into his new stylistic synthesis.

There are obvious affinities of style between the *Gradualia* motets and Byrd's settings of the Ordinary of the Mass in the 1590s. It is those three remarkable works that first exhibit a new fully controlled conciseness of technique and (at least after the Four-Part Mass) a new restraint in expression. The stylistic analogy is clearest with the music for five voices, particularly if the Five-Part Mass is placed alongside the large group of motets for the Marian Propers which opens book 1 of the *Gradualia*, and which was evidently one of the first sections written for the collection. Both bodies of music are set in the D Aeolian mode with the same overall range, from low A to high f' (see Ex. 3d).

No such close parallels occur in the other voice groupings, for Byrd had learned some lessons from composing the Masses. In four voices, it was sufficiently remarkable that he set his first Mass in the intense, highly-coloured style that was always associated with the G Dorian mode. It would have been inconceivable for him to have done the same with the 4-part Propers in the *Gradualia* for Corpus Christi, Christmas and Epiphany. In three voices, if he did not exactly decide to rest on his laurels, he declined to follow his own lead where it would have counted most. He included in the *Gradualia* miscellaneous pieces in this texture, but no actual Propers.

Even in five voices, he revised his original scheme slightly. Whereas the Five-Part Mass employs a choir including two tenors, the Marian Propers employ five different voices (notated in the treble, mezzo-soprano, alto, tenor and baritone (F3) clefs, rather than treble, mezzo-soprano, alto, alto and baritone). And the style is not quite the same. The austerity that Byrd came to consider appropriate to the Ordinary of the Mass is relaxed in the Propers. The full-choir sections are rhythmically more intricate, the trios more elaborate. The modal treatment is not as consistent, and the *Gradualia* motets employ dissonance more liberally; we must consider either that they were less 'carefully' composed or that the composer was deliberately spicing his style. The adjacent (or simultaneous) use of the lowered and raised form of the seventh degree at the cadence—the famous 'English cadence'—is entirely absent from the Five-Part Mass, but it occurs again and again in the *Gradualia*. If we turn to book 2 of the *Gradualia*—again, drawing the comparison between works closest in mode, between the Marian Propers of book 1 and the Easter Mass of book 2—the style can be seen to have relaxed even further to a significant extent.

The contraction of phrase lengths between the motets of the 1570s and 1580s has been indicated by some typical statistics on pages 107, 135, 144 and 184. In the *Gradualia* phrases longer than ten breves are the exception. This is not to say that these shorter phrases always, or even often, end with clearly marked cadences, for the ambiguity of cadence structure mentioned on page 144 is also carried further. In the 1580s a growing flexibility of rhythm can be attributed to the madrigal influence on certain works in which short phrases of a sharply different rhythmic aspect are skilfully juxtaposed, such as 'repente', 'inveniat vos' and 'dormientes' in *Vigilate*, and the two 'et non tardabit' phrases at the end of *Apparebit in finem*. This tendency reaches a climax in *Laudibus in sanctis, Domine non sum dignus* and *Domine salva nos*, the most modern pieces of the 1591 *Cantiones sacrae*. In the *Gradualia*, much more than before, rhythmic contrast operates also on a lower level, within phrases as well as between them. Crotchet rhythms constantly (and quaver rhythms occasionally) poke their way into phrases that move essentially in a minim pulse, as appears in Examples 43, 61 and others on the following pages. The whole rhythmic surface of the music is less stable. A new ambiguity in the way crotchets are to be heard—as ornamental or as rhythmically functional—opens up a whole new field of artistic resource.

It must be said that the 5-part Marian motets of book 1 are less typical in this regard. They are written in a quieter style than the other motets, one that sometimes even verges on the colourless. And this can be ascribed to a whole congeries of related factors. Most obvious, perhaps, is the closeness of this group of motets to that great monument of classic restraint, the Five-Part Mass. If the Marian group was indeed one of the first sections of the *Gradualia* to be written, Byrd might have begun in a relatively sober style which he later modified or thought better of and relaxed. Furthermore, since many of the motets were designed to be transferred from one liturgical situation to another, where they find themselves in conjunction with or even attached to new neighbours, a certain anonymity of style was perhaps well advised. Most (though not all) of these Marian texts are not very distinctive in phraseology, so a composer might find less than usual to inspire him in the words; most of the services are of modest liturgical importance, so he might reasonably wish to give them a corresponding musical treatment. Finally the texture chosen, involving only one soprano in the choir, is a quiet one, and the mode chosen, the Aeolian (in D), avoids bright modulations to the dominant. Which of these factors, if any, was primary—the chronological, textual, liturgical, textural, harmonic, or what we may call the shunting factor—is impossible to say. In any case the twenty-five motets of the Marian group present a more muted impression, and a less characteristic one, than the other liturgical items of the collection.

As a result this is not the easiest section of book 1 to approach. The All Saints Mass, which lies close at hand, separated from the Marian group by a 'spacer' consisting of a few non-liturgical items, will serve as a more effective introduction to the music of the *Gradualia*.

All Saints

INTROIT 1605 *a 5*/29   Gaudeamus omnes ℣ *Exultate iusti*. Gloria Patri.
Gaudeamus
GRADUAL   30   Timete Dominum ℣ *Inquirentes autem.*
+ALLELUIA   *Alleluia*
℣ Venite ad me. Alleluia
OFFERTORY   31   Iustorum animae
COMMUNION   32   Beati mundo corde

As far as rhythmic flexibility is concerned, the All Saints introit **Gaudeamus omnes** (1605 *a 5*/29) is the most extreme piece in book 1, though it can be matched without any difficulty by many numbers in book 2. The text does not categorically demand a highly inflected setting—and as we shall see, on another occasion Byrd set nearly the same words in a more level style:

Gaudeamus omnes in Domino, diem festum celebrantes sub honore Sanctorum omnium: de quorum solemnitate gaudent Angeli, et collaudent Filium Dei. ℣ Exultate iusti in Domino: rectos decet collaudatio. Gloria Patri, et Filio, et Spiritui Sancto. Sicut erat in principio, et nunc, et semper, et in saecula saeculorum. Amen. Gaudeamus omnes in Domino . . .

Despite the dense use of crotchets in some of the phrases, and despite the unbarred-C time signature employed here as everywhere else in the *Gradualia*, there is no question that this music still moves in the basic minim pulse, and not in the crotchet pulse of such works as *Laudibus in sanctis*. The opening subject defines the tonic triad in minims. The crotchet figure for 'Domino' has an essentially decorative function, though the way it always begins on a peak note stresses the duple metre in a thoroughly un-Palestrinian fashion, as does also the persistent dotted rhythm for the word 'Gaudeamus'. The tonality, too, is kept very simple and lucid. The six subject entries come on F, F, F, B♭, F and C, with the last of them harmonized so as to stress a passing modulation to the dominant exactly two breves before the final tonic cadence. The entries all come at the interval of one or two breves and the subject itself always lasts the same length of time, three breves plus a cadence note of a minim or a semibreve.

All this brings forcibly to mind the square, schematic writing which Byrd evolved for the expression of jubilant sentiments in his very earliest years as a motet composer. Undoubtedly he was working with the same *topos*. What distinguishes the present point from the beginning of old motets such as

Laudate pueri Dominum and *Laetentur coeli* is its deftness, its lucid and faultless counterpoint—this from a composer who would not blink at parallels and false relations elsewhere in the same piece—and its strikingly transparent texture; the five voices are scarcely ever heard sounding all at once and the passage actually ends *a 2*. But of course the most important distinction is that this style does not continue or recur. It is used merely as a point of departure for a kaleidoscopic array of brilliant stylistic contrasts. Contrasts begin with the rapid explosions of 'diem festum celebrantes', with their ringing crotchet rhythms in 4-part homophony. After no more than four breves of this—four breves set askew against the basic metre of the piece—a much slower section intervenes momentarily, 'sub honore Sanctorum omnium'. We are back in the classic minim pulse, against which just a few crotchets and quavers are subsumed in a strictly ornamental capacity.

For 'sub honore Sanctorum omnium' Byrd employed a simple type of repetitive structure which assumes great importance in the *Gradualia* as a whole. A short melodic idea with light contrapuntal support reaches a clear cadence and is at once repeated in another voice, generally with the texture redeployed and with some melodic, harmonic and contrapuntal variation. There may be more repetitions, but no further extensions nor any codetta worth mentioning. As musical construction this is elementary in the extreme, even drastic, but it does make for conciseness and also encourages a composer to sharpen his sense of phraseology and phrase balance. Here Byrd could draw on his rich experience with instrumental music; broadly speaking, the music of the *Gradualia* makes its points through subtleties of phrase balance, rather than through the traditional resources of polyphony. The force of this observation appears from a general comparison between the repetitive structures of the *Gradualia* and their precursors in the music of the 1580s. At that time Byrd used 'cell' technique to build extended periods out of two (or more) successive cadence-directed cells for semichoirs followed by a richer, more genuinely contrapuntal phrase for the full choir as climax. This technique has been discussed on pages 117 and 140 and elsewhere. The construction that is so common in the *Gradualia* resembles 'cell' construction in its emphasis on clear phraseology; what it lacks is exactly the free development section which, in the older technique, completes the scheme. The emphasis is on balance rather than on development or the planning of climaxes.

After the majestic 'sub honore' phrase, 'de quorum solemnitate' jolts back into vigorous crotchet movement. Then 'gaudent angeli' builds upon a slow sequence in the bass, with the smaller angels chattering excited diminutions above it. The rhythm has to be slowed down again by the last two phrases.

The introit ends with its first emphatic triple rhythms, triple minim rhythms whose easy swing is enhanced by the near-ostinato treatment of the motive for 'Filium Dei'.

In melodic terms the 'Filium Dei' motive amounts to a sort of expanded augmentation of 'et collaudant', and by its rhythm it recalls 'Gaudeamus omnes' and also looks forward to 'Exultate . . .', the beginning of the 3-part verse. A bright and rather brittle piece, this verse covers no more than two text fragments, the first involving few word repetitions, the second extending a little further and ending with the customary florid cadence. All this is typical enough. Next comes the doxology, such as was required for every one of the thirteen introits of the *Gradualia*. In setting these same words Byrd always held fairly closely to the same scheme.

The doxology of *Gaudeamus omnes* is typical in starting both the 'Gloria Patri' and 'Sicut erat' phrases in block chords after a minim *Generalpause*. The one exception to this routine in Byrd's output comes in the introit for Sts. Peter and Paul, *Nunc scio vere* (1607/38). Here one of the tenors blunders in genially ahead of time with the word 'Sicut', filling in the minim rest and effectively shattering the composure of the homophonic surface. In all Byrd's doxologies, the homophonic writing at 'Gloria Patri' turns half-polyphonic at the next words 'et Filio, et Spiritui Sancto'; in *Spiritus Domini* (1607/ 1631: Whitsun) an amusing little sequence links the Son and the Holy Spirit. Likewise with 'Sicut erat' and the next words 'in principio, et nunc'. *Viri Galilaei* (1607/25: Ascension) continues with half-homophonic, half-polyphonic writing of this kind for 'et in saecula', but ordinarily both this text fragment and 'saeculorum. Amen' are set as brief but clearly developed points of imitation. And often enough (as in *Gaudeamus omnes*) Byrd takes the path of least resistance and links these phrases by means of related motives for 'saecula' and 'saeculorum'. There is only one instance of a real point of double imitation made out of the two motives (*Nunc scio vere*); this technique had lost interest for Byrd by the time of the *Gradualia*. Sometimes, as in *Gaudeamus omnes* and most prominently in *Resurrexi* (1607/20: Easter), a fast-moving 'Amen' motive emerges from the tail of 'saeculorum'.

He composed one doxology for each combination of mode and texture required—but not much more. The 'principle of economy' is at work in the five introits belonging to the Marian group in book 1, which all employ the same mode (D Aeolian) and texture (five voices, with one soprano). Since three of these introits share the same verse, 'Eructavit cor meum', once Byrd had written the music for this and for its doxology under the Nativity introit *Salve sancta Parens* (1605 *a* 5/6), he simply gave the direction 'Eructavit: ut supra. Gloria: ut supra' under *Vultum tuum* (1605 *a* 5/16: Christmas to the Purification) and assumed that the user of the books would take the same hint without further prompting when he came to *Gaudeamus omnes* (1605 *a* 5/23: Assumption). Although *Rorate coeli* (1605 *a* 5/12: Advent) has a different verse, nevertheless Byrd used the identical 'Eructavit' doxology after it. (This time he printed the music over again.) The one remaining Marian introit, *Suscepimus Deus* (1605 *a* 5/1: Purification), has its own verse and its own distinct setting of the doxology, but the second portion of this, from 'et in saecula' to the end, appears to be an earlier version of the other, communal setting (Ex. 43).

It will be seen that in harmonic terms the 'et in saecula' section from *Salve sancta Parens* is more stable, a circumstance that must be considered in terms of the harmonic progress through the verse and the entire doxology:

	verse	Gloria . . .	Sicut . . .	et in saecula . . .
Suscepimus Deus				
(Magnus Dominus)	d–F	F–G	C–A	(a)–(F)–d
Salve sancta Parens				
(Eructavit)	d–d	d–D	g–F	d——d

Overall the harmonic plan in *Salve sancta Parens* is the more lucid, that in *Suscepimus Deus* the more diffuse; presumably it was some dissatisfaction with this original harmonic plan that caused Byrd to recompose the doxology.[*] Once he was at it, he indulged himself in some florid writing for 'Spiritui Sancto' and also changed the textural quality of the concluding 'et in saecula' section. In *Suscepimus Deus* this is governed by the canon in free augmentation between bass and soprano, with the other voices imitating only sporadically and very freely indeed. In *Salve sancta Parens* the soprano canon has been speeded up so as to provide a deft extra leg to the sequence, and the other voices made to imitate more systematically. Furthermore the crotchet motive for 'Amen' in *Suscepimus Deus*, an elegant 5-beat motive which appears only in the soprano, and only twice, is transformed into a simpler figure which moves through three of the voices in *Salve sancta Parens* before the bass extends it into a fine run at the cadence. It moves more directionally and prepares a better climax. In short the counterpoint in

---

[*]Perhaps his dissatisfaction centered on the junction (F—F) between the end of the verse and the doxology. For whilst amongst the thirteen introits there are two other examples of verses ending away from the tonic, and three other examples of doxologies beginning away from the tonic, *Suscepimus Deus* is the only introit showing *both* of these deviations. In any case, once Byrd had written the *Salve* verse and ended it in d (– – D d f♯), he could not re-use the *Suscepimus* doxology which begins on F (F a c f c′).

Ex. 43

a Suscepimus Deus

b Salve sancta Parens

a Suscepimus Deus

b Salve sancte Parens

this doxology, as well as the harmony, contributes to an effect of greater lucidity. Only at the cadence, however, would one wish to say that the new music is definitely an improvement. The level of craft that Byrd brought to even the most 'functional' parts of the *Gradualia* is very impressive.

Another situation in which Byrd was required to apply himself twice to much the same job came up with the doxologies for two 4-part introits in the D Aeolian mode, *Puer natus est nobis* (1607/1: Christmas) and *Ecce advenit dominator Dominus* (1607/10: Epiphany). At first glance the nearly identical soprano and bass lines in these pieces for 'et Spiritui Sancto' and imitative motives for 'et in saecula' may look like the work of a composer who is bored or at least impatient or at least trying to save time. But in fact the chore served as a stimulus to fresh thinking about the whole problem of setting these doxologies. The 'et in saecula saeculorum. Amen' termination in *Ecce advenit* turned out to be Byrd's most extended, with two related motives presented in successive four-fold ostinatos. And the termination in *Puer natus* turned out to be his shortest and most informal in contrapuntal treatment, as well as probably his most vivid setting ever of these words. The main motive for 'saeculorum' emerges sequentially out of the 'in saecula' motive. But it emerges only in the two middle voices; the bass acts like a real harmonic bass, as it does also in the remarkably baroque little explosion that occurs just previously, at the unlikely words 'et nunc et semper' (Ex. 44). Byrd may have been bored with text setting, but his purely musical imagination was as busy as ever.

Ex. 44

Timete Dominum (1605 *a* 5/30), a sectional motet combining the All Saints gradual and alleluia, is an uneven piece of work by comparison with the introit *Gaudeamus omnes*. The opening consists of an inconspicuous little stretto on a motive built on interlocking thirds—treated with some originality, however: the motive is adapted to two successive text fragments, and in the soprano and tenor it actually changes mode, from CEDF ('Timete Dominum') to CE♭D– ('omnes sancti eius'). In a move reminiscent of the earlier rhetoric, the affective semitone e♭'d' which has emerged in this way is at once answered by another semitone, fe. The next phrases, however, are of the neutral quality that Byrd tends to resort to in the *Gradualia* when nothing in the words, it seems, strikes him particularly, and the 3-part verse is followed by one of the few dull alleluias in the whole book. Although the resumption of the 5-part texture at 'Venite ad me' is well managed, the motive for 'et ego reficiam vos', in a rhythm of $1 + 2 + 3 + 3$ crotchets, seems less refreshing than rather galvanic and mechanical in its actual developments. A more genuinely lively effect is achieved at the beginning of the second alleluia section by a series of homophonic shouts in triple rhythm—scored, rather surprisingly, for fewer and fewer voices as the series mounts higher and higher.

Iustorum animae (1605 *a* 5/31), the offertory, is one of Byrd's most celebrated and admired compositions. It is not a long work—at thirty-eight breves, shorter than certain single points of imitation in early motets, and with none of its segments drawn out for more than eight breves. Yet 'concise' seems oddly wrong as an epithet for it; there is an almost timeless quality to the slow oscillating motive near the end for the words 'illi autem sunt in pace'. More than with most pieces in the *Gradualia*, one feels here that every note has been edged into place with complete artistic calculation. A distant model for the setting may be *Emendemus in melius*, with its rather strict homophonic declamation ceding to polyphony in the final phrase. Here, however, the modulation from homophony to polyphony is more gradual and much more subtly controlled.

The first three phrases of the motet are homophonic; this in itself sets *Iustorum animae* apart from nearly all its companions in the *Gradualia*. 'Iustorum animae in manu Dei sunt' is sung plainly, rather in the manner of some of Byrd's simpler anthem openings. At 'et non tanget illos' the two sopranos assert their competitive rights and echo the words between them; at 'tormentum mortis' modulations to G and D make an astonishing expressive effect in view of the extreme simplicity of means. Then slowly the texture grows more complex. At 'visi sunt oculis insipientium mori' the counterpoint is still informal (and exceedingly original): the motive for 'insipientium'—a descending scale figure in crotchet declamation—appears in its *recto* form only in the top two voices, the dissonant outlines e♭′a′ (S^2) resolved up a step in sequence by f′b♭′ (S^1, echoed by S^2). Meanwhile the lower voices contrive to make exquisite false relations, sometimes with the help of the 'insipientium' motive in free inversion—E♭ against E♮ in the first phrase, F against F♯ in the second, both E♮ and F♯ in the third. Can Byrd have meant these false relations to sound sardonic, as a commentary on 'the sight of the unwise'?

There is a matchless place where the 'in pace' motive descends in two parallel stretto cycles through S^1, S^2, A and B (see Ex. 45). The bass sinks

Ex. 45

down first to the subdominant, B♭, a low pitch which has not been heard since the beginning of the work, and then to A, which sounds inexpressibly deep and peaceful because (in part) at the moment of its sounding the middle of the texture empties out, and when this is filled in, the mediant harmony sounds so fresh and strange. It is remarkable how Byrd binds the second half of this motet together. After the digression to D and G at 'tormentum mortis', the harmony moves back around the circle of fifths— around to B♭ and up again to F. The 'in pace' motive is the same as 'insipientium', and likewise generates false relations. And one non-motivic statement of the words 'in pace' in the soprano recalls with quiet precision the slow oscillation of the 'illi autem' motive.

The text of the communion **Beati mundo corde** (1605 *a* 5/32) is a little longer than usual, consisting of three verses from the Sermon on the Mount. Byrd chose a form for this that is unusual yet as natural as could be: he set the three Beatitudes for three, four and five voices respectively in successively longer musical sections. This is one communion cast in a sectional form, then, rather like that of certain tracts. The opening 'Beati mundo corde' section carries itself more gracefully than the other trios of the All Saints Mass, and its airy emphasis on upward semibreve leaps of a fourth or a fifth prepares the other two sections, which likewise open with the word 'Beata' set to such leaps.

As in *Iustorum animae* the tonal scheme is very clear and clearly geared to the text. The first two sections end in F and both incline conventionally to the dominant, but a subdominant flavour is introduced near the end of the second (4-part) section, with a little shower of E♭s. Subdominant harmony is picked up at the grand homophonic opening of the third (5-part) section and swung powerfully up the circle of fifths to a half cadence on A. The text 'Blessed are they which are persecuted for righteousness' sake' would have had a special meaning for Byrd; in any case the second part of it centres around D minor and throws up many pointed dissonances and false relations. 'Quoniam ipsorum', a fast homophonic section, moves back down the circle of fifths, touching B♭ just long enough to support the delicate return to tonic harmony in the concluding phrase 'est regnum coelorum'. The haunting motive here is built once again on Byrd's favourite pattern of interlocking thirds.

Beati mundo corde forms a perfect conclusion to the cycle of four pieces that makes up the All Saints Mass—a conclusion that seems more carefully calculated, it must be said, than in most of the other Masses. The three nearly balanced periods for the 'quoniam . . .' phrases provide weight of one kind, and the rich texture of the beginning phrases of the 5-part section, reminiscent of the older Tudor style, provides weight of another. The final cadence is the most serene and drawn-out of the four cadences of this motet, even though it lacks the stereotyped plagal support that is so common in this mode. It is worth noticing, too, that the opening section for the three high voices fills out a scheme for the Mass as a whole, in that the 3-part introit verse was set for the middle voices (S²—Byrd's *quintus*—AT) and the 3-part gradual verse for the low ones.

Beyond this, the question of 'unity' for the Mass as a whole is one which in Byrd's time would have resolved itself to questions of the mode and its characteristic melodic and harmonic traits. Clearly he did not wish to 'unify' the Mass Propers of the *Gradualia* as he had unified the Ordinaries, by the explicit repetition of motives. If we discern the same motives and parallel harmonic constructions in different motets—interlocking minim thirds, crotchets filling a downward fifth, circle-of-fifths progressions, cadences approached from the low mediant A—these are best understood as formulae of the Lydian-Ionian mode in this particular cleffing, that is, in the range A–f' (see Ex. 3a). And certainly these features unify the Mass. The tighter 'unification' that we may seek uneasily in the *Gradualia* as the result of habits ingrained from the study of nineteenth- and especially early twentieth-century music pertains to that music only: a music in which the old vitality of the modes, now reduced to two, was sadly impoverished, and which was racked by disruptive contrasts of a kind beyond Byrd's imagining.

And at many places in the All Saints Mass the listener catches his breath, struck anew by Byrd's comment about the power of sacred words to suggest music that is absolutely appropriate and unique 'to a mind that is not indolent and inert'—and that happens to belong to a composer of genius. The beautiful sequential treatment of 'Beati pacifici' in the communion is an example, and so is the transparently simple setting of 'qui laboritis' in the alleluia verse, and so is almost every phrase in *Iustorum animae*. Once heard with Byrd's music, these words can never quite be heard again without it. Or to put a different emphasis on the matter, one that Byrd would doubtless have found more gratifying, for many listeners and communicants over the centuries these scriptural words have acquired a special radiance thanks to his music.

Purification of the B.V.M. [2 February]

INTROIT 1605 *a* 5/1		Suscepimus Deus ℣ *Magnus Dominus*. Gloria Patri. Suscepimus Deus
GRADUAL	1	Suscepimus Deus . . . 2 ℣ *Sicut audivimus*. Alleluia
+ ALLELUIA	3	℣ *Senex puerum portabat*. Alleluia
after LXXᵐᵃ:		
GRADUAL	1	Suscepimus Deus . . . 2 ℣ *Sicut audivimus* (without alleluia)
+TRACT	4	Nunc dimittis ℣ *Quia viderunt* ℣ *Quod parasti* ℣ Lumen ad revelationem
OFFERTORY	22	Diffusa est gratia . . .
COMMUNION	5	Responsum accepit Simeon

The group of Marian Masses which opens book 1 of the *Gradualia* is a comprehensive one, including music for four of the main feasts of the Virgin Mary and the complete cycle of Saturday Votive Masses in her honour (see Table 9). Several other Marian feasts which are not named can also be furnished from the material provided: the Visitation (2 July), the Presentation (21 November) and the Conception (8 December).* The book begins with the Purification and proceeds to the Nativity, the Votive Masses, the Annunciation and the Assumption—and this order immediately raises a question. For of course the four Masses from the Proper of Saints should all be grouped together in chronological sequence starting from Advent (Purification, Annunciation, Assumption, Nativity) and the Votive Masses should be placed before (or possibly after) them.

Jackman was inclined to believe that the order of contents got mixed up at the printer's, and it is certainly true that the publication shows signs of careless or casual arrangement.† There is, however, another possibility.

*The texts for this feast in Byrd's time differ from those of the present-day Feast of the Immaculate Conception.
†Jackman, *Gradualia*, 30ff.

The order of publication may correspond by and large with the order of composition, which was not rearranged either because this order meant more to the composer than liturgical correctness, or because he did not wish to separate musical numbers that he thought of in conjunction.

It is fairly clear from the various little anomalies within the Marian group of Masses—the order itself, the occasional incorrect or jumbled texts, the awkwardnesses caused by transfers of music—that it was not conceived of as a unit from the beginning. Like the *Gradualia* as a whole, this Marian section must have evolved over a period of time during which the scheme itself was developed or clarified. What seems likely is that Byrd first wrote one or two Masses for particular services, and then at a later stage decided to build upon these to form the larger unit. At this later stage the numbers would sometimes be composed in the abstract, as it were, and not for specific performances, and so anomalies both musical and liturgical would more easily escape detection. Most (though not all) of the anomalies, make-shifts and plain errors occur in the section from the Votive Masses onwards. The Purification and Nativity Masses might have been composed first, then, the Lady Masses and the Annunciation composed next to fill in the liturgical scheme, and the Assumption composed last to complete it. We shall see that with some minor modifications, this hypothesis fits the musical facts as well as any other.

A number of musical features suggest that the Purification Mass was the first to be composed. One has already been discussed, the situation with the introit doxology (p. 243). Besides this, the Mass includes an unusually long communion, relative to its text, and a gradual verse that is curiously uncertain in texture. After starting in three voices, like most such verses, it somehow picks up a fourth just a few bars before the end. What is more Byrd seems not to have grasped all the implications of his own 'principle of economy'. The transfer of the section 'Suscepimus Deus' to the gradual works correctly but the transfer of 'Diffusa est gratia' to the offertory does not (see p. 222n); and in the introit **Suscepimus Deus** (1605 *a* 5/1) his way of indicating the interior stopping point for the end of the gradual ('in fines *terrae*') is awkward and in any case unique in book 1 of the *Gradualia*. The cadence at 'terrae' reaches a tonic chord lasting for a semibreve, but instead of marking this with a *signum* and/or a barline Byrd follows it with a minim rest in all the voices. The music is awkward, too, with its bumpy rhythm and its abrupt turn to the subdominant G minor (which may have been prompted by the *tierce de Picardie* at 'terrae') for the introit's final cadence ('dextera tua').

In its position as the introit, the opening of *Suscepimus Deus* leads in one direction, to the introit verse, doxology and *da capo*—where the G minor ending sounds especially peculiar. In its position as the gradual it leads in two others, depending on whether the Purification comes before or after Septuagesima Sunday. If before, the 'Suscepimus Deus' section is followed by the gradual verse **Sicut audivimus** (1605 *a* 5/2) with its bright alleluia and then by the hasty alleluia verse **Senex puerum** (1605 *a* 5/3) with its weightier second alleluia. This second alleluia, spun out of two motives, is twenty percent longer than any other in the *Gradualia* and really sounds like two different alleluias one after another, in spite of one or two ingenious 'plants' of the second motive in the territory of the first. If after, 'Sicut audivimus' ends without its bright alleluia and runs into the tract **Nunc dimittis** (1605 *a* 5/4. The text is that of the canticle.) As in the other Marian tracts, Byrd evokes the characteristic sonority of the old Tudor style in the rich opening period, in the 4-part verse 'Quia viderunt' with its twining figures and plaintive false relations, and especially in the concluding 'full' section.* Here the scales for 'Lumen' recall not only the motives for 'salutare tuum' and 'quod parasti' earlier in the piece, but also the setting of the word 'lux' in *Descendit de coelis*, an ancient-sounding cantus firmus respond published in the *Cantiones sacrae* of 1591. However, in between this grand flourish and the even more grandly flowing final period 'et gloriam plebis tuae Israel', Byrd placed a sharply contrasting middle section, madrigalian in its rhythms, its harmony, and its uncommonly rigid metrical structure.

Although *Diffusa est gratia* (a part of 1605 *a* 5/22) appears under the Annunciation, and although its first section lacks a few words needed for the Purification offertory,† that section may have been written originally for the Purification after all. The spaciousness of its very supple opening point of imitation is equalled only by that of the Purification communion. Furthermore its concluding phrase 'in aeternum' recalls the 'saeculorum. Amen' section of the introit doxology, both in its melodic material and in its texture, a free canon between soprano and bass with only approximate imitation in the other voices (cf. Ex. 43a).

To launch the broadly-scaled communion **Responsum accepit Simeon** (1605 *a* 5/5) Byrd turned to a device he had developed in the 1580s for motets such as *Cantate Domino* (1591/29). A 7-breve cantus firmus is sung by the alto and then by the bass, accompanied by loose faster imitations *a 3* during the first statement and *a 5* during the second: a very weighty kind of construction. The conclusion of the piece is drawn out on a scale reminiscent

---

*Terry published this section as a separate motet in *Novello's Series of Tudor Motets*, No. 22 (1934).
†The other sections are discussed on pp. 265f and 268.

of the 1570s. While augmentation is common enough in Byrd's contrapuntal writing, we do not often encounter a subject redefined in augmentation after 13 breves and then systematically imitated in its new form for another 17-breve period. (The first augmented entry seems designed to recall the cantus firmus for 'Responsum accepit Simeon': see Ex. 46.) The particular emphasis on the closing words of this motet can be explained, one rather

Ex. 46

Re-spon - sum ac - ce - pit Si - me - on   ni - si vi - de - ret Christum Do - mi - ni

ni - si vi - de - ret Christum Do - mi - ni

suspects, on the assumption that the composer was identifying with the aged Simeon:

Responsum accepit Simeon a Spiritu Sancto, non visurum se mortem, nisi videret Christum Domini.

Byrd had passed his sixtieth birthday, and the dedications to both books of the *Gradualia* abound in references to his great age, his approaching death, the sweet song of the dying swan, and so on. In the event, of course, he lived on till 1623.

There is only one other motet in the Marian group with the same distinctive type of opening as *Responsum accepit Simeon*, and that is the Purification tract *Nunc dimittis*. If we take this as an indication that they were composed together, we may also take the alleluia *Senex puerum portabat* to be a later addition to a Mass which had originally been written with a tract—written, that is, in a year when the feast fell after Septuagesima. This occurred in 1598, 1600 and 1603. The alleluia following the gradual verse (after a barline) would also have to be a later addition, and in fact the music suggests that this was so. Byrd here falls back on one of the most obvious of all rhythmic patterns to declaim the word 'alleluia', ♩. ♪♪♪; the *Gradualia* includes more than a dozen alleluias built on this dotted-minim rhythm, often falling into emphatic dance-like periods and making much use of homophony, as in the present instance. But most of these alleluias come in the later sections of the *Gradualia*. Only four figure among the nineteen alleluias of the Marian cycle, and each of the four seems to be a later addition.

The Nativity of the B.V.M. [8 September]

INTROIT 1605 *a* 5/6		Salve sancta Parens (without alleluia) ℣ *Eructavit.* Gloria Patri. Salve sancta Parens
GRADUAL	7	Benedicta et venerabilis 8 ℣ Virgo Dei Genitrix. Alleluia
+ALLELUIA	9	℣ Felix es sacra Virgo. Alleluia
OFFERTORY	10	Beata es Virgo Maria (without alleluia)
COMMUNION	11	Beata viscera (without alleluia)

Votive Mass of the B.V.M. from the Purification to Advent

INTROIT 1605 *a* 5/6		Salve sancta Parens (in P.T.: alleluia) ℣ *Eructavit.* Gloria Patri. Salve sancta Parens
GRADUAL	7	Benedicta et venerabilis 8 ℣ Virgo Dei Genitrix. Alleluia
+ ALLELUIA	20	. . . ℣ Virga Iesse. Alleluia
after LXX^{ma}:		
GRADUAL	7	Benedicta et venerabilis 8 ℣ Virgo Dei Genitrix (without alleluia)
+ TRACT	21	*Gaude Maria Virgo* ℣ Quae Gabrielis ℣ Dum Virgo ℣ Dei Genitrix
OFFERTORY	19	Felix namque es
in P.T.:		
ALLELUIA	20	Alleluia ℣ Ave Maria. Alleluia ℣ Virga Iesse. Alleluia
OFFERTORY	10	Beata es Virgo Maria. Alleluia
from Pentecost to Advent:		
ALLELUIA	18	℣ Post partum. Alleluia
OFFERTORY	14	Ave Maria (without alleluia)
COMMUNION	11	Beata viscera (in P.T.: Alleluia)

That the Nativity Mass was composed next after the Purification is suggested by its anomalous position as the second Mass in the *Gradualia* and also, in a somewhat roundabout way, by the anomalous manner in which the music itself is presented. It will be noted that four of the five texts for this feast are also used in the cycle of Votive Masses. In fact they are more familiar from that context; the introit *Salve sancta Parens* and the communion *Beata viscera* are firm fixtures for most of the year, framing what was known in the

Middle Ages as the 'Missa Salve'. And indeed Byrd provided the Nativity introit, offertory and communion with alleluias which are not sung on the feast itself, but only when the same texts are sung in the Lady Mass in Paschal Time. Under the Lady Mass rubric, of course, the alleluias would be quite correct. As printed, under the Nativity, they constitute an anomaly— and it remains to inquire how this might have come about.

Were the alleluias part of the original conception? If so—that is, if Byrd wrote the pieces originally with the dual liturgical function in mind—it is hard to imagine why he would have gratuitously created the anomaly by listing them under the Nativity. On the other hand, if the pieces were originally written without alleluias for the Nativity alone, and the alleluias added later to make the music usable in the Lady Mass, the anomaly is easily accounted for. All we need assume is a certain lethargy on the composer's part in the matter of changing or expanding rubrics, and perhaps a desire to cling to an original conception. It seems likely, then, that the Nativity Mass was composed early in the project, at a time when the Lady Mass cycle was not yet in consideration.

In any case, one of the three Paschal alleluias, that of the introit **Salve sancta Parens** (1605 *a* 5/6), looks like a later addition. It brings together two rhythmic clichés which are heard again and again in alleluias of the later *Gradualia* Masses but seldom in the Marian group, ♩♩♩♩ and ♩. ♩♩♩. The two-crotchet figure is used nowhere else in the group and the dotted-minim figure occurs only a few times, always in alleluias which seem to be additions.

The first words of the introit are set to a point of imitation so swift it does not even leave time for a bass entry. Everything that follows is wonderfully deft, and yet somehow wonderfully anonymous—the staggered homophony at 'puerpera Regem', the witty little inversions at 'qui coelum', and the miniaturized phraseology achieved by repeated structures in the last two phrases (from BW 4, 36, bar 3, the cadences are spaced 3, 3, 4, 4, (4), (4) and 6 semibreves apart). Even the verse 'Eructavit cor meum' is composed more blandly than any other 3-part section in the *Gradualia*. The most expansive effect in this whole introit comes at the end of the doxology (see Ex. 43b): which seems a strange place for it.

The introit section proper of *Salve sancta Parens* lasts for 28 breves. At 23 breves the gradual **Benedicta et venerabilis** (1605 *a* 5/7) is even tinier and even more exquisitely composed, one of several perfect miniatures contained in the *Gradualia*. The opening repeated structure involves an expressive 2-part cell subtly altered so that its central i–iv–i progression becomes a slightly brighter or milder i–VII–III; this supports the over-lapping entry of the next phrase, 'es, sacra Virgo Maria', in a particularly eloquent configuration. Each of the phrases grows out of its predecessor and the last of them, 'inventa es mater Salvatoris', in effect carries the upward motion initiated by the earlier motives up the entire octave.

Benedicta et venerabilis runs directly in to the gradual verse **Virgo Dei Genitrix** (1605 *a* 5/8) and the alleluia verse **Felix es sacra Virgo** (1605 *a* 5/9). Both are rather routine pieces, with a decidedly stiff alleluia after the first of them. As is always the case with the composite pieces in the Marian Masses, the second alleluia is more substantial, an effect that stands out with special clarity here thanks to the symmetrical, heavy half closes before each of the alleluias.

The offertory **Beata es Virgo Maria** (1605 *a* 5/10) falls into balanced periods of 12, 6, and 12 breves, with the most beautiful music forming a sort of light interlude in the middle ('genuisti qui te fecit'). It seems unthinkable not to sing the alleluia after this motet, with its playful ostinato by inversion on a little phrase which might have danced in from *The Barley Break*; but the alleluia belongs only in Paschal Time, when the piece is transferred to the Lady Mass. Both *Beata es Virgo Maria* and its alleluia are almost entirely in F. The listener becomes sharply aware of these protracted episodes in the 'relative major' which break up the D minor expanse of the Marian Masses. They represent Byrd's one serious license in modal treatment—not the mere fact of Lydian 'commixture' in itself, which is always possible in the D modes, but the fact that the Lydian mode is established for so long and so strongly. Progressions to the subdominant, such as we have seen in the Purification Mass, are handled in the more usual transitory manner. On the other hand progressions to the dominant A minor are very rare, and for this reason, as has been explained earlier, the D mode of the *Gradualia* is to be regarded as a transposed form of the Aeolian (see p. 69). E♭s are equally rare; perhaps the most striking one of all introduces a characteristic Mixolydian touch at the cadence of *Beata es Virgo Maria*. Almost the only true Dorian motets in the entire collection are two that fall outside the liturgical scheme, *Plorans plorabit* and *Salve sola Dei Genitrix* (see p. 158 and 327). Both employ the G mode with two flats in the signature.

Perhaps in compensation for the Lydian bias of the offertory, the communion **Beata viscera** (1605 *a* 5/11) avoids not only F cadences but even F triads, concentrating instead on D and G minor, B♭ and A. This wonderful little piece opens with an ingenious and expressive ostinato in which the first figure is always followed by the figure for 'Mariae Virginis' at the same pitch level, though usually not in the same voice nor in the same rhythmic relationship, since the main entries of the 'Beata viscera' figure come after time intervals of 3, 4 and 5 semibreves. Neither figure is imitated more than once at any melodic interval other than the octave or unison. Byrd was pleased enough with this melodic material to use it again, in variation, for the text fragments 'quae portaverunt' and 'aeterni Patris Filium'.

So ends the Nativity Mass; but its motets are heard again and again in various permutations and combinations as transferred to parts of the Lady Mass cycle. This is perhaps the best place to follow their vicissitudes. The introit *Salve sancta Parens* gives its name to the 'Missa Salve' for the period from the Purification to Advent, as has already been mentioned. In this period the gradual is always *Benedicta et venerabilis* with its verse *Virgo Dei Genitrix*, except of course in Paschal Time. Seasonal variations concern mainly the alleluia verse and offertory.

In the 'Missa Salve' Byrd's gradual-verse combination *Benedicta et venerabilis-Virgo Dei Genitrix* has to lead in three new directions, as musical alternatives to the route taken in the Nativity Mass itself (to the alleluia *Felix es sacra Virgo*). Early in the season, when there is likely to be a Saturday or two between the Purification and Septuagesima, *Benedicta* forms a unit with the alleluia verse *Virga Iesse*, which must be transferred from the end of the greater alleluia *Alleluia. Ave Maria* (1605 *a* 5/20) later in the partbooks. (In Byrd's setting *Virga Iesse* separates off from the rest of the music easily enough.) After Septuagesima *Virgo Dei Genitrix* sheds its stiff terminal alleluia and goes into the tract **Gaude Maria Virgo** (1605 *a* 5/21). If Byrd did not follow the scheme of his other Marian tracts here—a full-choir beginning and ending, with reduced-voice sections in the middle—this was no doubt because the opening words reminded him irresistably of the trio openings of a dozen old votive antiphons with similar incipits. There was Taverner's famous *Gaude plurimum, Gaude Maria Virgo* set by both Robert Johnson and John Sheppard, *Gaude flore virginali, Gaude Virgo Mater Christi* and many others. His tract opens with a trio of an unusually archaic cast, and this trio seems to pay specific homage to *Gaude gloriosa Dei Mater*, the grandest of the antiphons of Thomas Tallis (see Ex. 47). This is thought to have been written for the Chapel Royal during the reign of Queen Mary, perhaps at her accession. It must have made a tremendous impression on the choirboys who sang at its premiere performance, and the imagination is not slow to identify one particular boy who may have sung in the trios.

Ex. 47

In this season the famous offertory **Felix namque es** (1605 *a* 5/19) continues in use from the post-Christmas season. Byrd composed it briskly, up to an excellently soaring final section consisting of two phrases grouped as a single stylistic unit, the soprano and bass conducting a free canon while the other voices accompany with essentially free counterpoint. *Felix namque es* can be regarded as an improved version of the Nativity alleluia verse *Felix es sacra Virgo Maria*; text and music are quite similar. The descending dotted-note figure that occurs in two of the voices for the word '*quia ex te ortus est*' may even be an unconscious reference to the setting of the same text phrase in the other composition.

The Lady Mass in Paschal Time is wreathed in alleluias, seven of them in all, one each in the offertory and communion, two (or rather the same one twice) in the introit and three in the greater alleluia, *Alleluia. Ave Maria*. Then in the long summer season the gradual *Benedicta et venerabilis-Virgo Dei Genitrix* forms a unit with the alleluia verse **Post partum** (1605 *a* 5/18). Byrd puts this under the Lady Mass after Christmas, but it is really more familiar from its summertime use.

Post partum corresponds textually with the last verse and a half of the tract *Gaude Maria Virgo*, and interesting points of contact appear between Byrd's two settings. The loose retrograde relation between the two 'Post partum' subjects may or may not be coincidental; in any case the form of the motive in the tract is more expressive, and so is the setting of the word 'inviolata' using the same motive. Here *Post partum* introduces an inexplicable fast dotted rhythm, which serves more appropriately elsewhere in the *Gradualia* for such words as 'viventis', 'et Spiritui Sancto' and 'et resurrectionem'. At the repeated invocation 'Dei Genitrix' the tract reaches a sober climax of intensity thanks to one of Byrd's rare moves (in this mode) to the dominant; by comparison the alleluia verse seems colourless at this

Ex. 48

point; yet the same rare modulation has been heard a little earlier and for no apparent rhetorical reason at the cadence to the phrase 'inviolata permanisti'. The motives for 'intercede pro nobis' are similar in both pieces (Ex. 48). Again the tract gets the better of the comparison—the declamation more natural, the musical discourse more persuasive, the cadence grander in every way. Of course *Post partum* still has the terminal alleluia to come— where it is remarkable to encounter much the same motive (Ex. 48). Though Byrd marks the prior cadence with a *signum* and a barline, there is in fact no liturgical situation in which this alleluia is left off. It is a cheerful item and basically a very simple one, consisting of a four-fold ostinato, with ingenious variations, on the 2-breve figure shown in Example 48.

In summer the offertory is the unhappily truncated *Ave Maria*, which will be discussed in the next section, and the communion *Beata viscera*.

Votive Mass of the B.V.M. in Advent

INTROIT 1605 *a* 5/12		Rorate coeli ℣ *Benedixisti Domine*. Gloria Patri. Rorate
GRADUAL	13	Tollite portas ℣ *Qui ascendit in montem Domini*. Alleluia
+ ALLELUIA	14	℣ Ave Maria. Alleluia
OFFERTORY	14	Ave Maria (without alleluia)
COMMUNION	15	Ecce Virgo concipiet (without alleluia)

Votive Mass of the B.V.M. from Christmas to the Purification

INTROIT 1605 *a* 5/16		Vultum tuum (without alleluia) 6 . . . ℣ *Eructavit*. Gloria Patri. Vultum tuum
GRADUAL	17	Speciosus forma 6 . . . *Eructavit* . . . *Lingua mea*. Alleluia
+ ALLELUIA	18	℣ Post partum. Alleluia
OFFERTORY	19	Felix namque es
COMMUNION	11	Beata viscera (without alleluia)

There is little internal evidence bearing on the date of composition of the next few Marian Masses in the *Gradualia*. It might be thought more likely that after the Purification and Nativity Byrd would have continued with other feasts from the Proper of Saints—the Annunciation and the Assumption—and then finished up with the Lady Masses later. But even apart from the order of publication, there are no musical clues indicating that the motets from the regular Annunciation Mass were written first, and some indicating that the Assumption was written last of all. (The situation with the Annunciation Mass in P.T. is equivocal.) What we do see are signs that Byrd had begun systematically to fill out the total liturgical scheme. After the Nativity he stopped writing new introit doxologies, as we have seen (p. 243), transferring them instead as needed from *Salve sancta Parens*. Careful rubrics for transfers now make their appearance.* Transfers and errors become more frequent and troublesome.

The yearly cycle of Lady Masses begins with three or four Saturdays in Advent. If the introit and communion texts here seem unusually vivid, that is because they were adopted not from the traditional stock of Marian devotion but rather from the Proper of the Fourth Sunday in Advent. But neither the meteorological omens in the introit **Rorate coeli** (1605 *a* 5/12) nor the buoyant sentiments of the gradual **Tollite portas** (1605 *a* 5/13) stirred much interest in the composer. The coolness of his response emerges only too clearly from a comparison with the dramatic Easter motet *Terra tremuit* of 1607 and with the enthusiastic early motet *Attollite portas* (which begins with nearly the same words from Psalm 23 as *Tollite portas*).

Yet the workmanship is again on the highest level, as witness the exquisite augmentation of both fragments of the motive for 'et nubes pluant iustum' near the begginning of *Rorate coeli*. Also notable are the subtle rhythms of the opening phrase of *Tollite portas*, echoed several times within the space

---

*Though Jackman, *Gradualia*, 29f, has another explanation for this. 'Rubrics calling for repetitions and substitutions of different Mass parts are completely supplied only in the third and fourth Masses of Book I, the two Lady-Masses for the seasons from Advent to the Feast of the Purification. . . . Why do the rubrics not begin in the *first* Mass of the book, where some sections are also missing? Why wait until the third Mass? A possible answer to these questions is that the first two Masses in Book I, and only these two—for the Feasts of the Purification and the Nativity of the Virgin—are out of place. In correct order, according to the usual arrangement of liturgical books, the seven Mass headings of Part 1 would proceed: Pro Adventum, Post Nativitatem Domini, In Festo Purificationis [etc.]. What appears in the *Gradualia* as the third and fourth Masses *ought* to be the first and second, as Masses belonging to the Temporale, and beginning with the opening of the ecclesiastical year at Advent. Hence the appearance in these Masses of the explanatory matter, i.e., of the rubrics, is not only natural, but is further evidence of the liturgical thought behind the work. In other words, if there are going to be rubrics at all, it is in precisely these Masses that they ought to occur.' One wonders why, if these Masses were rubricated because they ought to be placed first, they were not actually placed first. Perhaps this is further evidence of confusion at the printing house.

of this short composition, as well as the elegant symmetrical structure and the dovetailing of the tiny points 'et elevamini' and 'portae aeternales'. Entries come at strict 3-semibreve intervals: 'et elevamini' on f and a' in thirds (A and S); the same an octave lower (B and T²); the same on high c' in the soprano—followed by a stretto in the alto—simultaneously with 'portae aeternales' on F (B); 'portae aeternales' an octave higher (T¹); and then 'portae aeternales' for the last time on high d' (A).

The verse of this gradual starts with a quiet eloquence that is quite out of the ordinary in Byrd's 3-part *Gradualia* verses. It ends with an archaic cadence and a very short sequential alleluia, leading to the alleluia verse **Ave Maria** (1605 *a* 5/14). This is a particularly precious work, though at first acquaintance it may seem almost unnaturally self-effacing. The opening is not so much sung as murmured; Byrd blurs the words 'Ave Maria' on a neutral arpeggio in the low voices, and even while articulating the words 'gratia plena' in homophony as the high voices enter, he hides the actual melody in the alto. The whole effect is remarkably baroque (see Ex. 49a).

Ex. 49

The next text fragments pass by just as hastily, and even the more extended phrase 'et benedictus fructus ventris tui' ends with a sort of rush up to a high dominant cadence. Patently this lacks cadential stability, despite the semibreve in all the voices, and despite the *signum* and barline put in by the composer to sanction the omission of the following alleluia when *Ave Maria* is used again in this same Advent Mass as the offertory. This is the first of those gentle alleluias which form such a memorable feature of the *Gradualia* (Ex. 49b). It glimmers with marvellous details—the unresolved C♯ in bar 1, the rhythmic reshuffle of the material of bar 1 in bar 2, the subsequent growth of the tenor rhythm introduced in bar 3—but it is the subdued glow of the period as a whole which seems to catch so exactly Mary's response to the words of the Angel. The harmony and rhythm of this alleluia are firm enough so that its 10 breves seem both to resolve and to balance the 21 breves of the more evanescent 'Ave Maria' which precedes it.

The quiet combination of *Tollite portas* and *Ave Maria* makes one of the most perfect post-Epistle groups in the whole of the *Gradualia*. How elegantly the two alleluias are scaled together—the second exceptionally muted and the first exceptionally short, by far the shortest in the Marian group as a whole. To perform *Gradualia* motets singly, without reference to their total liturgical context, is always a pity; in this case it is more like a crime. And doubly criminal to sing *Ave Maria* by itself without its final alleluia.*

The Advent Mass concludes with its most vivid moment, the repeated cries of the Child's name in the communion **Ecce Virgo concipiet** (1605 *a* 5/15). 'Et vocabitur nomen eius *Emmanuel*': a name is a wondrous thing, and Byrd makes the point by an abrupt but triumphantly convincing return to a D minor that has not been heard since the complex, elegant point of imitation at the very beginning. The return is enforced by a joyous cluster of dissonances over a grand bass augmentation. As for the alleluia at the end of this piece, used only at the Annunciation in Paschal Time, it is clearly a later addition, for it belongs to the late type mentioned on page 253 and it fits badly: at the beginning the alto has to leap a diminished fourth, and at the end music which has performed the welcome function of cementing the brilliant D minor cadence turns inconsequentially to the subdominant. Even apart from harmonic considerations, the clipped phraseology of this

---

*H. C. Collins, in his edition of *Ave Maria* for Chester (H.B.C. 7, 1925), took a strong line on this final alleluia: 'The music will not bear the omission of the *Alleluias*. The Motet is therefore not available for use from Septuagesima Sunday to Easter'—nor, presumably, during Advent in its role as an offertory, when the word alleluia must also be omitted. Yet Byrd specifically prescribes the piece on this occasion (see Table 9).

The Lenten use without an alleluia referred to by Collins is at the Annunciation, and *Ave Maria* without its alleluia also transfers to the Lady Mass in summer. The latter two Masses were presumably projected at a later time than the Advent Mass, by which time the composer may have turned a deaf ear to effects of the mutilation which Collins rightly considered intolerable. It is harder to understand Byrd's providing the mutilated offertory for the Advent Mass itself, for he must have had the Advent offertory clearly in mind when he wrote *Ave Maria* in its role as the alleluia verse.

It would be a little more understandable if we could believe that *Ave Maria* in both of its roles—as alleluia verse and as offertory—had been transferred to Advent from some other liturgical position. But the only other position where *Ave Maria* comes *with* its alleluia is in the rare Annunciation Mass in P.T., which cannot have been written before the Advent Lady Mass on account of the situation with the communion, discussed below.

alleluia makes a sad anticlimax after the controlled broadening of the end of the communion proper.

Five or six Saturdays fall in the forty days between Christmas and the Purification. The motets of the Lady Mass in this season are on the whole less concise than those of the Advent Mass, and also less distinguished.

The text of the introit **Vultum tuum** (1605 *a* 5/16) corresponds to the last three verses of the Annunciation tract *Audi filia* (part of 1605 *a* 5/22) except for a few small cuts in the introit—just enough of them to have made it impossible for Byrd to consider a transfer. Instead he seems to have gone out of his way to choose different styles for his settings of every common phrase. In the tract, the words 'Vultum tuum' are set as a point of 4-part imitation in inversion, unremarkable except for a Beckmesser-like cadence; in the introit the same words are set as a long stretch of staggered homophony. At 'adducentur regi virgines' the tract goes into three parts and into canon; the introit works with swiftly-moving homophonic cells *a 3*, and only gets around to free canonic writing at 'proximae eius adducentur tibi', by which time the canon in the tract has stopped.* (It is a nice question which of the two phrases exhibits greater subtlety in word illustration.) The introit ends with a considerable flurry of crotchets for 'in *laetiti*a et *exultati*one'; the tract places this phrase in a dancelike triple metre. The tract itself concludes very magnificently with an extra phrase, back in duple metre, comparable in style with the ending of the Purification tract *Nunc dimittis*.

Because its text was adopted from the Sunday within the Octave of Christmas, the gradual **Speciosus forma** (1605 *a* 5/17) has a longer verse than usual. Byrd pieced this together by transferring the 'Eructavit' trio (SAT[1]) from *Salve sancta Parens* and adding a second trio for 'Lingua mea' (SAT[2]). In the 'Lingua mea' section the word 'velociter' is set in a predictably rapid fashion, just as it was in the middle-period motet *Domine exaudi . . . clamor meus* (see p. 146). Perhaps in order to balance the long verse, the last phrase of the gradual is drawn out at unusual length ('diffusa est gratia', a text fragment also set in the composite No. 22).

Ordinarily *Speciosus forma* makes a unit with the alleluia verse *Post partum*, which has been discussed under the summer Lady Mass. When, as happens occasionally, Septuagesima Sunday comes early enough so that there is a Saturday after Septuagesima but still before the Purification

---

*For the free canon in the introit, Byrd reached back to a stretto idea he had picked up from White and used in some motets of the middle period, involving a figure with interlocking descending fourths (see p. 138f). Needless to say, the treatment here is less ponderous than in *Peccavi*, less dramatic than in *Exurge quare obdormis Domine*, and more lucid harmonically than in either of those older motets.

(2 February), the terminal alleluia of the gradual and the alleluia verse are omitted and the tract *Gaude Maria Virgo* is sung instead directly after the gradual verse. This transfer can be managed, but is doubtful that Byrd considered this eventuality; the tract begins with another trio and he surely did not envisage *three* of these in a row. Nor did he think to write a *signum* over the cadence before the terminal alleluia in *Speciosus forma*.

The Mass in this season ends with the offertory *Felix namque es* and the communion *Beata viscera*.

The Annunciation of the B.V.M. [25 March]

INTROIT 1605 *a* 5/16   Vultum tuum (in P.T.: Alleluia) 6 . . . ℣ *Eructavit.*
                                     Gloria Patri. Vultum tuum

GRADUAL   22   Diffusa est gratia ℣ *Propter veritatem.*

+ TRACT   Audi filia (without alleluia) ℣ *Vultum tuum* ℣ *Adducentur regi* ℣ Adducentur in laetitia

in P.T.:

ALLELUIA   20   Alleluia ℣ Ave Maria. Alleluia ℣ Virga Iesse. Alleluia

OFFERTORY   14   Ave Maria (in P.T.: Alleluia)

COMMUNION   15   Ecce Virgo concipiet (in P.T.: Alleluia)

Profoundly implicated with the Lady Mass cycle, the Annunciation Masses in Lent and Paschal Time can hardly be said to exist as independent entities. The Annunciation shares its introit *Vultum tuum* with the Lady Mass after Christmas (actually this text is taken from the Common of Virgins) and its offertory *Ave Maria* and communion *Ecce Virgo concipiet* with the Lady Mass in Advent. All that seems to have been composed specifically for this feast is the music of the Paschal alleluias added to the introit and communion, the gradual-tract combination *Diffusa est gratia. Audi filia*—though even here, as we have seen, the section 'Diffusa est gratia' may have been written earlier for the Purification—and possibly the greater alleluia, *Alleluia. Ave Maria. Alleluia. Virga Iesse.**

*See p. 252. The text of this alleluia is right for the Annunciation in P.T. However, the motet's placement in the Lady Mass section, prior to the Annunciation heading, suggests strongly that Byrd meant it to serve also for the Lady Mass in P.T., in spite of the fact

In the first part of this piece Byrd treats the Angel's words of annunciation a little more emphatically than he does in the motet *Ave Maria* (see p. 261f). **Alleluia. Ave Maria** (1605 *a* 5/20) wanders through the modes rather more freely than is usual with Byrd's composite pieces following the Epistle:

Alleluia	Ave Maria	Alleluia	Virga Iesse	Alleluia
a–G	C–(d)–g	g–D	d–C	F–d

One outcome of this tonal plan is a striking harmonic aura, very mild and special, for the homophonic statement of 'Ave Maria'. The words are declaimed to the same rhythm as in *Ave Maria* but with a much clearer melodic outline. The 'gratia plena' figure—the same one as in the other piece, and in much the same harmonic context—stands out more sharply because it is repeated in a little ostinato and then followed by an evocative rest in all the voices: a rest that depends crucially for its effect on the preceding alleluia, in regard to both rhythm and harmony. The figures for 'Dominus tecum' and 'benedicta tu' are similar in both pieces; both echo the dotted-note declamation of 'gratia plena'. And since 'benedicta tu in mulieribus' now has to bear more weight as the last phrase before the second alleluia section, it is extended and strengthened by means of augmentation and by a somewhat unusual repetition of the motive for the second text fragment. Though linked motivically to the first, the second alleluia is nonetheless rather perfunctory, and the verse 'Virga Iesse' is disappointing after 'Ave Maria'; but the third alleluia brings this piece to a broad and splendid conclusion.

Diffusa est gratia (1605 *a* 5/22), a very miscellaneous piece containing some fine moments and some dull ones, follows the same extended (even straggling) plan as the Purification gradual-tract combination *Suscepimus Deus-Sicut audivimus-Nunc dimittis* (1605 *a* 5/1, 2 and 4). The broad 5-part polyphonic opening with its graceful, intimate subject proceeds to the 3-part verse 'Propter veritatem' and then to the opening 'full' verse of the tract 'Audi filia'. This moves homophonically to F and in F it stays for its two relatively long remaining phrases. Here the loose imitative structure, the rather bland harmonic style, and certain melodic details such as the frequent

that in that situation the two verses should be reversed (and in spite of the erroneous rubric 'Post Septuagesima': see p. 222n). It may be that Byrd wrote the piece correctly in the first instance for the Annunciation and then moved it around later when he decided to pass it off for the Lady Mass. There is, however, no other clear case of such a rearrangement in the *Gradualia*. Or he may have harboured a persistent misapprehension about the order of the verses, in which case he could have conceived the piece in the first instance for the Lady Mass. That is what the order of publication suggests.

descent from e′ to c′ recall the older Tudor style, which Byrd evokes in all the Marian tracts. In a final page, replete with archaic sonorities, Byrd is able to restore the D minor tonality altogether convincingly, with the help of a simple bass progression, DCB♭A, which is actually quite rare in this mode (BW 4, 133, bar 6). The same progression contributes to the rich final cadence of the tract *Gaude Maria Virgo* for the Lady Mass in Lent.

The Assumption of the B.V.M. [15 August]

INTROIT 1605 *a* 5/23		Gaudeamus omnes . . . 6 . . . ℣ *Eructavit*. Gloria Patri. Gaudeamus omnes
GRADUAL	22	. . . *Propter veritatem* ℣ Audi filia. Alleluia . . .
+ ALLELUIA	23	. . . ℣ *Assumpta est Maria* . . . *angelorum*. Alleluia
OFFERTORY	24	Assumpta est Maria . . . Dominum. Alleluia
COMMUNION	25	Optimam partem elegit

The Assumption Mass which comes last in the cycle was probably also the last to be composed. Once again the style of the alleluias proves to be suggestive. Besides the one inserted into the composite No. 22, belonging to the later category using the dotted-minim figure, two others have distinctive features which are new in the Marian group. After No. 23 the alleluia moves in triple metre, and after No. 24 the words 'alleluia, alleluia' are declaimed in continuous crotchets—up to seven in a row. These features come up again in book 2 of the *Gradualia*.

The general liveliness of the Assumption music could also indicate that when Byrd wrote it he was getting tired of the restrained style that we have been examining. The texts themselves, however, might have been enough to invigorate the style used to set them. They form something of an exception to the neutral quality of Marian devotion typical of so many of the Propers and keep throwing out promising words such as 'Assumptione' or 'assumpta', 'gaudent' and 'collaudantes'. These Byrd often sets to similar motives. With the former words, indeed, there seems to be a progression from the upward fourths and sixths traversed by 'de cuius Assumptione' in the introit to the octaves at the beginning of the alleluia verse, and finally to the soaring, accelerating tenths of the offertory.

The very first phrase of the introit **Gaudeamus omnes** (1605 *a* 5/23) seems to presage rhythmic adventure; throughout all the 5-part writing of the Marian group no more than half a dozen imitative subjects are to be found with rapid crotchet declamation on three successive crotchets, as in 'Gau*deamus* omnes'. But while this certainly counts as the most spirited of the Marian introits, a comparison with the All Saints introit—which has the same text, allowing for the substitution of the words 'beatae Mariae Virginis: de cuius Assumptione' for 'Sanctorum omnium: de quorum solem- nitate' (see p. 241)—puts the matter in a different perspective.

One is struck first, perhaps, by the manifest intrinsic superiority of the opening point of imitation at the Assumption. The subject is in two contra- puntal parts, the vigorous 'Gaudeamus' idea and a slower one, almost like a cantus firmus, which helps launch the point and then destructs after two entries. It is with the setting of the words 'diem festum celebrantes' that the basic difference in conception begins to appear. All the phrases, with the exception of 'de cuius Assumptione' and 'collaudant Filium Dei', are treated along essentially the same lines as in the All Saints piece: bright and solid at the opening, clamorous at 'diem festum celebrantes', very stately at 'sub honore', and effervescent at 'gaudent Angeli'. But at the Assumption nothing is quite so bright, or clamorous, or stately, or effervescent. And the main thing is that while Byrd does his duty by the text he also shows himself much more concerned with rhythmic and harmonic continuity, avoiding the sharp contrasts which he courts in the other composition.

It is impossible to view the transfer of two successive sections from the Annunciation to supply the Assumption gradual and verse as anything other than a makeshift. So awkward is the transfer, in fact, that one feels Byrd cannot have had the Assumption even vaguely in mind when he wrote the Annunciation—that the Assumption Mass must have been an afterthought. Still, he was sufficiently intrigued by the odd result of this transfer to echo it quite deliberately in the alleluia verse, **Assumpta est Maria** (part of 1605 *a* 5/23), which forms the second portion of the post-Epistle group. After assembling the first portion of this (the gradual) from the 3-part section 'Propter veritatem' and the 5-part 'Audi filia' and 'Alleluia', transferred from *Diffusa est gratia* (1605 *a* 5/22), Byrd also used three voices for the alleluia verse 'Assumpta est Maria' and its terminal alleluia. But then he repeated the last words of the verse, 'gaudet exercitus angelorum', and added yet another alleluia, all *a 5*, ending with nine breves of 5-part music:*

*The passage is transcribed wrongly in TCM and BW so that the triple metre goes twice too slow; see Andrews, *Byrd's Polyphony*, 47f.

Propter	Audi filia alleluia	*Assumpta alleluia*	... gaudet exer-	alleluia
veritatem		*est Maria*	citus angelorum	
a 3	*a 5*	*a 5*	*a 3*	*a 3*	*a 5*	*a 5*

A repetition of this kind is as unprecedented as a 3-part gradual (and for that matter, even the 3-part alleluia verse was unusual enough to rattle the printer, who mistook it for an introit verse and attached it onto the end of *Gaudeamus omnes*).

The first alleluia (after 'Audi filia') hides a considerable measure of ingenuity behind the good-humoured strains that it builds up out of the stereotyped dotted-minim figure. It is firmly in F, like most of 'Audi filia'. The little 3-part alleluia following the alleluia verse is also a cunning piece of work, but the 5-part alleluia brings the Assumption post-Epistle group to a more straightforward close. This is one of the few alleluias in the *Gradualia* written in triple metre. Heard after the very dance-like duple rhythms of the first two alleluias, the fast galliard rhythms of this one provide an unmistakable echo of the Renaissance *Tanz/Nachtanz* tradition.

Both the offertory and the communion are excellently characterized little pieces. The opening subject of **Assumpta est Maria** (1605 *a* 5/24) is repeated in thirds an octave lower (SA[1], then TB), making a double structure to which Byrd adds one extra entry in the other alto—a sort of tonal answer—and then, as though impatient of the delay, sharply undercuts the cadence with a strong rollicking figure for 'gaudent Angeli'. Joined skillfully in to the end of this phrase is an interesting point for the words 'collaudantes, benedicunt Dominum'. A pair of octave imitations on a subject which itself marches up an octave (B♭–B♭ in bass and first alto, F–F in soprano and tenor) constitutes yet another repeated structure; moreover an augmentation of the 'collaudantes' crotchets appears in several voices (most comically, in the bass) while an inversion of them serves as a second, cadential motive for 'benedicunt'. After this the alleluia explodes in intricate crotchet sequences. Since the breath-taking false relation at the introduction of 'gaudent Angeli'* everything has been in F, up to a sudden turn back to D in the alleluia's penultimate bar—which jolts nearly as hard.

Perhaps in compensation for the Lydian bias of the offertory, the communion **Optimam partem** (1605 *a* 5/25) stays close to D minor and, more surprisingly, A minor. (One thinks of a similar situation in the Nativity

---

*This sharp articulation also illustrates a fine point of Byrd's response to syntax. When the first two text phrases of a motet are closely connected (e.g., 'Benedicta et venerabilis/es, sacra Virgo'; 'Beata viscera Mariae Virginis/quae portaverunt'; 'Optimam partem elegit/ sibi Maria') Byrd tends to overlap the second phrase. But here the first two phrases are quite distinct: 'Assumpta est Maria in coelis:/gaudent Angeli'.

Mass.) The admirably plastic opening phrase recalls that of the offertory *Assumpta est Maria* in its structure, involving a subject in thirds (A¹ A², this time accompanied by a brief cantus firmus in the S) followed by a repetition at the lower octave (TB) and then by a single 'tonal answer' (S). The middle section hugs the duple metre, but choppiness recedes in a final point of great rhythmic subtlety. In the subject itself there is a curious but entirely effective little gap between the words 'ab ea' and 'in aeternum', and each fragment chiselled out in this way exploits semitones more pointedly than usual in the *Gradualia*. The motet (and the Mass as a whole) comes to a fine florid conclusion enforced by two strongly placed false relations between C and C♯.

[2]

The three 5-part Propers of book 2 for Easter, Ascension and Whitsun may well have been the last music of the *Gradualia* to have been composed. Placing them next to the 5-part music of book 1 brings into sharpest possible relief the stylistic range encompassed by Byrd over the whole collection. Most striking is a comparison between the Easter Mass and the group of Marian Masses which we have been discussing, since all this music is in the same mode (though not all in the same clefs). In such a spectrum the beautiful All Saints Mass can be seen to occupy a middle position between the essentially restrained style of the Marian group and the vivid *al fresco* writing of the later pieces. The two sopranos in the choir stand as an emblem of a new commitment to brilliance.

These book 2 Masses are full of surprises; Byrd employs a whole array of novel effects, some of which will obviously not bear much repetition. In certain of the motets the rhythm is kept extremely fluid, and rhythmic discontinuities are matched by sharp harmonic and textural contrasts. Short homophonic sections of a madrigalian cast become common. The 3-part verses, too, are more modern in style—and there are fewer of them. The fundamental difference, perhaps, is that Byrd is now ready to respond in a much more extreme way to texts which are themselves much more evocative than those typical of the Marian Propers.

There is another side to the comparison, however. By and large the workmanship of the book 2 Masses manifests less refinement than that of the Marian Masses; there are signs of carelessness, even impatience in their composition. Sometimes Byrd's novel devices succeed brilliantly, but at other times the rhythmic effects can give an impression of eccentricity, and the homophonic effects an impression of mere facility. At a number of places the part writing is needlessly rough. All this goes to confirm a conclusion suggested by some other evidence, that at least parts of book 2 must have been written quite rapidly. These Masses include some of Byrd's greatest motets, such as *Haec dies, Psallite Domino, Confirma hoc Deus* and *Non vos relinquam orphanos*, works in which the elegance of detail is fully commensurate with the inspired quality of the overall conception. But they also include less inspired pieces and also some decidedly sticky ones, pieces which have probably contributed to the view sometimes ventured that book 2 of the *Gradualia* does not hold up to the artistic standard of book 1.

As these three Masses all fall in Eastertide, they are shot through with alleluias—even more of them than in the Lady Mass in Paschal Time, for which Byrd had made provision in the Marian group. This feature obviously has much to do with the brilliance that characterizes so much of the music. Each greater alleluia comes around to the word in three separate sections, while some of the introits, communions and antiphons have two, even three, alleluias prized in and after their sometimes miniscule texts. All the offertories, communions and antiphons end with alleluias, and this helped Byrd achieve settings of particular conciseness. A final alleluia, as we have seen, relieved him of the necessity of making a motet's final point weighty or extensive. As a formal block, the alleluia could take responsibility for terminating the discourse, employing brilliance for this means rather than contrapuntal extension or rhetorical emphasis.

Most of the 5-part alleluias of book 2 are appreciably simpler than those of the Marian group. Perhaps Byrd was growing weary of the intricate constructions that he had provided again and again for the Marian alleluias, or perhaps he now felt that such intricacy was inappropriate in pieces where the word had to be set so very many times. Many of the alleluias fall back on the two familiar figures discussed above, those involving dotted-minim and two-crotchet rhythms, occasionally with a more or less routine effect, but occasionally with great beauty. In almost a third of the pieces, furthermore, Byrd uses a simple sequential structure, something he had experimented with in the Marian Masses only once, and in a very quiet spirit: after the gradual *Tollite portas* (1605 *a* 5/13). The sequential alleluias of book 2—and there are examples in the 4-part as well as the 5-part fascicle—would not be described as quiet, but rather as showy and playful, schematic, ingenious and irresistible. We examined one of these alleluias on page 233 (Ex. 42).

They have a quality that we may recognize from the extended 'fa la' sections in that popular favourite of all Elizabethan musical genres, the ballet. The English ballet had been developed in the 1590s by Byrd's pupils Morley and Weelkes; the development was not entirely inspired by the

Italian *balletto*, not entirely cut off from native sources of musical energy. Byrd, who appears to have considered the ballet to be beneath his dignity as a serious musician, came closest to its spirit in the sequential alleluias of the second *Gradualia*.

Easter*

INTROIT	1607/20	Resurrexi ℣ *Domine probasti me*. Gloria Patri. Resurrexi
GRADUAL	21	Haec dies ℣ Confitemini Domino. Alleluia ℣ Pascha
+ ALLELUIA		nostrum
+ SEQUENCE	22	Victimae paschali laudes. Alleluia
OFFERTORY	23	Terra tremuit. Alleluia
COMMUNION	24	Pascha nostrum. Alleluia

Easter is a season that calls for much music. In a source such as the Gyffard Partbooks of Queen Mary's time, many more liturgical items are furnished for Easter than for any other season, and Byrd followed this tradition in the *Gradualia*. The 5-part Mass in book 2 followed after a sizable group of 3-part Easter motets in book 1, plus the early cantus firmus motet *Christus resurgens*, a 4-part setting of the famous Easter processional antiphon. He was able to draw on his own experience, too, in dealing with Easter texts over many years: from *Similes illis fiant*, his boyhood collaboration with Sheppard and Mundy in the Gyffard Partbooks, and the little canons of *Alleluia. Confitemini Domino*, to the precocious *In resurrectione tua Domine* of the late 1570s and the brilliant 6-part *Haec dies* of 1591. This is worth mentioning both because it is a unique situation—apart from Easter he had scarcely set any texts belonging to the other *Gradualia* feasts prior to that collection—and also because he appears to have referred back to some of the earlier pieces in composing the 5-part Masses of book 2.

Appropriately enough, and surely by design, the Easter Mass is the most brilliant of all in the *Gradualia*. It is the one in which Byrd's new stylistic tendencies are displayed in their most extreme form. The first word of the introit **Resurrexi** (1607/20) is, of course, the key word of the feast and

---

*There is no 5-part setting of an antiphon, perhaps because in book 1 Byrd had already provided a setting (in three parts) of the *Magnificat* antiphon for first Vespers, *Vespere autem sabbati* (part of 1605 *a 3/6*).

indeed of the whole Paschal season. Byrd sets it to one of his most brilliant
stretto points, nine breves long, with a motive curling and accelerating up an
octave. At its basis is a cell of four breves which is imitated twice, after
5 and 6 semibreves, at the lower fifth and octave—but imitated so freely, and
with so many extra strettos, that the whole makes a wonderful effect of
effervescent spontaneity.

Then suddenly the next several text fragments follow with bewildering
rapidity (Ex. 50). Everything seems calculated to create a sense of dis-

Ex. 50

continuity: the changing textures, the extraordinary bass solo at 'Posuisti',
and the repeated juxtaposition of clashing triads—D major and F major,
A and B♭, D and B♮. We scarcely catch our breath at the phrase 'super me
manum tuam' before an even more hectic little alleluia explodes with a
cadential flourish of ten quavers in the alto. Nearly all the fragments in this
brilliant mosaic involve echoes between the two sopranos; if 'Posuisti'
breaks the pattern, that is only because the words are sung only once. The
final alleluia starts after another juxtaposition of D and F major chords. It
employs an ostinato figure which is then modified, shifted to the strong beat,
and underpinned by a slower bass sequence aEFC/FCDA in preparation
for the cadence. Though a half close it is entirely solid.*

*At BW 6, 127, bars 5–6 (TCM 7, 264, bar 2) emendation of the penultimate 'alleluia'
in the second soprano to c′b♭′a′b♭′c′ ga′gfg seems preferable to the alto emendation
feedcdef proposed in TCM and followed in BW.

It cannot be said that mercurial writing of this kind continues into the verse 'Domine probasti me', but nonetheless this is one of the most modern of the verses in the *Gradualia* (see Ex. 41b). There are various suitably nervous touches in the doxology. The last-minute imitative figure for 'Amen'—a crotchet scale moving up a seventh, in three of the voices—links well into the *da capo*.

In this Mass the gradual and alleluia form a single number with no voice reduction; the texts are short and Byrd chose to make the setting one of his most concise. The opening repeated period of **Haec dies** (1607/21) is only four breves long and the four large sections of the piece last for no more than 14, 12, 6 and 13 breves respectively. Thanks to the skill with which Byrd controls the rhythmic flux the impression is not so much of haste or even excitement as of vivacity. The gradual itself speeds up and moves to C in reaction to the text fragments 'exultemus' and 'et laetemur', but this intensification is beautifully checked by the more deliberate pace of the gradual verse 'Confitemini Domino', which turns back at once to D. The declamatory patterns are surprisingly similar to those in Byrd's youthful setting of the same words for the Sarum liturgy (see p. 62), the main improvement consisting of matching rhythms for the two settings of 'quoniam'.

The alleluia picks up the pace again by means of a rather urgent cadential overlap and then by insistent chiming of the familiar dotted-minim rhythm— which chimes from an unfamiliar position, however, always across the beat, thus adding to the sense of urgency. No essential action is required of this alleluia and it merely runs its dotted-minim figure (gage) down in sequence from G–E–C–A. Its cadence, in F, feels just a little curt, a quality that is enhanced by a minim rest in all parts; then the solemn words of the alleluia verse 'Pascha nostrum' are sung in slow homophony with a very effective turn to A minor. (The supporting E major chord here is the only one in the Easter Mass.) The phrase 'immolatus est Christus' is set more expansively, its 10-breve span making use of a more archaic style that avoids dissonance, though it does not avoid false relations. This provides an admirable balance to a highly accomplished four-sectional musical structure.

Haec dies runs into the Easter sequence **Victimae paschali laudes** (1607/22). The highly inflected style of the introit and gradual could obviously not be carried on through this very long text. Byrd instead resorted to the old-fashioned style and form he had developed for the Purification and Annunciation tracts (whose texts, however, are only half or two-thirds as long). The basic form as extended here, with 'full' sections at the beginning middle and end intercalated symmetrically with sections for reduced voices, looks even more like the old votive antiphon:

verse 1	Victimae paschali laudes	*a 5*	16 *breves*
2	Agnus redemit oves	*a 4*	21
3	Mors et vita duello	*a 2*	13
	Dux vitae mortuus	*a 5*	14
4	Dic nobis Maria	*a 3*	6
5–7	Sepulcrum Christi viventis	*a 2*	28
8	Scimus Christum surrexisse	*a 5*	19
	Amen. Alleluia		6

In verse 3 the duel between Death and Life suggested a free 2-part canon between alto and tenor, while verses 4–8 suggested a 'dramatic' setting in which the question put by the three low voices is answered on Mary's behalf by the two sopranos. As Byrd was not at his best in the trios of the *Gradualia*, generally speaking, the dullness of these duets does not come altogether as a surprise. But they are shored up by three superb 'full' sections: 'Victimae paschali laudes', with its haunting three-fold repetitions, the vivid 'Dux vitae mortuus', and—most vivid of all—'Scimus Christum surrexisse', whose dark exuberant course is checked by a plagal amen and alleluia, unexpectedly sober and concise.

Byrd countered one of the longest and most retrospective pieces in the *Gradualia* with one of the shortest and most modern. **Terra tremuit** (1607/23) is a musical epigram:

Terra tremuit, et quievit, dum resurgeret in iudicio Deus. Alleluia.

Having decided to set the nine words of this offertory very concisely, in eleven breves of music, Byrd was well advised to concoct something strange and novel for the word 'tremuit'—and to repeat the oscillating crotchet chords a moment later for 'quievit', devil take the meaning . . . The sequential alleluia works with rather facile madrigalian scales in stretto. Guided as simply as possible by the second soprano and the bass, the sequence moves first round the circle of fifths (that is, down by seconds) and then down by thirds.

The communion **Pascha nostrum** (1607/24) is the most eccentric Easter piece of all. The rich, complex, flowing point of imitation at the start is sharply contradicted in harmony, rhythm and texture by a 3-breve alleluia which overlaps its cadence in an almost insulting fashion. Then, after an even more abrupt harmonic move, the second half of the piece moves in a faster pulse and with increasingly madrigalian accents, culminating in a triumphant exclamation of the word 'sinceritatis' by the full choir in block chords:

Pascha nostrum immolatus est Christus. Alleluia. Itaque epulemur in azymis sinceritatis et veritatis. Alleluia.

Here is a case where the 'abstrusa atque recondita vis' of sacred words is operating in a way that seems indeed abstruse and recondite; some private association to the word 'sinceritatis' must have prompted this pointed setting. The accelerating rhythm continues into the alleluia. Byrd had experimented with an alleluia in continuous crotchet declamation in the Marian offertory *Assumpta est Maria*, and he now saw that such alleluias would terminate the communions of his brilliant Masses for Easter and Whitsun very aptly. The bright F major chatter of the present piece is led back to the Dorian mode by a minim sequence in the bass reminiscent of that in the introit (b♭FGD/FCDA).

Ascension

INTROIT	1607/25	Viri Galilaei ℣ *Omnes gentes plaudite*. Gloria Patri. Viri Galilaei
ALLELUIA	26	Alleluia ℣ Ascendit Deus. Alleluia 27 ℣ Dominus in Sina. Alleluia
OFFERTORY	28	Ascendit Deus. Alleluia
COMMUNION	29	Psallite Domino. Alleluia
MAGNIFICAT ANTIPHON, 2ND VESPERS	30	O Rex gloriae. Alleluia

The Ascension of our Lord, like the Assumption of the B.V.M., tempts a composer with many texts that cry out for rising figures in the musical setting. Once again Byrd makes many of these figures similar and arranges them in an order of increasing levitation. Characteristically, though, the entire range is more extreme: in place of the fourths, sixths, octaves and tenths of the Assumption, the Ascension introit motive 'ascendentem in coelum' in its basic form covers a fifth, 'Ascendit Deus' in the first alleluia a seventh, 'ascendens in altum' in the second alleluia (on average) and 'Ascendit Deus' in the offertory an octave. All culminate in a grand rising passage in the communion, 'qui ascendit super coelos coelorum', in which the bass marches up in minims through a twelfth, from low F′ to c.

In the Ascension and Whitsun Masses Byrd shows a new disinclination to commence motets with polyphonic writing. It is hard to say whether this resulted solely from a desire for still greater conciseness or whether it represents one facet of a broader retreat from polyphony as a guiding compositional principle. In any case straightforward 'cell' constructions and homophonic beginnings of one kind or another now become the rule. The introit **Viri Galilaei** (1607/25) begins with a four-fold ostinato, but an ostinato of a kind Byrd had never used before, at least in a motet: one that is essentially regular in rhythm and essentially homophonic in texture. The result is unusually neat and square, a quality that is maintained in the rest of the introit and verse by means of self-consciously regular rhythms and phraseology. The consonant nature of the harmony—the first serious dissonance does not appear until after fifteen breves—contributes to the squareness; indeed consonant harmony is characteristic of the Ascension Mass as a whole. The contrast could not be more complete with the volatile, irregular Easter music. The last phrase, 'ita veniet', built on Byrd's favourite figure of interlocking thirds, breaks the regularity of phrasing as the bass gingerly lowers itself down an octave with the help of an amusing touch of augmentation. This is an unusual motet for Byrd but in its own way decidedly an effective one, at least up to the disappointing alleluia.

In the Marian greater alleluia *Alleluia. Ave Maria* (1605 *a* 5/20) Byrd showed himself quite aware of the different needs of alleluias at the beginnings and ends of pieces (see p. 265). This awareness is sharpened in the greater alleluias of book 2. Without the words, the first phrase of **Alleluia. Ascendit Deus** (1607/26) would never be recognized as an alleluia; it consists of a simple repeated structure of a cell with one slower voice (S^2S^1A, then S^1AB), comparable to those at the start of such motets as *Rorate coeli* and *Optimam partem*. After the last words of the verse, 'in voce tubae', have been set in an anonymous half-homophonic style, Byrd repeats them in an entirely new setting. This trumpets away at the G major chord of the cadence for all the world like *The Battle* or the setting of *Blow up the trumpet in the new moon* in the *Psalmes, songs and sonnets* of 1611.

The short central alleluia runs very smoothly into **Dominus in Sina** (1607/27), which begins with an old-fashioned 3-part cell (indicative of Byrd's newest manner, however, is the radical harmonic reinterpretation when the top line of the cell is repeated a fifth higher). The upward thrust of the next short phrase, 'ascendens in altum', also infects the next one, 'captivam duxit'; then playfully—since what goes up must come down—Byrd leads 'captivitatem' down the scale in the two sopranos, and down an octave to low D' in the bass. The final alleluia makes a brisk but splendid sound with a dotted crotchet figure, guided sequentially up the circle of fifths by a simple dotted-minim figure in the bass, FCGD. This prepares a cadence in G. Indeed the whole greater alleluia tips precipitously towards the Mixolydian mode, despite the Ionian incipits of both parts.

Byrd could have saved himself the trouble of composing the offertory **Ascendit Deus** (1607/28), for the text corresponds to that of the first alleluia verse, and all he had to do was make sure that the initial alleluia in the latter piece would separate off (as is the case in the greater alleluia for Whitsun). If he had done so we would not be much the poorer, though admittedly we would miss the most intricate of Byrd's sequential alleluias. A distinctly brainy elaboration of the alleluia in *Ego sum panis vivus*, a 4-part motet for Corpus Christi (see p. 233 and Ex. 42), this employs the interlocking thirds that come up at several other points in this Mass. After starting on B in the tenor the figure moves down in thirds in the bass from G–E–C–A; the soprano anticipates the tenor at the upper third, on d′, and hovers there until the stretto interval is a seventh (ed′), at which point the sequence proceeds in the two outer voices. Over and above this basic outline the rhythm is shifted with a conjurer's skill, with invertible counterpoint at the tenth used to very good advantage.

A small point of rhythmic subtlety also brings to life the simple opening of the communion **Psallite Domino** (1607/29), one of the most spirited and expert pieces in the whole of the *Gradualia*. Cries of 'Psallite Domino' in the soprano are answered by the rest of the choir in block chords, but although the tonal plan is elementary—subject, tonal answer, tonal answer, subject— Byrd adds just the necessary rhythmic variety by introducing entries after 4, 6 and then 3 minims. There follows his most imaginative response to the idea of the Ascension, an ecstatic slow stepwise surge upward in all the voices ('qui ascendit super coelos coelorum'); in his own way Byrd recreates the effect of the magnificent 'et ascendit in coelum' passage from the Credo of Taverner's *Missa Gloria tibi Trinitas*. The motet ends with a particularly charming alleluia.

These are both tiny pieces, barely half as long as the *Magnificat* antiphon **O Rex gloriae** (1607/30). The words 'O Rex gloriae, Domine virtutum' are sung only once, in a non-repeated 3-part cell, invested with a special luminous intensity by their ascent through the major triads of C and D (see Ex. 51a), F and ultimately G. This basic harmonic action then projects into the total form. The phrases 'super omnes coelos' and 'ne derelinquas nos orphanos', which begin on D and F respectively, each feature a stepwise upward sequence reflecting the striking progression CD at the very beginning: the material for 'super omnes coelos' is repeated a tone higher, on E, adapted to

Ex. 51

the next word, 'ascendisti', and that for 'ne derelinquas' makes sharply defined cadences on G and A. And although the words 'ne derelinquas nos orphanos' themselves are not sung on A, this degree holds fast throughout the next phrase, a serious and strangely affecting repeated setting of the words 'sed mitte promissum Patris in nos' in which the bass moves down in interlocking thirds from a to A. Repeated structures underlie all the sections of this motet, once again, past the opening cell. Even the alleluia involves a little sequence (F to G) which is repeated. Like several other alleluias in the Ascension Mass, however, it does not maintain the musical level of the music that precedes it.

Whitsun

INTROIT	1607/31	Spiritus Domini ℣ *Exsurgat Deus*. Gloria Patri. Spiritus Domini
ALLELUIA	32	Alleluia ℣ Emitte Spiritum tuum. Alleluia 33 ℣ Veni Sancte Spiritus. Alleluia
+ SEQUENCE	36	Veni Sancte Spiritus. Alleluia
OFFERTORY	34	Confirma hoc Deus. Alleluia
COMMUNION	35	Factus est repente. Alleluia
MAGNIFICAT ANTIPHON, IST VESPERS	37	Non vos relinquam orphanos. Alleluia

It is startling to turn the page and see the introit of the next Mass, **Spiritus Domini** (1607/31), begin with a cell closely resembling the distinctive opening cell of the Ascension antiphon *O Rex gloriae* (see Ex. 51). While this obviously means nothing to the listener or communicant at Mass on Whit Sunday, it gives the student a good deal to think about. It suggests that Byrd composed these pieces in strict order and that musical parallels between certain adjacent or nearly adjacent numbers emerged from a momentary mental set rather than from any deliberate plan to 'unify' the Masses. It bespeaks hastiness in the composition of the Whitsun Mass as a whole—there is indeed a certain amount of perfunctory writing in this cycle, which however also includes two of the most accomplished and beautiful of all Byrd's compositions. Finally, the striking parallel between adjacent pieces belonging to two different Masses cautions us against making too much of parallels within the Masses themselves. The second alleluia **Veni Sancte Spiritus** (1607/33), for example, starts off like a carbon copy of the introit. There is a cell of identical length and very similar material, albeit in only two voices rather than three, followed as in the introit by a simple homophonic answer.

Thirty-one breves long, the offertory **Confirma hoc Deus** (1607/34) is another of the perfect miniatures contained in the *Gradualia*. The first few phrases flow rapidly and very smoothly, growing more and more polyphonic after the plain opening in G, and moving up the circle of fifths to a cadence on A at 'a templo tuo'. Byrd's interest in schematic structures is evidenced once again by the route back, which consists of regularly spaced imitations of the motive for 'quod est in Hierusalem' down four steps in thirds.* The most original and beautiful place in this motet comes at the junction of the last phrase 'tibi offerent reges munera' and the terminal alleluia. Alleluias ordinarily make a clear new departure, even when an overlap is involved, but this one seems to evolve naturally and almost imperceptibly out of the previous musical flux; 'tibi offerent' does not reach a cadence, and in fact it is just stretching to a leisurely climax in the soprano when the two alleluia motives make their first appearance below, as though to control both the surge up to high d' and the somewhat vigorous dotted rhythm for 'offerent'. Each motive bears a family resemblance to figures that are already in the listener's ear (what is more, the word 'alleluia' has actually been sung even before the advent of these motives). The rhythm, which has been moving steadily in twos, now broadens out to threes, and with the help of distinct new forms of both alleluia motives, and one glowing false relation, the piece achieves a serenity or a majesty that would hardly have been predicted on the basis of its concise opening gestures.†

The notion of integrating alleluias with the rest of the music is carried one step further in Byrd's superb setting of the *Magnificat* antiphon **Non vos relinquam orphanos** (1607/37). Like the Paschal introit text, among others (see Ex. 50), this text contains interior alleluias as well as a terminal one:

---

*The sequence is bce (etc.) / ga'c' / efa' doubled by bdf / ABD (echoed at the octave by abd and a'b'd').

†For a closer analysis of this motet see J. Kerman, 'William Byrd, 1543–1623', *Musical Times*, cxiv (1973), 687ff.

Non vos relinquam orphanos. Alleluia. Vado, et venio ad vos. Alleluia.
Et gaudebit cor vestrum. Alleluia.

Instead of treating the first phrase and first alleluia as successive units, Byrd
runs them together as a sort of double point, so that from the very start the
heavenly promise is punctuated by quiet, grateful alleluias. This famous
passage sounds less like an old double point than an ostinato, however, for
although the main entries are arranged with some cunning in a flexible
pattern, the alleluias are generally tucked in at the same places and on the
same pitches. The motet moves forward rather suddenly in crotchets at the
phrase 'Et gaudebit cor vestrum', a simple repeated structure with changing
harmonies for each of the three statements; the faster motion continues and
then slows down beautifully in the terminal alleluia. This passage goes back
to *In resurrectione tua Domine*, a motet from the late 1570s which fore-
shadows the *Gradualia* pieces in form and also in actual content (see p. 90f.)
and Ex. 52). In the earlier piece the flowing stretto lasts for eight semibreves

Ex. 52

only before giving way to another idea. In *Non vos relinquam* an augmentation in the bass provides a new figure for the cadence—a figure which turns
out to be an extended inversion of the previous alleluia motive heard together
with 'Non vos relinquam' at the very start, and heard again in the brief

central alleluia. What Byrd was dealing with here was simply the two-crotchet stereotype which comes up more than a dozen times in the *Gradualia*; this is a fine example of the artistry that such materials could yield when he was writing at the height of his inspiration. The words of this motet may well have touched him more closely than those of the other Whitsun items.

In *Confirma hoc Deus* and *Non vos relinquam* it is the beginnings of alleluia sections that are shaded away. In the communion **Factus est repente** (1607/35) the end of the interior alleluia receives similar treatment; the augmentations in this little alleluia do not have time to settle before the next phrase is brought down upon them. Byrd may have done this to convey the overwhelming impact of the Holy Spirit, for the piece as a whole is certainly one of the most vivid and madrigalian of his whole output:

Factus est repente de coelo sonus tanquam adventientis spiritus vehementis, ubi erant sedentes. Alleluia. Et repleti sunt omnes de Spiritu Sancto, loquentes magnalia Dei. Alleluia.

Suddenness and vehemence are depicted by complex crotchet rhythms (duly mitigated at 'sedentes') while the repeated chiming of soprano and tenor Ds in the last phrase seems not to illustrate the text itself so much as the adjacent passage in Acts: 'And there appeared unto them cloven tongues like as of fire, and it sat upon each of them. And they were all filled with the Holy Ghost, and began to speak with other tongues, as the Spirit gave them utterance'. Glossolalia is evoked by the alleluia, too, with its instrumental-sounding crotchet figure multiplying itself in exuberant but hard-to-follow cross rhythms. It is a 5-minim figure, superimposed upon a schematic 4-minim sequence in the bass.

Schematic, once again, is the layout of the matched alleluias beginning and ending **Alleluia. Emitte Spiritum tuum** (1607/32). Both alleluias move at the same basic steady pace—an 8-semibreve ostinato (overlapping after 5 semibreves) in the first, a 4-semibreve sequence in the second—with faster contrapuntal adjuncts. And the second half of the ostinato figure is equivalent to that of the sequence. In between, the three different phrases of the verse work with much the same musical idea: an unusual but not a very expressive procedure.

The Whitsun greater alleluia ends with a terminal alleluia which is not included if the sequence is sung.* But as with some of the Paschal alleluias

---

*An examination of Byrd's treatment of three Masses that include sequences shows some inconsistency. (1) In the Easter Mass the alleluia *Pascha nostrum* lacks a terminal alleluia and is followed directly in the partbooks by the sequence *Victimae paschali laudes*. (2) In the present Mass an optional alleluia is present, and what is more the sequence is in the Marian group, one would hate to skip this optional alleluia. The ascending 4-crotchet scale figure, with its propensity for forming gentle *echappées*, appears also in the Ascension communion *Psallite Domino* (1607/29) and in the well-known 4-part motet *Sacerdotes Domini* for Corpus Christi (1605 *a 4/3*) (see Ex. 54).

As for the sequence **Veni Sancte Spiritus** (1607/36), that long text presented the composer with a problem and he tackled it in a more forthright manner, if also in a more schematic one, than he had with the Easter sequence *Victimae paschali laudes*. There are five 6-line stanzas, rhyming *aab ccb*. Byrd ploughs right through the words, declaiming them syllabically and usually only once in each voice, employing some kind of homophony or light polyphony. As each line of verse lasts for an average of three breves, he is able to dispose of over 80 words—over 200 syllables—in about 100 breves; three *partes* of approximately the same length encompass stanzas 1–2, stanzas 3–4, and stanza 5 with the last line drawn out prior to the amen and alleluia. *Veni Sancte Spiritus* may not count as anyone's favourite Byrd motet, but it deserves our respect for the variety that he was able to pack into this constraining scheme. The first halves of stanzas 2 and 4 (stanzas 2^1 and 4^1) are set for reduced voices, and in as many as five half-stanzas successive lines are treated in free or strict sequence (stanzas 1^2, 2^1, 3^2, 4^2 and 5^2)*. The phrases 'Consolator optime' and 'Flecta quod est rigidum . . .' recall the opening cell of *O Rex gloriae*, once again.

placed out of order, as a sort of appendix after all the other Mass items. (3) In the Corpus Christi Mass in book 1 Byrd does not set the sequence *Lauda Sion Salvatorem* at all. Again he provides as terminal alleluia to the alleluia, *Caro mea*, but as in the Ascension Mass, this alleluia follows a *signum* and a bar line so that it can easily be detached if the sequence is sung in plainchant. Sequences were not easy to set, and at the time of book 1 Byrd had apparently not yet decided to tackle them.

*There seems to be a systematic element here too, but in fact these sequences seem always to have been prompted by verbal parallels between the lines in question, such as 'Veni pater pauperum, / Veni dator munerum, / Veni lumen cordium' and the like.

Corpus Christi, Votive Mass of the Blessed Sacrament, Christmas, Epiphany

After the Marian group and the All Saints Mass, book 1 of the *Gradualia* contains only one other coherent 'office', the 4-part Mass for Corpus Christi. This includes the Corpus Christi processional hymn and is augmented by three special motets associated with the Blessed Sacrament, making eight numbers in all. In book 2 this complex is further augmented by two antiphons and by a pair of texts designed to make the Corpus Christi Mass usable as the Votive Mass of the Blessed Sacrament on Thursdays throughout the year. Two other 4-part Masses appear at the beginning of book 2, for Christmas and Epiphany.

As we have seen with the Mass Ordinaries, the style that Byrd evolved for 4-part writing is simply a chamber-music version of his normal style in five parts. The differences determined by the number of voices are obvious enough. Most (though not all) of Byrd's masterpieces of intimate expression are for four parts; one thinks of *Ave verum corpus, Ego sum panis vivus, O magnum misterium, Senex puerum portabat* and *Sacerdotes Domini*. In four parts broad and massive effects are avoided, and with them the evocation of the archaic Tudor style which forms so striking an occasional feature of the Marian Masses in particular. With the 4-part repertory, as with the 5-part, a progression can be traced from a more careful, restrained, sometimes even relatively colourless idiom in the first book to a more vivid and venturesome one in the second. Indicative is the disposition of the voices: in book 1 the Corpus Christi Mass (like the Marian group) uses a balanced choir with one soprano while in book 2 Christmas and Epiphany (like the 5-part music for All Saints, Easter, Ascension and Whitsun) use two sopranos of equal range, a texture which allows for more brilliant effects. If there are no 4-part motets to match the most brilliant of the Easter and Whitsun pieces, there are also no 4-part motets or passages as hasty as some that are to be found in the 5-part section. Save for one or two exceptional pieces, Byrd's music for the 4-part Masses is more consistent in style than the 5-part music, is more consistently 'modern' in sound, and also maintains a more consistent level of workmanship.

It will be recalled that book 1 includes a good-sized group of miscellaneous 4-part compositions, some of them non-liturgical and some older than the main body of the *Gradualia* (see Table 8). Not set apart by any special rubric, they follow directly the eight Corpus Christi items as Nos. 9–20 in the partbooks. Indeed it is a moot point whether the miscellaneous group should be construed as beginning at the end of the Corpus Christi music or half way through it, for the last four Corpus Christi items—Nos. 5–8, which follow the introit, gradual–alleluia, offertory and communion—do not fit too well with the others, on a number of counts. Their liturgical association with the Mass is only approximate, as has already been suggested. *Ave verum corpus* and *O salutaris hostia* fall into the 'paraliturgical' category at best, for these hymns never achieved formal liturgical status even though they were commonly sung at the Benediction of the Blessed Sacrament. *Pange lingua gloriosi* is the main hymn for the important Corpus Christi procession. And *O sacrum convivium*, the *Magnificat* antiphon at Second Vespers, probably owes its place in this company to its additional paraliturgical uses in honour of the Blessed Sacrament and in the same procession. Manuscript evidence shows that *Ave verum corpus* predates the main body of the *Gradualia* (see p. 225) and stylistic evidence argues the same for *O salutaris hostia*. Only *O salutaris hostia* and *O sacrum convivium*, furthermore, are in the Mixolydian mode, the mode of the main Corpus Christi items.

Within the miscellaneous group itself, Nos. 9–20, Byrd did not arrange the music according to mode or clef combination, but he did group the Marian texts together (Nos. 11–19). What seems most likely is that finding four* pieces among his miscellaneous group that were associated with the Eucharist, he took care to group them all at the beginning so as to bring them in conjunction with Corpus Christi. We shall follow this hint and consider these four pieces together with the four actual Mass numbers, adding to them the four extra motets of book 2 (five, in Byrd's numeration)—even though we evidently cannot conceive of a very integral relationship amongst this mixed dozen.

*Four—or three: *O sacrum convivium* could very well have been written at the same time as the Mass itself.

Corpus Christi

INTROIT	1605 *a* 4/1	Cibavit eos ℣ *Exultate Deo*. Gloria Patri. Cibavit eos
GRADUAL	2	Oculi omnium ℣ *Aperis tu. Alleluia.* ℣ *Caro mea.*
+ALLELUIA		Alleluia
OFFERTORY	3	Sacerdotes Domini. Alleluia
COMMUNION	4	Quotiescunque manducabitis. Alleluia
HYMNS TO THE	5	Ave verum corpus
BLESSED		
SACRAMENT	6	O salutaris hostia
MAGNIFICAT ANTIPHON,		
2ND VESPERS	7	O sacrum convivium. Alleluia
PROCESSIONAL		
HYMN	8	[Pange lingua gloriosi] Nobis datus nobis natus
BENEDICTUS ANTIPHON,		
LAUDS	1607/17	Ego sum panis vivus. Alleluia
MAGNIFICAT ANTIPHON,		
1ST VESPERS	18	O quam suavis est

Votive Mass of the Blessed Sacrament

INTROIT	1605 *a* 4/1	Cibavit eos (in P.T.: Alleluia) ℣ *Exultate Deo.* Gloria Patri. Cibavit eos
GRADUAL	2	Oculi omnium ℣ *Aperis tu. Alleluia.* ℣ *Caro mea.*
+ALLELUIA		Alleluia
after LXX^{ma}:		
TRACT	1607/13	Ab ortu solis ℣ Et in omni loco 14 ℣ Venite comedite
in P.T.:		
ALLELUIA	16	Alleluia. Cognoverunt discipuli. Alleluia. *Caro mea.* Alleluia
OFFERTORY		
	1605 *a* 4/3	Sacerdotes Domini (in P.T.: Alleluia)
COMMUNION	4	Quotiescunque manducabitis (in P.T.: Alleluia)

The texts of the Corpus Christi Mass, returning as they do again and again to the ingestion of the blood, body, bread, meat, honey and wheat flour, are not ideally calculated for musical setting. Byrd is perhaps more to be congratulated for providing striking settings of the offertory and communion than blamed for writing, in the introit and gradual-alleluia group, music in a light polyphonic style that is deft, concise, and rather vacant in character. For all that, the introit **Cibavit eos** (1605 *a* 4/1) achieves a delightful bright quality as a result of its cheerful, innocent homophonic alleluias and also from a peculiarity of modal treatment. The soprano high e′ is used freely in preparation for all the main cadences of the piece, all five of them—something that does not happen in any other of Byrd's Mixolydian motets, which if they employ this high note at all treat it much more cautiously.

The gradual **Oculi omnium** (1605 *a* 4/2) includes a number of phrases involving sequence; this technique seems to come up very naturally and extensively in the 4-part music of the *Gradualia*. After the gradual proper, the verses 'Aperis tu manum tuam' and 'Caro mea' are duller and stiffer in style, as is the 3-part alleluia that separates them. In view of the unusual length of the alleluia verse for Corpus Christi, presumably, Byrd set only the first half of it ('Caro mea') as a trio, resuming the 4-part texture at the words 'qui manducat meam carnem' in a way that recalls the beginning of one of his introit doxologies. The sequence *Lauda Sion Salvatorem* is not set; instead *Oculi omnium* ends with an alleluia.

The gem of the Corpus Christi Mass is the offertory, **Sacerdotes Domini** (1605 *a* 4/3), another of the consummate miniatures of the *Gradualia*, which has rightly become a great favourite. Perhaps the simple words struck Byrd particularly and made him think of writing a quiet tribute to priests he had known. None of his other motets sounds as natural and as inevitable as this one. Word repetition is at a minimum. There is none at all in the soprano, prior to the alleluia, so that this line controls the whole structure like that of a song (see Ex. 53). The interval of the fourth announced at the beginning

Ex. 53

Sacerdotes . . . incensum . . . et ideo . . .   et non polluent . . .   Alleluia . . .

becomes the basis of a sequential ascent at 'incensum et panes offerunt' and a matching sequential descent at 'et non polluent nomen eius'; fourths in another configuration dominate the alleluia, where the soprano does not fail to touch down again at low d, the springboard for the original ascent. At 'et ideo sancti' the rising fourths contract to thirds but the rhythm broadens. The serenity and conviction of this climax also gains from the one lucid contrapuntal gesture in the piece so far, the imitation of 'erunt Deo suo' between the tenor and soprano. Elsewhere the texture is that of Byrd's characteristic half-homophony, with its mysterious shifting chords and murmuring free strettos—a texture that works just as well in four voices as in five or six, and maybe better when extended passages are in question, as here.

Genuine polyphony waits for the alleluia, one of the simplest of all Byrd's polyphonic alleluias in structure as well as one of the most beautiful (Ex. 54).

Ex. 54

The opening crotchet motive on the tonic is answered on the dominant, and on the dominant we wait while the bass mulls over the motive twice before an unhurried stretto of tonic entries (S and T) makes the cadence. The exquisite placement of the other motive entries depends upon the strong sense of this dominant, not only in bars 3 and 6, where D is sounding in the bass, but paradoxically even more so in bar 4, where it is not. The soprano line, which begins by curling up from b' to e', the highest note in the piece touched ever so lightly as an *echappée*, moves down in sequence to a' and g; how expertly the last *echappée* is neutralized by the syncopated tenor entry below. As in the alleluia of another very fine Mixolydian motet, *Confirma hoc Deus* (see p. 279), F♯s and F♮s are handled here with the greatest subtlety and freedom. The dotted-minim figure of bar 2, an old friend in alleluia settings, seems like a stranger in these surroundings, yet the lower voices in bars 4-6 quietly unmask it as an inverted augmentation of the original crotchet motive.

Coming after *Sacerdotes Domini*, the madrigalian block chords at the start of **Quotiescunque manducabitis** (1605 *a* 4/4) sound unusually vigorous, and the alleluia at the end of this motet—dare one say?—unusually rough, at least by Byrd's ordinary standards of 4-part writing. Yet the total progression from the neutral-sounding introit and gradual-alleluia of this Mass to the serene offertory to the robust communion—this is also unusually forceful and uncommonly effective. The phrases 'et calicem bibetis' and 'manducaverit panem' also have a distinct madrigalian cast. At two junctures, 'itaque...' and 'reus erit', Byrd makes sharp parallel articulations by juxtaposing D and F chords; the energy built up by the powerful sequential point 'et biberit calicem Domini indigne' spills over into the resounding half-homophony of 'reus erit' and from there into the alleluia. For once, in all the 4-part music of the *Gradualia*, Byrd seems to hanker after a fuller texture; five parts seem to be clearly implied by the final plagal cadence.

There is an 'abstrusa et recondita vix' to sacred words, Byrd writes, which can suggest an appropriate musical setting almost as a matter of course to the alert mind. Ave **verum corpus** (1605 *a* 4/5), perhaps the best known and best loved of all Byrd's compositions, provides an interesting illustration of this maxim. At the very beginning a famous false relation stresses the word 'verum', rather than 'corpus', which might have been elected by an innocent reader of the text (see below, p. 289). But what is being hailed is not the Body of Christ but the Eucharist which miraculously *is* the Body. The declamation 'Ave *verum* corpus' makes a doctrinal point of great importance to Catholics of Byrd's time, who were locked in controversy over the issue of transubstantiation. And perhaps it is not too abstruse to suggest that by echoing this false relation later in the piece—at 'O dulcis, o pie', 'o Iesu', and most directly at 'miserere mei'—Byrd meant to keep the Eucharist more clearly before our eyes than the text itself manages to do.

He may very well have taken the idea of the initial false relation (though not the idea of using it elsewhere in the composition) from the setting of *Ave verum corpus* by Lassus (see Ex. 55).* Though the progressions are not

Ex. 55

of course quite parallel, each introduces a harmonic clash extraordinarily early in the game, by the standards of each of their composers' other works. If Byrd meant to refer to Lassus, however, he may also have meant to teach him a posthumous lesson in word setting; the more intense clash in the English piece, achieved by an upward leap in the bass and dwelt on by a more deliberate rhythm, supplies not only emphasis but also a remarkable emotional aura to the miracle itself. Byrd was interested in the doctrinal

*Published in *Moteta sex vocum* (Boetticher 1582η; *Sämtliche Werke*, xii, 66). This 6-part motet begins *a 4*.

point, then—the declamation would seem to allow no other conclusion—but he was also interested in much more. At the phrase 'in cruce pro homine' the homophonic texture is agitated slightly into a chain of suspensions, which expand into a dense concatenation when the name of Jesus is finally spoken, three lines later: twice $^6_4$–$^5_3$, twice 6–5, then 7–6. Here, where the words 'Iesu fili Mariae' inevitably summon up a picture of the Madonna and Child, Byrd's commentary may perhaps bring to mind ancient representations of this theme in which the Passion Tree can be seen greening in the background.

Scholars who have studied the *Ave verum corpus* text have remarked on its early circulation in both missals and books of hours, reflecting its double life as a ritual item and as a text of private devotion. Private use is indicated by the variant used by Byrd, ending with the words 'miserere mei. Amen', and it was doubtless the presence of this personal prayer that led Byrd to the G Dorian mode which is so rare in the *Gradualia* but so characteristic of his early motets of prayer and penitence. He was no longer prepared to develop such prayers by means of solemn, dramatic appeals in massive homophony, nor by lengthy periods of intricate polyphony rising to some great climax. But he was ready to extend and intensify them in another way, as simple and poignant as it is unique in his work: by the verbatim repetition of the final 'O dulcis . . . miserere mei' section at the end, prior to the 'amen'. This was a device that Byrd used regularly in consort songs.

It is worth noting, finally, that like many Byrd motets with poetic texts *Ave verum corpus* has a simple metrical prototype at its basis. A semibreve-minim units corresponding to the trochaic foot of the verse gradually asserts itself as the piece proceeds, at the points indicated by italics:

Ave verum corpus natum	de Maria Virgine:
Vere passum, *immo*latum	in cruce pro homine:
Cuius latus perforatum	*unda fluxit* sanguine:
Esto nobis praegustatum	in mortis examine.

O dulcis, o pie, o Iesu fili Mariae miserere mei. Amen.*

This rhythmic unit also permeates the rest of the music—in augmented

*This text differs in several details, most conspicuously in the addition of 'miserere mei. Amen', from the version given in modern liturgical books, and also from that given by Mone and Dreves, who however record the 'miserere mei' variant from as early as the fourteenth century. Lassus' text is identical with Byrd's. Peter Phillips set the same minus the 'amen'. Other sixteenth-century settings that are available in modern editions show appreciable textual variants (Josquin, L'heritier, Clemens, Gallus, Georg Premmer). The versions found in Henrician Primers all seem to lack the 'miserere mei' conclusion.

form at the beginning, and in diminution at the end of each of the four lines. But where the word accent goes against the poetic metre, after the midpoint of lines 2 and 4, Byrd follows the word accent in each case, underlining the metrical (and verbal) parallelism by similar melodic figures.

Word setting must have been the last consideration to enter Byrd's mind when he composed **O salutaris hostia** (1605 *a* 4/6), a companion hymn to *Ave verum corpus* which stands out just as startlingly from the normal run of *Gradualia* pieces. This is an extremely thorough imitative exercise in which each of the four balanced phrases of text and music—they last for about 16, 8, 16 and 12 breves—contains a full exposition of its subject followed by a full counterexposition. The basic organization is not contrapuntal, though, but melodic. The soprano has two principal presentations of each line of the hymn, the second a slight variation of the first, while the other voices are markedly less regular and less melodic. (The T starts out in free canon with the S but soon proceeds more freely; the A is always more florid than the other voices.) In the diagram below, which should give some idea of the schematic nature of this piece, phrase lengths in semibreves are shown for each main soprano phrase and (in italics) for sections in which the soprano is silent or plays a secondary role. Below, initial and terminal notes are given for the soprano phrases:

O salutaris...	Quae coeli...	Bella premunt...	Da robur...	
3 6 *4* 10 *5*	6 *2* 7 *3*	9 *4* 10 *5*	*5* 4 *7* *10*	*semi-*
g–a' g–g	a'–a' a'–a'	d–d' d–d'	g–g g–g	*breves*

The harmonic scheme is lucid and simple enough, as the diagram indicates, and the subject entries show a strong tendency towards ostinato. Of 36 entries of the four subjects, two-thirds begin on G or D.

Described in this way, *O salutaris hostia* sounds like a throwback to (or even a remnant of) the earliest repertory of Byrd's motets published in the Tallis-Byrd *Cantiones* of 1575. Old it may very well be, but not as old as that, because no symmetrical plan is to be discerned among the entries in any of the points, and also because the part-writing is rather smooth and such roughnesses as do occur are of the sort found throughout the *Gradualia*. Was there, at least in Byrd's mind, a tradition of abstract, schematic setting for this particular text? Tallis's famous version is one of his most rigid essays in what was at that time evidently the newly-imported technique of continuous imitation, while Byrd's own earlier setting is a 3-part canon (see p. 118f). Except for the Mixolydian mode it has no point of contact with the present composition.

The processional hymn **Pange lingua gloriosi** (1605 *a* 4/8) contains six 6-line stanzas. Byrd sets stanzas 2 and 4, 'Nobis datus' and 'Verbum caro', and then departs from strict alternation so as to include the stanza 5, 'Tantum ergo', where the celebrants all kneel as the Sacrament is revealed. Stanzas 1, 3 and 6 are to be chanted, but Byrd also provides a final amen. The distinctive sound of this composition comes not from a special musical style or texture, as in the other hymns, but from the mode, which followed from Byrd's decision to incorporate the plainchant into his polyphony. This he did in a partial and curious way. Each stanza begins with one voice singing a successively shorter fragment of the chant *incipit* in long notes: in stanza 2 aaaGc (tenor), stanza 4 a'a'a'g (soprano), stanza 5 merely a'a' (soprano; and here the pitch A casts a long shadow). Since the chant is in the first mode with B♭ always indicated,* and Byrd quotes the *incipit* a fifth higher, he arrives at the A Aeolian mode which frequently has a Phrygian colouring. Stanza 2 is set very concisely indeed, but the ends of the other stanzas expand considerably. Crotchet figures enliven stanza 4, notably a scale motive mounting up a seventh for the line 'Ad firmandum cor sincerum', and stanza 5 closes with an expressive descending point for 'Sensuum defectui' lasting for fifteen breves.

It is tempting to speculate that Byrd wrote **O sacrum convivium** (1605 *a* 4/7) with an eye to both of its neighbours in the publication. The setting of the phrase 'mens impletur gratia' forcibly recalls the unusual Phrygian colouration of *Pange lingua gloriosi*, and the opening point 'O sacrum convivium', with its deliberate rhythms and equally deliberate imitative treatment (a very orderly exposition reaching up to C matched by a counterexposition reaching up to D), sounds like a condensed echo of the opening apostrophe of *O salutaris hostia*. But after beginning in this way the piece moves much more flexibly. It is the most substantial of the Corpus Christi motets of book 1 in imitative style, and the one which looks forward most clearly to the richer idiom of book 2.†

This idiom is manifest in the antiphons *Ego sum panis vivus* and *O quam suavis est*. What is unforgettable in **Ego sum panis vivus** (1607/17) is the word setting, though it is not of a kind that admits obvious categorization. The broken octave of the opening motive provides a clear surface clouded by a little spurt of ripples at the word 'vivus'; the octave is resumed at 'qui de

---

*In modern liturgical books this first-mode chant is given as an alternative to the more familiar third-mode version of the chant, which has a slightly different incipit; in Byrd's time the first-mode chant was standard. The account of the cantus firmus treatment in this motet in D. Stevens, *Tudor Church Music* (London, 1955, 2/1961), 41, is garbled.

†The alleluia at the end of *O sacrum convivium* is detachable, so that the piece can be used as a general motet in honour of the Blessed Sacrament in Lent.

coelo' and dissipated in tumbling motion at 'descendit'. After this, a single octave leap in the tenor for 'vivet in aeternum', with its peak note extended and pointed up by a seventh in the soprano, can invest these key words with an indescribable shudder of muted joy and vivacity. Like many of Byrd's shorter Mixolydian pieces, *Ego sum panis vivus* works almost entirely with G, C and D triads, but there is a wonderful gentle plagal quality at the beginning which is picked up again when the half-homophonic 'vivet in aeternum' idea is reharmonized over an F major triad. The alleluia, discussed on page 233, follows perfectly from the bass line in the 'vivet in aeternum' phrase. It forms an expansive, luminous conclusion to this classic example of Byrd's motet polyphony in the last phase of his activity.

O quam suavis est (1607/18) moves much farther afield harmonically than its companion and needs to, being more than twice as long. The harmonic range of this motet can be thought of as a projection of the unusual chromatic inflexion of the first bars (Ex. 56). Byrd, who seems in general to

Ex. 56

have backed away from chromaticism for purposes of word illustration, here employs the technique in a masterly fashion, the more so in view of the restraint which his temperament evidently set as a condition for the exercise. The caress of the first line is echoed only once, in a milder form, by means of the opening tenor motive imitated in the bass; a second motive for 'suavis est' allows the composer to dwell on the words and underline them with diatonic semitone motion instead of chromaticism. Later echoes are equally delicate. At the word 'dulcedinem' a veiled progression from a G major to an E major chord is followed by a single linear chromatic step in the tenor, and at 'suavissimo' there is no more than a single juxtaposition of G and E major. Here the effect depends as much on the suspended Phrygian cadence as on chromaticism *per se*. This motet really begins in A minor and makes cadences on various other degrees before the Mixolydian mode is established beyond any possible doubt by the rather square final point ('dimittens inanes'). The penultimate pages provide an example of Byrd's virtuosity in handling the words '. . . de coelo praestito, esurientes reples bonis, fastidiosos divites' as a continuous, unhurried series of fresh ideas, each growing naturally out of the preceding one, almost entirely without cadential articulation.

There remains to mention the pair of motets in book 2 for the Votive Mass of the Blessed Sacrament. In an indirect way they provide one of the worst puzzles in the *Gradualia*, for of course they imply that the Corpus Christi items of book 1 are to be drawn on to make up the rest of the Votive Mass, as indicated on page 285. And if these book 1 items are to be used for the Votive Mass outside of Paschal Time they must shed their alleluias: which they simply cannot do. In *Cibavit eos*, *Oculi omnium* and especially *Quotiescunque manducabitis* the alleluias are knitted in to the texture of the rest of the music, and while this is not the case with *Sacerdotes Domini*, one scarcely knows which is more shocking, the prospect of curtailing this marvellous little work or the realization that Byrd actually appears to have sanctioned such a practice. In any case, there is not much interesting music in the first half of the greater alleluia for Paschal Time, **Alleluia. Cognoverunt discipuli** (1607/16)—the second half reprints the music of 'Caro mea' from *Oculi omnium*—and the tract **Ab ortu solis** (1607/13) is notable mainly for the presence of a real *da capo*, a great rarity for Byrd (when the words 'magnum est nomen meum in gentibus' are repeated at the end of the motet). The *secunda pars* **Venite comedite** (1607/14), accommodating the final verse of the tract, sounds at many points like *Cibavit eos*. All in all the new votive items do nothing to raise the quality of the large and largely admirable group of compositions that Byrd provided, in the two books of the *Gradualia*, for the feast of the Eucharist and related services in its honour.

Christmas

INTROIT	1607/1	Puer natus est nobis ℣ *Cantate Domino*. Gloria Patri. Puer
GRADUAL	2	Viderunt omnes fines terrae ℣ *Notum fecit Dominus.* Alleluia
+ ALLELUIA	3	℣ Dies sanctificatus. Alleluia
OFFERTORY	4	Tui sunt coeli
COMMUNION	5	Viderunt omnes fines terrae
VESPER ANTIPHON, 2ND VESPERS	6	Hodie Christus natus est. Alleluia
VESPER ANTIPHON (CIRCUMCISION)	7	O admirabile commertium
MATINS RESPOND	8	O magnum misterium 9 Beata Virgo ℣ *Ave Maria.* Beata Virgo

Byrd's major effort in the 4-part section of book 2 of the *Gradualia* was devoted to the Mass for Christmas. Besides this he wrote only the incomplete Epiphany Mass and a few miscellaneous pieces, some of which we have just been discussing. The Christmas Mass includes, perhaps, none of Byrd's specially radiant compositions, such as *Ave verum corpus* for the Blessed Sacrament, *Iustorum animae* for All Saints and *Non vos relinquam orphanos* for Whitsun. But for sustained distinction and high quality it has no match among the other Masses of the *Gradualia*: and this level is sustained over eight motets, a larger number than in most of the others.

As with Corpus Christi in book 1, so with Christmas in book 2 we are obliged first to take account of certain small musical and liturgical anomalies. In principle the Christmas music employs a choir with two sopranos, like nearly everything else in book 2, whether for four, five, or six voices. *Puer natus est nobis* and *O magnum misterium*, however, are scored for SATB, like the Corpus Christi motets. On the liturgical front *O magnum misterium* and *Beata Virgo* belong to a category not found elsewhere in the Gradualia, the Matins respond, and *O admirabile commertium* is not for Christmas at all but for the feast of the Circumcision, a week later.

The latter texts were special favourites, and one can easily envisage Byrd stretching his limits—at Christmas, of all times—to include them. And though the possibility must be considered that the three motets in question are earlier pieces incorporated into the scheme of book 2, one is hard put to support this idea on stylistic grounds. There may be more brilliant 4-part motets in book 2 than **Puer natus est nobis** (1607/1), but its rhythmic intricacy and freedom of dissonance treatment, especially in the remarkable syncopated point 'magni consilii Angelus', exceed anything in book 1. We have already noted the bold treatment of the doxology (Ex. 44). What is more the verse 'Cantate Domino' stands out as the most modern-sounding in the whole of the *Gradualia*. It is one of the few that does not employ a style that is primarily canonic. Instead Byrd went back to his earlier setting of the same *incipit* in the 6-part motet *Cantate Domino* (1591/29), adopting both the kind of cantus firmus technique he had developed for that brilliant piece (see p. 182) and also the actual melodic idea. The fast dotted figures that accompany the cantus firmus in the first phrase assume burgeoning life of their own in the second. Cantus firmus work of the same sort appears at several other points of the *Gradualia*: in as many as four other Christmas motets, in the Purification tract and communion (see Ex. 46) and elsewhere.

Puer natus est nobis, in any case, ranks high among Byrd's motets and very high among his introit settings. The upward fifth in semibreves at the very beginning no doubt refers to the familiar plainchant, which had formed the basis of a monumental Mass written by Tallis when Byrd was still his pupil, half a century earlier. Tallis seems to be recalled by the sober chords towards the end of Byrd's opening point.

If the Christmas Mass is really to be tested for earlier elements, one's suspicions would more likely focus on the 3-part verse 'Notum fecit Dominus' in the gradual **Viderunt omnes fines terrae** (1607/2). This verse occupies the opposite end of the stylistic spectrum from 'Cantate Domino'. A free canon at the unison between the two sopranos is underpinned by the tenor imitating more loosely yet, but systematically and always at some interval other than the unison or octave. The soprano *dux* tends to repeat its lines in sequence up a tone, while the *comes* imitates each line only once. Beyond this there are no free phrases and scarcely any free phrase endings; the tenor keeps returning monotonously to G. The gentle circling motion of the melodic lines, which proceed mainly by step, contrasts with the sharply defined fourth, fifth and octave outlines of 'Cantate Domino'.

Morley recommends free canonic exercises of much this same kind in *A Plaine and Easie Introduction to Practicall Musicke*; he had doubtless learned to improvise them when studying with Byrd in the 1570s. But the unobtrusive smoothness of harmony in Byrd's verse raises new suspicions about the hypothesis that it might predate the rest of the Christmas Mass, a hypothesis that is in any case hard to uphold in view of the decidedly modern appearance of the gradual *Viderunt omnes* itself and of the associated alleluia **Dies sanctificatus** (1607/3). This is not the first occasion on which we have seen Byrd deliberately adopt an archaic style or at least certain archaic features.

The gradual raises an interesting question. Its text reads as follows:

Viderunt omnes fines terrae salutare Dei nostri: iubilate Deo omnis terra.
℣ Notum fecit Dominus salutare suum . . .

and the text of the communion **Viderunt omnes fines terrae** (1607/5) consists simply of the first seven words of this. At the time of book 1 Byrd would merely have marked a fermata on the music of the gradual to indicate a transfer. He did not follow this procedure now, either for logistical reasons —he may have become disillusioned with the transfer process, as has been suggested above (p. 236)—or for textual ones. Perhaps he felt that when the text reaches its climax on the words 'iubilate Deo' the sense of rejoicing should animate it from the very beginning, but that without this climax the text calls for a more restrained sentiment, something like quiet wonder. That, at any rate, would account for the essential difference between his music for the same words in the gradual and the communion. (The difference is all the more striking because the two pieces begin with very similar themes treated in the same way—in the type of cantus firmus technique derived from *Cantate Domino*.) In the gradual, the accompaniment figures already stir more energetically in the opening phrase; then the words 'salutare Dei nostri' are declaimed almost wholly in crotchets, and 'iubilate Deo' summons up a fast, emphatic, swinging motive featuring dotted crotchets and quavers in sequence. In the communion the opening phrase with its murmuring FE intervals is quieter and more subtle in expression, and the beautiful concluding point 'salutare Dei nostri' rich and meditative rather than jubilant.

The *Gradualia* includes more than a few very short motets in which every note seems perfectly set in place. *Viderunt omnes* (the communion) differs from the other minor masterpieces of this class in its construction: it consists of just two overlapping phrases, 9 and 12 breves long, without any alleluia. The last three Christmas items are also exceedingly fine works, this time in a different genre, that of the more spacious settings found typically with antiphons and other longer non-sectional texts. *O magnum misterium* is the most frequently sung of the three, but its two very different neighbours *Hodie Christus natus est* and *O admirabile commertium* are scarcely inferior.

At the beginning of our discussion of the *Gradualia* motets stress was laid on Byrd's typical constructions in double periods. These double periods depend on subtleties of phrase balance for their effect, rather than on contrapuntal development as in the earlier motet style. The three large Christmas motets provide in their opening periods an epitome of Byrd's virtuosity in this matter. The simplest of them is **O magnum misterium** (1607/8), in which the basic idea in thirds (T and B) is only 6 semibreves long, embedded in an 8-semibreve phrase closing quietly on the tonic. This is repeated (S and A) directly after the cadence and now lasts no longer than the basic 6 semibreves; Byrd compensates by inverting the two lines at the twelfth and exploiting the resulting slight modification of harmony to work a rich half close proceeding ii_6-V_7-i_4^6-V. In **Hodie Christus natus est** (1607/6) the opening 2-part imitative idea (S^1 and S^2) is 7 semibreves long; the excitement implicit in this text demands an overlap in the repetition, which is nonetheless spaced so as to keep an uninterrupted series of triplet rhythms (Ex. 57). What a joyous way of treating the declamation! Though

Ex. 57

the second statement ends just like the first, on the tonic—the B repeats the S^2 line exactly at the lower octave—the harmony is now biased towards the mediant. Broadest and richest of all is the opening of **O admirabile commertium** (1607/7), where the phrase outlines are blurred considerably. The opening unison canon (T and S^2), with its characteristic overlapping 2–3 suspensions, loses definition after 7 semibreves, but before long approximately the same combination is heard (with much else) in the subdominant (S^1 and S^2). This is expanded to 12 semibreves, surging up smoothly but very powerfully before settling back on a D major chord. Only at the end of the second statement does a persuasive motive emerge for the last word of the phrase, 'commertium'.

Each in its own way, the second statements of these opening double constructions expand on the originals and lend expectation to the new phrase that is to follow. Byrd's control of the weighting and balance of phrases, using all the combined resources of melody, rhythm, harmony and counterpoint, can make one think of Brahms; the analogy is not altogether fanciful. What is more, these motet beginnings all seem to be echoed rather clearly by their endings. The triple rhythms of *Hodie Christus natus est* return for the first time, and very emphatically, in the concluding triple-metre alleluia. The semitones which produce the expressive 2–3 suspensions at the beginning of *O admirabile commertium* also form a key element of the final subject, 'suam deitatem' (Ex. 58). In *O magnum misterium* the final point 'iacentem in praesepio' resumes both the characteristic texture of the opening and also the memorable cadence, with its stirring low G' and A.

The powerful cascading prose rhythms of the *Hodie Christus natus est* text helped determine the breathlessness of the music:

Hodie Christus natus est: hodie Salvator apparuit: hodie in terra canunt Angeli, laetantur Archangeli: hodie exultant iusti, dicentes: Gloria in excelsis Deo, alleluia.*

Byrd's four settings of the word 'hodie' in this motet use the same dotted figure, but always in different rhythmic contexts. The second ('hodie Salvator') breaks in on the cadence of the opening phrase with a dance-like fragment; its function seems to be to counteract the opening triple rhythms with firm duple ones in sequence, and in a free ostinato. The third ('hodie in terra') works up an excited antiphonal exchange overlapping between the bass and the upper voices. Most dramatic of all, the fourth ('hodie exultant iusti') is a single homophonic exclamation marking a sharp harmonic shift, its D major chord juxtaposed with the F major semibreve chord of the previous cadence.

A matching harmonic shift prepares the climactic last line, after the acclamatory phrases 'canunt . . .', 'laetantur . . .' and 'exultant . . .' have each been set to their inevitable fast-moving subjects in stretto. Following a half close on A at 'dicentes'—another full stop on a semibreve in all parts—the just proclaim the Gloria as a cantus firmus repeated between the two sopranos, while F major is defined by the free flowing motion in the other parts. An ecstatic passage of largely free counterpoint concludes this magnificent phrase (notice the octave outlines in the bass part here—cC, b♭B♭, GG' and cC). The very concise alleluia flares up in homophonic sequences and subsides just as suddenly into a half close on the low A major chord. Byrd had reached this same low cadence chord at the word 'dicentes'.

O admirabile commertium is a work of unusual breadth and dignity—unusual, at least, within the sphere of the *Gradualia*. In technical terms two of its phrases, 'animatum corpus sumens' and 'et procedens homo sine semine largitus est nobis', closely resemble phrases in *Hodie Christus natus est*, 'canunt Angeli' and 'Gloria in excelsis Deo' respectively. But the effect in the latter case is altogether different: in *O admirabile commertium* there is

---

*A translation of this text, *This day Christ was born*, is set for six voices in the 1611 *Psalmes, Songs, and Sonnets*. Many of the other sacred texts in this publication had also been previously set by Byrd in Latin.

no repetition of the lengthy cantus firmus, and this comes in the bass, which relentlessly inches its way up the scale from C to b♭ in breves, culminating in a mighty roar of 'largitus' on the notes ab♭a. Hearing this, the upper voices break into agitated crotchet declamation. Then the superb final point picks up this same semitone articulation; for in its original form the subject 'suam deitatem' intones AB♭A three times in a slow ostinato (Ex. 58).

At an earlier period Byrd would have separated off the three semibreves for 'suam' to form a double subject for diffuse contrapuntal developments. Here, of course, no such thing happens. Instead the initial semitone of the subject expands to a third and the continuation is inverted, enlivened rhythmically, and finally wound around into a canonic *cambiata* figure of wonderful solemn grace. The movement ceases for one breathtaking moment to mark the exact point of the subject's metamorphosis (bar 9).

In place of the brilliance and solemnity of its two neighbours, *O magnum misterium* projects a mood of mild lyricism, a mood exactly appropriate to a

Ex. 58

Nativity scene. (Lyricism, not wonder; Byrd makes no effort to provide a musical illustration of the 'great mystery' which caught the imagination of Palestrina, for example, in his well-known motet on the same words.) No doubt one feature that attracts modern choirmasters to Byrd's piece is its extremely lucid tonal structure. The first large section works almost exclusively with D and G minor and A minor and major triads, and the first strong cadence comes after 17 breves on G, with an especially luminous *tierce de Picardie*. The second section, in which the animals bear witness to the birth of God, turns even more luminously to B♭ (an unexpected cadence degree in this mode). For the words 'ut animalia', Byrd chose a canonic idea in interlocking fourths which he had adopted in the old days from White, realizing for the first time, perhaps, the expressive potential of its transparency when heard in stretto and of its emphasis on the sixth degree. Then the last section, 'iacentem in praesepio', with its caressing thirds and sixths, returns softly but quite single-mindedly to the sphere of D minor sonorities. The final cadence is grounded by a low A which is in effect prolonged in the bass for four full breves.

But is it not a solecism to speak of a 'final' cadence here—to speak of this motet without including **Beata Virgo** (1607/9)? Certainly the sentence beginning 'Beata Virgo . . .' is required to complete the text of the respond *O magnum misterium*, after which there should follow the 3-part verse 'Ave Maria' and then 'Beata Virgo' once again as the *repentendum*. (Byrd specifically directs the *da capo*.) Yet the way this ostensible *secunda pars* follows from the first indicates that it was conceived of as an entirely separate composition. *Beata Virgo* is a marvellous little piece, but after the very solid D minor cadence at the end of *O magnum misterium* its series of tiny echoing phrases, its brisk survey of the various available major-mode cadence points, and its hasty half close on A make a strangely ineffectual impression. The whole of *Beata Virgo* lasts for only 17 breves, not much longer than the single point 'iacentem in praesepio', and none of its constituent phrases lasts longer than 4 breves save the last, which is also the only one in which the words ('Dominum Christum') are repeated in all the voices.* The deft verse comes to a relatively strong cadence on F after 14 breves. The *repentendum* has weight enough if the music starts with 'Beata Virgo', but falls far short of *O magnum misterium* is heard at the beginning.

The concentrated, almost song-like structure of *Beata Virgo* suggests one direction in which Byrd's style might have developed, for the composition of intimate texts; it is one of the most 'advanced' works in the *Gradualia*. Another is the equally unassuming motet **Tui sunt coeli** (1607/4), the

---

*There is a strange problem of underlay in this piece. The liturgical text is 'Beata Virgo cuius viscera meruerunt portare Dominum Christum'. But in all four original voice parts, in both the 1607 and 1610 editions, the word 'meruerunt' is missing, and a short phrase of music is left untexted. (This happens in a few other motets in the *Gradualia*, as we shall see.) The editors of TCM silently supplied the words 'cuius viscera' in this gap, rather than 'meruerunt'—which made grammatical nonsense but musical sense, for in fact the untexted music is a sequential repetition of the 'cuius viscera' motive. They must have been mistaken; at the same time, it is certainly unusual for Byrd to use the same music for two successive text fragments. Compare the phrase 'Dominum Christum'.

Christmas offertory. This piece can be described as a single process culminating in a remarkable setting, lasting for 13 breves, of the words 'preparatio sedis tuae'. Prior to this, the first 18 breves are devoted to a whole series of tiny ideas which prepare the more expansive final point by contrast with their exceedingly clipped phraseology. The run of two-semibreve units in the opening phrase 'Tui sunt coeli, et tua est terra'—units seesawing back and forth between tonic and dominant—practically cries out for barlines. In a different way, the single dissonant configuration in this phrase, a single augmented fifth within an otherwise wholly consonant span of 12 breves, prepares the strongly dissonant matrix for three closely spaced cadences to come (BW 6, 22, bars 5–6, 22, bar 3 and 23, bar 1).

The inner workings of the last phrase are particularly elusive and fantastic. The opening 3-part cell, with its ecstatic ornamentation (never to be repeated or even echoed) for the upward auxiliary c'd'c' on 'prepar*atio*', when resumed by the other soprano becomes *more* rather than less homophonic; its accents are realigned so as to congeal into the third of the strong cadences. In the polyphony following this cadence (a Phrygian cadence on A) precision of motivic forms means much less than a general rumination on the notes F, G and A. In fact the six remaining breves of the composition, till the final chord, are really given over to a rich prolongation of the pitch A. Low A is the centre of gravity of the subject's last main entry, in the bass, and high a' is a barrier through which the strangely irresolute sopranos can no longer penetrate. The small clashes between the voices in this passage, the spare voice spacings, the chord sequence itself—all are utterly individual, at once surprising and inevitable.

In passages of this kind Byrd's polyphony seems to be dealing with linear relationships in their most basic and most eternal form; the norms of 'sixteenth century style', whether English or Continental, are scarcely to be discerned. The music has a quality that one senses only in the late works of the greatest composers. Characteristic of the *Spätstil* quality is the concentration, the grace, the quiet, and a certain abstractness of procedure: for little or nothing that has been said in the previous paragraph has much to do with the words of this particular offertory. What absorbed the composer was the mystery of musical process, one feels, rather than the mystery of the Christmas liturgy, or any individual words or concepts such as heaven and earth, plenitude and justice, the throne of Christ. He was working in the same spirit elsewhere in the Christmas Mass: in *Beata Virgo*, the communion *Viderunt omnes fines terrae* and parts of the introit *Puer natus est nobis*. This 4-part cycle contains some of the most visionary music of the *Gradualia*, as well as some of the finest.

Epiphany

INTROIT	1607/10	Ecce advenit ℣ *Deus iuditium tuum*. Gloria Patri.
		Ecce advenit
GRADUAL	15	℣ Surge illuminare Hierusalem. Alleluia
OFFERTORY	11	Reges Tharsis
COMMUNION	12	Vidimus stellam

Byrd's shortest motets are those set to offertory and communion texts. But in the unfinished Epiphany Mass he composed both of these liturgical numbers more broadly, at least in respect to their conclusions; the final sections of *Reges Tharsis* and *Vidimus stellam* extend to 20–1 breves, longer than any other 4-part points in the *Gradualia*.* While this expansiveness fits well enough with the texts 'omnes gentes servient ei' in the offertory and 'adorare Dominum' in the communion, it is hard to believe that those words would have prompted such breadth unless Byrd had also had some purely musical idea in mind.

    Reges Tharsis (1607/11) actually ends with a full-scale point of double imitation, something seldom seen at this stage of his career; which is just as well, perhaps, for to judge from this example the technique that had served him so well in earlier days no longer offered much of inspiration or interest. Or perhaps he just found four voices for double imitation rather few for comfort. The structure of the phrase is obvious—upward motion from bb' to c' to d' marked by imitations in the two sopranos—and the joint development of the subjects can hardly be called expressive. He was able to strike fire from ancient embers more convincingly with the phrase 'et insulae munera offerent', which follows directly (and somewhat ungrammatically) from the concise opening double period for 'Reges Tharsis'. Here Byrd went back to the stretto ostinato technique that he had practiced in some of his very earliest music (see Ex. 6k). And the old technique now produces a brilliant new effect, a rhythmic ostinato of sixteen dotted-crotchet-quaver figures, with the crisp sequential motive for 'insulae munera' highlighted against the even shorter motive for 'offerent' (which is related to it by augmentation and inversion) in a way that recalls Marenzio. The most beautiful point in *Reges Tharsis*, however, crystallizes around a lyrical canon at the words 'et adorabunt eum omnes reges terrae'.

---

    *The last point of *Ab ortu solis* is equally long, but it really consists of a 15-breve point of imitation overlapping with a large, 6-breve plagal cadence.

Beginning with the same verb as the two Christmas pieces entitled *Viderunt omnes*, the Epiphany communion **Vidimus stellam** (1607/12) also begins with the same kind of cantus firmus writing. In the cantus firmus itself the word 'stellam' glints and sparkles as the outcome of an upward octave leap to high d' interrupted by a semibreve rest—an effect that would not, however, bear repetition, and Byrd squeezes out the semibreve rest in the next (and last) cantus statement. The three kings announce their coming with the greatest of humility. Their words 'et venimus' are set to block chords pitched low, syncopated across the *tactus* after an almost embarrassed little wait, and tinted with major-mode harmonies never before heard in the piece. There is something very homely and innocent, too, about the 'cum muneribus' figure which follows, prior to the lengthy final phrase 'adorare Dominum'. Here a scale figure mounts up a sixth, a seventh, then at last an octave; and by the time the two sopranos have used this scale to recapture the stellar d', the tenor and bass have already introduced a new circling motive for the same words. This motive moves towards a deliberate cadence, a sixth below the climax: as though after allowing themselves a moment of enthusiasm the kings return to adoration in a more restrained and respectful spirit. *Vidimus stellam* is one of Byrd's most charming compositions, as well as one of his most accomplished.

Like many introits, **Ecce advenit dominator Dominus** (1607/10) seems to possess less character than other members of its Mass. **Surge illuminare Hierusalem** (1607/15), on the other hand, is a first-rate piece whose status as a liturgical waif—it is placed out of order in the partbooks, it omits the whole gradual and uses slightly wrong words for the verse*— unfortunately militates against its use on those select occasions when Byrd's Epiphany Mass is sung as a unit. The opening figure for 'Surge' may look simple enough on the page, but Byrd keeps the rhythm spinning brilliantly; then in the middle phrases, built out of more neutral material, he maintains a driving quality which reaches a climax in the fine swinging motive for the last phrase 'super te orta est'. The fastest rhythms are saved for the alleluia. At the beginning of our discussion of the *Gradualia* motets it was pointed out how Byrd makes use of alleluia sections to punctuate sectional motets and to terminate non-sectional ones brilliantly and concisely. The point is well illustrated by *Surge illuminare Hierusalem*, especially when this is heard or considered along with its associated offertory and communion, where in the absence of alleluias Byrd felt called upon to conclude with unusually heavy points of imitation.

A word on the question of mode in *Surge illuminare Hierusalem*. Pre-
*See p. 226n.

sumably Byrd thought of the mode as D Aeolian, as in the Christmas and
Epiphany Masses as a whole. The middle of the motet stays close to D minor
sonorities and octave species. The opening surge is on G minor, however,
counterbalanced by an unusual and unusually forthright cadence in A, the
quintessential Dorian touch; ultimately 'super te orta est' moves firmly to F
and the alleluia returns to a cadence in G. These subdominant cadences
sound peculiar to modern listeners—even more peculiar, probably, than half
closes on the dominant such as those which conclude the Christmas motets
Hodie Christus natus est and *Beata Virgo*. But in the D mode Byrd writes
final cadences in G often enough: to speak only of 4-part compositions, he
does this also in the Christmas communion *Viderunt omnes fines terrae* and
gradual-alleluia group *Viderunt omnes–Dies sanctificatus* and in the Purification antiphon *Hodie beata Virgo*. None of the ten or eleven Mixolydian
pieces associated with Corpus Christi makes a final cadence elsewhere than
in the tonic, G. In the 6-part Mass for Sts. Peter and Paul, however, we shall
come upon an occasional motet in the C Ionian mode which seems to end in
(not on!) the dominant.

Sts. Peter and Paul, St. Peter's Chains

Five parts constitute Byrd's norm of vocal texture in the *Gradualia*, as in the rest of his vocal music and in that of his contemporaries. So much is obvious; and it also seems obvious that when he came to compose the 4-part Ordinary of the Mass and the 4-part Propers he was able to adapt the style developed for five voices to four quite effortlessly. The result is so natural that we can scarcely imagine him giving a moment's thought to any 'problem' of texture. Things seem to have been rather different with the music of the *Gradualia* for six parts. To understand this it is necessary to recall rapidly the history of Byrd's involvement with 6-part writing.

In the 1560s and 70s a choir of six (or even more) voices, used in the traditional way as a means of achieving monumentality, was Byrd's normal resource. But already in the *Cantiones* of 1575 there are signs that he was turning to five voices in the interests of flexibility and greater subtlety of expression, and in the next period the turn becomes a veritable about-face. When he assembled, ordered and published his newer motets in 1589 and 1591 he included no 6-part music at all in the first book and only a very deliberate selection of it in the second: two pairs of archaic or archaizing pieces in monumental genres not matched elsewhere in the book, and two pairs of modern ones deeply indebted to the madrigal tradition. These are the jubilant *Cantate Domino* and *Haec dies*, which are notated in a basic crotchet pulse, and the highly expressive *Domine non sum dignus* and *Domine salva nos*. All appear to have been composed especially for the publication. Only the great alleluia at the end of *Haec dies* approaches the scale of Byrd's earlier writing, and even here the effect is brilliant rather than monumental. For the two jubilant motets are notably fast on their feet and, for Byrd, unusually light in texture.

Besides these four almost self-consciously modern essays, only one or two others for six voices are known from the fertile period of the 1580s. Later Byrd made settings of the Ordinary of the Mass for three, four and five voices but not for six. There are no 6-part pieces in book 1 of the *Gradualia*, whose disposition of voices matches that of the Ordinaries. It would have seemed quite natural if there had been none in book 2 either.

But book 2 does introduce 6-part writing—for one Mass, the last in the book, the Mass of Sts. Peter and Paul. It is as certain as such things can be, short of an affadavit signed by the composer, that this texture was chosen in order to invest this feast with unique emphasis and solemnity. Given Byrd's programme in the *Gradualia*, Sts. Peter and Paul and the associated feast of St. Peter's Chains were the only ones he could have taken in hand as a way of affirming his allegiance to Rome.

The importance that he attached to this is indicated by the risk he was ready to take in publishing the material; and the risk itself is indicated by his decision to suppress certain of the texts, leaving the motets in question wordless, identified only by their incipits. These motets are marked with a dagger in the listing below. Byrd evidently felt secure in publishing those texts of Sts. Peter and Paul that are taken into the liturgy directly from the Bible.* But he suppressed those that are not (*Solve iubente Deo, Hodie Simon Petrus* and *Tu es Pastor ovium*). This scarcely diminished the public nature of his gesture of affirmation, for of course the crucial statement 'Tu es Petrus et super hanc petram aedificabo ecclesiam meam' comes from St. Matthew and was therefore printed.

Another consideration was the triple pun on the rock, the Saint's name and that of Byrd's patron, Lord Petre.† By a happy circumstance, the Mass of Sts. Peter and Paul as the one Mass from the Proper of Saints comes last in liturgical order when joined with Christmas, Epiphany, Easter, Ascension and Whitsun. Thus by crowning his great two-volume project with a single 6-part Mass, and with this particular 6-part Mass, Byrd found himself in the ideal position, if one may say so, of being able to pay tribute simultaneously to God and Caesar.

---

*Significant in this regard is an unobtrusive phrase in Byrd's dedication to book 1, as he explains that besides motets for certain offices he is issuing 'others for five voices with their words drawn from the fountain of Holy Writ'. This can refer to only two pieces, *Unam petii a Domino* and *Plorans plorabit*. Byrd was saying that whatever seditious double meanings might be read into those texts, they were in fact blameless selections from the Psalms and Jeremiah which any Christian might read, contemplate, set to music and sing for the edification of his soul.

†This pun had been formalized, as it were, by the founder of the family fortunes, Sir William Petre, Secretary of State from the time of Henry VIII to Elizabeth I. When as Dr. Petre he acquired the Essex manor of Ingatestone in 1539, he promptly recast its ancient Latin name 'Ginge ad Petram' (Ing at Stone) as 'Ginge Petre', and was still calling it 'Ingatstone alias Ging Petre' in his will of 1571. See F. G. Emmison, *Tudor Secretary* (Cambridge, 1961), 24.

Sts. Peter and Paul [29 June]

INTROIT	1607/38	Nunc scio vere ℣ *Domine probasti me.* Gloria Patri. Nunc scio vere
GRADUAL	39	Constitues eos principes . . . Domine ℣ *Pro patribus tuis.* Alleluia
+ ALLELUIA	41	℣ Tu es Petrus. Alleluia
OFFERTORY	39	Constitues eos principes . . . generatione
COMMUNION	41	Tu es Petrus (without alleluia)*
MAGNIFICAT ANTIPHON, 1ST VESPERS	43	Tu es pastor ovium†
MAGNIFICAT ANTIPHON, 2ND VESPERS	42	Hodie Simon Petrus. Alleluia†
BENEDICTUS ANTIPHON, LAUDS	44	Quodcunque ligaveris

St. Peter's Chains [1 August]

all as in the above, except:

ALLELUIA	40	℣ Solve iubente Deo. Alleluia†
MAGNIFICAT ANTIPHON, 2ND VESPERS	40	Solve iubente Deo (without alleluia)†

Monumentality may be measured in two dimensions. Byrd employed more voices than usual and employed them in an unusually dense fashion; there are no more than three or four passages in the whole Mass where one or more of the voices is left out for any length of time. He also made the 6-part motets, or at least certain salient phrases in them, appreciably longer than others in the *Gradualia.*

A small but characteristic sign of this is that two of the pieces, *Nunc scio vere* and *Tu es Petrus,* open with simple triple repetitive structures rather than Byrd's familiar duple beginnings. More significant is the exceptional breadth of the final phrases, in all the 6-part motets except those in which considerations of form made this impossible: the introit, which has to go on to the verse, and the gradual and the antiphon *Hodie Simon Petrus,* both of which end with alleluias. (The situation with the alleluia verses *Solve*

---

*This text is also sung at Vespers of both feasts, as the antiphon for the psalm *Laudate Dominum* (see 1607/45).

†The text of these motets is omitted in the publication.

iubente Deo and *Tu es Petrus* will be discussed in a moment.) One of these lengthy final phrases was the key passage from St. Matthew on which everything depended, and Byrd set this as his longest point of all. But there is no readily apparent textual impetus for the extension of the other final phrases. Byrd's idea was simply to obtain the effect of monumentality, and this effort led him to remarkable new heights of contrapuntal virtuosity.

Given Byrd's aim here, it is clear enough why the expressive 6-part style that he had developed in *Domine non sum dignus* and *Domine salva nos* in 1591 could have no direct issue in the *Gradualia*. This may be cause for regret, for those are wonderful pieces, and it is certainly something of a paradox, for in those motets he was working out a new concise, flexible style which would be carried further in the music of the *Gradualia* for four and five parts. But for the 6-part Mass of Sts. Peter and Paul Byrd had another ideal in mind—and in any case the liturgy here offers no 'expressive' texts that would make such a style conceivable. Indeed, of the seven texts only two contain enough vivid images to support a brilliant madrigalian style comparable to that of *Cantate Domino* and *Haec dies*. The other texts are relatively neutral and so is Byrd's music for them. Neutral and, at best, wonderfully grand; but at worst, both stiff and awkward. Unused as we are to imputing technical difficulties to Byrd at this stage of his career, it is impossible not to conclude that at certain places he was embarrassed by the 6-part texture.

In the introit **Nunc scio vere** (1607/38), for example, after producing an excellently sonorous opening point, he seems oddly irresolute as to the correct form of the motive for 'quia misit Dominus' and careless in dropping a single E major triad at 'de manu Herodis'. An amorphous impression persists when, after the S^2 and B introduce a 2-part combination for the fragment 'et de omni exspectatione', only two other voices (S^1 and A) engage in this before the S^2 breaks in with a new syncopated motive for 'plebis Iudaeorum'. This distinctive idea consumes everyone's attention. Although the bass continues bravely with 'et de omni exspectatione' in sequence, it receives only half-hearted response from the T^1 and none at all from the T^2, which goes right on to 'plebis Iudaeorum' without ever referring to either member of the earlier 2-part combination. 'Plebis Iudaeorum' is worked into a stiff ostinato: which may be viewed, however, as a suitably derisive comment on the false expectations of Peter's enemies.

The gradual **Constitues eos principes** (1607/39), which must be said to mark some kind of low point in the *Gradualia*, opens with a very simple repeated cell of the kind familiar from the motets of the 1580s. Much the same cell, in fact, opens part 2 of *Laudibus in sanctis* (1591/2). The point 'nominis tui, Domine' grinds along mechanically to an unconvincing cadence, defined by a semibreve in all parts and a minim rest to facilitate the omission of the next phrase (which is not sung in the gradual, but only when the number is transferred to provide the offertory). Byrd follows almost precisely the same procedure for the transfer in the Purification introit *Suscepimus Deus*.* Archaisms bristle in the music following the cadence, and the 3-part gradual verse—even more than the introit verse, discussed on page 231f —is one of the stickiest Byrd ever wrote. Paying scant attention to the declamation throughout, he breaks the phrase 'propterea populi confitebuntur tibi' into three short motives and ends the verse with a *de facto* rhythmic ostinato drawn out for thirteen merciless breves.

The massive but simple alleluia after this gradual verse begins in quasi-homophony in a fast triple metre. It moves rapidly in sequence to the dominant, G, and then slows down for an expanded I–IV–V–I cadence in C. One of two alleluia verses must follow upon this heavy stop, *Solve iubente Deo* for the feast of St. Peter's Chains or *Tu es Petrus* for Sts. Peter and Paul; and Byrd matched the alleluias appended to these numbers closely in dimensions, form and harmonic plan, and even in the motives employed, though these merely ring changes on the ubiquitous dotted-minim figure. Both final alleluias begin with sequential or echoing bars between semichoirs, again essentially homophonic in style, moving in triple rhythms to D or A (these echo the triple-metre bars moving to G in the previous alleluia); then both run into extended V–I–V cadences. To us these sound inevitably like plagal cadences in the dominant, G, but Byrd, who had no objection to such effects, as we have seen, knew exactly what he wanted and insisted on having it both times.

His special effort to establish coherence in these gradual-alleluia groups was well advised, no doubt, for prior to their alleluias (which are both detachable alleluias) the two alleluia verses themselves are composed less as members of composite groups than as free agents. The essential fact here is the unusual size of the last phrases of these pieces, 22 breves in one case and 30 in the other. In all other alleluias of the *Gradualia*, the presence of the terminal alleluia allows Byrd to construct the final phrase on relatively concise lines. It seems clear that Byrd got into this difficulty (if difficulty it be) on account of the phrase 'et super hanc petram aedificabo ecclesiam meam'. This had to be set as forcibly as possible, in spite of the fact that it stands as the last phrase of an alleluia verse, *Tu es Petrus*.

The two works employ a brilliant but weighty madrigalian style somewhat

*See p. 251. The only difference is notational: here a *signum* is marked on the cadence and a barline added, features not present at the Purification.

reminiscent of Thomas Weelkes, whose *Madrigals of five and six parts* must
have made a sensation when they appeared in 1600. Byrd came up with a
marvellous inspiration for the beginning of **Solve iubente Deo** (1607/40), or
perhaps one should say, with a marvellously inspired reinterpretation of
Weelkes's *Thule the period of cosmography*. As monotone breves pick out the
word 'Solve' on G (and once on D), the other voices dissolve the same word
into crotchet figures running, or rather, endlessly flowing up and down the
G major triad (Ex. 59). Byrd controls these interlocking crotchet figures with

Ex. 59

the greatest art, starting them out in lucid combinations and congealing the
texture only after 7 breves, when the harmony finally moves down a fifth to C.
With another move of a fifth, to F, the texture grows more and more complex:
and through it a slower upward motive for 'iubente Deo' surges again and
again, but in no regular time sequence, like a series of great bubbles rising
inevitably and anonymously in some thick slow-boiling liquid. Suddenly
things clear up. The metre is determined by the crotchets, and a canzonet-
like texture accommodates tiny motives for 'terrarum', 'Petre' and—with a
characteristic little rattle—'catenas'. The harmony now moves up the circle
of fifths to A. A strange twitching figure in the motive for 'Qui facis' eases
the return to the slower metre, and the motet ends broadly, backing down
around the circle from A to F and then to C. Unless sung with the gradual,
of course, this motet and *Tu es Petrus* should stop on their reasonably solid
C major cadences, prior to the alleluias.

The well-known motet **Tu es Petrus** (1607/41) has two phrases only, a relatively neutral 8-breve period for 'Tu es Petrus' and then the great 30-breve sequel. Even the broad phrase structure here helps to highlight the all-important doctrinal statement. Byrd paints the Church's firm foundation as a series of breves and *longae* deep in the bass, over which the other voices 'build' endlessly energetic strettos on an upward motive involving a dotted figure in crotchets (see Ex. 60). Again and again this

Ex. 60

motive reaches its peak on notes standing a sixth above the bass, notes suspended across the strong beat and resolved in a dizzying array of tiny 6–5 progressions. As resolutely English in its execution as it is Italian in conception, this point is one of Byrd's most original and prodigious conceptions. The upper voices enter very regularly over the first few bass *longae* (G′ and F′), but after briefly resuming the motive for 'et super hanc petram' in a free inversion, they built their strettos over the remaining *longae* (C and G′) much more freely and broadly. Freest of all is the peroration, where the bass abandons its pedal notes to join in the development of the scale motive. This now moves in thirds or tenths and soars up to peaks harmonized by fresh and airy root-position triads (Ex. 60). A final mischievous distorted entry in bars 6–7, recalling the jagged contrapuntal effects of Byrd's earliest *Cantiones*, restores the harmonic balance.

Paul is robbed to pay Peter in the liturgy for this feast. **Hodie Simon Petrus** (1607/42) is the only one of the seven *Gradualia* texts which so much as mentions St. Paul, and the reference is limited to the last of its three parallel pronouncements. Byrd sets the three sections of this lengthy antiphon, each beginning with the word 'Hodie', rather differently. For the first he employs a dense polyphonic idiom and for the second a rapid madrigalian style recalling the middle section of *Solve iubente Deo*, though with less textual justification and less musical interest. For the third—his tribute to St. Paul—he uses a series of mostly solemn but lucid points and cells in the older manner. (This style recurs in other 6-part motets, *Quodcunque ligaveris* and *Laudate Dominum*). The one lively phrase ('lumen orbis terrae') is slowed by an unexpected cadence in A; this degree was evidently chosen so that the strong dominant E would set the next motive in maximum relief, a slow ostinato for the words 'inclinato capite' sinking through the octave F–F'. Coming after this heavy F sonority, the next phrase with its marching motive for 'pro Christi nomine' can celebrate the Martyr's glory with natural brilliance by stressing G and D. The final alleluia, after an unusually long overlap, settles into a rhythmic (and ultimately also a melodic) ostinato on the dotted-crotchet figure which comes up many times in book 2 of the *Gradualia*. Its use in the present instance is much enlivened by the syncopated initial minim of the alleluia motive.

The second tenor voice, whose normal range in this mode is from C to e, has to touch low A in this motet. In the two remaining antiphons (and also in the two non-liturgical 6-part motets which follow the Mass) the second tenor is replaced by a second true bass with a range from G' or A to c. Byrd had occasionally worked with a 6-part choir of this kind before; the attraction of this texture was that it allowed for clear echoes between semichoirs alternating the two basses as well as the two sopranos. In the present context, it seems also to have freed him to lighten his 6-part texture. Thus **Tu es pastor ovium** (1607/43), which is 45 breves long, drops the first bass for seven breves in the initial phrase and for five more at the beginning of the last phrase.

This is another excellent short motet to place beside *Solve iubente Deo* and *Tu es Petrus*. Its text is very much like that of *Tu es Petrus*:

Tu es pastor ovium, princeps Apostolorum: tibi traditae sunt claves regni coelorum.

and the last phrase in Byrd's setting lasts very nearly as long. He devised a

novel type of double point, which really amounts to three extended statements of sharply contrasted subjects for the two text fragments. 'Tibi
traditae sunt' makes a grand effect of antiphonal homophony, though it is
never scored more heavily than in sixths and thirds; 'claves regni coelorum'
appears first in an insouciant little baroque flourish, then in a new ostinato
motive cadencing heavily in A, and then in freer imitation on a subject
loosely combining certain features of the other two. The tonal plan is as
lively as the thematic structure:

(1) tibi tradi- tae sunt	claves regni coelorum	(2) tibi . . . claves . . .		(3) tibi . . .		claves . . .
(C) E A		G	C C	A	D G C (G)	C

During the second statement of 'claves regni coelorum' the motive for 'tibi
traditae sunt' is heard in the accompanying voices, sometimes reduced rather
comically to its rhythmic essence on a monotone. The last 'claves' motive
breaks into smooth madrigalian scale motives, which echo similar motives for
the phrase 'princeps Apostolorum'. They then settle gingerly on a C major
chord, forming another of Byrd's typical half-tonic, half-subdominant
cadences in this mode.

A composer might well regard the text of **Quodcunque ligaveris**
(1607/44) as a joyless challenge rather than any kind of stimulus:

Quodcunque ligaveris super terram, erit ligatum et in coelis: et quodcunque
solveris super terram, erit solutum et in coelis [Matth. 16:19]: dicit Dominus
Simoni Petro.

A poetic paraphrase of this had baffled Byrd in the early hymn *Petrus beatus*
(see p. 77f). The magisterial opening point with its striking 9-semibreve
cantus firmus—note the ligatures!—determines the scale on which he now
chose to work; for 25 breves the harmony scarcely budges from C. Two
phrases are introduced by wonderfully solemn quasi-homophonic passages:
'et quodcunque solveris super terram', which stays in A minor for 11 breves,
and 'erit solutum et in coelis', which moves back to C in 18 breves. There is
a weighty stop and an enormous final phrase is built on a double subject of an
unusual kind: instead of the second subject contrasting with the first, it
expands up on it ('dicit Dominus': GABAG; 'Simoni Petro': ABCD . . .).

In 'expressive' terms the words at this point are negligible, and Byrd took
the opportunity to provide a purely musical display of extraordinary scope

and extraordinary intricacy. But in doctrinal terms the words are all-important: as H. C. Collins remarked, 'the extraordinary section . . . beginning "dicit Dominus Simoni Petro" rings like a challenge to England's rulers.'* Starting as a strictly canonic duet for four breves, the two motives are diminished and augmented, combined and recombined in a dozen different ways, and transformed by a sort of 'evolving variation' technique until they close into one of the most gorgeous sunsets that Byrd ever painted. Example 61 begins just as the strong triple rhythms asserted by 'dicit Dominus' in the bass (indicated by a bracket) begin to break down under the pressure of a telling new version of 'Simoni Petro' with a rich cadential

Ex. 61

*H. C. Collins, 'Byrd's Latin Church Music for Practical Use in the Roman Liturgy', *Music & Letters*, iv (1923), 259.

echappée figure. The augmentations of this version in bars 4–7, the single inversion of 'Simoni . . .' in bar 6, the single B minor chord in bar 7, the beautiful details contributed by the T¹ in bars 6, 7 and 9—even in Byrd (or in Bach) one seldom comes upon so incandescent and intimate a union between contrapuntal technique and expression. Then, as though aware all along that he was settling irrevocably into G, Byrd draws up to another full stop and adds one final homophonic statement of the text tugging hard at the tonic. Perhaps to his ear the long C major stretch at the beginning of this great motet was sufficient to restore the balance.

[2]

When was the Mass of Sts. Peter and Paul written? Although on pages 227f some general conclusions were drawn as to the date of composition of book 2 of the *Gradualia*, it is not immediately clear that this Mass can be considered on the same terms as the rest of the book's contents.

The primary evidence in this matter emerges from a stylistic comparison between the 4- and 5-part music of the two books. The difference indicates that this music, at least, was composed in the order of publication—book 1 before January 1605 (the date of registration), and book 2 after. This is supported by various bits of more speculative evidence. For example, book 1 was not labelled 'liber primus' on the original title page; in early 1605 Byrd was not advertising a second book of *Gradualia*, perhaps because he was not contemplating one, perhaps because most of the liturgical music he had as yet written had now been published. The contents and ordering of the two books—more miscellaneous in the one case, more methodical in the other— suggest that book 2 represents a new coherent effort. In any case the book 2 Corpus Christi antiphons ought to have found a place with their Mass in book 1, had they been ready in 1605. Then there is the matter of the transfers; the cumbersome system of the Marian Masses in book 1 is abandoned in the 4- and 5-part Masses of book 2, which provide several opportunities for transfers that Byrd pointedly ignored. No doubt all these arguments would be preceded by the common-sense argument that music published later is generally written later, if Byrd did not seem to negate this by his description of the book 2 motets as 'long since completed by me and committed to the press'. This was in 1607. On analysis, however, his assertion turns out to be consonant with the hypothesis that the bulk of book 2 was written rather rapidly in the second part of 1605.

Now all these arguments break down with the 6-part Mass of Sts. Peter and Paul in book 2. There are puzzling differences in style between some of its members, and there is no 6-part music in book 1 to provide a basis for comparison. Drawing analogies with stylistic features in the 4- and 5-part music is a risky business. As for the arrangement and order of the publication, this tells us nothing, for as the one 6-part Mass and the one item from the Proper of Saints, this one had to come last on both textual and liturgical grounds. Its position cannot be taken to indicate that it was written later than the other Masses of book 2. The use of transfers suggests that in fact it predates them.

Once this possibility has been broached, new lines of speculation are suggested by the likelihood—the great likelihood—that a Mass of St. Peter was designed as a special tribute to Petre, the dedicatee of book 2. Even if the Mass had been available for inclusion in book 1, in 1605, Byrd might not have wished to feature it in a publication dedicated to somebody else. Perhaps even in 1605 he had some idea of a further publication which would be dedicated to Petre—if not a second volume of *Gradualia*, perhaps a smaller, more furtive undertaking on the model of the Mass Ordinaries. The politically sensitive contents of this particular Mass would seem to require analogous caution in the publishing.

At this point speculation begins to take wings; but we can bring it down to earth by asking what a Mass of Sts. Peter and Paul would have looked like, if Byrd has written it before 1605. It would have had three numbers only: the introit, the gradual doubling as offertory, by means of a transfer, and the alleluia verse doubling as communion. Byrd might or might not already have composed the other alleluia for St. Peter's Chains to accompany these three numbers. But he almost certainly would not have written the three antiphons. Book 1 shows that in 1605 he had not yet settled on the idea of antiphons integrated in mode and texture with the main items of a Mass.

And once we think of the Mass of Sts. Peter and Paul in two layers—an earlier layer consisting of the Mass itself and a later one comprising the three antiphons—the stylistic puzzles begin to clear up. The antiphons fall into place with the products of Byrd's ripest style, while the introit and gradual can be envisaged as emerging from a period when he was working somewhat awkwardly to meet the special requirements of the *Gradualia* motets in a 6-part texture. The unusually archaic nature of the introit and gradual verses (expecially the former, discussed on page 231f) suggests that this period may have been at the very earliest stage of the *Gradualia* project. There are also some fleeting hints of similarity between the Mass of Sts. Peter and Paul and that of the Purification, which was probably the first of the Marian group to be composed, so probably the earliest of all the 4- and 5-part Masses. The same system for the transfer comes up in the Purification introit and in the gradual for Sts. Peter and Paul, and the syncopated ostinato subject for 'plebis Iudaeorum' in *Nunc scio vere* recalls several in the Marian Masses, notably 'nisi videret Christum Domini' in the Purification communion *Responsum accepit Simeon*. Even certain small anomalies in the doxology of *Nunc scio vere*, mentioned on page 243, make better sense if the piece is thought to have been composed early in the project. So does the ending alleluia of *Constitues eos principes* which, though effectively integrated with the alleluia verses to come, seems nonetheless rather simple-minded by the standards of the *Gradualia* as a whole.

As for the alleluia verse which doubles as the communion: vastly as *Tu es Petrus* surpasses the introit and gradual in quality, there is nothing in its madrigalian second and final point 'et super hanc petram . . .' that could not have been written many years before 1607. What may be significant is the similarity between its first point—which serves so well as a foil to the second —and the first point of *Nunc scio vere*. It may also be significant that the only other communion in the *Gradualia* with a final point as long as that of *Tu es Petrus* is *Responsum accepit Simeon* for the Purification. We can see that both of these texts might have (or even must have) tempted a composer in Byrd's position to set them with special emphasis. But it is less certain that in 1607, when he was cultivating the highly compressed style of the later 5-part Masses, he would have yielded to such temptation.

This inquiry into the date of the Mass of Sts. Peter and Paul has perhaps led us to isolate the earliest stage in the composition of the *Gradualia*. Byrd's difficulty in dealing with the 6-part texture was compounded by the newness of the more general problem posed by liturgical composition, a problem he was rapidly to solve in the course of working through the Marian group of Masses from the Purification to the Assumption. There is, finally, more than poetic justice in seeing the *Gradualia* take its impetus in an act of composition dedicated to St. Peter, in a forthright gesture of Catholic solidarity. That Byrd would have deployed his maximum resources for such a task is understandable; less so that he would have experienced such evident trouble in the execution.

As a final flight of speculation, it may be hazarded that the composer was constrained to produce his first-layer Mass of St. Peter in a particular hurry. Suppose it was ordered in the year 1603 to celebrate not only the rising hopes of the English Catholics on the accession of James I, but also the elevation of Petre to the peerage on 21 July. The Feast of St. Peter's Chains falls on 1 August. Byrd's rubric in the partbooks refers to the major feast, Sts. Peter and Paul, and makes no mention of St. Peter's Chains; but might not the music have been written originally for the latter occasion? It is slightly odd that despite the rubric, the alleluia that comes first in the publication is not *Tu es Petrus* for Sts. Peter and Paul but *Solve iubente Deo* for St. Peter's Chains—followed by the motet *Tu es Petrus* in its role, perhaps, as communion for the latter feast, rather than as alleluia verse for the former.

One would not, of course, wish to pinpoint the commissioning, composition, copying out and clandestine rehearsal of all this difficult music in a ten-day period. Petre would have received prior notice of the honour, and in any case he and his party doubtless entertained high expectations of James from the start, observing how soon the King's reputed generosity in such matters was proved in action. James distributed knighthoods recklessly, by Elizabethan standards, even before arriving in London on 3 May, and ennobled Cecil and three others but ten days later.* It is a long shot. But the awkwardness of Byrd's introit and gradual calls rather urgently for explanation.

*S. R. Gardiner, *History of England from the Accession of James I* (London, 1883), i, 87f.

5d
Miscellanea

Nearly all the miscellaneous compositions of the *Gradualia* appear in book 1, which is less rigorously organized than its sequel and seems clearly to have been intended by the composer for a more general audience. Book 2 contains, outside its central schedule of 'offices', only a single 4-part composition and a pair of 6-part motets at the end. Byrd allowed himself even this small latitude, perhaps, because the plan of book 1 had included no 6-part fascicle and therefore left no place for any miscellaneous compositions in that texture. Some of the miscellaneous motets are set to non-liturgical texts, some to liturgical texts in categories other than the regular Mass items.

It is of course not necessary to believe that every one of these pieces which happens to have a liturgical text was actually designed for a service. Among them, *Salve Regina* and the other Marian antiphons might indeed have been sung at actual Compline services; on the other hand *Visita quaesumus Domine* and *In manus tuas*—motets with texts similar but not identical to certain Compline texts—were more likely intended for informal occasions when pious chamber music was wanted. (All but a few of the miscellaneous pieces are for three or four voices, appropriate to music making on a modest scale.) On such occasions, Byrd's Marian antiphons such as *Salve Regina* would surely have been welcome too, on the same basis as his strictly non-liturgical motets, his vernacular psalm settings from the English songbooks, and other such pieces.

In any case, with the miscellaneous motets Byrd seems to have relished the opportunity to provide some variety from the relatively restricted ambit of style, mode and texture imposed by the main scheme of the *Gradualia*. In the 5-part fascicle of book 1, for example, he included as one of the three miscellaneous items a short consort song for mean voice and four instruments, **Adoramus te Christe** (1605 *a* 5/26). We can imagine the puzzlement with which Continental musicians or connoisseurs would have regarded this 'cantio sacra' (to cite the title page), if by chance copies of the *Gradualia* travelled the cross-channel Catholic supply routes in the wake of the Gun-powder Plot. The other two items are both motets in the old 'political' genre. Their texts have been cited above on pages 42 and 225. *Plorans plorabit* (1605 *a* 5/28: see p. 158f), a magnificently dour Tallisian essay in the G Dorian mode, employs low clefs and a traditional thick texture including a single soprano and two alto voices. Striking as pointed a contrast with this as possible, **Unam petii a Domino** (1605 *a* 5/27) is a very bright and modern-sounding composition in the C Ionian mode with two sopranos reaching up again and again in the treble clef to high g′.

If *Unam petii* has its own distinctive place in the sound-world of Byrd's motets, one reason is that these are scarcely ever set in the Ionian mode peaking on the high fifth degree (see Ex. 3a). A rare exception, *Domine secundum multitudinem dolorum meorum* (1589/27), produces a rather different effect, partly because the bass goes down only to C rather than to A, as in *Unam petii*, but mainly because since the soprano is not doubled, Byrd plots its climaxes with great care and introduces high g′ sparingly. In *Unam petii* the sound of the high fifth in the two sopranos permeates the texture, which is kept notably light and airy throughout. Characteristic is the motive of the opening point, which encompasses an octave with two upward leaps (fcfga′c′). Here, as in the opening point of the *secunda pars* and in the last point, the space of an octave or a tenth opens up frequently between adjacent voices.

The 'Unam petii' motive supports a full-scale point of imitation including six entries; from the outset it is clear that this motet is a weightier thing than the typical *Gradualia* Mass item, with its double construction as opening gambit. The *secunda pars*, too, begins with a regular point of imitation, which in this case actually continues with a sort of counter-exposition.

Each *pars* includes a fairly long passage in tenths (or seventeenths), a technique contributing further to the open quality of the texture ('omnibus diebus vitae meae'* and 'ut videam voluntatem Domini'). The motive for the final point 'et visitem templum eius' starts with a dotted-crotchet figure that comes up a number of times in the *Gradualia* (cf. Exs. 6k, 60, 61), but the stiff rhythm of the *incipit* gives way repeatedly to a rhythmically irregular, highly complex melismatic cadence. The rhythmic dissociation works together with the open texture and some very unusual dissonance treatment to give a remarkably individual, strange, ecstatic feeling to the conclusion of this fine motet.

[2]

In the 4-part fascicle of book 1 Byrd does not so much relish variety as revel in it. The dozen miscellaneous items here furnish about as many surprises. Among them is a short psalm-motet (No. 9), a cantus firmus composition (No. 10), a made-over fantasia for strings (No. 15) and a series of homophonic formulae for the recitation of the Litany (No. 16). Two of the compositions last for nearly a hundred breves (Nos. 12 and 13) and one lasts for only eleven (No. 20). Byrd's music ranges through the Dorian, Aeolian, Mixolydian, Ionian and perhaps the Phrygian modes. Several numbers are distinctively scored for high voices. There are two small groups of matched pieces—the three Marian antiphons (Nos. 12–14) and the pair of *Magnificat* antiphons for the Purification (Nos. 18 and 19). If these are left out of consideration, it really seems as though Byrd went out of his way to avoid including two pieces that are at all alike.

The total range of **Ecce quam bonum** (1615 *a* 4/9), a quiet setting of the short Psalm 132, in the F Ionian mode, extends only through two octaves and a third, from B♭ to d'. Although the piece exists in an earlier manuscript version (see p. 225), this probably does not predate the *Gradualia* by many years. It is true that the first pages evoke an old-fashioned chanson idiom, involving dry imitations in crotchets, as surely as does the 'motet' **In manus tuas** (1605 *a* 4/15) which was actually arranged from an instrumental fantasia, Fantasia G4 (see Vol. III, p. 92). But this style is relaxed later, especially in the *secunda pars*, where the music is similar enough to that of

---

*This phrase and the unusual recurring phrase 'magnum est nomen meum in gentibus' in the 4-part motet *Ab ortu solis* (1607/13) employ almost the same motive, doubled at the tenth in both cases. Though presumably *Ab ortu solis* is the later piece, the treatment of the motive in it is weaker, perhaps on account of the 4-part texture or because the words 'in gentibus' suggested less interesting sequels to Byrd than 'vitae meae'.

the Corpus Christi Mass which precedes it in the partbooks. Byrd set the last half-verse of the psalm, 'Quoniam illic mandavit Dominus benedictionem et vitam usque in saeculum', somewhat in the manner of an introit doxology, perhaps on account of the textual reminiscence. The one compositional problem that seems to have sparked his interest was finding characteristic and distinct settings for the word 'descendit' at its three separate appearances. It is curious how naturally the last three or four phrases of this motet fall into large metrical units of five semibreves.

Didactic texts like Psalm 132 always brought out the sententious side of Byrd's nature. Evidently a prayer for God's blessing on the house struck a much more cheerful nerve. A brilliant exercise in his most modern, concise* manner, **Visita quaesumus Domine** (1605 *a* 4/11) matches *Unam petii* in mode and general texture, the C Ionian mode with the high fifth g′ sounding repeatedly in the two entwining sopranos. It does not match exactly, since the bass of the 5-part motet is missing; this is a piece for high voices, with the lowest of them, a tenor, beginning and ending on middle c. There is much lively homophonic writing and madrigalian polyphony. 'Visita, quaesumus Domine' is set as a short cell in two voices, repeated at once by the full choir in block chords—a simple, vivid type of beginning that Byrd would employ again, with a difference, in the Whitsun alleluia *Veni Sancte Spiritus* in book 2. Thereafter in principle every other phrase returns to homophony, as indicated by italics in the text below; and all phrases, whether homophonic or polyphonic, end with particularly strong, clear, flamboyant cadences. This scheme is broken only towards the end, where a series of fast-moving points run into one another without clear articulation:

Visita, quaesumus Domine, habitationem istam, *et omnes insidias inimici* ab ea longe repelle: *Angeli tui sancti* habitent in ea, qui nos in pace custodiant, et benedictio tua sit super nos semper. *Per Christum Dominum nostrum.* Amen [cf. prayer et Compline].

These points are less distinguished, however, than the earlier phrase 'ab ea longe repelle', with its unusual sprung motive, and the concluding 6-breve amen, which seems in its short span to achieve astonishing buoyancy. The music might take off like a balloon if not for subdominant ballast received over the last thirteen breves of the composition.

A batch of Marian motets follows, beginning with three of the familiar

---

*The text itself (see below) is a concise version of the Compline prayer *Visita quaesumas*, which ends 'Per Dominum nostrum Iesum Christum Filium tuum: qui vivit et regnat in unitate Spiritus Sancti Deus, per omnia saecula saeculorum. Amen.'

antiphons for Compline. These are all set for SATB in the Mixolydian mode, like the items of the Corpus Christi Mass. (The fourth Marian antiphon, *Regina coeli*, for Paschal Time, Byrd composed in the D Aeolian mode for three voices, along with the other miscellaneous Easter music.) **Salve Regina** (1605 *a* 4/12), one of Byrd's most beautiful larger motets, gives us a rare opportunity to compare his view of a single text over a period of twenty years or so, for he had composed a *Salve Regina* in the 1580s, for five voices (1591/6–7: see p. 173f).

The new piece is more concise, of course, and also more gracefully proportioned. The *prima pars* of both settings begins with a trio. In 1591 this is followed by two extended 5-part sections of roughly equal length, the second of them ('Et Iesum benedictum') constituting the *secunda pars*. In 1605 both *partes* begin with trios, and a shapely pattern emerges of two balanced pairs of sections with lengths in a ratio of about 4:5. In each pair the sections for three and five voices stand in a ratio of about 2:3—

		breves			*breves*
1591: Salve Regina	*a 3*	21	1605: Salve Regina *a 3*		16
Ad te clamamus	*a 5*	67	Ad te clamamus *a 4*		25
			2ª pars: Eia ergo *a 3*		19
2ª pars: Et Iesum	*a 5*	63	Et Iesum *a 4*		34

As this chart suggests, the new setting contracts the dimensions of the old one more and more—almost phrase by phrase—as the piece proceeds. The portion up to 'Eia ergo' is shorter by some twenty percent, but by the end of the text the figure is approaching forty. The final phrase 'o dulcis Virgo Maria' lasts for 27 breves in 1591, 14 breves in 1605.

Yet the very first words, 'Salve, Regina, mater misericordiae', are actually set more expansively in the *Gradualia*. One reason for this, no doubt, was simply to give more dignity to the opening salutation. Compared to the later setting, the earlier one seems to move through the text with rather disrespectful haste at the beginning, only to grow more and more hopelessly prolix as it goes along. Another reason has to do with a point of musical recapitulation. For all the differences between the two pieces in form, dimensions, mode, and the themes employed, they exhibit certain parallels in basic procedure.

In 1591 Byrd carried over the melisma of the initial 'Salve, Regina' quite emphatically at the second 'salve', which occurs at the end of the opening trio, and then again towards the end of the whole piece at 'O clemens', 'o pia', and 'Virgo Maria', and he does much the same thing in 1605. But does it much more subtly. As the second 'salve' is downplayed in the new motet, he cites the original 'Salve, Regina' melisma in a restrained version, and at 'O clemens, o pia' he arranges things so that the now more insistent melismas seem to grow out of the motive for the previous word 'ostende', as well as recalling both 'salve's'. And the expanded setting of the opening section in 1605 allowed for an enhanced return at 'O clemens, o pia'. Here Byrd echoes not only the melisma but also the cantus firmus-like fragment sung by the soprano, as well as the highly characteristic harmonic colouration of juxtaposed G and A major chords (Ex. 62). Expansion was needed at the beginning of the motet for emphasis, so that the return could make its point.

Ex. 62

Another parallel between the two motets—hard to specify in technical terms, but strongly felt all the same—comes in the emotional quality that Byrd projects in the final phrase 'o dulcis Virgo Maria'. Gentle rocking motion controls both settings, and they are both in the same mode—for in 1591 Byrd found that when his mind turned to Marian devotion he slipped inevitably into the Mixolydian mode, no matter if the music he was writing happened to be Aeolian. In the later motet it is particularly the repeated conjunction of A and G major chords that illuminates the setting of the final apostrophe, which cannot perhaps be called an improvement on the earlier setting (see Ex. 30) but is surely no less fine in its own way. The last few bars employ sequences on the 'Maria' motive shown at the end of Example 62b (alto, bars 6–7) together with yet another manifestation of the opening melisma, for the word 'Virgo': a miracle of elegance.

Where Byrd clearly does improve upon his earlier effort is at the end of part 1 (in the new division). Using affective semitones, he makes the last several motives of this section cleave together in a wonderfully humble, almost apologetic evocation of the vale of tears from which the Virgin is sued to relieve us. Upward and downward inflexions—EFE, BCB, AB♭A, AG♯A and DC♯D—are adjusted to the syllables 'Ad te su*spiramus*', '*gementes*', '*et flentes*' and 'in hac la*chrymarum* valle'. A magnificent piece of draughtsmanship, this passage subsides into a very individual low cadence for the word 'valle', preceded by an unanticipated low F in the bass and several false relations of unusual poignancy.

The 'Salve, Regina' trio at the beginning of this motet is one of Byrd's most modern in style. The two 'salve's' are treated freely, as has already been indicated; thereafter the motive for 'mater misericordiae' imitates hardly at all and 'Vita, dulcedo' does so only by grace of motivic flexibility of a sort that puts the idea of canon far from the mind. 'Eia ergo' on the other hand is of all Byrd's trios one of the most strictly canonic. The use of the two styles of 3-part writing in this most carefully planned of compositions confirms the impression of Byrd's deliberate cultivation of archaic styles for purposes of contrast.

The long trio at the beginning of **Alma Redemptoris Mater** (1605 *a* 4/13) starts rather strictly—the canon causes a strange progression at the last 'coeli'—but ends with a motive for 'succurre cadenti' which not only falls and falls but also seems to make interesting systematic use of false relations to enhance the feeling of weakness. The voices descend well below the stave—the soprano to G, alto to D and tenor to B. Perhaps the finest touches in this motet are the final soprano statement of 'natura mirante', rising up through a tenth to a high e' which sounds wondrous indeed, and the delicate treatment of F♮ in the phrase 'summens illud Ave'.

Ave Regina coelorum (1605 *a* 4/14) is a very original composition. Like the other two antiphons, it begins with a section for reduced voices; but instead of a trio it has three crisp little duets moving in purposeful crotchet rhythms with a decidedly modern ring. The themes are characterized and contrasted with unusual sharpness: see especially the quiet, terse flourishes for 'Salve, radix', the miniature marching motive for 'salve, porta', the melismas for 'Valle' and the elegant echoing duets in thirds for 'Super omnes speciosa'. There are scarcely any phrase overlaps, and the clearly demarcated phrases get steadily longer as the piece proceeds (beginning with 'Salve, radix': 5, 6, 8, 9, 10 and 11* breves).

Perhaps on account of this preparation, the 21-breve final point 'Et pro nobis Christum exora' does not sound at all long—or perhaps this point succeeds simply as a result of its fine, soaring theme and its crystal-clear structure. The soprano theme in its original form is echoed an octave lower and then resumed by the soprano a third higher, leading to IV (C). Then the theme starts again in its original position, but now in the alto, answered this time by overlapping soprano and tenor entries leading symmetrically to V (D). The pitch D is struck again and again by the motive for 'exora', and its resolution five breves later is simple, inevitable and grand.

Among the Marian antiphons *Ave Regina coelorum* stands somewhat apart in style, but in harmonic plan all three are strikingly similar. Despite their considerable length, Byrd holds strictly to cadences in I, IV and V up to the penultimate phrase, which in each case moves emphatically to a cadence (or a series of cadences) on ii. This is, on the whole, a more conservative treatment of the mode than Byrd accords to the Corpus Christi or Whitsun Masses. Yet perhaps even more than the Mixolydian Masses, the Marian antiphons (and *Ave Regina coelorum* in particular) show clear signs of a break with modal practice in their repeated employment of F♯ in contexts which are not strictly cadential. This is an old story with Byrd. The Ionian mode, as we have seen (p. 70), allows for dominant cadences but not subdominant ones, while the Mixolydian allows for both, with the important qualification that the dominant chord in question is minor. For Byrd the way to major tonality, or something very like it, consisted not in supplying subdominant cadences in the Ionian mode, but in raising the third of the minor dominant in the Mixolydian.

Little needs to be said about simple chordal setting of the **Litany** (1605 a 4/16).† Except in the Agnus Dei portion of it, Byrd follows the plainchant rather loosely (or else he was following a variant version of the chant); the ultimate descent from A to E (see *Liber usualis*, 838)—in Byrd's transposition, from E to B—is reflected in the alto voice and results in an unusual Phrygian cadence. Elsewhere the chant migrates from the tenor only to the soprano (at the first Christe eleison, the second Agnus Dei and the responses 'te rogamus audi nos'). The similarity between the second Kyrie–Christe–Kyrie

---

*It seems justifiable to count 'Valle' and 'o valde decora' as a single 11-breve unit, for while the two phrases have different (though related) themes, they do for once overlap and both strike A minor cadences and no others.

†Prior to the responses 'ora pro nobis', and so on, all the Saints' names and other sentences are omitted, probably as much to save space as for reasons of political caution.

of this Litany setting and the Kyrie of the Three-Part Mass, noted on page 205, may be taken as an indication that the work was composed in the early 1590s.

Salve sola Dei Genitrix (1605 *a* 4/17) is another composition for high voices, like *Visita quaesumus Domine*, this time scored for tenor and three sopranos. Obviously this special texture encourages balanced constructions, and in half a dozen of the phrases the three sopranos echo one another quite closely. In this regard it is instructive to compare the first phrase of this motet with that of *Surge illuminare Hierusalem* (1607/15) for Epiphany. Byrd works with much the same motive, but treats it in a much less symmetrical, more dynamic fashion in the later piece: a measure of the difference between his response to the words 'surge' and 'salve'.

This motet's text, which does not appear to come from the liturgy, turns suddenly at the end to thoughts of death:

Salve, sola Dei Genitrix et Virgo Maria: tecum una est Dominus, tibi gratia summa, superque es fœmineos benedicta choros; benedictus Iesus, ille tui ventris fructus; miserere tuorum nunc et in extrema, precor, O ne morte relinquas.

Byrd responded to this unanticipated sombre note in an unusually dramatic way (and it was principally to accommodate the line 'ne morte relinquas', surely, that he decided on the G Dorian mode—in the *Gradualia*, a great rarity). The impressive litany-like plaint for 'ne morte relinquas', sung three times by the sopranos and once an octave lower by the tenor, is preceded and prepared by the first homophonic phrase in the piece, 'nunc et in extrema', which begins with a jolting false relation and goes on to declaim the word 'nunc' with a remarkable intense stammer. Both the false relation and the stammer are resumed for the exclamation 'O' a moment later (Ex. 63).

Two 4-part *Magnificat* antiphons for the Purification follow at this point. Evidently Byrd in 1605 did not yet have clearly in mind the idea of matching

Ex. 63

antiphons to the main items of the Mass, or perhaps he had just been struck by the idea, and was making a special effort to implement it with two compositions which were already at hand. In any case, things do not quite match in mode (nor, of course, in texture), for although both the Mass and the antiphons are ostensibly in the D Aeolian mode, the range of the former is A–f' while that of the latter is G'–d'. Byrd uses the low G' sparingly but always to great effect, and it is an effect completely absent from the 5-part Marian motets.

The antiphons do not display any of the unusual stylistic features of the high-voiced motets, or of *Ave Regina coelorum* or *Ecce quam bonum*; they fit quietly and very naturally into the general stylistic continuum of the book 1 Mass music. On internal evidence it would be hard indeed to say whether or not they predate the 5-part Purification Mass. Perhaps the most memorable feature of **Hodie beata Virgo** (1605 *a* 4/19) is the insouciant final phrase 'et benedixit Deum in aeternum', which breaks out of quasi-homophony into elegantly calculated free polyphony—but a swift circle of fifths seems to leave it so dizzy that it misses the right cadence point. The sober opening of **Senex puerum portabat** (1605 *a* 4/18) is as remarkable for its neglect of declamatory niceties as for its highly original sonority (Ex. 64). A sequence

Ex. 64

recalling one for the words 'et non polluent nomen eius' in *Sacerdotes Domini* (1605 *a* 4/3) illuminates the next phrase 'puer autem senem regebat'. In this phrase and in all but one of the others, the original figure for the 'por*ta*bat' melisma recurs either as a functional or a decorative detail, often in its distinctive melodic form. Its turning notes are spread out as a scale in the subject of the final phrase, a marvellously ample and expressive meditation on the single word 'adoravit'. *Senex puerum portabat* looks forward to the 4-part antiphons of the book 2 Christmas Mass, in the same mode; they are larger pieces, but hardly greater ones.

As an *explicit* to the 4-part section of miscellaneous compositions Byrd provided an expertly crafted 11-breve setting of the response **Deo gratias** (1605 *a* 4/20). Its structure is that of an alleluia with two subjects. And indeed a very similar piece of music appears in the following 3-part fascicle of the *Gradualia*, for the first alleluia of the Easter motet *Alleluia. Vespere autem sabbati.* A comparison is drawn on page 333.

[3]

When Byrd said in the preface to the first *Gradualia* that he had set all the hymns of the Blessed Virgin Mary, he was referring to those in the Little Office of Our Lady. The texts in today's liturgical books differ somewhat from those in use before the Council of Trent, which were *Quem terra pontus aethera* at Matins, *O gloriosa Domina* at Lauds, *Memento salutis auctor* at the Little Hours and *Ave maris stella* at Vespers (and Sarum Use added *Virgo singularis*, which is simply the tail end of *Ave maris stella*, at Compline).* It is hard to explain why Byrd's texts for these hymns, almost alone among the texts of the *Gradualia*, should not follow the Pian Breviary, but rather hold to the traditional versions current both in England and abroad before 1571. The Little Office was a central element of the *Horae* or Primers designed for private devotions, and it may be that in this area old textual forms commanded special loyalties.

The first three of these Marian hymns, which are poetic siblings, using the same stanza pattern (four lines of iambic tetrameter) and sharing the same doxology—'Gloria tibi, Domine, / Qui natus es de Virgine, / Cum Patre et Sancto Spiritu / In sempiterna saecula. Amen'—are set in the same distinctive style.† Byrd's intentions are clearest with **O gloriosa Domina** (1605 *a* 3/2), the most consistent, the most concise, and also the dullest of the three. His idea seems to have been to simulate in the three voices the half-homophonic style he had developed in his earlier full-choir hymns *Siderum rector* and *O lux beata Trinitas* in the *Cantiones* of 1575 (see pp. 115f). Like those hymns and like *Iesu nostra redemptio* in the *Gradualia* (but unlike *Pange lingua*), the 3-part Marian hymns are not liturgical *alternatim* settings but complete ones, without reference to the traditional plainchant; and the music moves *a note neri*, in a basic crotchet pulse. Very laconic phrases are the order of the day, often regimented to a standard metrical pattern for the

*Sarum breviary, 283, 285f, 288f. In the Pian Breviary the text of *Ave maris stella* reads the same as in the older books and *Quem terra pontus aethera* differs only in its doxology, 'Iesu tibi sit gloria', but the two other hymns begin *O gloriosa Virginum* and *Memento rerum conditor* and diverge appreciably thereafter (see *Antiphonale sacrosanctae ecclesie* (Rome, 1912), 'Hymni antiqui', 46). For a random example of Byrd's adherence to the new forms, the motet *Adorna thalamum tuum* (see p. 336) includes the word 'genitum', which is an addition of the Pian Breviary.

†The soprano range of these three hymns is the same, c–d', which fits the soprano clef, but *O gloriosa Domina* uses the mezzo-soprano. Compare the Three-Part Mass, which uses the mezzo-soprano clef for the range a–d'.

iambic line, ◡ ◡ ◡—◡—◡—. Nearly every line is set either in block chords *a 3* or else as a very light point of imitation in which a pair of voices proceeds in thirds or tenths. Byrd also develops a curious little mechanism for starting up. He has the entire first line of each stanza sung solo by one voice, after which a second voice answers by repeating the melody at the octave, fourth or fifth; the third voice may double this answer in thirds or tenths (stanzas 1 and 2) or enter a little later in stretto (stanzas 3 and 4).

In the other two hymns the quasi-homophonic style is used less consistently and fewer stanzas begin with solos. There are flickers of interest in **Memento salutis auctor** (1605 *a 3/3*) at the lines 'Mater misericordiae' (a reminiscence from the *Salve Regina*) and 'Et hora mortis suscipe', with their echoing emphasis on the B♭A semitone, and at the beginning of the doxology, where the soprano suddenly swings along for two lines in a regular triple metre. The rest of the doxology is either repeated from *O gloriosa Domina* or closely modelled on it.

In **Quem terra pontus aethera** (1605 *a 3/1*) the solo starts are restricted to the doxology (stanza 5) and stanza 1, where the mechanism unexpectedly reveals its origin: Byrd's 5-part polyphonic song or madrigal *Of gold all burnished* from the 1589 *Songs of sundrie natures*, which begins with the same tenor solo and precisely the same notes as 'Quem terra, pontus', and much the same choral answer. Byrd treated this somewhat longer hymn a little less barely than the others; and he seems to have roused himself at the doxology. For 'Gloria tibi, Domine' he copied the motive from *O gloriosa Domina* but added an augmentation which bridges smoothly over the next line. For 'et Sancto Spiritu' he took the rather comical crotchet figure used earlier for the words 'Fecunda Sancto Spiritu' and grafted it on to the 'Cum Patre' idea which is common to the three hymns. And he replaced the similar setting of 'In sempiterna' in the other hymns by a six-fold madrigalian stretto which, though slighter, might perhaps be deemed more stylish as a setting of the words.

As compared to the first three hymns **Ave maris stella** (1605 *a 3/4*) employs a weightier style, appropriate to a text of somewhat greater solemnity, though perhaps less than prudent in a setting that runs to seven stanzas. The metrical unit is the minim; none of the 28 lines in this hymn is set in block chords and only two employ imitation involving a pair of voices lined up in thirds. One of these owes its special treatment to the text, 'Ut videntes Iesum' (stanza 6); Byrd conveys his vision of the supplicants' eagerness and innocence by means of this simpler texture as well as by a charming combination of halting and darting rhythms. He now allows himself more contrapuntal artifice: in the phrase 'Spiritui Sancto' (stanza 7), where the imitative figure comes quite strictly on six different scale degrees, and in many phrases at the ends of stanzas, notably 'Semper collaetemur' (stanza 6) with its astonishing crotchet animation—which is no less astonishing for its smooth preparation in the 'Ut videntes Iesum' phrase just beforehand.

In stanza 5, 'Virgo singularis', the middle voice, heretofore a tenor, changes its clef from alto to soprano so that it can swop high d's with the actual soprano. Its total range over the whole motet is a cool two octaves. Meanwhile the soprano plunges lower than anywhere else in the piece, down to low F, as though in a fit of pique. This all seems inexplicable, even on the assumption of some sort of insertion or substitution of foreign, perhaps older material; *Virgo singularis*, as has just been remarked, was the beginning of a separate Sarum hymn in this same series. It is puzzling, too, as well as disappointing, that this special stanza should offer less rather than more of musical interest than all the others.

Obviously Byrd devoted much more care and art to the composition of the Easter Marian antiphon **Regina coeli** (1605 *a* 3/5). Indeed, of all his 3-part compositions one would unhesitatingly choose this motet as a model for richness and elegance of 3-part contrapuntal writing. Byrd's setting was controlled by the peculiar form of the text, punctuated or rather lacerated by Paschal alleluias. He set this very expansively indeed, as eight roughly balanced sections, with the cadence points in the Dorian mode carefully plotted:

14 *breves*	11	14	16	13	13	15	16
Regina		Quia quem		Rexurrexit,		Ora pro	
coeli	alleluia:	meruisti	alleluia:	sicut	alleluia:	nobis	alleluia.
laetare,	(No. 1)	portare,	(No. 2)	dixit,	(No. 3)	Deum,	(No. 4)
i	i	III	iv	VII	$\frac{1}{2}$i	$\frac{1}{2}$i	i

This adds up to a substantial composition of 110 breves, outlasting any of the other, 4-part Compline antiphons with their vastly longer texts. Not only are the words of the 'verse' sections set at unusual length, but the alleluias are also more fully elaborated than the others in the 3-part fascicle.

In harmonic terms the two middle sections stand somewhat apart from the others, and this is borne out by their quieter musical style. The middle 'verses' move essentially in minims, whereas 'Regina coeli' expands into swift, graceful melismas and 'Ora pro nobis' gains unusual agility from a fertile double subject contrasting semibreve with crotchet and syncopated minim movement. The two middle alleluias are more mellifluous, the outer ones more intricate, built on lengthy crotchet figures containing leaps. These

motives strikingly recall some alleluia motives in the early cantus firmus
motet *Christus resurgens* (see p. 62)—but there is no comparison as far as
the working-out is concerned. Alleluia No. 4 amounts to an enhanced version
of alleluia No. 1, using a shorter form of its motive. Both alleluias depend on
subtle accentual changes in their motives, and both are laid out quite
similarly (Ex. 65). These impressive samples of Byrd's contrapuntal art have

Ex. 65

a distinctive haunting quality of their own; they are at some disadvantage,
though, next to the simpler and more modern alleluia No. 3, which must be
one of the most beautiful in the whole of the *Gradualia*.

While the Marian hymns seem to have been conceived in the spirit of
private devotions and were probably intended as pious chamber music,
Regina coeli might also have been sung at actual services and the remaining
Easter pieces in the 3-part fascicle almost certainly were. Yet there are small
liturgical oddities to be noted in many of them. The words 'Haec dies ...
laetemur in ea' sound repeatedly in Easter week, but never exactly as Byrd
sets them in his motet *Haec dies*, with an appended alleluia (he had done the
same in his more famous *Haec dies*, the 6-part motet from the *Cantiones
sacrae* of 1591). Both *Alleluia. Vespere autem sabbati* and *Post dies octo* appear
to be liturgical composites for Vesper services. The latter belongs to Low
Sunday; oddly, in Byrd's piece the *Magnificat* antiphon *Post dies octo* is
followed by the versicle and response which *precede* it in the service ('Mane
nobiscum Domine, alleluia. Quoniam advesperascit, alleluia.'). Byrd labels
this simply 'versus'.

The other composite belongs to Vespers at the Paschal Vigil on Holy
Saturday. This highly compressed service, which is fitted in just before the

end of Mass, consists in its entirety of the following: a brief antiphon whose text is the single word 'alleluia'; Psalm 116; the antiphon *Alleluia* again; 'the *Celebrant* then at once intones the antiphon of the *Magnificat* [*Vespere autem sabbati*] which is continued by the Choir'* at the words 'quae lucescit'; the *Magnificat*; the antiphon *Vespere autem sabbati* once again; a prayer; and the Ite missa est. What Byrd sets is an alleluia as the *prima pars* of his piece and then the portion of the *Magnificat* antiphon which is sung by the choir, 'quae lucescit . . .', etc., as the *secunda pars*. The best way to interpret this is in a strictly liturgical manner. After Byrd's alleluia, Psalm 116 should be chanted (in the fifth mode), the alleluia repeated, the *Magnificat* antiphon begun by the celebrant in plainchant and completed by the choir in polyphony, the *Magnificat* chanted, and finally the *Magnificat* antiphon repeated. In skeleton form, Byrd has provided a musical setting of the whole service.

Alleluia. Vespere autem sabbati, Haec dies, Angelus Domini (this is the offertory for both Easter Monday and Low Sunday) and *Post dies octo* all match in mode, clef combination, general dimensions and musical style. They are slight but busy pieces, bristling with ingenuities and not a few quirks, ready at any moment to slip in and out of minim or crotchet move-movement. In **Alleluia. Vespere autem sabbati** (1605 *a* 3/6) the final alleluia feels like a free canon over a cantus firmus that has been elaborated, the elaboration including an augmentation of the very brief, very fast alleluia motive. The opening alleluia moves more solemnly, however; as we have seen, it is no mere appendage but does duty as an actual antiphon. This alleluia is, in fact, a rewriting of the little 4-part motet *Deo gratias* (1605 *a* 4/20). The chart shows the spacing and the pitch level of the entries of the main subject:

Deo gratias	2	2	4		2	4		2	5 *semibreves*
(Mixolydian)	*free*	G	g		G	g		G	d
								(*syncopated*)	
Alleluia	2	2	5		2	5		4	
(F Ionian)	*free*	f	b♭		f	f		f	
								(*syncopated*)	

Both the main and the secondary subjects correspond fairly closely.†

Haec dies (1605 *a* 3/7) pronounces its message of joy with a rhythmic crescendo of almost excessive neatness; its alleluia, which lasts for ten breves, is rather similar to alleluias 1 and 4 of *Regina coeli*. **Angelus Domini**

---

*Liber usualis, 761.

†The emendation a′b′ for a′a′ in the soprano should be considered at BW 5, 185, bar 6.

(1605 *a* 3/8) has a shorter, simpler alleluia of the same general variety. **Post dies octo** (1605 *a* 3/9) is built so slightly it will not even tarry for its alleluias. The words 'Pax vobis' in this motet and 'Quem quaeritis' in *Angelus Domini* employ clipped sequential ideas of a type also encountered at 'Cum Petre' in the doxology of the Marian hymns and at 'in ulnas suas' in *Adorna thalamum tuum*. The arpeggio vocal lines in *Angelus Domini*, one of which moves upwards through the notes EAce in crotchets, escaped the notice of H. K. Andrews, who was at pains to tabulate such things in *The Technique of Byrd's Vocal Polyphony*. Perhaps he could not believe his eyes.

Only the *turbarum voces*, the words spoken by the crowd, are set to music in the **Passion according to St. John** (1605 *a* 3/10). The rest is to be sung in plainchant. Fellowes remarked on the vividness of Byrd's setting, 'notably the salutation "Ave, Rex Judaeorum", with its mock ceremony in the opening phrase, and the jeering taunt contained in the little scale passage at the end'*—a passage which might be taken as a parody of his own early style in a work like *Similes illis fiant*. The opening 'Ave' ceremony, too, parodies the beginning of the *Ave maris stella* that Byrd has just written,† and for the second 'Crucifige eum' he re-used his music for 'et laetemur' in *Haec dies*.

Where did Byrd get the idea of writing a work like this? He would have remembered the venerable English tradition of Passion setting; there is an example in the Gyffard Partbooks, an anonymous 4-part St. Matthew. But it is also likely that he had been shown the 4-part St. John and St. Matthew Passions in an important publication by Victoria, the *Officium hebdomadae sanctae* of 1585. In the late sixteenth century these were the most famous settings of the Passions—indeed, the only famous settings—and Victoria, like Byrd, confines himself to the words of the crowd. The Gyffard composer also takes in Peter, Pilate, the Maid and all the other minor characters.

In Victoria's St. John Passion, all but one or two of the extremely suave and simple verses trace the same course, from an F chord with a' in the soprano to a C chord with g in the soprano. The same is true of Byrd's except that the final highest-sounding note is e.‡ (Byrd's opening chord, framing a tenth, we recognize from the Three-Part Mass.) Perhaps Byrd

*W. Byrd, 89.

†Also the opening 'Salve' of *Salve Regina*, a few pages earlier. Otherwise this relatively stereotyped figure is quite rare in the *Gradualia*—though there is another example in *Alleluia. Vespere autem sabbati*.

‡Byrd holds more strictly to his plan than Victoria does to his; see *Opera omnia*, v, 170f. He does not follow Victoria in altering the cadence note when the verse ends in a question ('Numquid et tu ex discipulis eius es?'; indeed, he omits the question mark), though of course there was precedent for this in the plainchant Passion tone. Byrd also unaccountably runs the two separate 'Iesum Nazarenum' exclamations together as a single 'verse'; this is the only verse that does not end with a high e.

started with Victoria in mind and then grew impatient, for he composed with
comparable simplicity only in verses 1–3. In response to dramatic pressures
which start to make themselves felt in verse 4, he began systematically to
repeat words—something Victoria never did until his very last verses—and
after introducing crotchet melismas in the 'Ave, Rex Iudaeorum' verse, he
went on to employ crotchet declamation in each of the remaining seven.
Byrd seems also to have referred to the plainchant Passion tone more consistently than Victoria, though this is still handled in the most approximate
way. Verse by verse, the rough outline c–f–c can be traced in the alto voice.

   Adorna thalamum tuum (1605 *a* 3/11), the last of the 3-part numbers
in the *Gradualia*, is also one of the most important. Byrd did not attempt
here to match the jewel-like virtuoso counterpoint of *Regina coeli*. The
interest of the piece is on another level: *Adorna thalamum tuum* is one of the
very few 3-part compositions in which he dealt with the issue of large-scale
construction. This is something that scarcely came up with the 3-part music
in the main body of the *Gradualia*. The verses of the introits and other Mass
pieces were clearly conceived of as interludes; the weight of the construction
rested with the full-choir sections, and Byrd merely worked his way through
the text keeping the two or three phrases (there are seldom more) suitably
linked and counterpoised. In *Ave maris stella* he could rely on the rigid
poetic framework, so he did not exert himself much beyond the point of
extending the last line of each 4-line stanza to obtain a somewhat mechanical
sense of climax. Even in *Regina coeli*, though the aggregate of four parallel
double units gave him the opportunity for some sophisticated balancing, the
form remains essentially stiff and impersonal.

   Only in *Adorna thalamum tuum* did he address a fairly long text that was
not parcelled up by alleluias or moulded by a poetic stanza form, and build it
into a musical structure comparable in scope and subtlety to his best compositions for four, five and six voices. His means of doing this were no
different from those he had developed for the full-choir works. It is just that
he had never applied them so extensively to the chamber-music texture of
three voices. There is an imaginative, developing balance between phrases of
contrasting lengths and characters, some imitative, some homophonic, under
the control of a clear tonal plan; and everything is of course influenced by
the text.

   This gentle Purification antiphon touched Byrd's most lyrical nerve:

Adorna thalamum tuum, Sion, et suscipe Regem Christum: amplectere
Mariam, quae est coelestis porta: ipsa enim portat Regem gloriae novi
luminis. *2ª pars* Subsistit Virgo adducens manibus Filium ante luciferum

genitum: quem accipiens Simeon in ulnas suas praedicavit populis Dominum eum esse vitae et mortis, et Salvatorem mundi.

The two parts of the motet are parallel in that they both come to distinct stops on the tonic after 17 breves in the one case, 14 in the other. But whereas the *prima pars* adds only one more phrase, a long one dilating on 'gloriae novi luminis' and doing so almost exclusively with F, C and B♭ chords, the *secunda pars* proceeds more expansively. It begins with the lowest-pitched phrase in the piece, 'Subsistit Virgo', as a foil to the highest phrase a moment later, 'ante luciferum genitum', and continues with a smoothly interlinked series of short half-homophonic points. These move in faster note values and thrust for the first time away from major sonorities towards minor ones. Perhaps this is to be explained retrospectively by the last word of the penultimate phrase, 'esse vitae et mortis', for Byrd seems to have looked ahead past life to death as he read this text. A meditative shadow falls over the superb concluding point, 'et Salvatorem mundi'; one thinks of the 'dona nobis pacem' of the Three-Part Mass. Byrd fashions its motive from the final 'mortis' figure in the way he had learned to do in the Mass, and introduces some meticulously chosen 6–5 progressions—a new sound in this composition—to heighten the expressive effect. The subdued final cadence on F returns to the low pitch area entered into at the opening of the *secunda pars*.

Byrd's evident desire to inject variety into book 1 of the *Gradualia* has been mentioned in connection with the miscellaneous compositions of the 5- and 4-part fascicles. Things are no doubt less obvious with the 3-part fascicle; but it is still remarkable how much stylistic variety is encompassed by these eleven 3-part compositions. They can be arranged quite clearly along a scale of increasing elaboration or artifice: first the formulaic Passion, then the three simple Marian hymns (in the order *O gloriosa Domina*, *Memento salutis auctor* and *Quem terra pontus aethera*), the somewhat more fully worked *Ave maris stella*, the four intense little Easter pieces in the F Ionian mode, the 'classically' disposed and proportioned *Adorna thalamum tuum* and finally the richly ornate *Regina coeli*. Somewhere to the side stands the Three-Part Mass, with its deeper simplicities, its unusual restraint of sentiment and purity of style. Byrd's 3-part motets are his most unassuming, but like his 3-part instrumental fantasias, they challenged the composer to come up with solutions to their own special problems—problems that were different from those posed by music on a larger scale, but surely of the same order of technical interest and complexity. It comes as no surprise to see Byrd meeting those challenges with the same intelligence and artistry.

[4]

Of the compositions in book 2 standing outside of the main cycle of Masses, one is for four voices, **Iesu nostra redemptio** (1607/19), a 5-stanza hymn for the Ascension.* In style and form it approximates the three simplest Marian hymns in book 1. Again all the stanzas are set, and the music moves in a basic crotchet pulse; even the vocal range holds to the limited range of the 3-part hymns—or, more precisely, to that of the most restricted of those pieces, *Memento salutis auctor*, extending from a low C to high d'. The lines are set very concisely, often in a quasi-homophonic texture. Half of them last no longer than six semibreves. But the writing is more imaginative here than in the 3-part hymns, which contain nothing as distinguished as the settings of 'Crudelem mortem patiens' in stanza 2 (Ex. 66) or 'Nos tuo vultu saties' at the end of stanza 4.

 Ex. 66

Stanza 5 presents a major surprise: it is an act of homage to Tallis, like several other passages in the *Gradualia*. In Tallis's hymns one high voice carries the melody, which adheres to a simple metrical pattern and always paraphrases the plainchant (except in the case of *O nata lux de lumine*, the best-known and latest of his hymns).† Within this scheme the musical texture varies from piece to piece: *O nata lux* and several other hymns are essentially homophonic, *Illae dum pergunt concitae* has short gaps between the lines filled with 'pre-imitations', rather in the spirit of the consort song, and *Solemnis urgebat dies* has similar gaps filled by a second voice in strict canon with the soprano. Tallis generally changes from triple to duple metre in his last stanza. Byrd instead changes from duple to triple in the last

---

Antiphonale sacrosanctae romanae ecclesiae (Rome, 1912), 'Hymni antiqui', 20; the modern form of this hymn is *Salutis humanae sator*. In stanza 3, 'Inferni claustra penetrans, / Tuos captivos redimens: / Victor triumpho nobili, / Ad dextram Patris residens', the words of the second line are omitted in all the partbooks. In 1607 the freeing of prisoners was too sensitive a subject to be mentioned in a Catholic publication.

†See TCM 6 and Doe, *Tallis*, 34. The Tallis hymns are for five voices. *Deus tuorum militum* (*Hic nempe mundi*) is most probably by Sheppard, to whom it is ascribed in one of its two sources (see Benham, *Latin Music*, 178).

stanza (stanza 5) of *Iesu nostra redemptio*, and then proceeds to set the first line of this stanza like *O nata lux*, the second and third like *Illae dum pergunt concitae*, and the fourth—which he repeats in sequence, lest the canon be missed—like *Solemnis urgebat dies*. As in *O nata lux*, no use is made of the plainchant.

Two magnificent 6-part motets conclude book 2 of the *Gradualia*. For an *explicit* to his great compendium Byrd turned to familiar hortatory verses from his favourite source of texts, the psalter.

Laudate Dominum omnes gentes (1607/45) is pre-eminently a retrospective work, mining old veins for rich new matter. Again the ghost of Tallis hovers over this composition, for Tallis had made a setting of this same Vesper psalm, but this time Byrd made no reference to the older composer's music. He did, however, take something from two of his own older motets with closely parallel texts, *Laudate pueri Dominum* (1575/7) and *Cantate Domino* (1591/29). He set all these psalms of praise for a 6-part choir including two basses, and always made the most of the opportunity this gave him for phrase repetition with voice exchanges. From *Cantate Domino* he took the distinctive opening point; we have observed this repeated cantus firmus-like structure in a number of other contexts, both before and after 1591 (see pp. 164 and 294). Byrd now enlivens the second cantus firmus statement with great virtuosity, adding a dazzling triple-metre idea and also the dotted-crotchet rhythm which comes up so often in the *Gradualia*—and which will come into its own in the last phrase of the present motet. From *Laudate pueri* he took a version of his ancient stretto ostinato technique (see Exs. 6a and l), though again this is now handled more artfully than in the earlier examples.

In a deeper sense, Byrd re-interpreted the innocent structural rigidity of *Laudate pueri*, achieving instead a far from simple monumentality by means of multiple interlocking symmetries, duplications, and long-range balances. Thus the five phrases of *Laudate Dominum* are placed symmetrically (or palindromically) in the tonal areas of G (Mixolydian), D, A, D and G: an arrangement that is underlined by a heavy series of closely spaced cadences in the three central, modulating phrases. These cadences emerge naturally from Byrd's use here of 'cell' technique—another technique associated with the early motets rather than with those of the *Gradualia*, though Byrd found a good deal of use for it in the 6-part Mass of Sts. Peter and Paul. The chart below shows the spacing of the cadences in the three middle phrases (deceptive and weak cadences are enclosed in parentheses) and also the lengths of the cells; for pairs of cells which are essentially duplicates except for voice changes, the numbers are given in italic.

	Phrase 2 laudate eum . . .			Phrase 3 quoniam confirmata . . .					Phrase 4 misericordia eius		
spacing of	7	8	8	9	7	7	8	4	4	5	6 *semi-*
cadences	D	D	D	A	A	A	(A)	(A)	(A)	D	D *breves*
length of cells *	8	*10*	10	8	*9*	9	6	6	6	7	7

(The spaces between cadences differ from the lengths of the corresponding cells, of course, because of overlappings.)

The nature of these cells is as interesting as their deployment. The motives in phrases 2 and 4 are almost identical; acting on this hint, we can also discern a thematic parallel between phrases 1 and 5—which makes the motet as a whole a melodic as well as a harmonic palindrome. The cell of phrase 3 is demarcated by the Continental cadence figure $^{765}_{44}\sharp$, used occasionally by Byrd ever since the later motets of the 1575 *Cantiones* (see p. 101). Never before, however, had he used this strong, expressive articulation for so purely formal a function as that which is involved in 'cell' technique. Strangely, the text 'Quoniam confirmata est super nos' seems not to have entered into the picture. But Byrd's sensitivity to the cadence figure itself is shown by his successive alterations of it: the consonant fourth configuration at each of the first two A minor cadences is replaced in the later ones by an augmented chord, a V^6_5 and finally a i^6_4 (BW 7, 135 bars 3–4 and 7–8, 136 bars 2 and 6, 137 bar 1).

The fifth and last phrase of the motet employs yet another retrospective technique that is handled here in a novel manner, double imitation. This brilliant point recalls the final point 'dicit Dominus Simone Petro' in *Quodcunque ligaveris* (see Ex. 62), the number which precedes *Laudate Dominum* in the partbooks, but the structure is less complex, hinging with special clarity on 2- and 4-breve phrases repeated between the two sopranos. Guided by the sopranos, the second subject descends six times from C to G and then five times more in expanded, overlapping, very free versions from D to G. This is cadential action with a vengeance; and the suitability of this overwhelming, joyous ostinato to the words 'et veritas Domini manet in aeternum' is obvious enough.

*These cells are construed as beginning at BW 7, p. 133 bar 5 (T), 134 bar 1 (S¹), 5 (T), 10 (A), 135 bar 3 (S²), 7 (S¹), 136 bar 4 (S²), 6 (S¹), 137 bar 1 (T), 3 (B¹), 5 (B²). In bar 6, notice the extremely deft diminution added by the S¹, which serves also to prepare the dotted-crotchet rhythm in phrase 5.

Venite exultemus Domino (1607/46) makes just as splendid an effect, perhaps, in its own more facile, madrigalian manner. The very loosely built opening point comes tumbling down in premature strettos. Past this point, cells combining one bass and one soprano voice, and sometimes extending only a few minims, are constantly echoed by the other bass and the other soprano. As in *Laudate Dominum*, the main cadences are arranged more or less palindromically—F, C, G, (D,) A, D, (F,) C, F, F; there is a strongly contrasted middle section. And in view of the thematic parallels between symmetrically placed phrases in *Laudate Dominum*, it is interesting to see Byrd carry the principle even further here. In two separate sections, 'iubilemus Deo' and 'et in psalmis iubilemus ei', the word 'iubilemus' receives the same unusual double setting, a homophonic idea in a triple cross-metre which is soon abandoned in favour of a new crotchet scale figure designed for strettos. In the later phrase, this *volte face* is accompanied by a new version of the 'et in psalmis' motive, too, which reveals itself as a close relative of the second 'iubilemus'. Indeed this jubilant, exultant figure—it also accommodates the word 'exultemus' in the opening phrase—is never far from mind in this brilliant and genial composition.

Venite exultemus Domino multiplies its codettas, as though to provide a double envoy to the *Gradualia*. First comes a charming alleluia in a dancelike triple metre; the antiphonal tendencies that have been sensed throughout the piece come frankly to the surface as one phrase after another is echoed between the same two 4-part semichoirs. And finally, back in a slow duple metre, a solemn benediction. Expanding the amen at the end of the 4-part hymn *Iesu nostra redemptio*, Byrd used his two extra voices to bias the texture in the bass and low tenor region. So *Venite exultemus Domino* ends, after working its way through a variety of madrigalian textures, with the deep, rich accents of traditional English polyphony: a concept of sound and composition which Byrd never forgot, and which continued to have a bearing on his latest music.

6

Conclusion

As a composer of Latin sacred music, William Byrd made his start with a few strictly liturgical compositions, presumably written for Queen Mary's Chapel Royal when (and if) he was a choirboy there. No doubt a question must remain whether *Similes illis fiant* and *Alleluia. Confitemini Domino* really belong in the canon. They are works of no great consequence, and the musician has less stake in their authenticity than does the historian, for whom the existence of music for the Sarum rite by Byrd makes concrete his link with—indeed, his brief participation in—the great musical tradition of early Tudor times. There is some satisfaction, perhaps, in seeing the first modern English composer as also the very last of an unbroken line going back to the Middle Ages.

In any case, with or without the testimony of these two pieces, Byrd's strongly traditional orientation is clear. Cantus firmus hymns and responds formed the staple of the Marian Chapel repertory, and it is Byrd, almost alone among his countrymen, who continued writing cantus firmus motets for twenty years after the accession of Queen Elizabeth. Byrd even deferred to the old large-scale votive antiphon, a genre associated with the early part of Henry VIII's reign and revived briefly under Mary by Tallis and William Mundy. He evoked its form and style in the most ambitious of his early compositions, the tripartite motet *Tribue Domine*, and later grafted the form onto the highly unlikely, highly anguished penitential text of *Infelix ego*, which he had discovered in one of several Continental motets, most likely that by Lassus.

The situation with *Infelix ego* shows vividly enough that Byrd's regard for tradition was not a matter of simple conservatism. Whether he was dealing with a traditional plainchant, a traditional form, or merely a traditional text, he always suffused the composition with something vital of his own. Often this feels less like an additive process than one of re-interpretation and transformation. One can state it as a rule that in every work by Byrd, at least in his early years, there is always some special technical idea that he is interested in trying, or some new concept for the structure of the composition as a whole, or some individual expressive vision. Always—if an exception may be allowed for the two Marian ritual items: and even those works seek to impress in an obvious and rather innocent way by means of their canons.

Byrd's imaginativeness in dealing with musical technique is already clearly evident in his music of the early 1560s, in both the instrumental music and the Latin motets. To be sure, the level of his craft is at first not up to the originality of his ideas, and sometimes the ideas themselves are schematic and limited in scope, however original. Such are, for example, the plan for the sequence of the stanzas in the very early hymn *Christe qui lux es* and the novel type of imitation that he devised to accompany the cantus firmus in *Christus resurgens*. But in the slightly later cantus firmus motet *Libera me Domine de morte aeterna*, the way the chant melody controls the harmonic direction of the accompanying contrapuntal complex, and hence the total structure, is a conception of much greater subtlety and power. The result is music of incomparably greater eloquence than Robert Parsons's setting of the same plainchant, which was Byrd's model: the first example, perhaps, of a motet in which a more profound idea about musical structure goes hand in hand with a new expressive vision.

Compositional ideas of various kinds and at various levels likewise animate the non-cantus firmus motets of these years. Here Byrd was chiefly concerned —even obsessed—with imitation, the musical technique that had been central in the Continental motet since the time of Josquin. In the days when Byrd was a student, Tallis and other English composers managed imitation stiffly; it is not surprising that he would seek guidance, a little later, from the facile Italian hand of Alfonso Ferrabosco. There are early motets that served him as systematic studies in various branches of contrapuntal technique—in canon, double imitation, and what we have called the stretto ostinato and 'cell' techniques. Even in so unprepossessing a piece as *Memento homo*, the composer can be seen balancing the conflicting claims of imitation and phraseology for the work's overall structure.

The publication project with Tallis in 1575 marks the climax of this technical phase of Byrd's compositional activity. It also, as it were, rationalizes it: for the ample prefatory matter of the *Cantiones* hints strongly enough at the motive behind the young composer's rather surprising devotion to the genre of the Latin motet. However precarious its role in the Anglican liturgy, the motet continued to enjoy great prestige, and if Byrd had determined to carve out a place for himself in English music next to Tallis, he had to meet Tallis on his own high ground. We do not need Morley to remind us that of all the genres of sixteenth-century music, the motet is 'the chiefest both for art and utility'. Perhaps for the benefit of Queen Elizabeth, who had just presented the composers with the monopoly for music printing, Byrd and Tallis are depicted in glowing terms as the champions of English music before an imaginary jury of world opinion. This too was a contest that had to be waged with motets, not with keyboard pavans or In Nomines for consort.

As a commercial venture the *Cantiones* was a well-known fiasco, and it hardly seems to have done much better as an exercise in international arts diplomacy. This may have discouraged Byrd from publishing motets—but not from composing them. The impetus provided by the publication project carried over into the next decade. By 1581 we can detect a fresh repertory of about twenty pieces circulating in manuscripts, and it is clear that a very different principle is now guiding Byrd's motet production. There is a new individuality in his choice of texts for motets, and a new concern for enhancing these texts by the musical setting.

Music 'framed to the life of the words' was not unknown to Byrd in the 1560s, but what was now to become the commanding principle had then been just one more technique to master among many. He had depicted the psalmist's cheerful rhapsody in *Attollite portas* simply but vividly, and Job's all-but-despairing plea in *Libera me Domine et pone me iuxta te* in a considerably more involved (not to say involuted) fashion. On the other hand, he set two other motets from the 1575 *Cantiones* with words that are not much less gloomy, *Aspice Domine quia facta est desolate civitas* and *Memento homo quod cinis es*, in the one case with little and in the other with no recognition of their rich potentiality for text expression. In Byrd's Lamentations, although the manipulation of affective semitones forecasts some of the greatest effects of his later years, it is worth noting that the device is applied indifferently, highlighting both the key expressive word 'lamentatione' and also the abstract and formal ones HETH and TETH. For Byrd the Lamentations was not only an early study in text setting but also in imitation of a new, less rigid variety and in the shaping of imitative phrases. This was something that he was to perfect and make into one of the strongest and most individual features of his style. It is hard to say which of these three areas of investigation was primary for him, and in which he would seem from our vantage point to have taken the greatest strides.

Textual considerations begin to dominate only with the latest half dozen motets written for the Tallis-Byrd *Cantiones*. Four of them take their impetus directly from motets by Alfonso Ferrabosco, and by far the most important of these stand out for their affective treatment of the words. While *Domine secundum actum meum*, like the Lamentations, served Byrd as a study both in expressive text setting and in imitation—this time in the important technique of double imitation—*Emendemus in melius* stands out as his first full-scale essay in affective homophony and, at least among the motets, as his first masterpiece. If in a narrow sense it holds remarkably closely to its model, Alfonso's *Qui fundasti terram*, in aesthetic terms it far outstrips it—in the urgency of its rhetoric, and especially in the superb inspiration whereby Byrd conceived of the final prayer for liberation as liberation into polyphony. Throughout the composition the delicate line between homophony and polyphony is drawn, blurred and redrawn with the greatest consciousness.

The 1550s, the formative decade for both Byrd and Alfonso, was a period of significant change in Continental music. Clemens non Papa died while his works were being circulated in the massive publication programmes of Susato and Phalèse, and both Palestrina and Lassus made their first appearances. Clemens impressed, but it was Lassus who caught the imagination of musical Europe; various of Susato's books drifted across the Channel but Lassus was actually published here, in 1568, 1570 and 1592. Alfonso modelled a number of his motets, chansons and madrigals on works by Lassus, and it seems clear that this composer provided him with his general ideal of musical expressivity. It is less clear that he grasped the fluid half-homophonic rhetoric that is so distinctive with Lassus. What Byrd found in Alfonso was no more than a pale reflection of the latest Continental expressive manner; he got much more out of him in the way of technical pointers for imitative counterpoint. Byrd approached Lassus most closely, perhaps, in *O Domine adiuva me*, a rather uncomfortable half-homophonic motet of the period 1575–80.

This text is a freely-composed prayer (freely composed not by Byrd, however, but by some Continental writer: Byrd found it in one of the Susato anthologies). The crucial fact about Byrd's new group of motets is that their texts are no longer chosen from liturgical or any other traditional sources. The element of personal choice, whether on the composer's part or that of his patrons, places an entirely new complexion on the new phase of Byrd's motet production. The preponderance of penitential texts, many of them spoken as though on the point of death, is certainly very striking, and less easy to explain than the other fairly large group of texts referring to the desolation of Jerusalem and the plight of the congregation, and looking forward to liberation and the coming of God. A few of the texts grow almost (but never, of course, entirely) specific. There can be little doubt that Byrd was voicing prayers, exhortations and protests on behalf of the English Catholic community, and that this was the new motive behind his stepped-up production of motets in this period.

Music could enhance the words; the prayers, exhortations and protests would penetrate the mind more profoundly if they were enhanced by the proper music. This was not the aesthetic philosophy that Byrd had grown up with as a choirboy. In the days of the Sarum rite, the function of music was to ornament the liturgy, to distinguish and order ritual elements on a scale of greater or lesser solemnity. Byrd's new programme of motet composition depended on a new concept of music's function: to see the motet as propaganda it was necessary first to see music as rhetoric. He would have gained some inkling of such a possibility from the Lamentations of Tallis and White and the motets of Ferrabosco, but the sheer novelty of the whole conception should not be underestimated. As an intellectual synthesis it has something of the same boldness and originality as his accomplishments of a strictly musical nature.

Following in the imitative tradition of *Domine secundum actum meum*, Byrd now produced a long series of motets in which expressive detail and the grave overall momentum are maintained in a classic balance. Perhaps the greatest of these imitative works are the penitential motet *Tristitia et anxietas*, which is also one of the earliest, and the 'political' motet *Plorans plorabit*, evidently the latest of all, with its moving reminiscences of Tallis, who had died in 1585. *Vide Domine afflictionem nostram*, the most extreme of the 'Jerusalem' motets, and *Haec dicit Dominus* develop most impressively the homophonic idiom of *Emendemus in melius*. Individual words, phrases and total compositions are now moulded with a rare logic and beauty, resulting in an eloquence unknown to earlier English music. The words of a motet, like the themes of a harangue, are not many; the rhetorical art consists of repeating them again and again (these are long compositions) and doing so in such a form as to make the thought utterly convincing and unforgettable. And indeed there are words such as these from Isaiah—

Be not wroth very sore, O Lord, neither remember iniquity for ever: behold, see, we beseech thee, we are all thy people. Thy holy cities are a wilderness, Zion is a wilderness, Jerusalem a desolation

which are now literally unthinkable without Byrd's music. The power of Byrd's rhetoric hinges on his musical form, on the resiliency of his musical structures.

The local illustration of individual words was one element in Byrd's developing rhetoric. Sometimes called madrigalism, after the sixteenth-century musical genre that employed it most consistently, this was a technique of more fascination to that century than to later ones, when many musicians and critics (though by no means all) have tended to react against it. The reaction, in fact, began with Vincenzo Galilei—and Thomas Campion—in Byrd's own lifetime. But word illustration was still fresh to Byrd. After experimenting with the technique in several of the motets published in the

1575 *Cantiones*, he applied it with more and more assurance in works of the
1580s. In works such as *Vigilate* and *Circumspice Hierusalem* (set to the
boldest of all Byrd's 'political' texts) madrigalism is perfectly absorbed into
the musical discourse; it supports and strengthens the total rhetoric.

In the sphere of the Latin motet, then, Byrd introduced English music to
madrigalism before the madrigal—before, that is, the madrigal was actually
taken up by English composers, familiar as they may have been with the
genre from Italian imports. And there is one true madrigalian 'moment' in
Byrd's career, when he seems to have grown interested not only in madrigalism but also in certain fundamental stylistic traits of the Italian madrigal
itself. It can be localized in the period between the publication of the
Cantiones sacrae of 1589 and 1591. These two anthologies of motets extending
back over fifteen years or so include a few new pieces which, as they did not
circulate earlier, were evidently composed expressly for the publications.
Only in 1591 are the new compositions madrigalian in style and concept:
the intimate and emotional 6-part motets *Domine non sum dignus* and *Domine
salva nos* no less than the more obviously Italianate *Laudibus in sanctis* and
Haec dies. This coincides with a striking episode in Byrd's production of
English songs. In his two very accomplished settings of *This sweet and merry
month of May* contributed to Thomas Watson's *Italian Madrigals Englished*
in 1590, Byrd had just provided the first native models for the English
madrigal development.

The two 6-part motets may well have been written for Sir John Petre. It
is likely, in any case, that this patron was responsible for most of Byrd's
remaining Latin music, as Edward Paston was responsible for most of his
remaining English songs. Byrd now ceased to write motets of penitence and
protest and began, at first surreptitiously, to issue liturgical music destined
for the undercover Catholic services held in certain English country houses.
It seems beyond coincidence that at just this time he should have moved to
within a few miles of the Petre manors in Essex. Eventually he acknowledged
in the dedication to the *Gradualia* that the motets had mostly proceeded
from Petre's house, likening them to flowers plucked from his garden and
therefore rightly due to him as tithes: a metaphor that may indicate rather
exactly the nature of the understanding between the composer and his
protector. What was true of the *Gradualia* in 1607 was probably also true of
the three Masses, which were published in the 1590s without dedications of
any kind in a much more clandestine fashion.

The liturgical orientation of the Masses and the *Gradualia* motets marks
the second decisive change of direction in Byrd's career as a composer of
Latin sacred music. This change was accomplished a great deal more

smoothly than the earlier change in the late 1570s, when his technique was still in the process of being perfected. By the early 1590s his craft had progressed to a point where anything was possible and everything was effortless. The writing was becoming more and more fluid. Perhaps the most immediate outer signs of this are the gradual abandonment of double imitation, the technique with which Byrd had achieved his most grandiose effects in the motets of 1575 and the years following, and also a growing reluctance to juxtapose homophonic and polyphonic passages as dramatically as in, for example, *Emendemus in melius* and *Ne irascaris Domine*. But flexibility of style appears on every level, down to the most subtle, and it was this flexibility that allowed Byrd to develop the wonderfully natural, quiet manner of his new liturgical phase. Liturgical texts do not call for a composer's impressive or persuasive powers. The words are thoroughly known and their import has been thoroughly digested; the composer needs only to point them up with an ever-fresh sense of their seriousness, and perhaps sometimes also to accord them decorous illumination. Nor are these texts to be dilated upon at will. They take their place in ceremonies with their own time scale and their own canons of proportion.

A new idiom for liturgical music that would be concise without seeming perfunctory, and alert without seeming over-emphatic: this hinged once again on Byrd's mastery of musical structure. His matchless ability to shape polyphonic phrases around melodic climaxes, developed in the motets of the 1570s and 1580s, was obviously more suited to the rhetoric of those days than to his present concerns. The music is now organized largely by the careful balancing of phrases that are both shorter and more clearly articulated than before. It moves swiftly, partly because the rhythmic surface is more variable and partly because its way is eased by an increasingly sophisticated use of sequence. On a higher level, balance is obtained between sections defined by certain formalized musical textures. As we have remarked, Byrd's trios and other semichoir sections in the Masses and the *Gradualia* may be regarded as relatively long sections of low musical density, and his alleluias as relatively short sections of high density. Each texture is used systematically as a means of sectionalizing the longer Mass and motet texts. The structures of the early period, built out of grand leisurely phrases growing smoothly out of one another, are replaced by something more crystalline than organic, by a new art of interface and equipoise.

The trios themselves may be taken, along with certain other striking features of Byrd's style at this period, as evidence of his continuing commitment to traditional values in English polyphony. By way of some archaizing early motets, such as, in particular, *Tribue Domine* and *Infelix ego*, he drew his model for these trios from the half-canonic semichoir style of the Tudor votive antiphon. The stylistic range of the *Gradualia* trios is considerable, but Byrd seldom treated them as anything other than eminently functional, neutral and hieratic. In one motet, *Gaude Maria Virgo*, he even began the trio section with a fleeting reference to an ancient work of Tallis; this is one of several small indications that there was a particular personal tinge to Byrd's traditionalism. The 'full' sections of his compositions often look (or listen) back to the characteristic sonorities that he remembered from his student days under Tallis: the rich, complex consonant textures, the rotas and ostinatos, the chains of 6–5 progressions, the English cadential false relations. These sounds strike us most often in music for five and six voices, of course—notably in the Mass for Sts. Peter and Paul and the three large Marian tracts—but sometimes in music for fewer voices, too. There is even one impressive passage of the kind in the Four-Part Mass; though otherwise it is a remarkable fact that in the Masses Byrd seems to have turned his back momentarily on reminiscences of this sort. When he returned to them in the *Gradualia* we can be sure he was doing more than following the new fashion for such things that has been detected among the anthem composers of the time. Perhaps he was leading the fashion. In any case he must have come to recognize that the accents of Tudor polyphony suited his temperament and a certain density in his musical thought.

One would not wish to overstress the traditionalism and the retrospection. When Byrd derived the Sanctus of his Four-Part Mass from Taverner's *Mean* Mass, he transformed a passage of rich Tudor polyphony into a paradigm of his newest writing, predicated on clear phrase articulation and lucid harmony. The liturgical scheme of the *Gradualia*, furthermore, is unmatched for comprehensiveness and rigour in the earlier days of English Catholicism, even during the Marian revival. Models for such a publication—to the extent that there *are* models—can be found only in the wake of the Counter-Reformation. The conception, organization and implementation of the *Gradualia* project is as impressive an intellectual accomplishment, in its own way, as the conceptual synthesis underlying Byrd's activity as a motet composer in the 1580s. And if the *Gradualia* is hardly conceivable without the Counter-Reformation, the same is true of English Catholicism itself in the decades around 1600. This was an uneasy, deeply conflicted compromise between old and new: between the conservative gentry, who sought a *modus vivendi* while hoping against hope for a return to the Catholic community they had known, and the Jesuits with their militant missionary fervour, their newly animated ideal of personal Christian sacrifice, and their thoroughly disruptive lines of command. Byrd, who was in touch with Jesuits while owing his essential loyalty to aristocratic patrons of the old Catholic party, was certainly aware of the conflict and probably right in the middle of it.

The stress can be detected in his liturgical music, with its emphatic, perhaps purposeful incorporation of traditional and abstract elements on the one hand, and on the other its markedly modern character. This is not, after all, purely 'functional' music; Byrd does not simply point up the liturgical words but again and again illuminates them from a personal standpoint. It is not necessary to appeal to the general ideal of personal piety which had spread through Europe as the main force of the Counter-Reformation. No one who had lived through the experiences of the 1580s and had written the music that Byrd had in those years could be expected to return to the untroubled, hieratic world of traditional Catholicism.

And so the description of the new repertory as 'quiet' requires some qualification. The adjective may be allowed as a broad characterization for this music by comparison with the angry and anguished motets of the 1580s. It may also be applied fairly enough to the greater part of the three Masses, and to many pieces in book 1 of the *Gradualia*, especially among the impressive cycle of twenty-five Marian motets at the head of the collection. But at a number of isolated points in the Masses Byrd speaks in an unexpectedly individual and moving way, and there are motets in book 2 of the *Gradualia* whose intensity suggests that the passions of the 1580s had not entirely abated, and whose vividness suggests that the madrigalian moment of 1590 was more than a moment. *Tu es Petrus* is an egregious example. Perhaps Byrd faltered a little in the task of pointing up or illuminating a liturgical text in this instance, and found himself almost inadvertently trying to persuade.

Or perhaps *Tu es Petrus* is a somewhat earlier work. It is to some of the other 6-part motets—the magnificent *Quodcunque ligaveris* and *Laudate Dominum*, for example—that one has to turn for hints of a new direction Byrd might have taken, had there been a new demand for compositions on a monumental scale comparable to, say, the 8- and 9-part psalm-motets of his Lincoln days. Certain of the quieter compositions hint just as strongly at another new direction, even more individual: works such as *Beata es Virgo Maria*, *Ave Maria*, and *Tui sunt coeli*. There is a sharpened awareness of tonality, and a stripping away of imitative counterpoint to its basic linear relational content, as it were, so that the stylistic norm of sixteenth-century polyphony, of the 'Palestrina style', seems further away than ever. Dissonance and rhythm are handled more freely, not for the sake of experimentation or freedom per se, but because once freed of convention the essence of these musical elements stands out more clearly for fresh imaginative use.

Conciseness gives way to concentration; the *Gradualia* has its group of
perfectly fashioned miniatures, motets for five and often four voices lasting
for no longer than twenty or thirty breves. Byrd, who in his youth would
have lost no contests for prolixity, now evolves a new art of musical
aphorism.

It is the comprehensiveness of his art that commands, ultimately, the
greatest wonder. The subtle, complex combination of old and new in his
late music—what might be called its quality of historical texture—is only one
aspect of this comprehensiveness. This quality we would perhaps expect to
encounter in any music written for a long-established rite, and particularly in
times when that rite is under serious scrutiny. Still, it may be doubted that
any other composer of Catholic church music at the time of the Counter-
Reformation projects it to such an extent. One thinks not of Victoria, but of
Bach. And one thinks of Bach again in connection with the most striking
manifestation of Byrd's all-embracing musical intellect, namely his creation
of a body of instrumental music of a stature comparable to that of his vocal
music for the Church. From the historical point of view, no doubt, this was
ultimately Byrd's most profoundly original achievement. His insight into the
aesthetic possibilities of the variation set, the ricercare or fantasia, and the
stylized dance—the pavan and galliard—and his embodiment of this insight
into an extensive, finely articulated repertory: nothing like this was known
before. It is one of the ineptitudes of standard music history that Byrd's
achievement in this area has gone so long unrecognized.

Byrd's eye was not on history, however, but on eternity, and certainly
in his own mind the music that he consecrated to his Church was the most
important. His last major sustained act of composition was a motet compendium for the Church year, not a set of canonic variations or an 'art of the
fantasia'. By its very nature, as we have seen, the Latin sacred music invites
or rather posits traditionalism in a way the instrumental music could not.
But both kinds of music provided Byrd with comparably rich parallel fields
for the elaboration of musical structures: and it is in this, perhaps, that his
comprehensiveness commands the most wonder of all. It is not the case that
Byrd allowed the syntactical thread afforded by a verbal text to substitute
for the purely musical constructive powers that he exercised in the instrumental music. It is closer to the truth to say that every text, being different
from every other, offered a new technical challenge and suggested a new
aesthetic solution. The almost encyclopaedic variety of these solutions, in
Byrd's Masses and motets, songs and services, pavans, variations and fantasias, gives him his place among the greatest of composers.

Affect was closely bound to structure for Byrd, and structure in the vocal music was at root a function of the same technique that he cultivated in the instrumental music. Only the ramification differed. Contrapuntal draughts-manship and the control of harmony in the large and in the small were always the primary issues. After the precocious, if sometimes schematic formal inventions of his early years, Byrd's maturing imagination sought out and found expressive possibilities almost without number in the manipu-lation of contrast, climax, and accumulation. In his late years he ranged from the precisely jewelled movement of the visionary miniature motets of the *Gradualia* to the loose but deeply impressive total forms of the three Masses.

One thinks again of the eighty alleluias in the *Gradualia*. A strictly circum-scribed technical problem was posed by the repeated presence of the word 'alleluia' in the liturgical texts Byrd had to set; he looked past or through the word to find inexhaustible sources of musical energy. On alleluias such as those in *Ave Maria, Beata es Virgo Maria, Regina coeli, Ascendit Deus, Confirma hoc Deus, Venite exultemus Domino* and so many others, he lavished an extraordinary variety of artifice and achieved an extraordinary diversity of affect. His satisfaction at returning to the problem in one motet after another, in different contexts and from different standpoints, is almost palpable. These alleluias, in which the act of creation and the act of praise are both repeatedly renewed, are a microcosm of Byrd's comprehensive art.

Index of Byrd's Works
(including doubtful and spurious pieces)

The reference to the main discussion of each piece is given in bold type

Ab ortu solis *a 4* (1607/13–14), **293**, 321n
Ad Dominum cum tribularer *a 8* (MS), 32, 56, 112ff
Ad punctum in modico *a 5* (MS), **156n**
Adoramus te Christe (1605 *a 5*/26), **224**, 320
Adorna thalamum tuum (1605 *a 3*/11), **227**, 329n, 334, 335f
Afflicti pro peccatis nostris *a 6* (1591/27–8), 32, 56, **75ff**, 80, 99, 128
Alleluia. Ascendit Deus *a 5* (1607/26), **276**
Alleluia. Ave Maria (1605 *a 5*/20), 223, 235n, 257, **265**
Alleluia. Cognoverunt discipuli *a 4* (1607/16), **293**
Alleluia. Confitemini Domino *a 3* (MS), 26, 55, 59, 62, 111, 210, 271, **341**
Alleluia. Emitte Spiritum tuum *a 5* (1607/32), **281**
Alleluia. Vespere autem sabbati (1605 *a 3*/6), 210, 271n, 329, **332f**
Alma Redemptoris Mater (1605 *a 4*/13), **325**
Angelus Domini (1605 *a 3*/8), **333f**
Apparebit in finem *a 5* (1591/12), 41, **144ff**, 150, 239
Arise O Lord, 163n
Ascendit Deus *a 5* (1607/28), **277**
Aspice Domine de sede sancta tua *a 5* (1589/18–19), 32, 56, 62, **73f**, 80, 125, 131
Aspice Domine quia facta est *a 6* (1575/4), 84, **101f**, 343
Assumpta est Maria (alleluia verse) (part of 1605/a *5*/23), **267f**
Assumpta est Maria (offertory) (1605 *a 5*/24) **268**
Attollite portas *a 6* (1575/5), 83f, **87f**, 98, 101, 343
Audivi vocem de coelo *a 5* (MS), **157f**
Ave Maria (1605 *a 5*/14), 259, **261f**, 264, 349
Ave maris stella (1605 *a 3*/4), 329, **330f**, 334ff
Ave Regina coelorum (1605 *a 4*/14), **325**
Ave Regina coelorum *a 6* (MS), **161f**
Ave verum corpus (1605 *a 4*/5) 53, 225, **283f**, 288f

The Battle, 276
Be not wroth, 163n
Beata es Virgo Maria (1605 *a 5*/10), 223, **256**, 349
Beata Virgo *a 4* (1607/9), **294**, 300, 304
Beata viscera (1605 *a 5*/11), 223, **254**, 256, 259, 264
Beati mundo corde (1605 *a 5*/32), **248f**
Behold I bring you glad tidings, 163n, 170n
Behold now praise the Lord, 163n
Benedicta et venerabilis (1605 *a 5*/7) **255**, 257

Index of Names